The Sage of Tawawa

The Sage of Tawawa

Reverdy Cassius Ransom, 1861–1959

Annetta L. Gomez-Jefferson

The Kent State University Press • *Kent and London*

Frontispiece: Bishop Reverdy Cassius Ransom in his study at Tawawa Chimney Corner, Wilberforce, Ohio, 1950s.

© 2002 by The Kent State University Press, Kent, Ohio 44242

All rights reserved.

Library of Congress Catalog Card Number 2002001848

ISBN 0-87338-748-1

Manufactured in the United States of America

06 05 04 03 02   5 4 3 2 1

Library of Congress Cataloging-in-Publication Data

Gomez-Jefferson, Annetta L., 1927–

The sage of Tawawa : Reverdy Cassius Ransom, 1861–1959 / by Annetta L. Gomez-Jefferson.

p.   cm.

Includes bibliographical references and index.

ISBN 0-87338-748-1 (pbk. : alk. paper) ∞

1. Ransom, Reverdy C. (Reverdy Cassius), 1861–1959. 2. African Methodist Episcopal Church—Ohio—Bishops—Biography. I. Title.

BX8449.R35 G66 2003

287'.8'092—dc21

2002001848

British Library Cataloging-in-Publication data are available.

Dedicated to my parents,
Hazel T. and Joseph Gomez,
who believed in me when nobody else did.

Contents

Foreword

by Dennis C. Dickerson
Department of Research and Scholarship, A.M.E Church

Annetta Gomez-Jefferson has chosen a model modern minister, Reverdy C. Ransom, to demonstrate how twentieth-century African American clergy confronted the many challenges that faced black people in the urban/industrial era. Ransom, born nearly forty years before the turn of the century, fashioned ministries that addressed various issues that most black preachers had avoided or neglected. As a pastor, general officer, and forty-eighth bishop in the African Methodist Episcopal Church, he pioneered black church involvement with the social gospel, helped to revive the protest/political tradition in black leadership, and spearheaded ecumenical cooperation among the historically black denominations.

Educated at Wilberforce University and Oberlin College in the late nineteenth century, Ransom was assigned to congregations in urban/industrial areas in Pennsylvania and Ohio. In these settings he contemplated what initiatives black ministers and black churches should develop to serve their working-class parishioners. As a result, he became a convert to the social gospel. While working in Chicago in 1900, he left a prestigious pulpit to form an innovative Institutional Church and Social Settlement that offered programs in job placement, a day nursery, youth activities, and social betterment organizations for men and women. After Ransom was elected editor of the *A.M.E. Church Review* in 1912, he established in 1913 in New York City the Church of Simon of Cyrene, a mission that resembled his Chicago congregation. Unlike most ministers, he became a familiar figure among the gamblers, prostitutes, and drunkards. Some responded, reformed, and adopted healthier life-styles. Ransom, though one of the few black preachers who fully embraced the social gospel, pioneered a paradigm of urban ministry that succeeding generations of clergy extensively emulated.

Ransom grew to ministerial maturity during the age of Booker T. Washington. The Tuskegeean's emphasis on accommodation to white supremacy, economic development, and industrial education undermined earlier efforts at black protest and political activities derived from the Reconstruction era. When W. E. B. DuBois and William Monroe Trotter challenged Washington's conservative leadership, Ransom joined them in the fledgling Niagara Movement. At the group's 1906 gathering at Harpers

Ferry, Ransom articulated the sentiments of those black leaders who favored confrontation with the rampant racism that caused the disenfranchisement and lynching of African Americans. Ransom spoke again when the newly formed NAACP rallied at a mass meeting in New York City. In 1918 he vied unsuccessfully for a New York congressional seat. These activities in protest and politics, like his social gospel involvements, became emblematic of what other black clergy would do as they envisaged their role as ministers in twentieth-century American society.

While rooted in A.M.E. affairs at congregational and connectional levels, Ransom always viewed his ministry within a larger context. His social gospel theology and his protest/political affiliations merged with his vision for black ecumenism. Although he was a veteran of World Conferences of Methodism and of the Federal Council of Churches, he and other like-minded ministers believed that blacks could be better served by an association of black denominations. Therefore, they founded in 1943 the Federal Council of Negro Churches. As the organization's first president, Ransom hoped that the group's collective strength could be leveraged to produce societal gains for the black population.

Though always known as an A.M.E. clergyman, Ransom viewed himself as a modern minister who tried to cope with the changing role of clergy and the changing needs of those whom they served. This biography chronicles Ransom's efforts to modernize the black church and to fit it for the challenge of an urban/industrial age.

Foreword

by Reverend Handley A. Hickey

Reverdy Cassius Ransom was deeply moved by social, economic, and political injustices. He used his intelligence, fearlessness, eloquent oratory, and powerful pen to effect change in his church and country. Emma, his first wife and helpmate of fifty-six years, worked with him to establish an institutional ministry that involved all aspects of the local and larger community. In addition, she was an ardent leader and supporter of the Young Women's Christian Association. The Emma Ransom House in Harlem was named in honor of her contributions.

In this biography, Gomez-Jefferson gives us a clear picture of Ransom's civic and church involvement and of his strong belief that the Christian church should lead the way in solving the race problem. "As God is above men, so man should be above the idea of race" was his philosophy. He was never a lackey for state or church and bitterly opposed the domination and abuse of some bishops. Even after his own ordination in 1924, he was heard to say that "a minister does not serve under a bishop but with the bishop." As prelate of the Third Episcopal District, which included Ohio, Ransom became president of the Board of Trustees at Wilberforce University from 1932 to 1948 and was involved in the A.M.E. Church's attempt to keep the State of Ohio from taking over Wilberforce. The battle that ensued resulted in the establishment of two separate schools, Wilberforce run by the church and Central State run by the state. The successes and failures of Ransom's efforts on behalf of Wilberforce are still being debated; nevertheless, his devotion to the university and to education for blacks remains unquestioned.

An iconoclast in political matters, Ransom was one of the first Negroes to abandon the Republican Party following the failure of Reconstruction. In addition to his unsuccessful run for Congress from the 21st District of New York in 1918 as an Independent, he led the Smith for President Colored League of New York in 1928 and campaigned vigorously for the candidacy of Alfred E. Smith, a Catholic and a Democrat. In elections where neither candidate of the two major parties showed concern for blacks, he threatened to vote for Eugene V. Debs and the Socialists. He was appointed commissioner of the Ohio Board of Pardon and Parole by Democratic governor Martin L. Davey in 1936.

In 1940 he opened the Democratic National Convention with prayer and was later appointed by Franklin D. Roosevelt to the 45th Civil Defense Fifth Corps.

His contacts were varied. He championed the poor and forgotten and supported struggling black artists, such as poet Paul Laurence Dunbar, composer Samuel Coleridge-Taylor, and actor Sam Lucas (his uncle). He advised presidents and business magnates like William McKinley and Mark Hanna, and he worked with civil rights leaders Frederick Douglass, W. E. B. DuBois, Ida Wells, Mary White Overton, Julia Ward Howell, and William English Walling.

Although a formidable opponent of traitors and sycophants, Ransom remained loyal to his friends. With all his strengths and imperfections, this slim man of six feet two inches, with reddish hair and a carefully trimmed mustache, was a force to be reckoned with. His "Son in the Gospel," Bishop Joseph Gomez, summed up Ransom's character upon his death in 1959 at the age of ninety-eight: "He was spiritually sensitive. He felt deepest because he suffered most. . . . Often he tore the veil from himself and viewed with candor and disarming frankness his own frailties. Yet—and mark you, this was most important in his life—he was ever sure of God and His redeeming presence."

Preface

When I was a child, I used to love to repeat the name *Reverdy Cassius Ransom*. It sounded elegant. But even more, I looked forward to the times when Ransom would visit our house. I would sit at his feet, transformed by the picturesque scenes he painted of his dramatic life. The best times of all were when I visited Tawawa Chimney Corner. I loved to rummage through the celebrated house, look at the voluminous books that surrounded me at every turn, or skip rope down the long driveway, shaded by tall trees. I never questioned my parents' love for Reverdy or Emma, his companion for fifty-six years. The Ransoms were larger than life. None of us ever thought Reverdy could die. We were right, at least until 1959, when at ninety-eight years, he just got tired and went to sleep in my mother's arms.

In 1995, I retired from the College of Wooster and completed my father's biography, *In Darkness with God*. Because his life was so intricately entwined with Reverdy Ransom's, it seemed logical that when I finished his story, I should write about Ransom. Joseph Gomez, my father, had come to the United States from Trinidad in 1908 and joined Ransom's church in New York. Ransom helped him attend Payne Theological Seminary at Wilberforce, Ohio, and was there on the day he graduated and married Hazel Thompson. He became the godfather to my sister Eula at her christening in Detroit in 1926 and helped ordain my father when he was elected bishop in 1948. Ransom was a permanent fixture in the lives of all the Gomezes.

When I began to gather material for my father's biography, I came across many letters from Ransom, Annual and General Conference minutes that recorded his participation in the business of the A.M.E. Church, books he had written, others he had given to my father from his personal library, and manuscripts. Later I revisited Tawawa Chimney in search of more material for both men and was greeted by Georgia Myrtle Teal Ransom whom Reverdy had married after Emma passed. She led me to a trunk filled with papers and articles and told me to take what I wanted. I will always be grateful for her generosity.

When the Gomez biography was finished, my editor at Kent State University Press, John Hubbell, said that Reverdy Cassius Ransom was an interesting personality and asked if I had ever thought of writing about him. I was delighted that he had read my thoughts. And so I began the arduous task of arranging the Ransom material in chronological order and putting it in binders. After two more trips to Wilberforce where I worked with the archivist, Jackie Brown, I had more material than I could possibly use. My first visit was made even more fruitful by the presence of Rev. Dwight Dillard who flew all the way from Birmingham to assist me. From the very beginning of this project, he had encouraged me, sent material, and spent hours on the phone talking about Ransom. On a second trip, Alphine Jefferson, history and black studies professor at Wooster, drove me to Wilberforce and stayed for a week giving valuable assistance to my research. Ruth Ransom, granddaughter-in-law of Reverdy, graciously welcomed me into her home, shared family stories, pictures, and other memorabilia. In addition I had the opportunity of interviewing Argua and Hanley Hickey and Mildred Henderson who had known Ransom personally.

Upon my return to Wooster, the president of the College, Stan Hales, set aside money to help me finance the project and saw to it that I had an up-to-date computer and printer. Dennis Dickerson, historiographer of the A.M.E. Church, supplied me with conference minutes that were missing from my collection. My sister Eula and her husband, Harold Williams, read over many of the chapters and made valuable suggestions, as did my sons, Joseph and Curtis. With so much encouragement, I could only succeed in completing the task.

Now that I have finished *The Sage of Tawawa,* I am amazed that it took so long for the historians and other scholars to discover Ransom. It seems many people are interested in him today. I often get phone calls asking where they can find information or if they can come and share my material. I am always glad to oblige. Reverdy Cassius Ransom's accomplishments in religion, civil rights, and politics were astronomical. He was acquainted with most of the leaders of his day, black and white, and was involved in the major movements and organizations of the first half of the twentieth century, particularly those aimed at gaining freedom and equality for blacks. His story needs to be told many times and from different perspectives. To date, Donald A. Drewett has written a dissertation on the racial and social thought of Ransom. In his book, Calvin S. Morris emphasizes Ransom the pioneer black social gospeler. David Wills examines him as a black apostle, and Anthony B. Pinn has published a book of Ransom's writings. All of these are well-researched, well-written, valuable sources.

Although I personally prefer "black" and "African American" when referring to those of African descent, I have used the terms that were most acceptable during the various periods: "Negro," "colored," "black," "Afro-American." Often I have let Ransom speak for himself through his autobiographies, *The Pilgrimage of Harriet Ransom's Son,* and *School Days at Wilberforce,* and his sermons, orations, and letters. Most valuable, however, are his handwritten journals, the many discussions I had with him as I was growing up, and the papers and books he gave my father before he died.

Why another book on Ransom? As was my father's biography, this book is a labor of love. While some of the information may be familiar, I have added details that are quite new, thus making this the first comprehensive biography on the subject. *The Sage of Tawawa* is an attempt to look closely and intimately at Ransom the man from 1861 to 1959. It does not focus on a specific aspect of his philosophy. It is not a dissertation based on a single thesis. Instead, it is a portrait of a remarkable human being. He was not a saint and would have been the first to acknowledge his own weaknesses. He was, however, a humanitarian, a visionary, a dynamic orator and preacher, a radical thinker in his day; and he knew how to be a friend. Most of all, he was a spiritual and never doubted the reality of God in his life.

Harriet Ransom's Son, 1861–1881

I have fed you with milk, and not with meat: for hitherto ye were not able to bear it.
    1 Corinthians 3:2

On the first Monday of September 1881, a rangy, redheaded young Negro boarded the train from Cambridge, Ohio, for Xenia, Ohio. The remembrance of Harriet's last words—"God bless you, son. Study hard!"—did little to ease his anxiety as he watched the green and gold farmlands flash by like so many picture postcards. His final destination: Wilberforce, the African Methodist Episcopal Church University, just a short carriage ride from Xenia.[1]

"Reverdy Cassius Ransom" had been conferred on him by Congressman John A. Bingham, who had given his mother a five-dollar gold piece for the honor of naming him. The Congressman selected "Reverdy" from Reverdy Johnson, a prominent citizen of Maryland, and "Cassius" from Cassius M. Clay of Kentucky. His surname came from his stepfather, George Warner Ransom. With such an imposing label, Reverdy always felt he was surely fated to be somebody important.[2]

Reverdy Cassius Ransom had been born in Flushing, Belmont County, Ohio, on January 4, 1861, about three months before the attack on Fort Sumter that signaled the beginning of the Civil War.[3] He was born in a time of turmoil but also a time that would initiate change, two conditions that would characterize his ninety-eight years.

The Ransoms lived with Reverdy's maternal grandmother, Lucinda, who had been born a slave in Virginia, was freed, but held illegally for a while by her master. Eventually, he gave her money and sent her to Ohio with other relatives.[4] The repressive Black Laws passed in most northern states and in the Ohio legislature in the early 1800s included the stipulation that "Blacks entering the state were required to register themselves and their families with county clerks, to carry certificates attesting to their freedom, and to post $500 bond within twenty days of arrival in Ohio."[5] Although this law was not universally observed in Ohio, Belmont County was in the southern part, a section inhabited largely by former whites from the South who brought their racial attitudes with them.[6] More than likely Lucinda's former master felt obliged to give her the necessary papers affirming her freedom and enough money to meet the legal

Lucinda Williams, Reverdy's maternal grandmother. Courtesy Ruth Ransom, Xenia, Ohio.

qualifications if it became necessary. Either by chance or deliberation, she settled in the small village of Flushing, composed largely of Quakers, a religious sect strongly opposed to slavery.

By 1805, the Quakers had become so numerous in Flushing, they built themselves a meetinghouse and established an Underground Railroad Station that would carry slaves further north or to Canada. Like Lucinda, the 110 blacks living among the Quakers were former slaves, most of whom had come from Virginia.[7] In order for Negro children to receive an education, a Daniel Huff donated land on which a building was erected. It served not only as a school but a church as well. Harriet and Lucinda probably attended the services.[8]

Grandma Lucinda was highly intelligent and, unlike many blacks, had been taught to read and write before she left Virginia. In 1847, she bought a plot of land on the outskirts of Flushing. It was there, in a two-room house made of "hewn logs" valued at about $250, that Reverdy was born.[9]

In 1865, the Ransoms moved to Washington, Guernsey County, Ohio, a village sprawling along the National Pike, "one of the principal stations of the stagecoach." Reverdy's mother boarded him with his paternal grandmother and grandfather, Louis and Betsy Ransom, while she did domestic work in the homes of white people to pay for his keep. In his autobiography, he recalls how Betsy made her own candles, soap, "carded and spun her wool and made her own dyes." In later years he could still smell "the great back log and green wood in the wide fireplace." However, all of his memories were not pleasant. The Ransom children disliked him, and his father's sister never called him by name but referred to him as "that little redheaded devil." He was left to play outside by himself. Often he imagined he heard voices calling him. The sounds would cause him to "run screaming into the house." Because the adults could find no one in the yard, they concluded that Reverdy was a bit odd.[10]

In his autobiography, there is only one reference to his impressions of the Civil War as a child, possibly because he was so young and because there was no actual fighting in Ohio. He writes: "While playing beside the pike one day, I encountered a wagon train of Negro soldiers returning from the war. The driver of one of the wagons observing me, exclaimed, "I am from the South, I have been in the East, now I am in the West, but that is the first redheaded nigger I ever saw."[11]

A morning ritual observed by his grandparents, which later had a negative effect on Reverdy, was that of drinking whiskey every morning "before prayers and breakfast." The children were given "ten or fifteen cents" and sent with pails to the distillery near the house. When they returned, the adults would sit at the crude wooden table, smoking their corncob pipes or dipping snuff and drinking their "toddy." On many occasions they would pour some for the children.[12] No doubt Reverdy liked the way it gave a warm glow to the otherwise hostile faces before him. The hostility did not end with his family members but was felt even more sharply from the white community composed largely of former Southern farmers. It was in Washington that he first learned what it meant to be black in America.

In spite of the morning drinking ritual, the family members were staunch churchgoers. They were African Methodist Episcopals, members of the first autonomous black denomination in the United States, founded by Richard Allen of Philadelphia in 1794 in protest against the segregation he experienced in the white Methodist Church. On Sunday, everyone was required to attend services. As they left the house, they were accosted by white men who would call after them, "Kah, Kah! Jim Crow! I see a dark cloud rising. It's going to Rain! Nigger, Nigger, Nigger." The Ransoms would enter hurriedly the small candlelit church and close the door to block out the ugly sounds outside. Reverdy recalled that his mother was the only one to protest these indignities, and she taught Reverdy to despise bigotry whenever and wherever he encountered it.[13]

During the week, black children went to school at the A.M.E. Church. Even though blacks were required to pay taxes for education, it was not until 1849 that Ohio had

Harriet Johnson Ransom, Reverdy's mother, at age forty-five. Courtesy Ruth Ransom, Xenia, Ohio.

passed laws requiring the "township trustees to use a prorated share of the common school fund for support of black schools ... supplemented in 1853 [by] a law providing guidelines for the creation of black school districts." What resulted, however, was not equal educational opportunities. Most Negro schools were conducted in one-room shacks, abandoned deteriorated old school buildings, or in churches. "The curriculum was weak, the school year short, and teachers few; seldom was provision made for black schooling beyond the training in basic literacy skills."[14] Reverdy recalled that "little [else] was offered for anyone to learn," despite the sincerity of his teachers. Nevertheless, Harriet was determined that her son would go to college someday just as the sons of the well-to-do whites for whom she worked.[15]

No matter how many domestic jobs Harriet held, there was never any money for toys or other luxuries, but "across the blur of days in Old Washington," Reverdy remembered: "candy peach at Christmas; ... [at the A.M.E. Church] great feasting on

Quarterly Meeting occasions; the singing and shouting . . . no amusement and little play; and through it all, the loving care of [his] mother, who taught and trained [him] daily in the speech, manners and ideals . . . of the white people for whom she worked."[16]

Reverdy always had a great deal of respect and love for his grandmother Lucinda, but he worshipped his mother. In later years he paid her the supreme honor of titling his autobiography *The Pilgrimage of Harriet Ransom's Son*. The only reference he makes to his stepfather was that he had been a father to him for over fifty years.[17] About his real father, he wrote nothing. Some said he had been a white man; others that he was a light-skinned Negro who had deserted his family. In a 1979 interview with Georgia Myrtle Teal Ransom, Calvin S. Morris quoted her as saying that Ransom knew his father who was a Negro, and that he resented anyone saying otherwise.[18] Reverdy himself writes:

> I know that in my blood is a strain of at least one of the white races, Irish, I suspect. I judge from the general physical appearance of my relatives . . . as well as from my own, the prevailing strain of my Negro blood is from one of the North African tribes, perhaps Sudanese. . . . One thing I know, there is little of the Anglo Saxon in me.

He bases this largely on his temperament and his characteristics. For he writes, neither the white man's "music nor characteristic amusements appeal to me. No more than the forms in which he expresses his religious faith and the manner in which his acts of divine worship are performed."[19]

Whatever the truth, his real father had no noticeable effect on his life. It was Harriet who taught him to revere education and pursue his dreams, to conduct himself as a man, to be proud and stand up for his race.

In 1869 the family moved to Cambridge, Ohio, a town of about 2,500 people, three hundred of whom were colored. Once again Reverdy attended the all-black school housed in the A.M.E. Church. When he was thirteen (1874), his mother attempted to have him admitted to the white public school, but the principal, Professor Mc Burney, refused him.[20] (A school desegregation law was not passed until 1887 in Ohio. Even then it was ignored in some cities.[21]) Next she enrolled him in the white Presbyterian Sunday School class, but the teacher broke into tears after seeing he was Negro.[22] When Samuel J. McMahon found Reverdy cleaning spittoons and mopping beer-stained floors in a saloon, he gave him a job in his bank to remove him from an unsavory environment. Later, A. C. Cochran, one of the cashiers, hired him as a houseboy.[23]

Reverdy did have some time for entertainment. He enjoyed joining his buddies at Wills Creek where, in addition to swimming, he learned to "swear," "use tobacco," "fight," and "play cards." But most of all he enjoyed studying with the white tutors his mother adroitly secured for him. A shoe store manager taught him "the mysteries" of algebra in return for janitorial services. In addition, the resourceful Lucinda did washing for whites who agreed to instruct him in "advanced subjects." Occasionally his white friends would let him look into their *Harkness Latin Grammar and Reader.* In the summer Reverdy "was the only colored student to take advantage of a summer normal school" which would better prepare him for college.[24] He learned to love to read and would pore over the books he discovered on the shelves of the houses where his mother worked. One day he would have a library that would far surpass these. Moreover, whenever "the Court of Common Pleas was in session . . . [he] spent many hours there, listening to testimony of witnesses." He decided he wanted to be a lawyer. The persuasive arguments of the defense lawyers fascinated him.[25] The time spent in the courthouse sparked his love for oratory and his desire to champion the underdog. Little did he know then he would be acclaimed one of the most dynamic orators and preachers of his age.

Because Reverdy spent a great deal of time outdoors, he developed a fascination for nature. With the assistance of science books and tutors, in his teens, he put together a large album of dried leaves and flowers. Between each entry he was careful to insert tissue paper to preserve the samples. At the bottom of the pages, he classified them as "O," "G," "L," and "C," most likely to designate their organologic, Greek, Latin, and common names. The twenty-three samples include blue violet, liverleaf, dogwood, yellow honey suckle, cowslip, columbine, and jack-in-the-pulpit and give evidence to the beauty of Cambridge and the surrounding area. Although later Ransom was fascinated by the bustle and din of city life, he always loved most the serenity of the countryside as evidenced by the summer homes he bought when he became a man.[26]

Reverdy's sojourn to college was unexpectedly delayed. He became enamored of a Cambridge girl, the attractive Leanna Watkins. In explaining the incident, he said: "We lived in a community of free morals. We were both in our teens. She was one of the finest and the best among us. She was comely to look upon, added to this, the correctness of her life and conduct caused her to stand apart from most all of the other girls of her group. She more strongly appealed to me than anyone else." Reverdy referred to his relationship with Leanna as "youthful folly . . . a shadow of social tragedy across [his] life as to almost blight" his hopes for getting an education. Leanna Watkins and Reverdy C. Ransom were married on February 17, 1881.[27]

The year before the marriage Reverdy had applied for and received a twelve-month teacher's certificate from the Guernsey County Examiners that qualified him to teach orthography, reading, writing, arithmetic, geography, and English grammar.[28] He accepted a year's teaching position in one of the district schools to save money for his tuition; but no matter how much he worked and saved, there was not enough money. Harriet mortgaged her home so that he would have sufficient funds to begin college in the fall of 1881. Although torn between a sense of responsibility to Leanna and a desire to further his education (the goal for which he and his mother had worked so long), he finally decided to leave.[29]

So now he was on a train bound for Wilberforce University, guilt ridden, frightened, and lonely. It was the first time he had ever been away from his mother. He kept asking the conductor when they would arrive in Xenia. How many more miles was it? Were they there yet? When it seemed he could wait no longer, the train slowed, gave a final "whoosh," and stopped in front of a sign that read "Xenia, Ohio." Only three-and-a-half more miles to Wilberforce.[30]

CHAPTER 1

Green and Golden College Days, 1881–1886

A wise man will hear, and will increase learning; and a man of understanding shall attain unto wise counsels.

Proverbs 1:5

In the mid 1800s abolitionist groups and religious organizations in the North began to establish colleges and universities for the higher education of Negroes. Wilberforce University was a pioneer in this movement.[1]

Ministers at the 1853 Cincinnati Conference of the Methodist Episcopal Church "felt the necessity of a more liberal and concentrated effort to improve the condition and furnish the facilities of education to the 10,000 colored people in Ohio and . . . other free states."[2] As a result, in 1856 they bought Tawawa Springs, a health resort near Xenia, Ohio, situated on fifty-three acres. The land was heavily timbered with pines and oaks, "traversed by a deep ravine with five mineral springs running out of its sides." In addition to a stable and barn, there were ten buildings: nine cottages, and a two-hundred-room structure that could be used for a dormitory and recitation classes. Instead of calling the school The African University in the tradition of the primary African Free Schools established earlier in northern cities, they decided to call it Wilberforce University, in honor of the renown English abolitionist, William Wilberforce.[3] The 207 students who enrolled were mostly "the natural children of southern and southwestern [white] planters." Others were the children of free blacks from the North.[4]

Soon after the Civil War broke out, the Methodist Church found itself in financial difficulty. The slaveholders could no longer afford to send their mulatto children north, nor could the church provide scholarships for free blacks. On March 10, 1863, Bishop Daniel A. Payne, John G. Mitchell, and James A. Shorter agreed

> to purchase the property for the [African Methodist Episcopal Church] to be used as an institution of education for the colored race, which was at the time excluded from all the schools of higher education, excepting two or three, of which Oberlin was chief.[5]

In its Articles of Association, the founders "provided that none shall be excluded from the benefits of said institution, as officers, faculty, or pupils on account of color."[6]

The university had grown from five students when the A.M.E. Church first took over, to an excess of 130 students when Reverdy entered in 1881.[7] More than likely, he had chosen Wilberforce for several reasons: his family's close affiliation with the A.M.E. Church, the low tuition that he could supplement by working in the community, and the goals of the curriculum, as set forth by its first president, Bishop Payne, emphasizing the development of the mind rather than manual skills.

At dusk, as the horse-drawn carriage carrying Reverdy and two other students neared Wilberforce, Reverdy became more and more introspective. He was both homesick and anxious. In his book *School Days at Wilberforce* he wrote, "I little thought that night how, in coming days, I would often walk that road tired, penniless, and sometimes cold and hungry."[8] The night chill did not seem to bother the two who sat beside him prating about the "profs," "juniors," and "sophs"; which courses to avoid; and which books had to be read. To Reverdy they possessed all the sophistication of upper classmen who scorned beginners like himself.[9]

Turning into the campus, they passed Evergreen, a cottage shadowed in the pines. Evergreen was the home of Bishop Daniel Payne, who in his seventies was still a force to be reckoned with at the university. Next they skirted the pristine cottage of James A. Shorter who, after serving as agent for the school, had been elected a bishop in 1868. At sixty-four, he continued to be a revered personality in the community. Homewood, the domain of Miss Hallie Q. Brown, teacher, elocutionist, and temperance lecturer, was the last cottage seen before the carriage turned up the gravel drive leading to the home of the current president, Benjamin Franklin Lee. Before graduating from Wilberforce in 1872, Lee had done chores for Payne, who became a surrogate father to him; he had succeeded Payne to the presidency in 1876.[10]

With his cardboard suitcase in hand and the remains of the lunch his mother had packed for him, Reverdy was ushered into the house by one of the students who worked for the president. He was told to wait in the library. It seemed Lee was out chasing a horse that had escaped from the stable of one of the professors who was visiting in Europe. Lee would see Reverdy as soon as he had returned the absconder to its stall.[11]

Reverdy was tired. He sat in the straight-back chair and glanced at the books that burdened the shelves. There were even more books than those in the libraries of the white people his mother had worked for back in Cambridge. And these books belonged to a *black* man. Reverdy stood to meet the plump, medium-tall figure who entered the room. Lee was impressive with his receding hairline, thick long beard, mustache, and piercing dark eyes. After a short greeting, the president assigned him to board for the night with a "Mr. Brooks from Kentucky." As soon as Reverdy met Brooks, Brooks began to question him at length as if to ascertain his fitness to be a student. When he was finally allowed to retire, Reverdy found himself sleeping on a "tick bed" filled with "country straw" that pricked his back and legs all through the night.[12]

He was aroused from fitful dreams early the next morning. Brooks told him to go to Shorter Hall for 6 A.M. breakfast and then chapel. After chapel he was to go to the secretary of the College's office. Reverdy soon learned that the secretary would be the most important person in his student life. Among other things, he assigned rooms; received tuition; supplied textbooks, hammers, nails, strings, letters from home; and kept a record of student demerits.[13]

As Reverdy walked across the campus, he could see Shorter, the main hall, standing in the center of the campus. This red brick, three-story edifice had been built after the original building was burned by white miscreants in 1865. Dedicated on June 20, 1878, the new structure had been named in honor of James A. Shorter. Inside there were eight recitation and one lecture room, an art and music room, a chapel, a library, "a large hall which was to be fitted up for a museum," and separate reading rooms for women and men. Upstairs were five dormitories with sleeping accommodations for eighty persons. The women slept in one wing, the men in the other. In the basement there were fifteen rooms, a kitchen, pantry, storerooms, a dining hall, laundry, and sleeping apartments for those who "worked with the culinary and laundry." When the dormitories were filled, students sometimes also slept in the basement.[14] Luckily for Reverdy, Shorter was a vast improvement over the original building whose classroom walls had been of "rough, unplastered brick," and lacked "modern seats, and desks."[15] It would be Reverdy's all-purpose residence while at the University.

He entered the hall and bounded down the steps to where breakfast was being served. The room was furnished with long wooden tables and chairs and was alive with the cacophony of chatter, silverware, and dishes being passed. Breakfast was brought in on large serving platters. With a gallantry that would have pleased Harriet, Reverdy allowed the ladies to help themselves to the food first. Much to his chagrin, when the platters came back to him, there was no meat and no longer any butter, only bread, apple butter, hominy, and rice. He was told by the student waiters that the meat and butter plates were never refilled. For future meals he made sure he served himself before passing the platters. Gallantry had to be set aside during meals.[16]

In days to come, Reverdy would take his turn waiting tables. Students were required to perform this task for a week during the term—a task they usually enjoyed because this was the one occasion when male and female students worked together; however if "a young man became too marked in his attention to any of the young ladies, he was not permitted to serve [on] the same day with her." The dining hall was actually a boarding hall that the university leased out "to some responsible person" from the community. Students were required to pay $1.75 per week for board. Each table was presided over by a matron. If anyone was late to a meal, he would not be allowed to sit at the table. His only recourse was to bribe the cook or one of the waiters to let him eat in the kitchen or take food to his room.[17]

After finishing breakfast, Reverdy followed the other students up the steps to the Church of the Holy Trinity where chapel was held. Though located in Shorter, it had had a separate dedication. Its motto, "Upon this rock will I build my church and the gates of hell shall not prevail against it," was deeply ingrained in the minds of the students.[18] Not even hell was allowed to interfere with chapel attendance. Everyone was required to go twice a day (7:45 A.M. and 4 P.M.) except on Mondays that were holidays. Because students spent Sunday mornings and evenings in church, they were only required to attend prayer meeting Monday evenings.[19]

When one of the professors at the chapel door gave Reverdy his assigned seat, he sat with the male students on the right side of the room. The women were seated on the left, the faculty in front and back. President Lee opened the service by leading the students in singing a familiar Methodist hymn. Next a young man knelt on the rostrum and prayed. Unmoved by his earnest and lengthy entreaty to God, the male students passed notes across the aisles to the ladies of their choice. Ransom was amused by this sacrilege. When the prayer was over, the president read the scripture and then closed by giving a brief moral treatise on how students at Wilberforce were to conduct themselves in order to uphold the traditions of the institution. Reverdy was to learn that at chapel "occasionally [they] were treated to some student oratory." The student would stand, call out, "Mr. President," and then "follow with a neat little speech" meant to impress everyone, especially the faculty.[20]

As soon as chapel was over, Ransom kept his appointment with the secretary of the college, Thomas H. Jackson. When he entered, Jackson was reading the letter that had been sent earlier certifying Reverdy's good moral character. No one was admitted without such a letter. When he looked up, Reverdy handed him his tuition. Only after it had been paid would he be allowed to "recite with his class" the following day. In return, the secretary gave him a receipt and assigned him a room in one of the upstairs dormitories.[21]

He located his room and found it to be furnished with the barest necessities: a bedstead, mattress, two pillows, a desk, two chairs, pitcher and bowl, a clothespress, and a wood-burning stove. In his memoirs, he described humorously the two pillows that were "filled with a dark substance which looked like coarse hair." Seemingly they had multiple personalities and would "undulate," "swell up," "shrink," "twist [themselves] into a long hard roll, then stretch . . . diagonally across the pillow case" at will.[22]

As did all students, Reverdy had to purchase a coal bucket, coal, cord of wood, a lamp, oilcan, and a broom if he wished to keep the room warm, lighted, and clean. Most of the supplies could be bought from the basement supply room. The administration was a firm believer in that old cliché, "cleanliness is next to Godliness"; consequently, any faculty member could inspect a student's room whenever he wanted. Every student was assigned a roommate, and although Reverdy had a great deal to say about roommates in general, he never mentioned any specific person with whom he roomed. It can be assumed that whoever the roommate was, the two of them had their good times and bad, for he writes: "It requires more skill, more patience, and more forbearance to live peaceably and harmoniously with the majority of room mates, than in almost any other voluntary association between two human beings." He warns against selecting "the borrower," "the love sick," and the one who has annoying habits such as making strange noises while studying, "like the buzzing of a swarm of bees."[23]

At the time Reverdy entered Wilberforce, the university was divided into six departments: the collegiate department (classical course or scientific course), the theological department, the normal department, the academic department, the sub-academic department, and the music department. Courses in the sub-academic department were more basic than those in other departments and included such subjects as English grammar, reading, history of the United States, composition, and so on. Because few Negroes had had the opportunity to prepare themselves properly for college, this department always had the largest enrollment. All classes lasted for forty-five minutes during which the students would recite from their assigned readings. The school year was divided into three equal terms.[24]

His first year Reverdy was enrolled in the academic department because he thought it would best prepare him for a career in law. Every evening during the study hour he would prepare assiduously for his recitation the following day. Recitations begin at 8 A.M. "Each student [was] given ample time to recite without interruption all he [knew] of the part assigned to him." After each recital, the student was graded from one to ten, with seven as a passing mark. If he made lower than seven, he could make up for his failure by reciting some part of the lesson failed by another student. There was an unspoken honor system among the students. During all his days at Wilberforce Reverdy said he never knew of a student who cheated by using a "key" or a "pony."[25] Unfortunately, the method of teaching largely through recitation and sporadic lectures did not allow for much discussion or investigation, but it did ensure that everyone in the class understood the basics of the text under consideration.

Ransom soon had to find work in Xenia to pay his expenses. Occasionally one of the professors would hire him to do a few chores; but mostly, in all kinds of weather, he walked the three-and-a-half miles to Xenia to do janitorial work in barbershops. Even with those jobs, he often found himself hungry, cold, and without funds for coal. Too proud to ask others to allow him to study by their stoves, he would either gather twigs from the woods to feed his stove or study in bed with the covers pulled tightly over his body. He did, however, always make sure he had enough money to buy oil for his lamp so he could read his text.[26]

Reverdy and Leanna Watkins grew farther and farther apart after he went to Wilberforce, though he did see her on holidays. Because he was married and still had a deep sense of guilt concerning Leanna, Ransom paid little attention to the campus women. The other male students liked to stroll to the pump in the middle of campus and fill their pitchers with water when the girl of their choice was also drawing water. Because there was strict separation of the sexes, this was one of the few opportunities they had to socialize with the female students. This did not bother Reverdy. His hours were filled with work and study.[27]

For a long time Reverdy had heard about Oberlin College, a Congregational private school. Known until 1850 as Oberlin Collegiate Institute, it had been active in the Underground Railroad before the Civil War and was the first college to admit women and Negroes. It was its Theology Department that had initiated the school's liberal racial policies. Originally the department was largely made up of former students from Lane Seminary, a school located at Walnut Hills near Cincinnati, Ohio. Though most of the students were the sons of slaveholders, at Lane they had become so moved by the philosophy of the abolitionist, William Lloyd Garrison, they asked permission to use the chapel to debate the issue of slavery. Because of these spirited discussions, the students set about opening Sabbath and day schools for Negroes in Cincinnati. The Lane trustees became alarmed at this preoccupation with Negroes. While the students and Professors Beecher, Stowe, and Morgan were on summer vacation, the trustees met and passed a rule forbidding the discussion of slavery at Lane. In addition, they fired Morgan, one of the teachers who shared the students' enthusiasm for abolition.[28]

On December 15, 1834, Rev. John J. Shipherd, a "prime mover" in the settling of the Oberlin community, wrote a letter to the Oberlin board of trustees asking that a theology department be added to Oberlin. He urged that Rev. Asa Mahan be appointed president, and Rev. Morgan, formerly of Lane, be added to the faculty. He warned that neither man would accept the invitation unless the principle rule of the college was "that students shall be received into this institution irrespective of color." Shipherd stated further:

> Indeed, if our Board would violate right so as to reject youth of talent and piety because they were *black*, I should have *no heart* to labor for the upbuilding of our Seminary, believing that the curse of God would come upon us, as it has upon Lane Seminary, for its unchristian abuse of the poor slave.[29]

At the time, most of the people in the Oberlin community were colonizationists and believed that the answer to the slavery question was to send blacks back to Africa.[30] As a compromise to Shipherd, Mahan, and Morgan, the trustees passed what was a rather weak statement, but one that did ensure the integration of the college without alienating the community:

> Whereas, there does exist in our country an excitement in respect to our colored population and fears are entertained that on the one hand they will be left unprovided for as to the means of a proper education, and on the other they will be in unsuitable numbers . . . introduced into our schools and thus in effect forced into the society of the whites, and the state of public sentiment is such as to require from the Board some definite expression on the subject. Therefore, resolved, that the education of the people of color is a matter of great interest and should be encouraged and sustained in this institution.[31]

Once the resolution was passed, "from 5 to 8 percent of the student body throughout the nineteenth century would be black," and Oberlin community was considered to be a "haven for blacks in search of an education and greater freedom."[32]

No doubt Reverdy's reasons for transferring to Oberlin at the end of his freshman year had to do with some of the beliefs he held when he first arrived at Wilberforce. In *School Days*, he writes:

> The writer of these lines, previous to visiting Wilberforce, had never seen a colored professor, much less a Faculty composed of colored professors, presiding over a college owned and controlled by colored men. While he believed Wilberforce would do much for him, he did not believe that a college owned and controlled by colored men was as good as one composed of white men.[33]

In addition, he had been given an Avery Scholarship by Oberlin that would take care of his tuition; the college had been highly recommended by Professor Scarborough, his classical language teacher, who noted the lack of racism when he had been a student there in the late 1860s. In his autobiography Scarborough wrote, "I forgot I was a colored boy in the lack of prejudice and genial atmosphere that surrounded me [there]."[34] Ransom was confident this place of freedom was where he should be. The letter sent earlier to Oberlin from President Lee stating he was "an honorable, true, discrete and studious man" would ensure his warm reception. In the fall of 1882, Reverdy left Wilberforce to prepare for a career in law at Oberlin.[35]

In *Oberlin the Colony and the College*, James H. Fairchild, president of the college, described the community in the 1880s as a pleasant village of thirty-five hundred inhabitants, surrounded by a prosperous farming community in the midst of which [stood] a college with its various departments, theological, collegiate, preparatory and musical, and an average yearly attendance of twelve to fifteen hundred students.[36]

In 1835, several new buildings had been added so that Oberlin was better housed and equipped than Wilberforce. The one disadvantage for Reverdy was that he would have to find a room in the community. The women were housed on campus; the theology students lived in Council Hall, but the other males had to find rooms elsewhere.[37]

Little is known about the home where Reverdy roomed. In *Pilgrimage*, he said he "maintained himself by working in a private family for board and lodging, by occasional jobs, sawing wood (25 cents an hour) and by working in a barber shop every Saturday from twelve noon, until twelve midnight." He found the educational standards at Oberlin and the "general atmosphere of culture" to be on a "higher plane" than he had known before. On the other hand, he soon found that along "with other colored students, while not treated as an outsider, [he] was held within definite boundaries upon the outer fringes of college life which embraces mental, social and recreational contacts."[38]

Reverdy enrolled in the department of preparatory instruction, which was divided into two schools, the classical and the English. In the middle class (classical school) of which Reverdy was a part, there were 107 students, almost the total enrollment of Wilberforce at the time. The school year was divided into three terms—fall that lasted fourteen weeks and winter and spring that ran for twelve weeks each.[39]

Reverdy was required to attend church twice on Sundays—daily prayers in the evenings at chapel, and in the mornings with his boarding family. He also had to attend a weekly exercise in the English Bible and a prayer meeting on Mondays. A Friday weekly prayer meeting for his class was conducted by one of the teachers.[40] Although religious requirements at the school were similar to those at Wilberforce, the students appear to have had more freedom. At least the "Don'ts" listed in the catalogue were only three: no tobacco and alcohol, no secret societies, and no visiting the other sex at her private room except by special permission in case of severe sickness. Women were to be in their rooms by 8 P.M. during the spring and summer and 7:30 P.M. during winter and fall.[41]

More than likely Reverdy had a minimum amount of money to maintain himself, twenty-five cents a week for his room and $1.75 for his board. In the catalogue it was suggested that one hundred dollars added to earnings of one or two hours work a day could be made to meet all expenses for tuition, incidentals, board, room, books, fuel, lights, and washing for a college year. Students were encouraged to sustain themselves because there were only a few low-paying scholarships and few jobs to be had on campus. Reverdy's Avery Scholarship covered his tuition of three dollars a term; nevertheless, no matter how many jobs he held, he found it extremely difficult to make ends meet.[42]

At Oberlin Reverdy met several Negro students whom he was to remember. Among them were Ida and Hattie Gibbs, daughters of Judge Gibbs of Arkansas; Mary Church, better known later as Mary Church Terrell, the noted educator, lecturer, club woman; Ralph Langston, son of John M. Langston, congressman from Virginia; and John Alexander with whom Ransom had two things in common, "poverty and the love for study." At Oberlin Alexander "got a perfect mark on daily recitations in classes for two years and also the highest mark possible in examinations for two years." He was the first Negro to graduate from West Point and the first to teach military science at Wilberforce.[43]

Early in November, Harriet informed Reverdy that he had become a father. On October 4, 1882, Leanna had given birth to Harold George Ransom. Soon afterward, Leanna turned the baby over to Harriet to raise and, by mutual consent, Reverdy filed for a divorce that was finally granted February 6, 1886.[44] Whenever he could afford it, Reverdy traveled to Cambridge to see his son of whom he was quite proud, despite the ill timing of his birth. It was up to him to get a thorough education so he could support his child. It would be unfair to burden his mother with such a responsibility in her declining years.

Once again Ransom mentioned nothing about having a roommate at Oberlin in his autobiography. He did, however, tell a friend in later life that he roomed with a man who was studying law. His roommate was probably Negro, because a few months before he came to Oberlin, there had been an incident in which a professor had objected to a colored student rooming with a white student. The Negro students protested by writing a letter to the "Honorable Faculty of Oberlin College," in which they expressed their abhorrence that a faculty member would express such an opinion and urged the administration to take a strong stand against such attitudes. If the "better element of the white culture" condoned such an attitude, "what could they expect from the lower element of white society?"[45]

It was this incident which provoked Julia A. Wilson, an affiliate of the Mission to the Colored Refugees, to write a strong letter to President Fairchild in March of 1882. She was concerned about the "issue of the present controversy at Oberlin in regard to certain points in the treatment of colored students," a Mr. Davis in particular. She reminded Fairchild that she had sent several "young colored men" to Oberlin and was about to send more, assuring them that Oberlin was the "best place in the whole United States for the education of colored men, because there they are put on an equality with white men." She preferred Oberlin to colleges like Fisk because it was important that Negroes "learn to mingle *as men of equal power and standing* with the best elements of the white race." She did not think that Fairchild "imagined how deadly and how painfully they feel any treatment which sets them on one side as 'colored,' nor [did he] know how intensely such treatment reacts in prejudicing their mind against white men." The trouble Mr. Davis had endured had nearly "blighted" his life and education. "You little know what [blacks] have to contend with in the ignorance and jealously of their own people, and the prejudices of others." She concluded that "for the educated colored man there is no home in this world as things are now."[46]

Whether or not Reverdy was aware of this incident is not known; however, he soon ran into a situation that made him ask, as did the writer in the *Oberlin Review* of February 3, 1883: "Is there a color line in Oberlin?" At the Ladies Boarding Hall, several white students had refused to sit at the same table with the black women. Although some faculty members tried, they could not change the white students' minds. The writer of the article excused the inactivity of the administration by stating: "They cannot pass a rule and say the white students shall do thus and so in the matter, for they constitute 98% of the total number." Nevertheless, he did agree that "the evil ought not to go on. . . . If to-day prejudice separates the races at the table, to-morrow that prejudice may be extended to the recitation room and in the public hall." In his opinion, it was not that the College had changed its policies, but that the class of students now attending Oberlin had changed. "Twenty five years ago," he said, the students who attended "did more or less manual labor, and we have many today, who are among our ablest men, who worked their way through; but the majority are not of that class." Seemingly it was the richer class who "have their means supplied them and whose surroundings at home are not what they are here" who had brought about the problem.[47]

Along with the other black students, Ransom organized a meeting "to voice a protest against a new regulation segregating colored girls at a separate table." He addressed the meeting and in strong terms criticized such a practice. As a result, at the end of the school year, his scholarship was canceled. He returned to Wilberforce with an entirely different view of the value of an all-Negro college.[48] Though there is no concrete evidence of Reverdy's participation in the protest or the loss of his Avery Scholarship, it is reasonable to accept his statement in *Pilgrimage* about the incident and his testimony to friends later, given his passionate involvement in similar controversies later on. It is interesting to note that the names of other Negro students who were involved in the protest are not mentioned in the campus publications or elsewhere either.

Pressure was put on President Fairchild to alter the dining room situation as evidenced by letters such as that written by B. A. Ames of Memphis, Tennessee, a former Negro student. Ames wrote that he was acquainted with the relationship between the faculty and the management of the [women's] hall "and with many others, must believe that [Fairchild would] sanction no precedent so contrary to Oberlin's good history"[49]

L. A. Roberson, another Negro alumnus wrote to Fairchild:

I am influenced to send you the enclosed letter that you may have some idea how the *thinking class* of colored citizens feel in regard to "proscription" as practiced in the Ladies Hall. It is with us a matter of principle and not regard for personal comfort of the young ladies. We have a *race pride* in Oberlin on account of past history—Therefore we had sincerely wished that the *color line* would not be drawn, thus crushing all the womanhood and manhood in our young people. What have we to hope for, if in the midst of those who have bid us look up, we are shown a place beyond which we must not hope to leap—to simply pamper the prejudices of a few young people whose education morally has been neglected.[50]

Some time after Reverdy had left Oberlin, the president abolished the segregated seating, and the white and colored women once again sat together at meals.[51]

The experience at Oberlin had been good for Reverdy more than merely academically. It was at Oberlin that he received the call to the ministry. He said he was attending a dance when a voice spoke to him. He stopped in the middle of the floor and announced he had to go back to his room. During the walk home, it became clear to him what God wanted him to do with his life, and when he arrived home, he told his roommate, he was going to be a minister.[52] In describing his "call" in *Pilgrimage*, he said his "'call' came with such a compelling urge" that he "found no peace until, with [his] whole heart, [he] surrendered to it and embraced it with joyous fear."[53] Being at Oberlin had also deepened his appreciation for Wilberforce. He realized that

Wilberforce [was] giving practical solutions to the "Negro problem," by preparing the Negro for citizenship, imbuing him with the spirit of Christianity, training his mind to think, his hands to work and qualifying him for the demands of a high civilization.[54]

He concluded that there were three kinds of schools to which Negroes were admitted, each of which had benefits: schools like Harvard, Princeton, and Yale, where they could be in "the same class room with the best brains of the country . . . and demonstrate their ability to equal and in some cases to excel"; colleges such as Howard University and Lincoln, established for colored students, under the "support and control of white men," where Negroes "have filled all requirements and surpassed all expectations"; and schools like Wilberforce, Allen University, and Paul Quinn College, "established, maintained and controlled by the Negro." It is in these schools Negroes are "learning along with the highest intellectual attainments, race pride, self-confidence and self-respect." Of these colleges, Wilberforce was "a bright and shining example."[55]

Reverdy was able to return to Wilberforce by using the money his mother had earned selling her cow. In addition to completing the regular college course, he immediately became a part of the theology department in which fifteen other students were enrolled. Among Reverdy's classmates was John Hurst from Port-au-Prince, Haiti, who later became a bishop in the A.M.E. Church. In his autobiography Reverdy described Hurst as being very "Orthodox" in his approach to religion.[56] By 1884–1885, the number of theology students had dropped to eight and rose to only ten when Ransom graduated in 1886, possibly because of the financial problems experienced by the University. However, "within a period of two or three years, the new president, Samuel T. Mitchell (1884–1900), had [re]established confidence in the university." (The former President, Benjamin F. Lee, had been elected to *The A.M.E. Christian Recorder* in 1884.[57])

During his final years at Wilberforce, Reverdy took zoology, geology, mineralogy, Greek-exegesis, English literature, introduction to the critical study of the Holy Scriptures, philosophy of history, pastoral and systematic theology, Hebrew, ecclesiastical law, church discipline, homiletics, mental philosophy, divine government, symbolic and church polity, mathematics, German, and French. Among his teachers was Thomas H. Jackson (also secretary of the university), who ordained Reverdy to preach. He taught a brand of theology that was "so orthodox that to him the science of evolution was anathema." Reverdy, who had always had difficulty with the "Trinity as it was taught," was considered so "heretical" in his views that "more than once" he was almost suspended. His studies in Greek and Hebrew with the brilliant William S. Scarborough were more pleasant.[58] (Scarborough became the sixth president of the University in 1908.)

According to the catalogue, French was taught regularly so that the students in the theology department "may be incited to consider and labor for the Protestantism of Haiti so as to wrest that gem of the ocean from Roman Catholicism and semi-heathenism which now degrade the uneducated masses of its population." The department also believed that "the scientific character" of the curriculum would give the graduates a "greater ability to meet and vanquish modern infidelity."[59]

The department had opened a chain of missions and circuits in a forty-mile radius of the college so that theology students were permitted "to exercise their gifts and graces, by means of which they [could] acquire some experience in pastoral work before entering the regular work of the pastorate."[60] As a part of his practical experience, Reverdy joined the A.M.E. Annual Conference at Zanesville, Ohio, under Bishop Jabez Pitt Campbell and was appointed to a small charge in Selma, Ohio, in 1885.[61] It was difficult keeping up with his studies, traveling twelve miles to his circuit every Saturday to administer to his small congregation, and returning on Monday to participate in the activities of the University; but it was good training for the active life he was to lead.

There were so many church doctrines he could not accept, that often he wondered about his calling and whether he should be preaching to others. Because most of those around him did not question what they were told, he felt alone. "There were no sympathetic human counsellors to whom [he] could go." Whenever the doubts became too overwhelming, he would turn to "the Bible itself, together with a wide range of reading and the knowledge that these doctrines were man-made." Eventually, he began to have the "confidence and courage to follow [his] inner voice."[62] It was during this period that he wrote a poem concerning his uncertainties. The following is an excerpt:

I will not, though it raise me to the skies,
With deceitful heart on holy things arise,
I will not into God's pure temple sneak,
And there proclaim His tidings once a week,
When not within my soul the Spirit's voice
Has named me as His messenger of choice.[63]

Why had God chosen him, of all people, for such a high calling? he asked. He could never answer the question, nor could he ever turn from the ministry. Those who knew him well said he often tried to escape through alcohol that only left him more tortured and self-abased. All his life he was to struggle in his search for spiritual truth, and because he was strong of will, he would prevail.

It was while pastoring in Selma, Ohio, during his senior year that Reverdy met the woman who was to be his companion, helpmate, and wife, Emma S. Connor, the attractive daughter of Jackson and Bettie Connor. She had long brown hair, a round pretty face, large brown eyes, and a slender body that would become plump in years to come. Emma seemed short when she stood beside the 6'2" Reverdy. Her parents had moved from Virginia to Ohio after the Emancipation Proclamation was signed so they could educate and rear their ten children in the North. Long before he met Emma, Reverdy said, "I earnestly prayed God to direct me in the matter of marriage and to send me the woman I should have for a wife in the Christian ministry." His prayers were answered. He and Emma were married by Thomas H. Jackson, October 25, 1887, after he had graduated from Wilberforce. Until she died, they had "more than fifty years of congenial and happy companionship."[64]

The Wilberforce community attracted individuals of learning and culture. In addition to Bishop Shorter, Presidents Lee and Mitchell, and Hallie Q. Brown, there were Maj. Martin R. Delaney (orator, abolitionist, titled "Major" by Queen Victoria) and his wife, who along with "Ma" Shorter often gave Reverdy "wholesome meals." Ransom was also privileged to listen to lectures by visiting dignitaries such as the former slave and famous abolitionist, Frederick Douglass; B. K. Bruce, Negro senator from Mississippi; John M. Langston, who became Negro congressman from Virginia in 1890; J. B. Foraker, U.S. senator from Ohio; and William McKinley, later president of the United States of America.[65]

The three men who seemed to have had the greatest impact on his career were

Thomas H. Jackson, Daniel A. Payne, and Benjamin William Arnett. After Jackson had died, Reverdy was to write in the January 1922 issue of *The A.M.E. Review:*

> More than any other man, [Jackson] met me at the decisive turning points of my early career. When just emerging from my teens, he gave me license as an exhorter; later he licensed me as a local preacher; he took me up to annual conference and secured my appointment to my first charge, Selma, Ohio, a student charge near Wilberforce. Reverend, now Bishop, John Hurst and I sat with him for two years as our teacher in Hebrew and Systematic Theology. He united me in marriage to a lovely woman whom I found indispensable to my comfort and happiness.

He noted that Jackson, a man of strong convictions, was one of the first graduates from Wilberforce in 1870.[66]

Reverdy had heard of Daniel Payne before he arrived at Wilberforce. More than any other person, Payne had put his imprint on the character of Wilberforce University and thereby helped to crystallize Reverdy's concept of a truly educated man of God. As Hallie Q. Brown described him in *Pen Pictures of Pioneers of Wilberforce*, "he was a small man not more than five feet in height. . . . [He was] slender with small hands and feet, almost feminine in form, [had] delicate features, keen black eyes, shaded by colored glasses . . . a man of 'high ideals.'"[67]

In Reverdy's essay "Daniel Payne, the Prophet of an Era" written years later, he equated Payne with other great men around whom history revolved. He too recalled his frail stature, noting Payne never weighed more than ninety-six pounds, but he also remembered that the "power of his faith, his courage, and wisdom were the mightiest influences that directed the development of the A.M.E. Church for two generations. Daniel Payne was a man sent from God," he concluded.[68]

Benjamin W. Arnett demonstrated to Reverdy how a man of the cloth could use politics to better the plight of the black race. In 1885 he had been elected to the Ohio State legislature and the following year helped to pass the Civil Rights Acts that did away with the Black Laws in Ohio. He became a close adviser to William McKinley during his governorship of Ohio and his presidency. In addition to Arnett's political savvy, "he had a penchant for gathering facts and was a natural born statistician,"[69] qualities that Reverdy was to exemplify as editor of *The Year Book of Negro Churches* during the 1930s and 1940s. Because Ransom worked for Arnett while attending Wilberforce, more than likely his interest in politics and statistics was sharpened by his friendship with this gifted mentor.

One of the college organizations that helped shaped Ransom as an effective preacher and orator was the Sodalian Society that had been organized for young men by Lee, Shorter, Mitchell, and Knight (its first president) in 1871. Its motto was "Non Scholae

Sid Vitae Discimas—We study not for school, but for life," and it met every Thursday from 6:30 P.M. to 8:30 P.M. During the meetings there were a report by critics, readings by the librarian and budget master, a declaration or oration, the reading of essays, and discussions. Every third Thursday the usual program was supplemented by a lecture from a faculty member.[70] In *School Days* Reverdy credited the Sodalian Society with furnishing "an excellent school for the cultivation of literary tastes and oratorical skills." Students were severely critical of one another's efforts; therefore, those who came to college "self-conceited and puffed up" found themselves often ridiculed and bested by others who were more skillful in debate and oratory. Reverdy participated vigorously in all the Sodalian's activities and was rewarded by being elected vice president in 1885.[71]

Reverdy also participated in the Tawawa Sunday School Assembly and Theological, Scientific, and Literary Circle chartered in July 1883. The first year it published *The Tawawa Journal.* Founded and managed by Benjamin W. Arnett, the purpose of the organization was to "promote habits of reading and study in nature, art, science and in secular and sacred literature in connection with the routine of daily living (especially among those whose educational advantages have been limited.)" Arnett hoped to encourage every home to utilize the "Chimney Corner" so that there would be developed "a band of thinkers—those who desire to elevate the race and increase their knowledge and usefulness." His home, which was later owned by Reverdy, was called Tawawa Chimney Corner.[72]

On Tuesday, June 17, 1886, Reverdy graduated from Wilberforce University, the third highest in a class of nine men and one woman, all of whom made considerable contributions to society, the A.M.E. Church, and the race. They were Joseph Morris of Philadelphia, who was to serve "as principal of public schools in San Antonio, Texas for fifty years"; Herbert A. Palmer of Pennsylvania who "had a useful ministry in the Pittsburgh Annual Conference"; John A. Kirk of Ohio who spent nearly fifty years as a public school teacher and a professor at Paul Quinn College in Waco, Texas; John L. Watkins of Pennsylvania "who taught in the schools of Alabama but spent the major portion of his life as a minister in the Philadelphia Conference"; Benjamin W. Arnett, Jr. (son of Bishop Arnett) who was born in Ohio, reared at Wilberforce, became a public school teacher, a chaplain in the U.S. Army, and pastor in the New York and Philadelphia Annual Conferences; Timothy Dwight Scott, born and reared in Ohio, who was high school principal in Xenia, Ohio, and Parkersburg, West Virginia, and a minister and presiding elder in Ohio; John Hurst, who became pastor of the church in Port-au-Prince, Haiti, secretary to the Haitian legation to the United States, pastor in the Baltimore Conference, and financial secretary of the A.M.E. Church after which he was elected bishop; Laura Lavinia Clark (granddaughter of Bishop Daniel A. Payne), teacher at Wilberforce and in the public schools of Tampa, Florida; William A. Anderson (grandson of Bishop James A. Shorter), reared at Wilberforce, taught for a few years, then returned to Wilberforce where he operated a general store.[73]

For his graduation oration Reverdy chose as a subject "Divine and Civil Law." He began by establishing the unity of all created things that others called "natural selection" or "the evolution of a vital principle," but which he called "the decree of Deity." He asked his audience to ponder that even though man had free will, God did not turn him loose as "prey to the elements" to give over to evil tendencies. He placed within the human breast a "universal conscience" that enabled him to have the "righteousness to prevail." It followed then that the "only foundations" on which "individuals" and "nations" could build was God. He spoke of *"true governments"* as being moral, not "founded on mere selfish interests. The security of equality of justice, of opportunity for the true development of our moral natures, are the highest objects that government can contemplate," he asserted. Although written constitutions were a great help, "the true theory of government has been written in the lines of our nature by the finger of God." "Love and brotherhood" would triumph over force in this "true theory," a theory that had come down to us through the teachings of Christ.[74]

He spoke of the Negro's loyalty to the United States, how he had endured war to maintain the "rights" and "preservation" of the union. The United States had denied the "equality and brotherhood of man." It had not then adhered to the "true theory of government," he inferred. "Since all human constitutions have been so defective, and since civilization only advances as Statesmen . . . conform to the moral law, every man has the right of appeal to the high court of which Jesus is the judge."[75]

The state was supposed to protect its citizens. The Negro had the right to appeal. Discrimination and lynching were wrong as evidenced by the "long solemn wail [coming] up from the South, but its sound is not heard." Reverdy asks, "This is the government of the people? . . . Why this unequal treatment? What have [Negroes] done?" They fought to save the Union from disintegration, helped to build up and protect the country. That is what they have done.[76]

Reverdy believed tomorrow would bring about a new day—a day when the "true theory of government" would be realized, because from Gethsemane, Christ is:

Marching down the ages with a slow and steady tread. In his hand is the chastening rod of nations. His pilgrimage will not end until the Civil and Divine Law meet on the plain of righteousness and join hands. Hang out flags and banners! Ring the bells! [Until] with returning light, all hail![77]

Though the speech showed his youthful idealism, it established a pattern that would become familiar. Reverdy would always use eloquent words that would demonstrate his love for language, especially poetry, for his race, country, and most of all for God. There are few speeches delivered later in which he did not lash out against the devastating effects of racism and appeal for a return to the principles of "Brotherhood and Love" as exemplified by the life and teachings of Christ.

When he had finished, the audience stood on its feet and applauded wildly. "His mother rushed to the platform and threw her arms around him in controlled pride."[78] It was his grandmother Lucinda who brought him back down to earth by advising later: "Now you have graduated and got your diplommy, you must be a very smart man. But smart as you are, always give other people credit for having just half as much sense as you have and in life you will have little trouble."[79]

It was a precept that guided him through life.

CHAPTER 2

Early Itinerant Ministry, 1886–1896

What went you out into the wilderness to see? A reed shaken with the wind? . . .
A prophet? Yea I say unto you, and more than a prophet.
  Matthew 11:7, 9.

The African Methodist Episcopal (A.M.E.) Church is composed of Episcopal districts presided over by a bishop who has been elected by the General Conference. Each district has several Annual Conferences; the number is determined by the size of the district. It is here each minister must make his financial and committee report, listen to the Presiding Elders' Report concerning his progress during the past year, and receive his church appointment from the bishop for the following year. The Third District of which Reverdy was a part was composed of the Ohio, North Ohio, Pittsburgh, and West Virginia Annual Conferences.

In September 1886, Reverdy arrived in Cincinnati expecting to be given one of the smaller churches in the Ohio Conference. Instead Bishop Jabez Pitt Campbell transferred him to the Pittsburgh Annual Conference that was to meet in Meadville, October 17. That meant he would have to wait a whole month before knowing what kind of appointment he would be given. When he finally arrived at Meadville, he was asked to preach. Though there is no record of the sermon, it must have been well received because when he had finished, Bishop Campbell ordained him a deacon and assigned him to Altoona, Pennsylvania, a city atop the Allegheny Mountains, "about five miles below 'Horse Shoe Bend'."[1] Its entire county of Blair "referred to as the gateway to the Alleghenies, is situated in an area of caves and caverns noted for their scenic beauty."[2]

In Altoona Reverdy found that his church was a tidy frame building on a street near the business section. Before inspecting his parish further, he went in search of lodging and was lucky enough to find a friend who gave him a room free of charge and told him he could also have kitchen privileges. This was a blessing because the church of thirteen members could only afford to pay him what they raised three Sundays a month, usually about $15. His experiences at Wilberforce and Oberlin had taught him to live under the most straitened circumstances. "Thus," he affirmed, "I kept out of debt and preserved my independence and self-respect."[3] The little church began to prosper as people heard about his preaching and pastoral abilities. Soon many of the white churches in the city and surrounding towns invited him to preach at their services, and he became an influential part of the community. Before he left, he was even able to organize an A.M.E. Church at Tyronne, Pennsylvania, a small town not far from Altoona.[4] Organizing new churches was a practice Reverdy was to follow throughout his ministry.

In addition to the churches at Altoona and Tyronne, Reverdy's circuit included a church in Hollidaysburg. To save money once a month he would walk seven miles to meet with the membership, "five widows, one old maid and one married woman." Nevertheless, he learned to value this lovely little town sequestered in the Alleghenies. Its citizens were "some of the finest examples of character and intelligence [he had] ever met."[5] It was in Hollidaysburg that he became acquainted with Dr. Daniel Hale Williams, the noted Chicago heart surgeon, who often came to visit his hometown. He was to become one of Reverdy's strong supporters when he pastored in Chicago. Reverdy learned Williams's father had represented Hollidaysburg at the Equal Rights Convention of the Colored People at Harrisburg in 1865.[6]

While in Altoona, Reverdy did not spend all of his hours engaged at the churches on his circuit. When he was not reading, he and his friends went trout fishing in crystal mountain streams or fishing for bass in the blue Juniate River. On other occasions, he would hunt for "birds, wild turkey, deer and bear, back in the mountains."[7] Reverdy relished being outdoors; it brought him closer to God. His poetry and much of his writing reflect his love of pastoral settings. When he grew older, he was to spend long periods of his summers at Woodland Park, Michigan, fishing in the lake in front of his cottage in summer or hunting deer in the fall.

In 1886, Reverdy published his first article in the A.M.E. Church's leading newspaper, *The A.M.E. Christian Recorder,* titled "Too Cultured for His Flock." The piece not only reflected his training at Wilberforce and Oberlin, but his individual ideas concerning the role of the black minister. He complained that when a minister

> uses the pastoral visits as a means of spiritual instruction . . . prays from hour to hour, instead of feasting and joking . . . spends his otherwise unemployed time in study and with his family instead of loafing around barber shops and the like . . . he is often styled "stuck up" or as being unsociable.

Although at times he might seem "too cultured for his flock," it was the minister's mission to elevate the tastes of his congregation.[8] That is why he insisted on an educated clergy rather than one merely "called," and why he continued a self-education program all his life. Very early in his pastorate, Reverdy eagerly read history and literature to elevate his mind and give him a distinct understanding of human nature. To step into his ever-growing library was to be transported to places and events and to confront the illustrious thinkers of the ages.

Reverdy's philosophy concerning education was similar to W. E. B. DuBois's (professor and writer), and Bishop Daniel Payne's. In 1881, the year Reverdy entered Wilberforce University, a school emphasizing classical learning, Booker T. Washington had founded Tuskegee Institute that focused mainly on the industrial education of the Negro. Washington was to articulate clearly his willingness to compromise on equal rights in his speech at the Atlanta Cotton States and International Exposition in 1895. He said, "No race can prosper till it learns that there is as much dignity in tilling a field as in writing a poem. It is at the bottom of life we must begin." Washington felt it was "folly" to "agitate" for social and political rights. Negroes could only earn these rights by helping to reconstruct the South.[9] Affirming that Negroes were already at the bottom and that they should aspire for the top by training their minds and actively agitating for their rights in every aspect of life, Reverdy would find himself in direct conflict with Washington in the coming years. Meanwhile he took every opportunity to encourage Negroes to develop intellectually.

One such opportunity was in the form of another article which he wrote for *The A.M.E. Christian Recorder* (March 1887) titled "Concerning Wilberforce University." In it he spoke of the A.M.E. Church being in the forefront of educational progress for the Negro. Of the 2,841 students who had attended Wilberforce, most could be found in the pulpit, the classroom, or the newspaper or law offices. In comparing Wilberforce to other schools, he said that it was doing for its own Negroes what other schools could not do, preparing them to lead useful, moral lives, with pride in themselves and race.[10] "So Ransom and those of his persuasion took issue with the approach to fostering self-help and racial pride through industrial-vocational training. . . . It only reinforced the stereotype that the blacks were capable of menial labor at best."[11]

A fourth article written by Reverdy during this period appeared years later in *The A.M.E. Review*, titled "The Student." Still extolling the merits of education, he said the student "has worn the mantle of Caesar, and, Prometheus-like has been bound to the rock of all defeated theories and untrue faiths." Likewise, the student is "older than creation's morn . . . has thought all thoughts, dreamed all dreams, seen all sights and heard all sounds . . . lived all lives and died all deaths, suffered all defeats and won all victories." For Ransom, education opened up the entire real world and the magical world of imagination.[12]

Reverdy's bachelor days ended when he brought his twenty-three-year-old bride, Emma S. Connor, to Altoona. The couple had been married in Selma, Ohio, October 25, 1887. Though he had less than $5 in his pocket after the wedding, they "were rich in faith and strong affection for each other." His friend's room would not be suitable for he and Emma, so he rented a small, old frame house on "Gospel Hill." Becoming the

Emma in her twenties. Courtesy Ruth Ransom, Xenia, Ohio.

proud "possessor of a door-key" made him feel important. It was "a mighty symbol of duty and responsibility."[13]

Emma proved to be the ideal minister's wife. She rarely complained about the inconveniences she had to endure, especially in the early impoverished years. Not only was she a good companion to Reverdy at work or play, she loved people from all walks of life.[14] Soon after joining him in Altoona, she had transformed their house into a home where the community loved to visit. Her constant battle, however, was with the bedbugs she inherited with the house; they were determined to be permanent boarders. When Bishop Campbell and his wife came to visit the parsonage (the first bishop they had ever entertained), the Ransoms were terrified that they would be annoyed all night by the bedbugs. Evidently, the pests decided to take a holiday, for the bishop and his wife said they had slept soundly. Campbell must have been in capital humor, because after he had finished preaching Sunday, he refused to take the $5 the congregation offered him and insisted on the entire collection of $15. When he returned to the parsonage, he took the money from his pocket and gave it to Reverdy, saying, "I got it for you. I knew those officers never would have given it all to you."[15] Times were hard, and Reverdy was grateful for the bishop's thoughtfulness.

To make ends meet, Reverdy spent long hours doing manual labor for whites when he was not involved in church work. In a journal entry dated August 21, 1888, he states that on one such occasion, he got home Saturday night around eleven and found Emma sick. A few hours later, he went in search of Dr. Oatman.

At 7:15 [Sunday] Emma gave birth to a boy child. He was an eight month child, but was large and well formed. He was sick from the first and died about five o'clock Sunday evening. This is the first time anyone near and dear to me has fallen asleep. But I have the consolation that the little soul is with god.

He hoped that he and Emma would see God and his son in the hereafter. As if to reassure himself of his will to survive, he closes the entry by noting that despite his continual "weariness of body," he had been able to preach three times the Sunday before, at Altoona, Tyronne, and Hollidaysburg. No matter the difficulties he encountered, Ransom was determined to fulfill his church responsibilities. Luckily the bad times were balanced by the pleasant ones.[16]

The Ransoms were to experience many acts of kindness in Altoona. On one occasion, a prosperous Negro barber took Reverdy to a store, supposedly to see a display. Instead he had Reverdy try on a coat that he bought for him. It was a welcome replacement for the "thin and rather shabby cotton" overcoat Reverdy had been wearing. Another time when the couple had nothing to eat and no money, Reverdy stumbled out into the blinding snow "praying that God would help [him]." He bumped into the white opera manager who gave him five dollars for his church dues because he said he didn't have confidence in most of the white ministers, but he thought Reverdy was doing a good job. "From that day onward," Reverdy said, "I have never doubted that God of the sparrows would abundantly supply all my needs."[17]

The year 1888 was to be one of drastic changes for the Ransoms. During the Eighteenth A.M.E. General Conference in May at Indianapolis, Indiana, Bishop Campbell was moved to the Second Episcopal District; that meant he was no longer Reverdy's prelate. Bishop Daniel Payne took his place.[18] A few months later at the Pittsburgh Annual Conference in Cannonsburg, Bishop Payne ordained Reverdy an elder. During the final day of the conference, he read the appointments. Payne had moved Reverdy from Altoona to Manchester Mission in Allegheny City (now called North Pittsburgh, Pennsylvania), a mission of only five members. Reverdy was so angry that he went to the bishop and told him he could not go to such a place because there was "nothing there." According to Ransom, Payne "stamped his foot and shaking his trembling finger . . . said . . . 'There are people there.'" He proved to be right. There were a large number of Negroes living in Allegheny, most of them in squalor.[19]

When the Ransoms reached the city, they were directed to the parish near the Ohio River where they found their five members "worshipping in a reeking alley-like street, in a small room containing three benches and some chairs." Most of the neighborhood people lived in alley tenements and shanty boats on the river. Though many claimed to be religious, they saw no reason to attend church. Desiring to be near their potential members, the Ransoms moved into a broken-down house at Number 10, Evans Alley. Soon after they were able to get enough contributions from friends and businessmen to rent an old paint shop that they converted into a church that seated about 100 people. With fresh pastries in hand and a great deal of faith, Reverdy and Emma frequented the tenements and shanties and invited the people to come to the Manchester Mission and to the parsonage. Before long the makeshift church was so crowded, they began to plan for a larger, more permanent structure. It was in Allegheny City that he and Emma recognized the urgent need for social service that would meet the community's daily living requirements as well as be a place of worship on Sundays.[20] Later this concept was more fully realized in what became know as an "Institutional Church."

In assessing what the church needed to do to assist the Negro, Ransom knew first he had to give a great deal of thought to his race's plight in America. He concluded:

> The universal poverty of the Afro-American is held before his eyes, and the eyes of the world as an evidence of his shiftlessness. It is further charged that he has contributed nothing to the development and advancement of this country. These charges are false. He had produced a larger share of the wealth of this country than any other equal number of persons. But his share of the wealth . . . was stolen from him. His labor was and is the back bone of whatever material prosperity the South has ever enjoyed.

His social gospel and his politics would be based on this premise. Negroes had paid their dues and were entitled to their share of the American dream.[21]

Reverdy soon became acquainted with the local clergy, all of whom were older than he: Rev. D. S. Bently from Kentucky, an evangelical singer and preacher, and Rev. I. N. Ross, pastor of Brown Chapel who did not have much schooling but who made up for it with his dynamic preaching. Ross had pastored a mission church in Oberlin while Reverdy was a student there. Reverdy also became acquainted with Rev. G. W. Clinton, pastor of John Wesley A.M.E. Zion Church in Pittsburgh, and Rev. Cornelius Ashbury, who had the most training of the ministers.[22]

With Clinton as editor, Bentley as president, and Reverdy as associate editor, the group founded and published a newspaper, *The Afro-American Spokesman* on May 4, 1889. The paper had socialist leanings and was designed to persuade the twenty-thousand Negroes living in Pittsburgh and Allegheny City to take positive action against their economic plight. It warned that "Situated as we now are, in the industrial world, so far as material worth is concerned, the next generation can be but little better off than this." If we continued to allow ourselves to be "shut out from the industries that produce the wealth and constitute the back-bone of the country, we must ever be poor." The paper had a circulation of about seven hundred and continued to be published at the corner of Wylie and Federal Streets in Pittsburgh until March 15, 1890.[23]

Reverdy was always concerned about the uneven relationship between labor and capital. As Calvin Morris points out in *Reverdy C. Ransom, A Pioneer Black Social Gospeler,* the "two main currents to which [Ransom] was exposed during the 1880's and 1890's . . . was the Social Gospel and the deteriorating position of black people in the United States and Africa." What he and many other social gospelers "embraced . . . was a Christianized version of socialism. Jesus, not Marx, remained their example."[24] For Ransom, the teachings of Christ embodied the principles of socialism in action: sharing the wealth and dividing the loaves and fishes.

September 2, 1889, Emma gave birth to Reverdy Cassius Ransom Jr., a robust baby who resembled his mother. The same year Reverdy brought his other son, seven-year-old Harold Ransom, to live with him. Harold was baptized on September 17 by Rev. W. S. Lowry and Reverdy Jr. on September 22 by Rev. D. S. Bentley. The family unit was complete; the Ransoms were to have no more children. But from then on the parsonage resounded with the laughter and shouts of the two lively boys. Reverdy prayed that "God would give [him] the wisdom and strength to rear these children to His honor and glory."[25]

It was at Manchester Mission that Reverdy encountered his first real controversy with a congregation. The unmarried organist of his church became pregnant, and the members were indignant. They wanted her to be tried and expelled from the church. Reverdy fought against what he called Christian hypocrisy and reminded them that the church was not established for just the righteous, but for those who were most in need of love and compassion. Despite the objections of some of his most loyal members, he refused to turn the organist away. A few months later, he married her to the father and lived to "see her children engaged in business . . . school-teaching and law."[26] As David Wills pointed out in "Reverdy C. Ransom, The Making of an A.M.E. Bishop,"

> No doubt, Ransom's leniency for those who in one way or another departed from the church's teaching about sex and marriage, in part reflected a personal sympathy based on his own experience. But it also seems to have been based on a deliberate shift of emphasis from "law" to "gospel."[27]

Eventually the Manchester Mission was able to raise $4,500 to buy property, a lot and house on Chartiers Street in a white neighborhood. The Jewish man who had sold Reverdy the property told him he had made an offer of $8,000 to buy the adjoining lot and threatened to sell his property to a Negro church if the owner did not take the offer. True to his word, he sold it to Manchester Mission. When the Ransoms occupied the house, the neighbors offered him $500 not to move in. Reverdy refused. One night, the family was awakened by hard objects hitting the house; glass and lights were shattered. One of the rocks just missed hitting baby Reverdy sleeping in his crib.[28] Recalling this event, Reverdy wrote in *The A.M.E. Christian Recorder*, March 20, 1890:

> I reported the matter to the police, but they could never detect the parties. Failing in protection from this source, I bought a little instrument [gun] and the last time they came I brought it to requisition. I have not been annoyed since. Strange to say the Jew had had his revenge. The presence of our church here has caused the ground in the square in which it stands to depreciate in value fifty dollars a foot.[29]

(In the autobiography, Reverdy says the owner was an Italian, in the article, a Jew.) Reverdy stood firm, and eventually the neighbors came to understand that neither the church nor the Ransoms were going anywhere.

Before the new church had been built on the lot, Reverdy and a few of his members decided to name it Wilberforce Chapel; however, "the name did not meet the approval of the majority of the congregation." Reverdy promised to give them an opportunity to choose another name. To his surprise, at a Wednesday night prayer meeting, they voted to name the church after him. He protested and urged them to make another choice. "I felt and still feel," he wrote in his journal, "that it would be thought that I had influenced the people in this to secure some honor for myself, but it was an honor which under the circumstances, I did not, nor do I desire." Nevertheless, he was unable to change their minds, so the new church became Ransom Chapel. Ransom hoped that he would be worthy of the name.[30]

In November 1889, the masons began to lay the foundation for the church and on December 14, the cornerstone laying ceremonies were held. Although Bishop Payne was in attendance, Rev. J. M. Morris placed the stone, because the Bishop found it difficult to speak in "the open air."[31]

Early in December, Reverdy went to visit his parents in Cambridge and to see his father join the A.M.E. Church. While there he bought four shares in a building and loan association and borrowed four hundred dollars to pay his father's debts and fix up the house. He enjoyed his visit, especially seeing his mother again, but was anxious to return to Allegheny and Emma.[32]

In *Pilgrimage*, Reverdy relates many humorous incidents and characters he came in contact with in Allegheny. One of his favorites was "Uncle Tom" Chambers who told him he "couldn't preach much" but he certainly did "enjoy them gospel lectures." He met Matthew S. Quay, U.S. senator, who ran the Republican Party in Pennsylvania, and William Thaw, the philanthropist who, from his back door on certain days of the week, gave out $500 donations to causes he deemed worthy. Reverdy was a recipient of his largess. He became friends with Dr. J. C. Price, founder of Livingstone College in Salisbury, North Carolina, when Dr. Price visited Pittsburgh. He and Reverdy traveled up the Monongahela River then sat on the shore talking about the race problem. He never forgot their conversation, part of which had to do with education. Price told Reverdy, "[The Negro's] door of escape lies through schools like Livingstone College. We must use education. We must acquire the white man's knowledge in every department of human endeavor."[33]

Having seen that Reverdy had done his best with the limited resources at his command in Allegheny, in 1890 Bishop Payne transferred him from the Pittsburgh Conference back to the Ohio Conference and appointed him to North Street Church in Springfield, Ohio, a church, according to Payne, with "carpets on the floor, cushioned pews, stained glass windows and a marble pulpit."[34]

The number of Negroes living in Springfield in 1890 was 3,549, 11.1 percent of the total population. The increase of black population since 1880 (1,189) was largely due to blacks living on the fringes of Springfield moving into the urban center "as a result of aggressive municipal annexation policies" and the opening up of factory jobs. After 1890 the black population declined because of racial violence and riots.[35]

Between 1870 and 1900 Springfield's A.M.E. membership grew from 123 to 484. North Street Church was indeed a step up for the Ransoms. Its comparatively large congregation came from the middle and upper-middle class of Negroes, and it paid its pastor considerably more than Reverdy had been accustomed to. He recalled that on Sundays a "line of carriages and buggies extended for two blocks or more, on either side of the church." Among those in attendance were "Uncle Jim" Buford, contractor and politician who controlled the Negro vote, and James Nelson and William Dixon, owners and operators of prosperous blacksmith shops. A large number of the members worked in Asa Bushnell's farm machinery manufacturing plant where they were well paid. (It was Bushnell and Mark Hanna, iron ore and coal manufacturer, who were largely responsible for the election of William McKinley to the governorship of Ohio and later to the presidency of the United States.)[36]

In Springfield, Reverdy determined the style of oration and sermonizing he wanted to adopt. Like most young ministers, for a time he was fascinated by those histrionic preachers who got the loudest "Amens" from their audiences. He probably also remembered the comments of "Uncle Tom" Chambers about his "gospel lectures" in Allegheny City. At North Street on one occasion he had invited a popular evangelist from Kentucky to help him conduct a revival. After noting the tremendous reaction to the minister's "musical intonation" and "full flowing cadences," Ransom decided to try to imitate him. All week he practiced what seemed to him to be "a smooth, unctuous, sounding intonation." The following Sunday he stood before his congregation trying out his new style. When the service was over Ransom said one of the women asked him, "What is the matter with you this morning? Are you sick? . . . We don't want you to stand up there and act the fool like that preacher you brought here from Kentucky." Reverdy reminded her that the congregation had seemed to enjoy him, and she answered, "Yes, that is all right for him, but we don't want our minister to make himself ridiculous by any such performance." From then on Reverdy decided to be himself in the pulpit and graciously received all thoughtful criticisms concerning his delivery.[37] His sermons were highly moving because of the deep convictions from which he spoke. He did not need the extra flourishes. So masterful did he become in his delivery that when he died, W. E. B. DuBois called him a "preacher par excellence, orator in the category of Demosthenes, Chrysostom, T.M.D. Ward, and B. W. Arnett" and a "literary genius."[38]

There were many firsts for Reverdy in Springfield. In 1891 he organized the first men's club and Epworth League in the A.M.E. Church and welcomed to his pulpit the female evangelist, Amanda Smith. (At the time, the A.M.E. Church did not readily welcome women to its pulpits.) The men's club would meet on Sunday afternoon to discuss politics, civil rights, and any other matters that were of concern. The same year he wrote an article in *The A.M.E. Christian Recorder*, "Concerning Wilberforce: The Trustee Board and the Theological Department," in which he again stressed the importance of an educated ministry. He urged the board to reorganize or organize a theology department proper. This could be done by each of the fifty Annual Conferences establishing a scholarship of $100 to $125 for Wilberforce. If this were not possible, they could at least ask the General Conference "to provide for the maintenance of a theological school at Wilberforce."[39] By October, Ransom's wish for a reorganization of the teaching of theology was realized. Payne Theological Seminary opened as a separate part of the university with Bishop Payne as its first dean.[40] There was no way for Reverdy to know in 1891 how much he would become involved with Payne Seminary in later years.

On February 14, 1893, Reverdy was asked to speak in Columbus, Ohio, at the Sixth Annual Lincoln Banquet. On February 11, he had received a letter from Wilberforce that reminded him that the eyes of the university, especially his class of "86," and the race would be on him as he spoke in Columbus:

> Dare you fail, or will you accept this as a golden opportunity when you will so ably acquit yourself that they of the opposite color shall have additional reason for accrediting the Negro all the principles of true manhood. . . . May the shades of the immortal "86" hover over you and touch your tongue with a live coal of fire that your words may be words that burn deep down into the soul. [Signed] Your Companions in Toil: [Revs] T. D. Scott, W. A. Anderson and J. P. Maxwell.[41]

Reverdy titled his speech "The Fifteenth Amendment." He began by listing the three great sea voyages that had "had greater influence upon the history and progress of the human race than any event . . . since the birth of Christ": Columbus's voyage, the Pilgrims on the Mayflower, and the Dutch man-of-war carrying the first cargo of twenty Negroes to Jamestown, Virginia, in 1619, "the only race that had not come of its own accord." Nevertheless, since then the Negro had always been there when America needed him, he said. "Though beaten, cursed and robbed: rewarded with the severance of the tenderest ties of affection—he answered, 'present' every day for two hundred and fifty years" including during the Revolutionary and Civil Wars.[42]

The question now that seemed to divide churches and other religious denominations and to perplex the politicians was "What shall we do with the Negro?" When the South failed to defeat the Fifteenth Amendment, it tried to "nullify it by murder, incineration, intimidation and fraud. . . . [It] invests the Negro with the stripes of the flag it failed to destroy, but denies both the promise and protection of its stars."[43] It is this subversion of the Amendment that threatens to pull down the republic. In defending the Negroes right to the franchise, he said:

Wise men may smile at his ignorance, the rich may mock his poverty, fools may despise the color of his skin; but an ignorant man, a poor man, a black man who is thoroughly loyal, is a better and safer voter than a rich man, an educated man, and a white man who in his heart is disloyal to the Union and who openly violates the Constitution and violates the laws.[44]

He noted that now almost all of the nation's attention was centered on the tariff but asked "What does a man care about the tariff whose birthright has been taken away?" How the government supports itself should be of secondary concern when the "constitutional rights are being denied in more than a dozen states." If the Fifteenth Amendment cannot be enforced, it should be done away with or amended so that any state that "excludes the Negro from the right of suffrage" loses its right to apportionment. Even though enfranchisement may be unpopular, Reverdy felt that the Republican Party should hold to those principles it maintained prior to and during the Civil War.[45]

Although he was somewhat disappointed in the present behavior of the Republican Party, he could not in all conscience endorse the Democratic Party. He closed by talking about the Negro's loyalty to Republicanism:

Despite outrage and desertion and wrong, despite passion and prejudice, as long as the banner of Republicanism bears upon it such illustrious names as Lincoln, Grant, Sherman, Garfield, Blaine, McKinley and Foraker with the principles which these names suggest . . . the colored citizens of the United States will be among the last to desert its standards or to let its sacred folds trail in the dust of dishonor or defeat.[46]

Reverdy's speech was timely in face of the 1893 depression resulting from the panic on Wall Street, the Pullman Strike, and the failure of the Philadelphia and Reading

Railroads.[47] As always during a depression, blacks had been the "last hired and the first fired." They needed someone to dramatically call attention to their plight. The Lincoln Banquet had given Reverdy an ideal opportunity to do so. Most felt that the second term of Democrat President Grover Cleveland had been a disaster. In his first Inaugural Address in 1888, he had delivered a few well-chosen phrases to appease the Negro population.[48] Even Frederick Douglass had said "no better words [had] dropped from the east portico of the Capitol since the inauguration days of Abraham Lincoln and Gen. Grant." However, in Cleveland's second inaugural speech, the president said little about the Negro. "As the Southern campaign to hang Jim Crow in albatross fashion around the necks of the blacks in the 1890s rolled along, Cleveland, as far as could be ascertained, said nothing" about civil rights and the Fourteenth and Fifteenth Amendments.[49] No doubt this is why Reverdy felt it was essential that he emphasize the dire need for the Fifteenth Amendment to be enforced if blacks were to be accounted full citizens in the country for which they had fought and labored. Reverdy had acquitted himself well. Undoubtedly his "Companions in Toil" at Wilberforce were more than justified in their faith that he would stir the emotions of those who believed in equality and at least disturb the consciences of others who were determined to keep the Negro down.

The same year, Ransom also attended the World Parliament of Religion held in connection with the World's Columbia Exposition in Chicago. He listened to Bishop Arnett as he moved the assembly by his address:

> We meet on the heights of this Parliament of Religions, the first gathering of the peoples since the time of Noah, when Shem and Japhet have met together. I greet the Children of Shem, I greet the children of Japhet, and I want you to understand that Ham is here![50]

Although most of the other A.M.E. bishops attended the World Parliament of Religion, none except Arnett was asked to speak. Nevertheless, the Wilberforce exhibit at the exposition was awarded a medal for superior students' work, and in the Haitian building at the exposition, Frederick Douglass "made an impromptu address on the Parliament challenging some antiadversions against Negroes by a white Southerner."[51]

It was during the exposition in Chicago that Reverdy made the acquaintance of Paul Laurence Dunbar, the black poet. Born in Dayton, Ohio, in 1872 to ex-slaves, Dunbar attended Central High School in that city. Because there was no money for college, when he graduated he found a job running an elevator in the Callahan Building where he would write poetry when he was not busy. In 1892 he had printed his first book, a small volume of poetry called *Oak and Ivy* but found he did not have enough money to pay the printer.[52] When he acquainted Reverdy of his predicament, Reverdy told him to ask for one hundred copies from the printer with Reverdy's personal guarantee the books would be paid for in a week. On Sunday morning back in Springfield, Reverdy introduced Dunbar to his congregation who bought all of the copies at one dollar apiece. Ransom recalled: "From [that] time until the close of his career, our friendship was warm; and our association close and intimate."[53]

In addition to their love for poetry, both men shared a weakness for alcohol that became more pronounced in Ransom's later years and in the closing years of Dunbar's life. (Dunbar died of tuberculosis at the age of thirty-four.) In his short career, Dunbar was to receive fame largely as a dialect poet in the plantation tradition of Joel Chandler Harris and Thomas Nelson Page, although he also wrote short stories, novels, and classical verse. After his death, some blacks would look on these dialect poems as wrongfully glorifying plantation life; however, there was a warm humor in his portrayals of antebellum Negroes that went beyond mere stereotype.[54] "Beloved of the folk who recited his works on all possible occasions and who named their schools and other public buildings for him, Paul Laurence Dunbar was more definitely the 'Poet of the People' than any other Negro writer has been." William Dean Howells, the writer and critic, praised his dialect poems as did most whites and many blacks. Little acclaim was given his standard English verses despite the fact that Dunbar liked them best.[55]

Dunbar often shared his frustration about the rejection of these works with Reverdy. His despair was best expressed in his poem, "The Poet," published in his 1903 collection, which ended:

He sang of love when earth was young,
and love itself was in his lays.
But ah, the world, it turned to praise,
A jingle in a broken tongue.[56]

Ransom disagreed with Howell's preference for the dialect poems, and felt "it was in the pure English poems that the poet expressed *himself.*"[57]

When Reverdy became editor of *The A.M.E. Review,* he dedicated his October 1914 issue to Dunbar that included tributes from Alice M. Dunbar, Dunbar's estranged widow, and W. B. Scarborough. In his own editorial, Reverdy spoke of Dunbar's love of beauty, pleasure, and music but added that "a spirit so highly strung and sensitive as his was not without its tragedies." He told of the times Dunbar would come to his study "wearing a look of almost hopeless dejection" and ask him to pray with him "for strength and heaven's gracious favor."[58] The tragedies of Dunbar's life—a failed marriage, rejection of the poems he most cherished, his addiction for alcohol that at times caused him embarrassment, and his lifetime battle with tuberculosis—touched Reverdy deeply. All his life he would treasure the too few moments he shared with his poet friend.

Reverdy also developed friendship with another poet, one who never received the acclaim of a Dunbar. He was Rev. Alberry A. Whitman, who published two volumes of poetry, *Not a Man and Yet a Man* and *Twasinta's Seminoles.* Ransom sensed that Whitman was a lonely man who, with his fertile imagination and artistic temperament, found the tasks of the ministry to be uninteresting and tedious. "One of the greatest American tragedies [was] . . . that the buried talents of black men and women [were] not permitted to emerge because of race and color prejudice."[59] He had great empathy for the black artist in all fields. Like Countee Cullen, another of his favorite poets, Reverdy never doubted God's goodness and wisdom, but still marveled at the "curious thing" that God would make "a poet *black* and bid him sing."[Emphasis added][60]

In the fall of 1893 at the North Ohio Conference, Reverdy received his last appointment from Bishop Payne who was to die two months later. This time Payne sent him to St. John A.M.E. Church in Cleveland, Ohio. It had been founded in 1830 and was the city's first black church. Prior to the late 1800s most blacks had attended white-dominated churches so that, during its first two or three decades, St. John's membership grew slowly "and was serviced by the lower-class . . . who felt out of place attending the staid services of the integrated congregations." By 1863 St. John had grown to seventy-six members and eighty-five Sunday-school scholars; however, when Reverdy arrived, there were about seven hundred members, and it was the largest Negro church in Cleveland.[61] Before he left, Reverdy had taken in over three hundred additional converts. Many of these people lived in East Cleveland and had to travel a long way to St. John. To accommodate them Reverdy founded a new church called St. James and asked the bishop to send a regular pastor there.[62] St. James was to become important to Reverdy in the 1930s and 1940s when he became bishop of the district and his friend and "son in the gospel," Joseph Gomez, was its pastor.

The wealthiest whites in Cleveland lived in mansions on Euclid and Prospect Avenues. Among the most prominent were Mark Hanna, iron ore and coal magnate and president of the Republican National Committee; John D. Rockefeller, oil magnate and philanthropist; Samuel Mathers of Standard Oil fame; and Sherwin of Sherwin-Williams Paint Company. Although blacks lived in a variety of areas of Cleveland, especially the mobile middle and upper class, the majority of the seven thousand Negroes lived in the Central Avenue area where St. John was located on Erie Street. There were also four other Negro churches on or near Central Avenue. Among them were St. Andrew's Episcopal Church and Mt. Zion Congregational Church that were considered by many to be elitist.[63]

On November 30, 1893, Reverdy was invited to deliver a Thanksgiving message at the prestigious Mt. Zion where Rev. Daniel Shaw was the pastor. Reverdy chose as his title

The Ransoms at Linwood Park, 1890s. *From left:* Harriet, Reverdy holding Reverdy Jr., Harold, and Emma. Courtesy Ruth Ransom, Xenia, Ohio.

"Out of the Midnight Sky," a reference to the slow emergence of world religions and Afro-Americans from the midnight of their existence toward the dawn of hope. He began by affirming how blessed the United States was, how God had provided for her well-being. "If capital has been idle and labor unemployed," it is because they have not used the gifts given them by God. Nevertheless, in every era, "there is a point which marks well [its] transition," a time when humanity "stands for a moment 'betwixt the conflux of two eternities.'" The Columbia Exposition in Chicago had marked such a time.[64]

The word generally used to describe the closing of the nineteenth century is "progress," Reverdy said. To most this means "the invention and multiplication of machines, the discoveries of science, the inductions of philosophy, the creations of genius, constitutional amendments, and the enactment of laws." But to him, this is not the meaning of progress. A nation may have all this and still be in the process of decay. "The ascending scale of human progress was best measured by Moses amid thunders of Sinai; by Jesus in Gethsemane; Paul before Agrippa; by Luther at the Diet of Worms; by Richard Allen's manly stand for manhood Christianity; by Abraham Lincoln" when he signed the Emancipation Proclamation.[65]

The "crowing glory" of the nineteenth century and the Exposition was the Parliament of Religion, he asserted. At the Art Palace in Chicago, people of all persuasions had gathered to tell of "their conception of God." When they had finished their testimonies, "it was discovered that in all nations 'God had not left Himself without a witness.'" With Aristotle, they agreed "that 'God is One, only receiving various names from the various manifestations we perceive.'" This World Parliament, Reverdy believed, marked the beginning of communication and understanding among the many religious of the world.[66]

After acknowledging the importance of the assembly where Bishop Arnett was the lone spokesman for the Negroes of all nations, Reverdy turned to the current plight of blacks in America. In the aftermath of the Civil War and emancipation, the Negro had thought his midnight had passed, but it was only "a momentary coruscation of light." The events of 1893 had merely "served to add more gloomy chapters to the sad and melancholy history of the race upon these shores." The Negro understands the importance of the church, the school, and the home and is "endeavoring to qualify himself for citizenship . . . by taking advantage of all the aid they afford." he said. Nevertheless, the Negro had been exposed to numerous outrages, mob violence, lynchings, and burnings:

> The smell of burning flesh from Negroes consumed at the stake has been a pleasant odor in the nostrils of tens of thousands of American citizens. . . . When a human life is taken by the mob, not only is the wretched prisoner slain, but the majesty and authority of the law is slain, and society is slain also.[67]

Next he spoke of the attitude of the press that, in the North, reported the crimes but offered no protest against them. The Southern press, including some clergymen, defended the mob violence. Through all of this the "Afro-American press [had] been wise in counsel, patriotic in tone, strong in defense, and fearless in pleading the cause of the race before the world."[68]

He posed the question, "Is there hope for the future?" A few Negroes had grown discouraged and given up, he said. "It is true that the field of opportunity is largely closed against us. But the man or the race who falters or retreats because the door of opportunity is slammed in his face, is unworthy of the goal he seeks." He cited the Jewish race who had been persecuted for years but had lived to see the birth and death "of empires for more than three thousand years." In terms of the Colonization movement proposed by those who saw no hope for the Negro in America, he had this to say: "If the free and enfranchised descendants of a race that endured two hundred and fifty years of slavery in this land cannot survive after thirty years because opportunities are limited [and] liberties curtailed, neither would they become strong and powerful" enough to survive in Africa. God was still in control.[69] Implied in his sermon was that if the Parliament marked a beginning of a change in religious tolerance, it was time for America to alter its behavior toward the Negro, because the Negro was here to stay.

Reverdy's objection to the expatriation of blacks was in direct contrast to A.M.E. Bishop Henry McNeal Turner's advocacy. As early as 1871, Turner was urging that blacks emigrate to Haiti, and a few years later that they ask the U.S. government to give them New Mexico. Finally he turned to Africa as the best location, stating that black Americans "must find a country in which they would be welcome to govern and to assume leadership." Because African Methodism was already established in Africa, he felt that God had ordained it to be the denomination that could best bring Christianity to the "Fatherland." In 1876, he became "lifetime honorary vice-president" of The Colonization Society, in spite of the disapproval of race leaders such as Frederick Douglass and William Monroe Trotter, editor of *The Boston Guardian*, who was to become Reverdy's good friend.[70]

Reverdy read in the *Cleveland Gazette* of Bishop Turner's invitation "to the friends of African repatriation or Negro nationalization elsewhere" to meet in convention. The meeting was to take place November 28, 1893, at noon in Cincinnati. Turner gave his reasons:

> The revolting, hideous, monstrous, unnatural, brutal and shocking crimes charged upon us daily on the one hand, and the reign of mobs, lynchers and fire-fiends, and midnight and midday assassins on the other, necessitate a national convention on our part, for the purpose of crystallizing our sentiments and unifying our endeavor for better conditions in this country, or a change of base for existence.[71]

Although Reverdy agreed that Negroes needed to unify "for better conditions in this country," he could never agree that they needed "a change of base of existence." He decided not to attend. It was true Turner was "a strange wandering comet . . . a daredevil that blazed new trails into hitherto untrodden paths," but Reverdy, like many others, must have thought the timing of such a convention was ill advised.[72] Many of the most dedicated leaders of The Colonization Society had died, contributions were at a new low, and the society had been severely criticized when "it failed to provide transportation for three hundred penniless blacks who had arrived in New York, mistakenly believing that they would be granted passage to Africa."[73]

As Reverdy had suspected, very little was accomplished at the convention. There was much rhetoric but a minimum of concrete planning. Turner was rebuffed in terms of the emigration issue. "Only the face-saving measure of returning his back-to-Africa proposals to committee saved him from outright defeat."[74] Reverdy admired Turner as a "staunch defender of his race," but as he said at Turner's eulogy in 1915: "How strange it is that epoch-making men, who seem to have the stamp of the divine approval, are so full of imperfections and inconsistencies. But our Jacobs and Davids, Luthers and Turners are of this mold."[75] He might have added "Ransoms" to the list.

On November 29, 1893, Bishop Daniel Payne died. Emma and Reverdy left eleven-year-old Harold and four-year-old Reverdy Jr. with church members and traveled to Wilberforce to attend Payne's funeral in the campus chapel on December 3. All of the bishops and general officers came to pay homage to a man who had meant so much to the Church and especially to Wilberforce University. The Ransoms listened to President S. T. Mitchell deliver "an eloquent address on behalf of the University faculty" and John G. Mitchell on behalf of Payne Theological Seminary. Finally "Bishops Tanner and Turner spoke feelingly of their loved and revered associate."[76] Even though Reverdy was sometimes uncomfortable with Payne's asceticism, he revered him and felt a sadness at the passing of this spiritual giant who had had a great influence on his own training. In his *Preface to History of the A.M.E. Church*, Reverdy wrote: "In the field of achievement in education, Bishop D. A. Payne stood head and shoulders above all the rest."[77]

The year 1894 was busy for the couple who were moving St. John toward a more comprehensive institutional church. In addition to rearing her own two sons, Emma organized a Sunday School of neighborhood children and established a kindergarten and children's day program so that mothers could have some place safe to leave their children while they worked. Most of the women were domestics because there were very few other jobs available to black women. She introduced the congregation to spirituals and classical music, emphasizing choral music, and founded the Tawawa Literary Society that sponsored forums and debates and brought in speakers such as Paul Laurence Dunbar, the young Dayton poet, and Ida B. Wells, ex-slave and activist in the antilynching crusade.[78]

The Women's Christian Temperance Union (WCTU) had its annual meeting in Cleveland, November 16–21, 1894. Both Emma and Reverdy attended some of the meetings that were held under a cloud of controversy. There was only one black delegate present. Ida B. Wells, an ardent supporter of the Temperance movement, did not attend. She was feuding with the president, Francis E. Willard. Reverdy was sorry to report that "the women of this convention, when it came to business on the lynching question, got down in the dust before a little handful of Southern women." Although they denounced every evil, including "the massacre of Christians in Armenia, they were silent when it came to lynching and burning of Christians at home." After much discussion, the president did announce at the end of the meeting that there would be a resolution against lynching but it would not mention any particular section of the country. This, of course, was done so as not to offend the Southern women.[79]

In light of the argument between Willard and Wells, Emma invited Ida B. Wells to come to St. John and speak at the Tawawa Literary Society on November 19.[80] Well's speech was summed up in an open letter written by Reverdy to the editor of *The A.M.E. Christian Recorder* under the heading "Two Great Women at Variance: The National Convention of the WCTU in Cleveland—Notes and Comments." Reverdy disputed the rumor that Wells had discredited Willard and the wctu while she was in London by saying "the organization drew the color line and was in favor of lynching." What she had actually said, Reverdy wrote, was that in some of the southern states, colored women were excluded from the wctu and that Willard and the union had been silent on the subject of lynching. Wells's remarks concerning white women had been in response to an interview Willard had given the *New York Voice* in 1890 in which she allegedly said

> that the Negro's inspiration was the grog shop and the toddy stick; that it was unsafe for white men to venture beyond the shadow of their homes lest their wives and daughters should be assaulted and that [the Negro's] enfranchisement was a mistake.

Wells had called attention to the admissions in the press of some white women who said they had had consensual sex with black men and had not been raped as was reported. Reverdy agreed that Wells was justified in bringing Willard to task. To him she was "a mighty champion," who like "Joan of Arc . . . crowns the front of battle, holding aloft the sacred Oriflamme of truth."[81] Evidently those present at the St. John meeting agreed with Reverdy. Ida B. Wells's remarks were enthusiastically received.

While pastoring St. John, Reverdy "organized and consecrated the first Board of Deaconesses in the a.m.e. Church or, perhaps, in any other Negro denomination at that time." Among the duties of this group of older women were preparing for and assisting with the communion and baptism, visiting the sick in their homes and hospitals, and comforting the bereaved, in essence, serving as the "mothers" of the church. In his autobiography, Reverdy laments that he never got credit for establishing the board and complained that Bishop Abram Grant adopted the idea and went about organizing them throughout the Connection as if the whole project had been his idea.[82] Reverdy also organized a Society of Christian Endeavor, hosted its convention, and created the Ransom Cadets patterned after the United Boys' Brigade founded by W. A. Smith of the Free College of Glasgow. Among other things, Reverdy's brigade stressed compulsory attendance at Sunday School and weekly meetings for Bible drill.[83]

In an article in *The a.m.e. Christian Recorder*, "The Institutional Idea of Church Work," Reverdy outlined more completely his philosophies concerning the function of churches. He began by distinguishing between the Evangelical school of religious thought that "conceived the relations between God and man as determined by certain beliefs, and the Romish, representing the relations of God and man as regulated by certain fixed institutions." What he believed to be a "more fundamental and truer idea [was] not to bring men to Christ through theology or 'the church' but to bring men to theology and 'the church' through Christ." In doing so the church had to consider the whole man and not be satisfied with performing only the fundamental rituals, such as the sacraments.[84]

People have begun to see "that our church edifices, save for four or five hours a week, can be devoted to nobler purposes than silence and gloom," he wrote. Although, at the time, establishing institutional churches could not become common practice because of the lack of certain facilities, many of its practices could be used by all churches. For instance, at his current Sunday afternoon men's meetings, an orchestra and choir had been formed to supply music, and notable people from diverse professions were invited to speak. In addition, each Sunday morning he spoke to nearly fourteen hundred people, mostly men, who in turn brought others to church.[85] (This was highly unusual because most churches were attended more frequently by women.)

In the spirit of the Institutional Church, Emma had developed a Queen Esther's Guild of young women who met "once a week for social intercourse and intellectual improvement." The group, which started with only six members, now numbered over forty. They did charitable work in the community and brought other women into the church program. Emma also started a Married Ladies' Union, and her Tawawa Literary Society met "weekly to hear lectures, musicales, discussions and other exercises of a literary nature. The attendance rarely [fell] below two hundred and fifty to three hundred." To Reverdy there was nothing sensational about these groups because if there had been, the novelty would have worn off after two years of their existence. "So we may confidently assert that we are rapidly solving the much debated problem of how to reach the masses. . . . The institutional idea applied makes the church a much frequented place, [and supplies] real needs in the community," he concluded.[86]

While at St. John, Reverdy is also accredited with encouraging the first South African students to enroll at Wilberforce University: Charlotte Manye, Marshall Maxeke, Henry C. Msiginye, Charles Dube, James Yapi Tantsi, and Adelaide Tantsi. This group of singers brought over by a white man (name unknown) had hoped to give concerts throughout the states and eventually enroll at Howard University. Instead they found themselves out of funds and stranded in Cleveland. The Ransoms and members of St. John agreed to take them in. Because Howard University could not accommodate them at the time, Reverdy contacted Bishop Arnett who agreed to enroll all of them at Wilberforce. At the end of their studies, most of them returned to Africa and made a contribution to their communities as teachers and ministers.[87]

This incident helped to stimulate further Emma's interest in missionary work among blacks, not only in foreign countries but right there in Cleveland. Many Negroes who had migrated from the South were desperately in need of guidance, housing, and jobs. To publicize these needs, she and Lydia Lowry, a minister's wife from Pittsburgh, Pennsylvania, founded a missionary magazine titled *Women's Light and Love for Africa*. However, the magazine was short lived because, as Reverdy reasoned, it was "fifty years before its time," and the A.M.E. Church "was not ready for it." Instead Bishop Turner came out with an entirely different kind of magazine/newspa-

per, *Voice of Missions,* which, according to Reverdy, had "far more to say about matters of general interest to the church at large than it did about missions." Nevertheless, it was Reverdy's hope that history would applaud these two women for becoming, for a while at least, the voice of the churchwomen "in the field of foreign missionary propaganda."[88] Unfortunately, no copy of the magazine seems to have survived.

It is interesting to note that at this early date in their ministry, Emma and Reverdy
shared a love for journalism as well as church administration. As he was to write later:
"A thinker harnessed to a printing press is the most powerful and influential force in
modern civilization." The religious press, however, was not merely to be "the mouthpiece of public opinion," but must "educate, influence, and guide public opinion in
the right direction."[89] It would be the combination of his oratory and writing that
would contribute to his power as a spiritual and race leader.

Although missionary work had been a vital part of the A.M.E. Church since its
founding, it was not until the General Conference of May 1844 that a formal organization had been established which was largely run by the men. In the late 1800s, two
women's auxiliaries were added, The Women's Parent Mite Missionary Society (1874),
and the Women's Home and Foreign Missionary Society (1892). Their purpose was
"to assist the Missionary Department in starting local missionaries societies throughout the General Church, and to raise funds to foster missionary activities."[90]

The second convention of the Third District Women's Parent Mite Missionary
Society convened at St. John Cleveland, July 5–8, 1894. At the morning session, Emma
heard the president, Mrs. Ira Collins, recommend that schools be established on the
west coast of Africa and predict that "it would be but a short time before the light of
Christianity would encircle the continent." The duty of the church was to "civilize"
and "Christianize" the African, Collins said.[91] This assumption that Africans needed
to be "civilized" seemed to be a common belief among missionaries at the time, even
black missionaries, a belief that would be questioned severely in the 1920s and more
in the late 1960s and 1970s during the Black Power movement.

At the same session, Emma had a chance to meet Miss Hallie Q. Brown, Reverdy's
former teacher at Wilberforce, and Bishop Tanner and his wife. Emma and Hallie were to
become close friends because of their active participation in missionary work, love of literature, and admiration for Ida B. Wells. During the evening, Reverdy extended a formal
welcome from the local church and spoke about the work that was being done at St. John.[92]

One of the most significant events of the year was the publication of Reverdy's
booklet, *The Disadvantages and Opportunities of the Colored Youth.* The first four chapters were Sunday evening lecture delivered by him at St. John. Because the lectures
were given "extemporaneously," as were most of his sermons, what appeared in the
booklet was taken from stenographer's notes. The book ends with a reprint of his
Lincoln Banquet address, "The Fifteenth Amendment," delivered at Columbus that

was quoted earlier in this book. He included it because it corresponded with the general tone of the other chapters. In the Preface, Reverdy explains:

> We have not sought in these pages to give a solution to the "race problem," for after all attempts at solution it remains the great unsettling question of our times. But we believe that our youth, by "taking advantage of their disadvantages" and improving the opportunities at hand, can do much to overcome the impediments by which our pathway has been so long beset.[93]

In "Race Soil," the first piece, he affirmed his belief that certain races are endowed with particular gifts. The Jews are "the spiritual progenitors"; the Greeks are the givers of culture, the Romans "developed the idea of law and physical greatness. . . . *Races like the soil differ in degree of productiveness*."[94]

Reverdy believed the contribution of the Negro had to be looked at in terms of the "moral, social and intellectual atmosphere by which he has been surrounded." His virtue has been "outraged by public sentiment, despoiled by law, the canker of slavery has gnawed at [his] heart, and religion created for it a standard which must not rise higher than the will of a master." Jim Crow, lynching, segregation, and racism have abounded, and inequality is evident in every aspect of the Negro's life. This atmosphere has been created by the white man who calls the Negro immoral.[95]

> Despite all these ugly realities, the Negro must persevere in his quest for knowledge and development. Only history can record his future accomplishments, but "with his natural musical talents, the Negro will cause sweeter harmonies and prettier melodies to vibrate on the air. . . . Eloquent of speech, he will plead the cause of God and the welfare of mankind. . . . The moral, intellectual and spiritual night of the Negro is passing away.[96]

The title of the second lecture posed the question "Are We Able to Go Up and Possess the Land?" His answer came from Deuteronomy 4:22: "Ye shall go over and shall possess that good land." He told about the pictures of babies painted on a calendar he had seen. Above each was a symbol of what they were to become. Between these babies was a colored child with a question mark above its head. This to Reverdy was "the most impressive lecture on the race problem [he] had ever heard." If one were to study the part of Africa from which Afro-Americans came, "it would reveal . . . a people, the greatness of whose past is shrouded in the dim centuries." The artist who painted the calendar found the answer to "what will Black people all over the world become?" too difficult to answer, so he left a question mark.[97]

Reverdy said, unlike those blacks who want to escape being Negro, who want desperately to be white, if given a choice, he would still choose to be Negro. White America has told him he has no past, and certainly no future in this country. But there is a past and certainly a future. There are poems to be composed, "songs to sing, histories to write, some aspirations and some thoughts to give to the world." There is room in the fields of commerce, in government, and statesmanship right here in America. Again he objected to those who suggested that the Negro needed to emigrate to another country to succeed. "God Almighty has not fixed the bounds of any man's habitation. My friends," he said, "especially my younger friends, if it were in my power I would take you up and give you a glimpse of that land that lies beyond." He closed with the assurance that those boys and girls, "who come with aspirations and inspirations . . . with ready hands to batter down these doors of prejudice and enter those fields," will make for themselves " a place and a name, just as other races have done."[98]

"Lions by the Way" pointed out the pitfalls to which some blacks had succumbed to along the way. Although he took no pleasure in talking about the weaknesses of the race, "once in a while we should step aside and take a look at ourselves and endeavor to learn the truth concerning us," he said. One pitfall was the *lion of intemperance*. He knew personally what temptation was but warned that our young people could not imitate the whites who have a foothold in the earth that Negroes did not yet possess. Negroes could not afford to succumb to drunkenness. He spoke against those mothers who send their children to the saloon for beer.[99] No doubt he was thinking of his own experiences in Washington, Ohio, when his stepfather's people sent him to bring back a bucket of whiskey every morning.

Negroes could ill afford to waste their money on the *lion of gambling*. When a person spends money "he should get value for value." He spoke of the *lion of politics*. "Our dependence on legislation and political power has been one of the barriers in our way." We have often been used by parties, and "they have done a great deal to destroy us." Laws have been passed against us, and those passed in our favor have seldom been enforced.[100]

We are also assailed by the *lion of the white man's lust*. "I have no hesitation in saying that the outrages that are alleged to be committed by colored men upon white women, bear no comparison to those which the whites commit with impunity upon colored women." Nevertheless for the most part "colored women are the grandest women under heaven. They have been loyal as mothers and sweethearts, in the darkest night and dreariest days, [in spite of] every incentive to turn them from their course."[101]

He closed by pleading with his audience not to turn from God back into darkness, for "God will lead us out of darkness into light and give us the strength of Sampson to slay and overcome the lions that are by the way."[102]

In "Grapes from the Land of Canaan," he summed up the general topic of disadvantages and advantages of colored youth. He noted that many persons had been displeased with some of what he had said; others were highly gratified. He had simply endeavored to speak the truth as he would continue to do throughout his ministry.[103]

He paralleled the plight of the Israelites, who had been in bondage for four hundred years to the Egyptians, with that of the Negro. As the Jews stood on the borders of the Land of Canaan, the Promised Land, they sent spies to examine Canaan. These men brought back grapes as proof of the richness of the land and to persuade the people to cross over. But some of the people complained that despite the fertility of the land there were also Amelakites, Jebusites, and Hittites of whom they were afraid.[104]

Afro-Americans were but recently freed from bondage and released from the "wilderness of slavery." Some representatives have crossed over and entered "the rich fields of human endeavor. Others have been afraid and have cried out 'we can't go over and possess it.'" The grapes were the *Negro's demonstrated ability,* first as a toiler who has brought rich fruits into this land. "There is always hope for a man [who] is not afraid to work." This is the day of the common man, the working man. The results of their toil should not be poured into the lap of a few rich men. Proof of this could be found in Gen. Jacob S. Coxey and his army of unemployed workers as they marched on Washington, May 1, 1894, a march that undoubtedly gave impetus to the Pullman Strike a few days after Coxey was jailed. Reverdy reminded his audience that "God Almighty through the ages has written His will in blood. After every saber's flash, every field of carnage and of blood the common people have come to larger liberty."[105]

Negroes have demonstrated their ability as soldiers. "You never heard of a troop of colored soldiers refusing to go forward, no matter if the odds were against them. That kind of blood does not run in their veins," Reverdy asserted. In the history books that he read as a child there had been nothing mentioned of the Negro's participation in war.[106]

Negroes are demonstrating their abilities in business. Ironically, segregation in the South has contributed to this. Negroes have bought their own hearses to carry their dead, have started their own drugstores and every other kind of businesses from which they have been barred by whites. But Negroes still need to learn the value of a dollar so that they do not spend their money frivolously on things they cannot afford. Negroes have now entered the professions, literature, the sciences, and the arts. In all these they still need more development. "Talent without cultivation yields poor results." They have built and maintained schools and colleges, and the young people "have repeatedly won the honors in all the departments of higher education."[107]

His final admonition was: "Go forward along whatever line your talent may lead. Many doors will be slammed in your face, but if you continue to knock and are qualified you will find an entrance."[108] As stated before, the last piece was his "Fifteenth Amendment" speech. The booklet was printed and distributed throughout the Connection, and Reverdy was pleased by the interest it created.

The year 1895 began with a somber occurrence. On the evening of February 20, after having spoken in the morning to the National Council of Women in Washington, D.C., the ex-slave, ardent abolitionist, and grand old man of the Negro race, Frederick Douglass, died of a fatal heart attack. On February 25 at 8 A.M., along with a throng of people, Reverdy and Emma assembled at Metropolitan A.M.E. Church where Douglass lay in state, even though many had already viewed his remains at his home in Anacostia.

> For four long hours the mighty throng poured in and out of the building anxious to get a last view of the dead hero. Every class of society was represented, white and black, they who came by carriage and those in rags. All knew that *Douglas was dead*.[109]

At 2:15 P.M. the service began. The sermon was delivered by Rev. J. T. Jenifer, the pastor of Metropolitan A.M.E. where Douglass had attended for the past several years. To many the most impressive oration was given by Dr. J. E. Rankin, president of Howard University.[110]

St. John Cleveland had its own memorial service for Douglass on March 12 that was attended by an overflow of mourners including Mayor Blee and two members of the Board of Control. During the service a poem by Paul Laurence Dunbar on Douglass was read. Rev. George Pepper, a personal friend of Douglass, delivered the eulogy. He reminisced about how it was Douglass who had prompted Abraham Lincoln to write the Emancipation Proclamation, freeing 200,000 Negroes. "Douglass is not dead," he said. "Wherever there is a colored man or white man who loves liberty the name of Douglass lives."[111]

Reverdy was ill and could not attend, so Emma read a statement written by him that also appeared in the *Cleveland Gazette* on March 16, 1895:

> all the honors that Douglass received in this country were infinitely less than they would have been in any other civilized country in the world. The day of our social, industrial and political emancipation has not fully dawned. May the name of Douglass remain as an inspiration to those who must achieve still greater things.[112]

While at St. John, Reverdy became more interested in the policies of the A.M.E. Church. Though he loved the church, he was not above pointing out its weaknesses. On September 5, 1895, his article, "Sign of the Times: Our Hold Upon the People," appeared in *The A.M.E. Christian Recorder*. After stating that "the A.M.E. Church is the most conspicuous example of the ability of the Afro-American to organize, equip, manage, maintain and perpetuate an organization," he said she must adjust to changes of the times. The founders of the church never claimed to have put together a perfect church. "Therefore to discard burdensome or inadequate methods and customs should not be regarded as an act of sacrilege." Especially was this true in the way the church raised money. Instead of having so many differed days such as Endowment Day, Allen Day, and so forth to raise money, ministers should see that their congregation observe the Dollar Money requirement. Each member, in addition to his regular offering, should be required to give one dollar for the maintenance of the various departments of the church.[113]

He said that many of the more intelligent and better-educated young people are leaving the A.M.E. Church for the Congregational and Episcopal Churches whose programs were better structured. In order to halt this movement, the A.M.E. Church would have to fill her pulpits with the most intelligent and best-trained ministers. Church programs had to be updated. "We must keep pace with the development of Christian work in the organization of young people's societies," he affirmed. "There needs to be a more universal recognition of the fact that to give our Church services an air of refinement and a tone of dignity is not incompatible with spirituality." No doubt these admonitions raised the eyebrows of the more traditional members of the Church who wanted things to remain as they were.[114]

Among the influential blacks with whom Ransom became acquainted while in Cleveland were John P. Green, George A. Myers, and Walter Wright. Wright was first a clerk and then personal secretary to R. D. Caldwell, a Cleveland-based official of the Nickle Plate Railroad. "Few Negroes enjoyed such social privileges or were able to rise as high in the white collar ranks as Wright, and the secretary's prestige among both Negroes and whites remained high as a result."[115] In his autobiography, Ransom calls him "exceptionally well trained for the times," and noted that passes to the Nickle Plate were not good without Wright's signature. Caldwell told Reverdy that Wright should have become a purchasing agent because "he knew more about the railroad than anyone else; but because of his race he would never be appointed." Instead the company gave Wright a bonus twice a year and when Caldwell died he left him $20,000.[116]

John Patterson Green was "the most successful politician" among the black upper class. After graduating from Union College of Law, he opened his law office. For nine years he was justice of the peace. In 1881 and 1889 he was elected to the House of the Ohio legislature, and in 1891 became the only northern black to be elected to the State Senate from a district that was largely white. He used his position two years later to fight for the expansion of Wilberforce University.[117] However, it was through George A. Myers that Reverdy met Mark Hanna. Myers owned the barbershop at the Hollenden Hotel and had great influence among the important businessmen of the city, especially the Republicans. Consequently, when Bishop Arnett's uninsured home in Wilberforce (Tawawa Chimney Corner) was destroyed by fire in 1895, Reverdy was able to solicit $800 from Hanna for the rebuilding of the house. Hanna had always had a deep admiration for the bishop.[118] At the time Reverdy did not know that he was helping to rebuild the house in which he would live during his Episcopacy in Ohio, his retirement, and death.

Hanna and Reverdy developed a deep respect for each other. Sometime in 1886, Hanna had sent for Reverdy and offered to recommend him to President William McKinley for the appointment of Chaplain of the Tenth U.S. Calvary. Reverdy considered this a great honor, but after a week of consideration, he and Emma decided that he should refuse because they did not want to raise Reverdy Jr. and Harold in an army fort. Instead Reverdy suggested that Hanna give the post to Rev. W. T. Anderson, a former Wilberforce classmate of his who had been "actively canvassing for the appointment. . . . Anderson had a long career as an army chaplain until, on account of ill health, he was retired with the rank of major."[119]

Reverdy and Emma read with pride in the March 2 *Cleveland Gazette* that Hallie Q. Brown, Reverdy's teacher at Wilberforce and their friend, was in Liverpool, England, doing dramatic sketches and giving speeches on "Temperance" and "The Progress of Negro Education Since Emancipation" with emphasis on Wilberforce. The purpose for her trip abroad was to raise money for a Frederick Douglass library to be built in connection with the university. At her first appearance in Pembroke Chapel, Rev. C. F. Aked had acknowledged, "I know no English elocutionist, man or women, who recites with the naturalness and charm, the vivacity and power of Miss Brown. I never knew until tonight what the human voice could do." Brown planned to travel to Bristol, Sheffield, Manchester, and various other cities in England before returning home. Reverdy would always be indebted for the training she had given him in speech at Wilberforce. The Ransoms hoped to have her speak in Cleveland soon.[120]

At the North Ohio Conference in the fall of 1895, Reverdy was elected delegate for the first time to the A.M.E. General Conference that convened at St. Stephens, Wilmington, North Carolina, May 4–22, 1896. "On the call of the roll 374 members responded to their names—8 bishops, 9 general officers, 239 ministers and 118 laymen representing 57 Annual Conferences," and 11 Episcopal Districts.[121] Ransom had never seen so many blacks at one gathering managing their own affairs. It was an impressive sight. On the other hand, he had never witnessed so much politics at a religious convention.[122]

Bishop Tanner, who Ransom said was elected bishop in 1888 "because of his launching of the [A.M.E.] *Review*, the most successful literary achievement of the race," delivered the Quadrennial Sermon.[123] His theme, "The Church the Right Hand of God," was divided into two subtopics "Loyalty" and "Strength." The A.M.E. Church had an obligation to God not to let the church be destroyed. When speaking of loyalty, he talked of loyalty to God, to His laws, and to the laws of nature. "God's Church must be strong," he said, "but it can only be as strong as the men composing it are strong." Blacks had come from an African race known for its physical strength; however, not only must they be physically strong, but also intellectually strong. He concluded by referring to the work of the pioneers of African Methodism: "Allen, Brown and Waters for loyalty; Payne and Brown for exactness; Ward for strength; Quinn, Wayman, and Disney for courage."[124] The sermon was described in *The A.M.E. Christian Recorder* as "logical," "instructive," and "interesting" and demonstrated Tanner's ability as an orator and scholar.[125] Tanner's belief that blacks must be intellectually strong was compatible with Reverdy's own philosophy that education was one of the most important tools for the race.

On the third morning of the conference, Bishop Arnett read the Episcopal Address. After congratulating the delegates as citizens of a commonwealth who live in "an age of religious liberty and toleration" and speaking of other church matters, he talked on a subject that deeply concerned Reverdy—the serious charges that were now being levied against the Negro from "those who profess to be our friends" as well as "those who made no pretensions to friendship." They charged the Negro with "ignorance, immorality, indifference, and disregard for the marriage vow, and the profession of a religion without morality." These accusers said the Negro was in worse shape than he had been in slavery. Arnett denied the charges:

> We speak from personal knowledge of the moral and social conditions of the people and affirm that the ideals of our leaders are as high as the ideals of their neighbors; that their practical life is more in harmony with the ten commandments . . . than those who are bearing false witness against us without any personal knowledge of the charges alleged.[126]

At the end of his speech, he made nineteen recommendations aimed at improving the administration of the church.[127]

Reverdy had never witnessed "the tide of unrestrained emotion of speech and actions by members of the delegated body."[128] Following the Episcopal Committee's majority and minority reports (the majority asking for the election of four bishops, the minority for no additional bishops), there was much confusion. In the end it was agreed that three bishops should be elected. W. B. Derrick was elected on the first ballot, J. H. Armstrong and J. C. Embry on the third. For the first time a layman was elected a general officer. H. T. Kealing, former president of Paul Quinn College, became editor of *The A.M.E. Church Review*.[129] Ransom observed that he was not honestly elected. "Men passed the ballot box and threw in bunches of ballots for Kealing," he said. Nevertheless, it was the beginning of the layman gaining more power in the administration of the Church.[130]

That same summer of 1896, Bishop Arnett came to visit the Ransoms in Cleveland. He told them that he had decided to move them to Chicago, to either Quinn Chapel or Bethel. After preaching at both churches, Reverdy chose Bethel.[131] This was perhaps one of the most significant choices of his life. Chicago was to define the direction of his long ministry and his devotion to a social gospel.

CHAPTER 3

The Institutional Church, 1896–1904

Verily I say unto you, if ye have faith as a grain of mustard seed, ye shall say unto this mountain, Remove hence to yonder place; and it shall remove; and nothing shall be impossible unto you.

Matthew 17:20

Chicago in the fall of 1896 had a history of racism, classicism, and disputes between labor and capital. The World's Columbia Exposition Reverdy had visited in 1893, with its White City stretching and glistening along the lakefront, had disguised the ugly cancer festering in the inner city. This malignancy was created by joblessness and poverty. A few months before the Ransoms arrived, the strike at McCormick Harvester Works, which culminated in the bloody Haymarket Riot, was but one of the strong indications that social reform was necessary if Chicago was to survive as the second most important city in the United States.[1] This need for social reform was well suited to the Ransoms' interests and talents.

Among the many ethnic groups in Chicago, including the Germans, Irish, and Scandinavians, the Negroes had been there longest. "According to tradition, the first permanent settler . . . was a black trader from Santo Domingo, Jean Baptiste Pointe Du Sable" who settled near the Chicago River around 1790.[2] It was not until forty-three years later that Chicago was incorporated "with 200 souls and 243 buildings." Then in the late 1840s a small band of fugitive slaves from the south and free blacks from the east established a community.[3]

Between 1870 and 1890, the Negro population grew to over fifty thousand, most of whom lived on the South Side, although some could be found in other parts of the city. Since the 1870s they had had the franchise and had attended integrated schools; however, despite the Civil Rights law passed by the state legislature (1884), Negroes were often denied access to certain public places and found it difficult to obtain decent jobs and housing. Between 1890 and 1910, in what has been called "the Migration of the Talented Tenth," a large number of blacks came from the South. Among them were preachers and politicians, the educated and not so educated, who had had some power for a few years after the Civil War. As Reconstruction in the South was being replaced by Jim Crowism, as blacks migrated to the city and their numbers grew, the attitude toward blacks more and more reflected the South's low esteem of the Negro.[4]

Quinn Chapel A.M.E., the oldest Negro church in the city, had been founded in 1847, just "fourteen years after Chicago was incorporated."[5] Its current pastor, Archibald J. Carey, was to become one of Reverdy's arch rivals during his pastorate in Chicago. Quinn was located on 24th and Wabash Avenues where few blacks lived. Its membership was made up largely of established Negro families who were community leaders. Bethel, on the other hand, was on the corner of 30th and Dearborn Streets, in the heart of the black ghetto. Its membership was more diverse. Some few established Chicagoans and many migrants from the South attended. No doubt Reverdy had chosen Bethel so he could be nearer to the homes of his congregation and so he could attract those of lower incomes as well as "the pillars" of the community. Bethel had an auditorium that could seat some nine hundred people; however, it was not long before Reverdy was preaching to standing-room-only audiences. He became aware that Negroes were moving from the South in such numbers that the "business as usual" kind of church would be inadequate to meet their needs. He set about creating organizations in Bethel that would be practical and yet uplifting to the community as he had done in other churches.[6]

In addition to the kindergarten, Sunday School, and women's groups Emma started, Reverdy organized a Men's Sunday Club that grew to five hundred members. It was the "first organization of the kind under the patronage of a Negro church and was the father of all the Sunday Forums that . . . followed."[7] The club met three Sunday afternoons a month in Bethel's lecture room. On the fourth Sunday it convened in the main auditorium, and women were invited to attend. Speakers included religious, business, literary, artistic, political, and educational leaders from Chicago and other cities throughout the country.[8] In *The Christian Recorder,* Ida B. Wells described the audience as being composed of "young men off the streets and out of saloons" as well as professional and businessmen of the city who had gathered for "intellectual culture." She also mentioned the Twentieth Century Literary Club and the kindergarten as a part of Reverdy's innovations and the twelve deaconesses he appointed "who cover the district seeking strangers, visiting the sick, and feeding, clothing and making warm the poor and needy."[9]

One of the greatest concerns Reverdy had while pastoring in Chicago was the negative assessment whites were making of Negroes throughout America. In an article he wrote December 19, 1896 in *The Freeman,* a black Indianapolis weekly, he expressed contempt for those whites who constantly point to the "Negro's immorality . . . the tone of his social life and material condition." He said an "unbiased investigation would show [the Negro's] moral condition to be no more than that of the class who assumes to sit in judgment upon him." He blamed America, particularly her Christian institutions, for attempting to destroy the Negro's sense of morality, first by sanctioning slavery and later by silently and vocally tolerating segregation.[10] Reverdy hoped that through his church programs and his sermons, he could eradicate that assessment, at least among the blacks of his congregation, many of whom already had a low esteem of themselves. He also sought to disturb the conscience of America in terms of her treatment of black citizens.

On November 26, 1896, Reverdy preached a Thanksgiving sermon at Bethel titled "The Industrial and Social Conditions of the Negro." He used as his text Isaiah 9:3: "Thou hast multiplied the nation, and not increased the joy." After once again speaking of how God has bountifully blessed America, he turned to the conditions of the Negro. Blacks could no longer continue as they had in the past where white men denied them the basic necessities and "that part of the capital" that would enable them "to win an independent living for themselves, their wives and their children." Because of unjust laws and practices, the source of wealth and power was locked, and the key was in the hands of aristocracy who ruled the corporations and syndicates. The rights of the individual no longer dominated the thoughts of America. Instead most of its citizens were now obsessed with making money.[11]

There was a time when blacks had more of a part in the development of America, he reminded the congregation. "But we have been forced in the North, in Chicago, as well as in the South, into a condition that may truly be termed industrial serfdom." Negroes used to dominate the barbershop business; now they are reduced to blacking boots. They used to dominate the laundry business, but because they would not organize, whites have taken over that. They used to have most of the catering business, but not anymore. Negroes are even beginning to be supplanted in the hotels, factories, and railroads where the only job they can get now is as porters. The black race is a race "of working men and working women. There are no capitalists among us, no millionaires. Because this is true the laborers of this country can never succeed without the Negro's aid." Negroes cannot be satisfied with their conditions but must continue to prepare themselves and rap at the doors of opportunity incessantly, "for I believe even though a door may be slammed in a man's face a good many times, if he continues to rap—he will finally enter," he affirmed.[12]

Reverdy warned that lynching was not only confined to the South, but could very well occur in Chicago as it had in other parts of the North. "During all these years, only one voice has been raised until two continents were compelled to hear," he said, obviously referring to his friend and church member, Ida B. Wells, who continued to protest in England as well as America against the insidious practice of lynching. Whites were killing Negroes in the South and had now gained the constitutional right to make them ride in "Jim Crow Cars" on the trains. And yet,

when a voice stands out and pleads, some, because it is not their voice, some because they are not getting the glory, [a] fat political job, and don't want to hurt the
feelings of the powers that be, will sink the interest of the race for their own personal gain and personal safety.[13]

Here he struck out against the black politicians and so-called leaders who wanted to
silence Wells.

He spoke of the blacks who were migrating to the United States from the West Indies
and from Africa. "While our numbers are being increased we must take a stand demanding recognition, for the destiny of our race is one" whether blacks live in America,
the West Indies, Europe or Africa. It is in America, Reverdy felt, that the Negro has the
best chance, "the grandest field for action." The Negro should "give to the world a dem-
onstration of our capacity and example of our power and of our strength."[14]

Two themes that emerge from this sermon were the need for persistence and the
interrelationship of racism and classicism. As well as addressing the Negro, Reverdy
seemed to be speaking to all classes who are excluded from the American dream—
particularly the workers who are thrown crumbs from the industrial giants. Because
Negroes have always been workers who reside at the bottom of the pole, they must
organize as a race or with others who are willing to join in the fight for a fair share.

As indicated earlier, at this time in his life, Ransom was leaning toward socialism—a kind of Christian socialism based on the teachings of the New Testament.
"The Negro and Socialism," Reverdy's article that appeared in *The A.M.E. Church Review* a month before, was a prelude to his Thanksgiving sermon. He had written that
socialism was not "a question of race [but] a question of men. . . . While one class of
toilers is outraged and oppressed, no man is free." He did not believe that socialism
was a form of anarchy. It rejects "the doctrine of selfishness . . . and affirms altruism
as a principle sufficient to govern the relations of men." In socialism the "interests of
the individual are made subordinate to the interests of society, while allowing freedom for the highest development of [the individual's] own personality."[15]

Evidently, even those who did not understand the concept of socialism favored what
he had to say in his sermon. They asked that it be printed and distributed to both
blacks in Chicago and throughout the Connection; consequently, it was printed in pamphlet form by the Chicago *Conservator,* one of the Negro newspapers in the city.[16]

There were those who violently disagreed with Reverdy's socialist doctrines. One
of his most vocal critics was William H. Coston, an A.M.E. minister from Ohio, who,
in the February 18, 1897 issue of *The Christian Recorder,* accused him of advocating the
abolishment of private property, of diminishing the power of the church, thereby
causing anarchy.[17] Reverdy defended himself by writing that socialism made "no war
upon the Church," but that more and more the church was being "largely permeated
with the social spirit." This social spirit had unlocked the door of the insulated church

so that it could be found on the highways, in the legislature, and in politics.[18] In discussing the argument between Coston and Ransom and Ransom's defense, Donald A. Drewett concludes that "Socialism, then, became for Ransom a means to an end and nothing more. He saw it as an opportunity for blacks to join with whites in a new social order of equality, not as a pretense for revolution as it was being used in Europe."[19]

In addition to the topic of socialism, Ransom was also concerned about the changing role of black women. On Sunday, June 6, 1897, he delivered a sermon titled "Deborah and Jael" to the Ida B. Wells Women's Club at Bethel. (A.M.E. Churches customarily devoted several Sunday worship services to different civic, profession, fraternal, or women's groups during the year.) Originally organized as the first women's civic club in Chicago, the Ida B. Wells Women's Club had obtained its charter and named itself in honor of it founder while she was on her second speaking tour in England (1894).[20]

Appropriately for the occasion Reverdy took his text from Judges that told the stories of Deborah, who led the Israelites to victory against their Kanaanitish foes, and Jael, who "took the tent pin and hammer and drove it through Sisera's temples . . . thus slaying the chief enemy and persecutor of her race." Both were revolutionaries for their race and nation and represented the highest kind of womanhood.[21]

The mission of Christianity, he said, was the production of the highest type of manhood and womanhood. He intimated that this also should be the goal of America with its vast opportunities. If the black man suffered severely during slavery, the black woman suffered even more. Slavery degraded her to "the lowest plane." Maternal and wifely instincts were rendered almost impossible. The black woman was not "permitted to inspire her man to deeds of noble action; and manhood which lacks the inspiration of womanhood will never produce very many heroes."[22]

Women are "natural hero worshippers, more so than men. . . . But the kind of heroes that we have presented have not been very inspiring, and the women among us who have had some cultivation and some intelligence, have found in the ranks of our men in the years that have passed so few who were their equals," he said.[23]

The inspiration Reverdy's mother had given him— "she was almost a God to me," he affirmed—"has been the inspiration of thousands of others all over the country within the last thirty years." Black women were beginning to develop a social life and culture.

> The day is almost at hand when the better elements among us are beginning to class themselves together and they are saying to those who are not fit for respectable association: if you want to stand on this plane, you must qualify yourself by virtue, by intelligence and culture so to stand.

Class for him was not based on money, possession, or high birth, but on moral fiber, high principles, and the willingness to develop and learn. "Men who disgrace their manhood [should not be allowed] to sit in the parlors of the respectable."[24]

Women are beginning to look beyond their doorsteps and "to study and think upon the great questions that affect them and the country at large," he said as he complimented the Ida B. Wells Women's Club for addressing themselves to racial and civic concerns. By doing so, they were honoring their founder, Ida B. Wells, who had taken her crusade to the people of America and England. When blacks were lynched in Tennessee, she courageously spoke out. Instead of the men of the race rushing to her defense, they shrunk in fear. Ida was compelled to leave Tennessee or become a victim of the lynch mob. Reverdy spoke of the times he had walked the streets with her in all kinds of weather on her way to a speaking engagement. Nothing could deter her from testifying against the evils of lynching, neither inclement weather nor threats.[25]

He pointed to other women who were making their mark in the larger world: Fannie Jackson Coppin, who had founded a school for the training of girls; Edmonia Lewis, who was being recognized for her artwork; Hallie Q. Brown, who was now in London gaining notoriety as an elocutionist; and Fannie B. Williams of Chicago, who was excelling in literature and journalism.[26]

Turning again to the men, he exhorted them to be protectors of their women:

> I am a minister of the gospel and a man of peace, but the day any man insults one of mine, I shall resent it with emphasis. . . . I believe that the men [who] lie in wait like a wild beast of the forest to destroy the virtue and uprightness of our women, should be treated like a wild beast.[27]

At times during the speech Reverdy's militancy overpowers his mission as a "minister of the gospel and a man of peace." He has deep anger for those who disrespect black women and comes just short of advocating "an eye for an eye."

As liberated as he was for his times, Reverdy still had a tendency to put women on a pedestal as "gentle creatures" who needed help from their "protector and King." His gallantry toward women was reflected in his behavior—a behavior that might well be resented today in light of women's lib. Whenever a woman entered a room he would try to rise, even when he was confined in a wheelchair. She must come through the door first and must have the seat if only one was available. When approaching her on the street, he would tip his hat and give a little bow. Women were attracted to him and usually surrounded him when he was in room of mixed company. He was handsome, stately, intense, highly intelligent, and well read on most subjects, qualities that endeared him to both men and women. Nevertheless, he was not a person one wanted for an enemy. He could diminish an opponent with mere words.[28]

In April of 1898, Reverdy became involved in a controversy concerning U.S. Army policies. The U.S. Congress had passed a resolution on April 19 recognizing the independence of Cuba and giving President McKinley permission to use the armed forces to expel Spain from Cuba. A few days later, the president "proclaimed a blockade of Cuba and called for 125,000 volunteers." After Spain broke off diplomatic relations with America, Congress declared war on Spain. At first most state governments refused to accept black volunteers in the army.[29] On April 27, Reverdy was a part of a committee who visited Governor John Tanner of Illinois to request that the only Negro unit in the state militia be "recruited to the full strength of a regiment [and] be headed by colored officers from corporal to colonel." The governor acceded to the request and commissioned John Marshall, a Negro, as colonel of the regiment. Reverdy offered to help with the recruitment of two companies, to allow his church to be used as a recruitment post, and to serve as chaplain to the group.[30]

It was some time after the governor's meeting that the Negro soldiers actually saw action. Among Reverdy's papers was found a pencil draft of a poem he was trying to write expressing their anxiety. Although there is nothing very remarkable about the poem, it does show that Reverdy was determined that the troops he had helped recruit should have their day, and his belief that despite the racism they experienced, Negroes should defend their country.[31]

Ten weeks after the declaration of war, the Spanish-American War ended. "Black soldiers [had] played a major role in the Cuban campaign and probably staved off defeat for the Rough Riders at San Juan Hill. In Cuba they won twenty-six Certificates of Merit and five Congressional Medals of Honor."[32] The all-black Eighth Regiment of Chicago returned on March 16, 1899. They passed the reviewing stand where Chaplain Reverdy C. Ransom and others greeted them. Reverdy praised them for their patriotism. He said, "We are proud of our heritage. Some have wondered whether the Negroes would fight or not, but you have proved that they would a hundred times."[33]

A week later at a banquet honoring the officers, Reverdy again expressed his gratitude but also took this opportunity to chastise the army practices. He told of how both white and Negro soldiers have been "covered with glory" when they came from San Juan Hill. The white soldiers were promoted to "lieutenancies in the regular army"; however, he asked:

> What of their colored fellows and fellow heroes? Some few of the bravest were made lieutenants in the immune regiments, and as soon as these regiments are mustered out, must go back to private life or the ranks of the private in the regular army.

The army should now give promotions to black soldiers in accordance with their performance during their time of service, he admonished.[34]

Reverdy had been a strong supporter of McKinley when he was governor of Ohio and when he became president in 1897. Now in 1899, Reverdy told his friend John Green, a black employee in the Postal Stamp Agency in Washington and a friend of the president, that he was displeased with the mustering out of black soldiers and/or their demotion after the war. He also abhorred the president's silence in terms of the mob violence in the South, particularly the murder of nine black men in Georgia. Reverdy wrote to Green, "Let the President be President of the whole, and act as he would if Indians were killing Negroes; or if the Negroes of the South were treating whites as whites of the South are treating the Negroes." He had just returned from commencement at Wilberforce where he had met Southern blacks who were anxious to know what McKinley would say in his annual address about racial oppression. If he remained silent, they would campaign against him in the South, Reverdy reported.[35]

Green sent McKinley a copy of the reply he sent to Reverdy. McKinley undoubtedly remembered Reverdy from Ohio and his friendship with Hanna. He discussed the matter of Negro troops with Elihu Root, his secretary of war, who reported that while the colored troops during the Spanish-American War had done well, the officers had not. "I am told that they have not the faculty of commanding; or of enforcing discipline, and are not respected by their troops as are the white officers."[36] McKinley replied that he was "inclined to organize a colored regiment" in which the field officers were white and the line officers colored.

> It does seem to me that if we exercise the same care in the selection of the line officers for the colored regiment that we have and are exercising with the line officers of the white regiments, we can secure a fine lot of soldiers.

He suggested they ask the president of Wilberforce (Samuel T. Mitchell, 1884–1900) to help recruit line officers from the "very best types of the race." (Under Mitchell's administration the national government had established a Military Science and Tactics Department at Wilberforce.) George Sinkler in his *Racial Attitudes of American Presidents* thinks that, "Racially, this might have been McKinley's finest hour."[37] Evidently, Ransom, for the time being, was somewhat mollified by McKinley's actions.

Reverdy's aggressiveness was not always shared by other Negroes. One of the men who was to become Reverdy's opponent in his agitation for civil rights was Booker T. Washington, the founder and president of the industrial school in Alabama, Tuskegee Institute. As a member of the Committee on Thanksgiving Services for the National Peace Jubilee held in Chicago, October 16, 1898, Reverdy had a chance to hear Washington speak. Along with Rev. Thomas P. Hodnett, Rev. John Henry Barrows, and Rabbi Emil G. Hirsch, prominent ministers who represented their various faiths, Booker T. Washington had been asked to be the spokesman for the Negro at the First Methodist Episcopal Church.[38] Reverdy remembered later that he had not been impressed and wondered how much he really did voice the thoughts of the race.

Because Washington seemed to have assumed the leadership of Negroes at the Peace Jubilee, Reverdy expected that he would attend the Afro-American Council when it met in Chicago, August 17–20, the following year. Instead, Booker T. Washington was conspicuously absent. The council was the outgrowth of the Afro-American League founded in 1890 by T. Thomas Fortune, editor of the *New York Age*. After two years of nonactivity (1896–98), it had been revived as the Afro-American Council in 1898 with Bishop Alexander Walters of the A.M.E. Zion Church as its leader. As first the League, and later the Council, the organization expended most of its energy debating the pros and cons of the Booker T. Washington accommodation school of thought.[39]

In his autobiography and in a published letter to the editor of the *Inter Ocean*, Reverdy said that the night prior to the meeting of the council in Chicago, Booker T. Washington had "stationed himself across the street from the parsonage" where Bishop Walters was staying with the Ransoms. Washington sent for the bishop, and they stood under a street lamp, talking at length. Washington "was trying to persuade Bishop Walters to soft pedal most of our program and to eliminate certain matters, at that time considered inflammatory," Reverdy said.[40]

During the meeting the more militant members presented a resolution that condemned President McKinley for his silence on lynching and a resolution condemning Washington for not attending the conference. Bishop Alexander Walters reported that Washington felt he should not attend the meetings because any radical utterances of the group might compromise his position and "his usefulness in connection with many causes."[41] In other words he was not about to jeopardize his sources of income that came from the many wealthy whites who supported Tuskegee.

Reverdy was so angered by Washington's absence that he stood up and proposed that Washington's name be stricken from the membership roster. He said:

> I know of no man who has received more advertising from his connections with the Negro race than has Booker T. Washington. He has posed as the leader of the colored people and the Moses who was to lead his people out of the wilderness. Yet he has hung around the outskirts of this council casting aspersions and contempt on its proceedings. . . . No such man ought to claim to be our leader. We want the country to know he is nothing to us. . . . He is trying to hold us in line. From his room in the Palmer House, he says, "Sh! Sh!," but he's afraid to come in. I move that Mr. Washington's name be stricken from the roll.[42]

Washington countered this criticism through interviews in the leading papers. He told a Saratoga reporter that despite the fact that many Negroes felt he should involve himself in politics, he had not "entertained this view." He would continue to "devote himself to the moral, educational, and educational development of the race," and was satisfied that he had the "Confidence," "Sympathy," and "Respect" of most Afro-Americans.[43]

Evidently Reverdy had underestimated Washington's influence in the Council. His resolution to censure Washington was defeated. President Walters defended Washington's rationale for being absent, and even W. E. B. DuBois said "the spirit of the gathering was not represented at all in the remarks of Ransom." He regretted that such a controversy had ever taken place and hoped that the news media would not report that the "convention had said anything detrimental to one of the greatest men of our race." He called Ransom's words "ill-timed and foolish."[44] No doubt DuBois did not want to leave the impression that the group was divided and that some of the members were openly attacking Washington.

DuBois was to change his mind radically in the coming years. In his publication, *The Souls of Black Folks* (1903), he was to denounce Washington in the strongest language. In a chapter titled "Of Mr. Booker T. Washington and Others," although he gives credit to Washington for his advocacy of "Thrift, Patience, and Industrial Training for the masses," he says:

> so far as Mr. Washington apologizes for injustice, North or South, does not rightly value the privilege and duty of voting, belittles the emasculating effects of caste distinctions, and opposes the higher training and ambition of our brighter minds ... we must unceasingly and firmly oppose him.[45]

For the first and possibly last time Ransom had to back down in his criticism of Washington. He wrote a letter of apology to Washington in which he said he regarded Washington's career "as one of the most fruitful and remarkable" of the race and offered his assistance "in any line of work" that Washington was "doing for the help of [Negroes] and mankind."[46] Later those words would rise up to haunt him also. In many ways, more than likely, Ransom did think that Washington's accomplishments at Tuskegee were commendable, but he found irritating and unproductive Washington's insistence that industrial education was the panacea for Negroes and that their agitating for civil and social equality was folly. Soon after the conference, he resigned from the Afro-American Council that seemed to be dominated by the Washington faction.

Another group that came to Reverdy's attention while he was in Chicago was the Manassa Society composed of about seven hundred mixed black-and-white couples. Being shunned by both whites and many Negroes, this group had organized to give support to each other. Reverdy says that he contributed to their membership in that he married "104 Negroes to white women and three white men to colored women." By interacting with the society, he soon learned that "contrary to erroneous belief that white women so married were generally . . . women of immoral repute," they were "good hard-working women who had been thrown into contact with colored men in hotels and restaurants and other public places where they were employed." Most of these couples soon bought their own homes. "Thrown back upon themselves they saved their money and made substantial provision for their personal security and comforts." On the whole, the Negro churches did nothing to welcome the group or their children into their programs. Reverdy invited them to Bethel and provided activities so that they might be "under Christian influence." He recalled that many of their children became professionals and contributed to the black community; a few others passed for white and were forever plagued with the fear they might be discovered.[47]

Since he had first come to Chicago, Ransom had been impressed by the work of Jane Addams who, after visiting Toynbee Hall, a settlement house in London, had been inspired to found a similar institution in Chicago which she named Hull House (1889). The house was a converted mansion on Halsted Street that served mainly Italian and Slavic immigrants who were crowded in tenements on Chicago's West Side. Reverdy also studied carefully the Mary McDowell's University of Chicago Settlement in Packingtown. Both of these institutions provided social services in their community.[48] He had implemented some of these programs in Bethel, but the building was not adequate for the program he had in mind.

Ransom was determined to find backers for his plans. In his autobiography, he relates that "throughout [his] ministry in the city of Chicago [he] had close, cordial association, and sympathetic cooperation of two . . . Chicagoans, native born sons of Ohio." He was referring to Clarence Darrow, who was already known as "the People's Lawyer," and Dr. Frank W. Gunsaulus, famous preacher and first president of Armour Institute of Technology. These two champions of the masses inspired him to hold on to his dream of establishing a church/settlement house as a part of the A.M.E. Church. Another man who gave great support to his cause was Robert G. Ingersoll, lawyer, orator, and agnostic.[49]

Ingersoll died in 1899. In 1901 Reverdy was chosen as one of three men to speak at a memorial service in his behalf at Studebaker Theatre, Chicago. Because Ingersoll was an agnostic, Reverdy expected to receive criticism from his Church and other ministers for his participation. This did not happen, perhaps because of the praise he was given in the press. In *Pilgrimage*, Reverdy wrote that Ingersoll never said there was no God:

> I think it fair to say that [he] repeatedly declared he had never said there was no God, but that if there were a God, he did not know Him, and if He exists He should write upon every blade of grass and upon each leaf upon trees, and emblazon in letters of fire across the heavens, "There is a God!"[50]

In his tribute, Reverdy said until only our passions and prejudices are "softened by time" and we view Ingersoll "standing out against the background of at least a century," can we clearly access his value to the age in which he lived. He spoke of Ingersoll as being a man who did not base his manhood on religion, politics, or wealth, "the mud-god and man-maker of our time," but on his "kinship and affinity . . . toward mankind of every condition and every race." He told of Ingersoll's battle against slavery, of his friendship and support of Frederick Douglass whom he invited into his home. Ingersoll had welcomed the Fourteenth and Fifteenth Amendments and said they were "but a price for the nation to pay for the Negro's two hundred and fifty years of slavery, and but a small reward" for his brave participation in the Civil War. He loved liberty, believed in law, and denounced lynching that many Christians "left their places of worship to greet with cheers." The church may "execrate" him, Reverdy said, but should also emulate his articulation, if not his eloquence in the cause of liberty. "Ingersoll was one of the first fruits of the evolution of humanity, away from tribe and clan and race into a manhood bounded only by humanity." Although not of his persuasion in matters of religion, Reverdy hoped in some small way to emulate Ingersoll's efforts on behalf of the neglected and despised.[51]

As early as December 21, 1899, Reverdy had written an article in *The Christian Recorder* in which he had warned that the A.M.E. Zion Church planned to buy a large building on Dearborn and set up an Institutional Church. If they were unable to do so the Baptists were prepared to adopt the plan. Wealthy whites in Chicago had expressed an interest in the project. And though they would not give money to a Negro church, "they would give liberally to a colored congregation if they were trying to establish and maintain an Institutional Church." He said further, "while [the A.M.E. Church is] building great churches in the cities throughout the country, and calling together great congregations, if we hope to hold our own, these churches must take on institution features or else Institutional Churches must be established."[52]

To give flesh to his dream, Reverdy informed Bishop Arnett he would like to resign from Bethel and open up a new church that would include in its program a settlement house. He had discovered that Railroad Chapel on Dearborn Street near 39th had not been bought by the A.M.E. Zion or Baptist Church and was for sale for $34,000.[53] Arnett said he would propose at the next General Conference that the A.M.E. Church purchase the property.

In May 1900, Reverdy was a delegate to the Twenty-first General Conference of the A.M.E. Church held in Columbus, Ohio, May 7–25, which had a membership of 418, including eleven bishops and nine general officers. He listened with interest to the Quadrennial Sermon by Bishop Abram Grant based on Genesis 28:19: "And he called the name of that place Bethel," and must have wondered at the irony of the text.[54] He wanted to exchange his Bethel for an Institutional Church.

On the third morning, Bishop B. F. Lee gave the Episcopal Address during which he outlined the growth of the church that now had 5,095 edifices, sixty-five annual conferences, 663,706 communicant members, and twenty colleges. He added that the history of the A.M.E. Church, written by Bishop Arnett that would include the history written earlier by Daniel Payne, was now ready to go to press.[55] Reverdy, whose interest in history was acute, would anxiously await the publication. It and the history by Charles Spencer Smith (1922) would be invaluable to him when he became historiographer of the church in 1948.

On Thursday May 17, the conference elected five bishops—Evans Tyree, M. M. Moore, C. S. Smith, C. T. Shaffer, and L. J. Coppin—to supervise two districts at home, one in South Africa, one in West Africa, and one in the West Indies. Of all the conference business, however, the most important to Reverdy was the passage of the resolution that stated the church would buy the Institutional Church in Chicago from the First Presbyterian Church.[56]

On July 1, 1900, the building officially became the property of the A.M.E. Church, and Reverdy was appointed pastor and warden of The Institutional Church and Social Settlement. The lot on Dearborn was 100 feet long by 125 feet deep. It had a brick building trimmed in stone containing sixteen rooms, including an auditorium that sat twelve hundred people, a dining room, kitchen, and gymnasium. The Ransoms immediately occupied three rooms in the rear that became the parsonage. Although they had no money, somehow they managed to raise $1,000 to clean the entire facility that was "dirty and out of repair from top to bottom." There were no "furnishings and equipment except seats" in the auditorium.[57]

Reverdy opened the building for the public on July 24, but it was not formally dedicated until October 21 when Bishops Grant, Arnett, and Turner were on hand to address the congregation. At the time of its July opening there were "no members, not one Sunday School scholar and no one with whom to begin the work but [Reverdy's] wife and two children." Before long, however, they had amassed seventy-five Sunday school children who not only came on Sundays but "every day in the week, to read, play and be helpful to others"; and thus the program was launched. "No provision was made for Reverdy's support nor was he given a dollar with which to begin the work."[58] Although he never received a set salary, for his support his congregation gave him $1,881.52 between July 1900 and April 1904, which averaged about $470 per year, hardly enough to maintain the couple and their growing boys.[59]

Hearing about his shortage of operating capital, Jane Addams came to him and asked how he expected to run such an ambitious program with no money. He said he was running on faith. She immediately wrote to a Mr. Winesap of Los Angeles who sent him a check for $100, his first donation for the program. Soon other contributions began to pour in from people like Mrs. George M. Pullman, wife of the railroad giant; Robert T. Lincoln, son of Abraham Lincoln; and Mrs. Victor Lawson, wife of the owner of the *Chicago Daily News*; Clarence Darrow; and Dr. Frank Gunsaulus. In addition to Addams, Rev. Graham Taylor of Chicago Commons and Mary McDowell of Chicago University Settlement provided "active sympathy and cooperation."[60]

During the first four years, 306 people were on the membership roll of the Institutional Church, but Reverdy preached to many more each Sunday. He was aware that quite a few had joined the church because of their interest in the various departments, not because they were converted. Reverdy explained that there was never a large church membership because he had "attempted to establish the church upon the various departments and activities, instead of first establishing the church and building the department and activities upon it."[61] As Reverdy so often said to young ministers, "You can't preach Jesus to empty stomachs, to jobless people, and to those who feel powerless." He was interested always in treating the *whole person*, a concept that was to become popular among educators in the 1950s and 1960s. As Katherine Leckie wrote in the Hearst's *Chicago American*, March 1, 1901:

> Not only in its narrower sense [was] the religious life developed in [Ransom's] Institutional Church, but humanity in all its breadth [was] taught. With it, the duty to the growth of the body, as well as the mind is ever put to the men and women, and the boys and girls.[62]

Reverdy's program was ambitious, inclusive, bold, and ahead of its time for a Negro church. Many people, including ministers of the A.M.E. Church, felt it had no place in the life of the Church. Unfortunately for Reverdy, Bishop Abram Grant replaced Arnett as bishop of the Fourth District because Arnett had been assigned to the Third (Ohio, Pittsburgh, California) at the May General Conference. A few months after the Institutional Church opened, Rev. A. J. Carey and A. L. Murray persuaded Bishop Grant that Ransom should not be allowed to preach on Sunday mornings because it would affect the attendance at their churches. Grant ordered Reverdy to preach only on Sunday evenings. It was not until a few months later when Bishop H. M. Turner, the senior bishop, came to visit Reverdy and heard him preach that the order was rescinded. Turner was quoted as saying: "Great God! Just think of anybody trying to silence a voice like that on Sunday morning. . . . How the man can preach." After that his opponents attempted another tactic. "They announced from their pulpit . . . that the Institutional Church was not really a church and forbade their members to take communion, or to cooperate with any activity of the Institutional Church."[63]

A close examination of Reverdy's program demonstrates how comprehensive and remarkable it was. In order "to meet and serve the moral, social and industrial need of [the] people," the building was open twenty-four hours a day. Activities included an employment bureau that helped find jobs for people and a kindergarten, established by Emma Ransom, which ran for ten months during the year and was staffed by a principal and two assistants "obtained each year from the Chicago Association." The sixty-two children who attended paid no fees, and the kindergarten was supported by "public subscriptions and entertainments." A day nursery/day care center was open from 6 A.M. to 7 P.M. and housed and fed the children of mothers who worked during the day. The fee for these services was five cents a day. "Those of kindergarten age were sent to it during hours when it was opened. Children of school age were sent to the public school and required to report back promptly after the class." Between 1901 and 1904, 7,822 children were serviced. Study classes in various subjects included black history and literature; a men's club of eighty met every Sunday at 4 P.M. to discuss "moral, social, industrial, economic and literary questions." Because of its influence several labor unions "recognized and admitted colored men to membership." A women's club of thirty members aided the sick and poor, sewed for the nursery children, distributed clothes in the community, and read literary papers and discussed them as well as other world news topics; a penny savings bank was established in which children were encouraged to save money.[64]

Other programs were a Sunday school that had an enrollment of 156 and an average attendance of ninety; a department of instrumental music, "organized by Maude Cuney-McKinley in February 1902," that included instruction in piano and organ and had an enrollment of twenty-seven pupils; a department of vocal music, organized in 1900 "under the direction of Pedro T. Tinsley, a graduate of the Chicago College of Music." In its Choral Study Club there were sixty members and eight in the Voice Culture Club. There was also a kitchengarten "supported entirely by Mrs. Victor F. Lawson, wife of the owner and proprietor of the *Chicago Daily News* and the *Record Herald*," which taught "scientific housekeeping" and homemaking and graduated approximately twenty-four girls each year; a gymnasium opened twice a week for women and twice a week for men; a catering class of twenty-one women taught by a teacher from the Chicago College of Domestic Arts and Sciences; a sewing class that numbered about fifty-two and met once a week to teach women "how to mend, cut and make their own clothes." The salary of the sewing teacher was paid by Mrs. M. A. Ellis. A men's Bible class recruited by Emma included such eminent citizens as Oscar DePriest (later a congressman), Louis B. Anderson (later an alderman), and Dr. Charles Drew, the Ransom's family doctor; The Mary Louise Arnett Girls' Club provided instructions "in hygiene, morals, deportment and [gave] direction in the choice of reading matter"; there was a boys' club managed by M. N. Work, an English major from Chicago University.[65]

During an interview Emma gave to Katherine Leckie of the *Chicago American*, she explained how the boy's club got started. One evening she was reading *Little Men* to eleven-year-old Reverdy Jr., and some boys from the neighborhood came in to meet the "new boy" on the block. Reverdy Jr. persuaded them to stay. Afterward Emma served a snack and noted that the watermelon was especially appreciated. "From that night the boys' club was not only an established fact, but a successful one." She said at first the boys did not want whites to join their club because they never allowed Negroes to use their swimming tank. But Emma told them that brotherhood knew "neither creed, color, not condition." Finally they agreed to let the white boys in but never would they let them hold office.[66] Reverdy and Emma were overseers of all of the departments, and Reverdy Jr. and Harold, who was now eighteen, participated in many of the programs. Living on the premises meant total commitment.

During August of 1901, Reverdy took his first trip abroad as a delegate to the Third Ecumenical Methodist Conference held in City Road Chapel, London, England, September 4–17. Traveling with Ransom were eight bishops including Arnett, who had pushed for Reverdy's appointment as a delegate; seven other ministers; H. T. Kealing, editor of *The A.M.E. Church Review;* and W. S. Scarborough, a professor from Wilberforce.[67]

The group arrived in mid-August so they could take the tour through the Rhine to Cologne, to the principal cities of Holland and Switzerland, past Mont Blanc to Lucerne, Milan, Venice, Florence, Pisa, Rome, Naples, Genoa, and Paris. Reverdy noted in Paris:

> that for the first time in [his] life he was enveloped in an atmosphere that seemed absolutely free of any prejudice on the account of color. . . . By contrast [he] shrank from the conditions that had to be borne and faced by members of [his] race in the land of [his] birth.[68]

While in Rome, he sent back a letter to the editor of the *Chicago Conservator* dated August 15. "What history, what philosophy and art, what eloquence, what glory and what shame, what defeat cluster around this name—Rome," he wrote. He was impressed by the Cathedral of Notre Dame and its Astronomical Clock. He visited the Vatican, Colosseum, the Forum, the palaces of the Caesars, "the triumphal arches, the monuments and [Rome's] Seven Hills." To him, Mont Blanc in Eastern France was "an enthroned eternity amid icy halls of cold oblivion." In Lucerne from his hotel window, he could see Mount Pilatus where legend has it that Pontius Pilate committed suicide by throwing himself over the cliffs. In Venice, he stayed in a hotel on the Grand Canal and sailed in the gondolas. Included in his tour was the Rialto, the Doge's palace, and the Bridge of Sighs. All the delegates were fine, he said, except "they felt a tinge of heart hunger, because as yet, [there was] no mail from the loved ones at home."[69] His letters to Emma reveal his amazement of how the people in Holland followed them through the streets, of how most of the places he visited in Europe showed little race prejudice, and of a particularly "delightful Sunday spent in Stratford" at the home of the president of the City Council. He missed her and the boys and wished she could have shared the experiences with him.[70]

On September 4, Reverdy had been asked to give a short address at John Wesley Chapel, City Road. His emphasis was on "the University side of Methodism as it looks toward education in the twentieth century." Here he had a chance to promote the idea of an Institutional Church among Methodists. He did not know how it was in England, but in America, he said, there was a tendency for young people to flock to the cities where the population is dense and where they are not directly under any educational or uplifting influences. From its inception, the Methodist Church had been the church of the masses but lately seemed to be veering away from its moorings. He mentioned the churches in the business district of Chicago pastored by Dr. Bushingham and the "Open Church" there as being the "only two examples . . . where any attempt is being made to get hold of the tens of thousands who are practically neglected." It was his belief that the church of the twentieth century must serve

> as the center of the life of the people, and in that center the people [should] be educated and uplifted instead of in the saloons and drinking halls. . . . If Methodism is to make good her splendid beginnings as the church of the masses, she must make her churches centers of educative influence.[71]

A.M.E. leaders were much in evidence throughout the conference. "Bishop Arnett presided at the morning session of the third day. On the afternoon of the fifth day, Professor H. T. Kealing delivered an address on 'Methodism and Education'"; the eleventh day, Bishop Benjamin T. Tanner read an essay on "The Elements of Pulpit Effectiveness"; and on September 18, Bishop W. D. Derrick (originally from Antigua) spoke at Bristol, Bishop Smith at Sheffield and Hull, and Professor Scarborough at Manchester.[72] Reverdy referred to Bishop Derrick's speech as "pompous." During the recess period he said Derrick told him, "Ransom, you are a young fellow. I want to teach you that you must think great thoughts. Listen to this, young man. Speech is but the shadow of our thoughts."[73] No doubt Reverdy thought the bishop should take his own advice. He hoped the speech Derrick had given was *not* the shadow of his thoughts. Reverdy was to have more unpleasant incidents with Derrick when Reverdy pastored in New York.

While in London, Reverdy had the pleasure of being the guest of Samuel Coleridge-Taylor, a Negro who was gaining renown in America and England as a composer and musician. He lived outside of London "about two miles from the Crystal Palace." Taylor had heard about Reverdy and his work in Chicago and admired him. The two men spent three days talking about America, Taylor's music, the Institutional Church, and

Emma and Rev. Reverdy Cassius Ransom standing in front of the Institutional A.M.E.
Church, Chicago, 1902. Courtesy Chicago Historical Society.

their aspirations for the Negro race. Reverdy also met the singer, Amanda Ira Aldridge,
the daughter of the late "Black Roscius," as the famous Shakespearean actor, Ira Aldridge,
was called.[74]

Emma and the boys had missed Reverdy and eagerly greeted his return from England. They listened attentively as he described the sights and sounds he had experienced and hoped someday they too would be able to visit Europe. He outlined the
inspirational sermon he had heard on High Holborn by the pastor, Joseph Parker;

Scarborough's address at Albert Hall; and the sermon he had preached one Sunday morning in Stratford that he modestly described as "acceptable."[75]

A few days later, he ran into the A.M.E. ministers, Rev. A. L. Murray and Rev. A. J. Carey, on State Street and was surprised that neither extended him a hand nor asked him about his trip. He was told by his friends that "they thought [Reverdy] would try to gain new prestige and attention by exploiting [his] trip abroad, and they intended to clip [his] wings and put him in his place."[76]

For some time Ransom had been concerned about the numbers (policy) racket on the South Side of Chicago headed by "Policy Sam Smith." The city officials and police seemed to ignore what was going on. When the gamblers began to "ply their trade" among schoolchildren, Reverdy and a group of concerned citizens decided to do something about it. They went to the aldermen and the police but were told "they could find no place or places where policy offices were located." Reverdy got a photographer who knew where some of the offices were. While photographing one of the locations, the photographer was assaulted and his camera broken. He was arrested on false charges and taken to the Harrison Street Police Station. Following the photographer's arrest, Reverdy launched a series of sermons against the racket.[77]

On February 15, 1903, he preached from the subject "The Great Physician." The "world is diseased. The wisest men of all ages have sought a remedy for the moral and spiritual ills of humanity. Christ removes the disease by removing the cause," he thundered. It was his intention to remove one of the blights in the black community by eliminating the racketeers whether they be black or white. He would not be stopped, no matter what the cost.[78]

In Chicago there were some fifteen hundred branches of the policy racket that took in "at least $30,000 out of the pockets of the ignorant, the poor and from deluded women, and even school children, for some of these branches [were] located near the school houses for that purpose."[79] A little over a year before, a grand jury had indicted 110 men connected with the racket, but they were never brought to trial and the syndicate since then had grown even stronger.[80] Ransom was aware that many of his own members played the numbers daily, sometimes playing numbers from the scriptures he read on Sundays. His crusade against the policy syndicate would not be a popular one; nevertheless, he continued his vigorous campaign.

On Sunday evening, May 3, 1903, while everyone was in the front of the building, someone planted an explosive in a side door that led to Reverdy's office in the rear. It cracked the walls, blew out several windows, shattered a two-foot-thick stone ledge, and "tore [his] books to shreds and caused general ruin."[81] Not only were windows broken in the church but also in nearby businesses and houses. When interviewed by the *Chicago Evening Post* and Hearst's *Chicago American* Reverdy said:

> I want to say once and for all to these people who are opposed to us—that they may burn this place, but if they don't burn me with it the police and firemen may cool the embers, and I will stand on the ashes and keep pegging away.[82]
>
> If this church stands I will make my next talk against the evil from its pulpit next Sunday. Be sure I will protect my life.[83]

As promised, with a loaded revolver beneath his Bible, Reverdy preached a second sermon against the rackets to an even larger congregation the following week. Outside plain clothesmen and volunteer pickets surrounded the building. At one point during his sermon, some boys playing outside gave a loud cry and the audience started to "stampede for the doors," but Reverdy told them everything was all right, and they returned to their seats. "Dynamite and violence are a poor answer to an argument. . . . You can't shoot great principles dead," he continued. He wished these racket men no harm. "If a man finds an animal in a steam he seeks to remove it without injuring it. Policy is an animal in the stream of humanity which we wish to cleanse. . . . Christianity is not violence," he affirmed.[84]

As a result of Reverdy's crusade, 128 members of the syndicate were arrested, and "two of the companies withdrew their books . . . from 150 branch offices in the 'black belt.'" According to the *Chicago Tribune*, the Wisconsin, Indiana, Interstate, and Springfield policy companies "called hurried meetings of the district managers" and decided "to 'lie low until the storm [blew] over'." This meant the withdrawal of

> all betting sheets from shops near churches and schools. [The closing of] shops that have aroused comment and open[ing] new ones only in private houses. Abandon[ing] the buggy service for delivery of betting sheets and drawings. "Policy Sam" Smith [was] ordered to devise another less conspicuous scheme for serving the branch shops.[85]

Admittedly, Reverdy could not by himself abolish a practice that had flourished for years and had the sanction of some policemen and public administrators, but he was able to inconvenience the syndicate for some time. In the future, they understood that there were blacks who would fearlessly fight for their community. He also made it more difficult for the law and other officials to wink at the activities of the policy ring.

In the summer of 1904, Reverdy became alarmed by the stockyard strike. (In *Pilgrimage*, Reverdy erroneously remembered the year as being 1902.) When the workers walked out, the owners had hired Negro "scabs" to fill in. This angered the strikers; however, "the only opportunity Negroes had to enter basic trades in early twentieth-century Chicago was as strikebreakers." The striker took out their frustration on the Negroes, and there were several altercations. "The most serious incident occurred when a mob, estimated at between two and five thousand, stoned two hundred Negroes who, with police protection, were attempting to leave the Hammond Company packing plant."[86]

Although warned he would be in physical danger, Reverdy decided to go to the yards and speak to the union leaders. He told them that

> colored men had no desire to take their jobs and would be quite willing to join the union if permitted, but colored men were laborers, had families to support and wanted jobs . . . that there were enough jobs for all if black and white workers could agree upon some plan of friendly cooperation.[87]

The following Sunday he invited representatives of the strikers and Negro workers to meet at the Institutional Church with Chicago leaders such as attorney Edward H. Wright, Adelbert Roberts, Louis B. Anderson, Clarence Darrow, Frank W. Gunsaulus, and Bishop Fallows of the Protestant Episcopal Church. Ransom said, "After conversing quite a long time in conference with the manager of the strikers, the representatives of the Negro workers, we settled the Stock Yard Strike that day in the Forum of the Institutional Church and Social Settlement."[88]

Ransom saved more than three hundred sermon outlines he used at both Bethel and Institutional Churches in Chicago. Before he died he intrusted them to Joseph Gomez. Even more than do his printed sermons, these outlines demonstrate homiletic methods that Ransom used throughout his ministry. Most of them are written on half-sheets of church stationery and range from a few lines to more detailed passages; some are dated, others are not. As Ransom had stated in his introduction to *The Disadvantages and Opportunities of the Colored Youth* (1894), he rarely wrote out his sermons, and he never read them. This is why he had so much trouble recalling them verbatim when asked to submit them for publication. Luckily he could write as eloquently as he preached, so his written sermons were as articulate and as moving as his spoken ones. He would start out with a subject and a Bible verse or verses. One outline dated 1896 was titled "Let Your Light Shine." He used as his text Matthew 5:16, from which he derived his thesis: "The light of Christ alone is able to dispel the moral and spiritual darkness of the world. Men and nations have perished without this light." He then listed four subheadings from which to expound extemporaneously. Ever aware of his heavy responsibilities as a minister of the gospel, he concluded that he, as well as all humanity, "should wave [Christ's] light in triumph above the world and in the face of death." Undoubtedly this method worked for him and his listeners who received his sermons enthusiastically.[89]

Reverdy's eight years in "The Windy City" had been tumultuous and enriching. He had had to fight opposition to his Institutional Church, not only among the ministers of the city but ministers and officials in the A.M.E. Connection. When C. T. Shaffer became bishop of the Third District, he was encouraged to remove Reverdy and make him presiding elder of the Indiana Conference. Reverdy learned of this and was angered because the bishop had not informed him of his plans. He told the bishop he declined to be a presiding elder. He would prefer to be moved to Evanston, "or some other less exacting charge than the Institutional Church." Shaffer informed him he made his appointments only at the Annual Conferences and not ahead of time. Knowing the bishop had already told other ministers he planned to make him a presiding elder, Reverdy retorted:

> You are a liar; you have already agreed with Bishop Grant . . .to bring Dr. David Cook from St. Louis to Chicago and to send Dr. A. J. Carey from Chicago to St. Paul Church, St. Louis, Mo., and you tell me you make your appointments at the Annual Conference when you have set up this matter months ahead of time? I am informing you that I would not accept an appointment from your hands to any church whatsoever.[90]

Learning of Reverdy's predicament, his friend and mentor, Bishop Arnett, gave Reverdy an appointment in the First Episcopal District.[91] No matter where they were sent or who opposed them, the Ransoms knew they would always carry with them the Institutional Church. And so with some reluctance and much anticipation, they departed Chicago for "the Whaling Capitol of the World," New Bedford, Massachusetts. The year was 1904.

CHAPTER 4

New England Years, 1904–1907

For I will shew him how great things he must suffer for my name's sake.
Acts 9:16

Reverdy's tenure at Bethel in New Bedford, Massachusetts, lasted only nine months but left him with "some of the fondest memories [he] had ever had." The historical importance of the city in terms of Afro-Americans intrigued Reverdy. It was here that Frederick Douglass settled after escaping from slavery, and the shipbuilding feats of Paul Cuffe were celebrated.[1]

Bethel, located on 460 Kempton Street, had a seating capacity of 250, but when Reverdy arrived, only half the pews were filled on a Sunday morning. Many of the families were native New Englanders and had been there since the days of Cuffe; other members' ancestors had come from West Africa as slaves and later had participated in the Revolutionary War. They had never known, however, the kind of slavery Negroes in the South had experienced.[2]

New Bedford, in many respects, maintained some of the same qualities Douglass had found when he arrived. "Everything looked clean, new, and beautiful. . . . Granite warehouses of the widest dimensions" made an interesting backdrop for the wharfs that were lined with ships of all sizes. "[There were] few dilapidated houses, with poverty-stricken inmates." Many of the colored people lived in decent houses and were enjoying some of the comforts of life.[3] Nevertheless, the city was not completely free from poverty or race prejudice any more than it had been in Douglass's time.

The Ransoms were most surprised by the manner of worship of the parishioners. In *Pilgrimage* he described it as "subdued and rather cold and formal, so unlike the spontaneous enthusiasm that generally characterizes the worship of the Negro congregation." The members knew little or nothing about Negro spirituals "and seemed to care less."[4] They were more attuned to the old Methodist hymns and anthems.

Reverdy's pastorate was devoid of the frenetic activities in which he had engaged in Chicago, and he found himself having more leisure to read, write, and spend lazy afternoons and evenings with people in the community. Among the more interesting personalities he remembered were Andrew Bush, the merchant and tailor; Attorney

Edward Jourdain; a man he only identifies as Mr. Moore, a bookworm; Miss Elizabeth C. Carter, a public school teacher, whom he later married to Bishop W. Sampson Brooks of the A.M.E. Church; and Sgt. William H. Carney of the Fifty-Fourth Massachusetts Regiment who had distinguished himself during the Civil War by preventing the flag from touching the ground when it was shot from the hands of the flag bearer.[5]

Nine months after pastoring in New Bedford, Reverdy was appointed by Bishop Arnett to Charles Street Church, Boston (July 2, 1905). Negroes had a long history in Boston. Eight years after Boston had originally been settled, they had arrived on the *Desire*, a trading vessel that had come from Africa by way of the Bahamas (1683). The people of Boston bought them as slaves. They, and all other slaves in Massachusetts, were freed by the Declaration of Rights authored by John Adams in 1780. "Boston, as the active center of the movement which brought slavery to an end in Massachusetts, became the birthplace of the Negro's freedom in America."[6] Negroes gained the franchise in 1778 when Paul and John Cuffe won their court case which established that a person who paid personal taxes should be allowed to vote. The question of franchise was finalized by the Body of Liberties in 1790 "which guaranteed manhood suffrage, without regard to race."[7]

At the time the Ransoms arrived, the Negro population of Boston proper was 11,948, and of greater Boston, 21,234.[8] Once again the Ransoms found themselves in a city rich with historical significance. With its acts of rebellion against the British, it provided the impetus for the Revolutionary War in which Crispus Attucks, a black man, was the first to give his life in the cause of freedom. Phillis Wheatley, a slave brought from Senegal to Boston around 1753, soon mastered the English language and became the first published American black poet. She was honored in both America and England. In 1829, David Walker published the inflammatory antislavery tract titled "An Appeal in four Articles, together with a Preamble to the Coloured Citizens of the World, but in Particular, and very Expressly, to Those of the United States of America." It stirred blacks to action and terrified slaveholders in the South so much that a price was offered for his capture. Boston was also the city in which William Lloyd Garrison first began the Abolitionists movement with the publication of his paper, *The Liberator*, on January 1, 1831. He was soon joined by blacks like Frederick Douglass; William Wells Brown, the writer; Charles Lennox Remond, first Negro lecturer for the antislavery society; and Peter Howard, a barber, who ran a station in the Underground Railroad.[9] Reverdy must have thought that providence had brought him to Boston at this time when the push for black liberation was waning in the North as well as the South. In its place was a growing tendency to rob Negroes of their rights through another kind of slavery—Jim Crowism.

Charles Street A.M.E. Church was in the West End on the corner of Charles and Mt. Vernon Streets. It stood "just below Beacon Hill and the State House, a block and a half from the Charles River Basin" and, in the other direction, a block and a half from the Public Gardens.[10] Reverdy described it as "the fourth oldest example of colonial architecture in the city . . . ranking in age with King's Chapel and Park Street Church." On its tall steeple was a clock that was cared for by the city. Its commodious auditorium with its oak pews was stately and graceful in appearance.[11] In the early years, when the church was owned by whites, Negroes were only allowed to occupy the first two rows of the balcony; this was incentive for them to buy the building, December 15, 1876. Among those who had attended the church and contributed to its programs at one time or another were such notables as Wendell Phillips, William Lloyd Garrison, Edward Everett Hale, Gen. Benjamin F. Butler, Frederick Douglass, and Phillip Brooks.[12]

When Negroes first came to Boston, those who did not live as servants in the homes of whites settled near the wharfs in the North End. Before 1800, they began to move to the West End, "beyond Joy Street and down along the northwesterly slopes of Beacon Hill to several blocks below Cambridge Street." Perhaps it was the establishment of the first black church, the African Meeting-House, in the West End that promoted some of the movement. By 1905 most had moved again, this time to the South End or to Roxbury.[13] Reverdy recalled that when he first took charge of Charles Street Church "there were not more than a score of families living in the West End."[14] This meant he would have to work hard to keep up the membership. Reverdy Jr. was fifteen and, at twenty-two, Harold had left home to live in New Jersey. In time he would marry and raise a family in Montclair.

The Ransoms settled in the parsonage at 196 Northampton Street, and Reverdy began his pastoral and civic duties with some uncertainty. The former pastor, John F. Henderson, had "not only been a fluent speaker, but had a rich fund of natural endowment which displayed itself in his rare gift of literary expression."[15] Reverdy hoped his sermons would be as well received. He was aware that Boston was one of the most celebrated educational and cultural centers in America with its Boston University, Massachusetts Technical Institute and Harvard University across the Charles River in Cambridge, and the historic Faneuil Hall that had provided a platform for most of the great abolitionist speakers. He need not have worried; he was warmly welcomed by the community. *Alexanders Magazine* spoke of his eloquence and scholarliness and said he was "just the kind of man needed by the progressive members and friends of Charles Street Church."[16] Early in his pastorate he reserved a special pew for students from Boston and Harvard Universities. In *Pilgrimage* he said the pew "was generally filled each Sunday morning, sometimes to overflowing with students from these schools, both white and colored, [and] quite frequently" with a Japanese, Chinese, or Hindu student.[17]

His first church bulletin outlined the schedule he would follow. On Sunday there would be two services at 10:30 A.M. and 7:30 P.M.; Class Meeting at 12:15 P.M., Sunday

School at 1:30 P.M.; and the young people's Christian Endeavor at 6 P.M. At the noon hour, dinner would be served by the King's Daughters in the church dining room. During the week at 8 P.M. classes would meet on Monday and Wednesday, Official Board on Tuesday, Prayer Meeting on Friday, and Trustee Meeting the first Thursday in each month. The bulletin noted the serious illness of Bishop Arnett and the fact that the pastor's sermon of the previous Sunday had been extracted in *The Boston Herald* and *Evening Transcript.*[18]

For his first sermon Reverdy had chosen the theme "Standards of Measurement and Comparison" taken from 11 Corinthians 10:12: "For we dare not make ourselves of the number or compare ourselves with some that commend themselves; but they measuring themselves by themselves, and comparing themselves among themselves, are not wise." He emphasized that people set standards for themselves and can never rise higher intellectually or socially than those standards they set. Therefore, it was important for humans to have high goals.[19]

The first transaction Reverdy had with his trustees was that of setting his salary. They told him they could only pay him $1,200 a year. This was the amount they had promised to pay the former pastor, but when they could not meet their commitment, they had to borrow the money. This amount was not satisfactory to Reverdy. He persuaded them to allow him to keep all the money raised on the first and third Sundays of every month. Reluctantly, they agreed. Reverdy was so successful in attracting new members that in less than four months, the offerings exceeded expectations. He needed only to keep the money collected on the first Sunday; the rest went to the trustees to run the church.[20]

Meanwhile Emma was involved in fixing up the parsonage and getting acquainted with the various church organizations. She had an opportunity to formally introduce herself to the community on August 11 when she spoke before the Convention of the Northeastern Federation of Women's Clubs in Potter Hall of the New Century Building on Huntington Avenue. She chose as her subject "The Home-Made Girl," which she defined as "one who is not the artificial product of society, nor the superficial creation of institutions of learning or romance literature." The homemade girl has had her character molded in the home and "has been trained through the exercise of experience to take a view of life that will be so serious that she will know life means opportunity for usefulness." Although civilization has emphasized progress as belonging exclusively to the man, his influence "is based upon the strength . . . of womanhood and the home."[21]

There has been much talk about the new woman, she said. But "there is a sense in which the colored woman is the newest woman in America." Whites are astounded by "the loftiness of her ambitions and the heights of her aspirations." The generation she must raise has not had the same benefit of education and wealth as have whites; consequently, it is her task to produce "a womanhood which shall be able to stand upon its feet and hold up its head in the face of this American nation." The best training in the domestics, in culture, and morality must come first from the home. This did not minimize the importance of churches, schools, and clubs, she noted; nevertheless, "the home is the most sacred of all altars. It is the first one that God ever established." Marriage and motherhood has "the seal and superscription of the most high." For those who are so unfortunate as to have no homes, it is the job of other women to bring the "best home life down to them, because they cannot come to us, even if they would."[22]

She spoke against those who get some education, money, and position and separate themselves from the masses of the people who are trying to rise, and against those light skinned Negroes who think they are superior to the darker members of the race. The women who are making the greatest contribution to the race are neither "wall flowers" nor "butterflies of fashion." They are the "plain women of sturdy virtues, of industry, of mother-wit and good commonsense."[23]

Next she turned to one of Reverdy's favorite themes, the battle that the colored woman has had against the lust of the white man for nearly three centuries. And yet the country has held up the Negro man as the "rapist before the eyes of the civilized world." By studying the statistics, Emma said, anyone will find that "there are no more fiendish Negro men than brutal white men." If our women are properly trained, they will "keep white men and all other men in their proper places, and . . . produce a manhood that will respect and honor womanhood regardless of race or class."[24]

She closed by saying that like the pioneers of old:

> The colored woman of today has before her an empire, unconquered, unsubjugated and untraversed; she has it in her power to make her beauty, the dream of art and the inspiration of poetry; her virtue and culture win her the devoted admiration of men and become the charm of society; her industry and frugality lay the foundation of material prosperity.[25]

It is interesting to note that she, like her husband, had a somewhat Victorian view of the woman. Her speech abounds with words such as "charm," "virtue," "homemaker," "graces," "refinement," "manners," terms that seem antiquated now. Though both she and Reverdy were advanced in their thinking, in some ways, they were products of their times.

On Tuesday, September 26, Emma was asked to speak again, this time at a benefit for the Harriet Tubman Home for Working Girls at 37 Holyoke Street, sponsored by the Committee of Ladies.[26] Unfortunately, no copies of her speech can be found. Both appearances, however, demonstrate that Emma intended to be just as involved in church and civic affairs in Boston as she had been in Chicago.

In October, Reverdy spoke before the National Reform Convention at Park Street Congregational Church on the topic "How Should the Christian State Deal with the Race Problem?" (*The Spirit of Freedom and Justice* listed the speech as having been given April, 1906; however, in *The Charles Street Church Weekly Bulletin* for October 1, 1905, there was an announcement that the speech is to be given on October 3. The following Sunday bulletin announced that the speech given at the National Reform Convention has been printed in a pamphlet and is ready for the public.[27])

Reverdy's first sentence set forth his thesis: "There should be no Race Problem in the Christian State." Christ had founded Christianity "in the midst of the most bitter and intense antagonisms of race and class." Nevertheless, he dealt with everyone the same, the Jews, Samaritans, Syro-Phoenicians, Greeks, and Romans. His aim was to break down the barriers "between man and man, and to take away all the Old Testament laws and ordinances that prevented Jew and Gentile from approaching God on an equal plain."[28]

American "Christianity will un-Christ itself if it refuses to strive on, until this Race Problem" is settled correctly. The Negro was brought to this country, not as a human being, but as a slave whose brute strength and animalism could be used to enrich the country, especially the South that made slavery the "cornerstone" of its civilization. Then God spoke through the Civil War. Blacks were "freed" only to be allowed on "the fringes of the industrial world." The propaganda that Negroes should solve their problems only through industrial education has became accepted by North and South. What "the South undoubtedly means . . . is that a peasant class, composed of ten million Negroes shall be built up and established in this land."[29]

The racist author of *The Leopard's Spots,* Rev. Thomas Dixon Jr., has said that Booker T. Washington's school was not "turning out servants, but men, who would go out into the world to be themselves leaders of men, as contractors, master mechanics and employers or directors of labor." It is for this reason, says Dixon, that Tuskegee will be a failure and will not survive. Reverdy would remind his audience that in the North, Negro youth are studying the same subjects as whites.

> Can one think of a greater crime, almost against the very life of human spirit, than this, that these youth should go thus out into life only to find that their ability, coupled with high character, counted for very little when they sought to enter the doors of industrial opportunity? . . . This nation cannot afford to waste any of its trained minds, skilled hands, and cultured brains.[30]

The Negro is the most American of all, he asserted. Next to the Indians, he has been here as long as the white man, has fought in his wars, been loyal despite the government's ill treatment. Therefore, the Negro's right to the franchise is unquestionable. No man has a right to govern another without his consent. Yet on the question of the franchise, the North has become "timid" and the government "quasi acquiescent." When it comes to social equality, members of the white race think this is the highest priority of the Negro. They justify prohibiting the Negro his rights on the excuse that they have to keep the Negro down to protect their homes and white womanhood. Against mob violence and lynching, the churches, newspapers, the president, and government are silent. Meanwhile the Negro is excluded from parks, museums, libraries, public entertainment places and has been segregated on trains, buses, and train stations, and even the Young Men's Christian Associations. Whites can never have a Christian State "by beating back and trampling under foot the simple rights and aspirations of ten million blacks. . . . As God is above man, so man is above race."[31]

> If the new Jerusalem tarries in its descent to earth, coming down from God out of heaven, then we, not like some foolish tower-builders upon the plains of Shinar, but taught from heaven in a better way, shall build upon the teachings of Jesus, with the doctrine of human brotherhood as taught by Him, until fraternity, realized shall raise us to the skies.[32]

There could be no doubt in anyone's mind that Ransom's presence, and especially his voice, would be significantly felt during his tenure in Boston.

When the Ransoms came to Boston, the controversy between the philosophy of Booker T. Washington and DuBois was at its highest. Washington's view was "generally accepted by the President in the White House, the Governors of the Southern States, as well as by most of the influential Negroes in the United States," but was strongly opposed by Reverdy and two other outspoken Negro citizens of Boston, George W. Forbes, former co-owner of *The Boston Guardian* (1901–03) and William Monroe Trotter, owner and editor.[33]

George Forbes had received his B.A. from Wilberforce and his A.B. from Amherst, served as the head of the largest branch of the Boston Public Library and as editor of the weekly *Boston Courant* (1892–97). In 1901 he became co-editor of *The Guardian* with Trotter. For the first two years, most of the editorials were written by him. After that, he left *The Guardian* and returned to his job at the library. William Monroe Trotter graduated from Harvard University and was the first Negro Phi Beta Kappa at Harvard. He had been jailed for a month in 1903 for repeatedly interrupting a speech given by Booker T. Washington at Zion African Methodist Church. Trotter insisted that Washington answer embarrassing questions about a letter he had written to the *Montgomery Advertiser*, a speech he had made before the Twentieth Century Club, and an interview he had given to the *Washington Post*, all of which reflected his accommodationist views. Washington refused to answer and Trotter and two companions were removed by the police to the Charles Street Jail. Only Trotter was given a prison term. This incident has been referred to as "The Boston Riot."[34]

From its inception, *The Guardian* was strongly anti-Washington. In 1902, Totter had written: "What man is a worse enemy to a race than a leader [Washington] who looks with equanimity on the disfranchisement of his race in a country where other races have universal suffrage by constitutions that make one rule for his race and another for the dominant race . . . ."[35] Again in 1903, he wrote: "This habit of always belittling agitation on the part of Washington, that very thing that made him free, and by which he lives and prospers, is one of his great faults if such a blundering can have any degrees in stupidity."[36]

Although he did not always agree with them, Reverdy became friends with both Forbes and Trotter and admired their courage and brilliance. In an editorial in the *A.M.E. Church Review,* October 1919, he was to call Trotter "the uncompromising advocate of political equality, social and industrial justice for his race. . . . To this cause [Trotter] has dedicated everything that men hold most precious—his family, his fortune, himself." Trotter and Forbes had modeled the *Guardian* "after the challenging form and spirit of the *Liberator* which Mr. Garrison used as a weapon against slavery."[37]

In *Dust to Dawn* W. E. B. DuBois described *the Guardian* as "bitter, satirical and personal," but added that "it was earnest, and it published facts." He did not "wholly agree" with the paper. Only a few Negroes did, "but nearly all read it and were influenced by it."[38] Among those who subscribed faithfully to the newspaper was Reverdy Cassius Ransom.

The year 1905 marked the Centennial Celebration of the birth of William Lloyd Garrison. Reverdy was chosen to give the closing address in Faneuil Hall the evening of November 11. Although the audience was largely Negro, on the platform with him were not only official representatives of Massachusetts, but also Julia Ward Howe, the poet, social reformer, co-editor of the anti-slavery *Commonwealth*, and author of "The Battle Hymn of the Republic," written in 1861, the year of Reverdy's birth.[39]

During his oration, Reverdy placed Garrison among those few great men who have the kind of "carrying power" that extends into another century. Garrison "never temporized nor compromised with the enemies of human freedom." His sources were the Bible and the Declaration of Independence. Those who admire and love Garrison must perpetuate his memory by confronting contemporary problems with the same "courage" and "uncompromising spirit" with which he "met the burning questions of his day."[40]

The Fifteenth Amendment, which was to give the Negro political power, is " more bitterly opposed today than it was a century ago," he said. Where is the Negro's place in America? is a question still asked in the newspapers, magazines, political campaigns, and literature of the day. Time has passed but the stage and the characters are the same. There are still those who would keep the Negro down by "unjust and humiliating legislation and degrading treatment." America is slow to learn the lessons of history; "the passions which feed on prejudice and tyranny can neither be mollified nor checked by subjection, surrender or compromise." Therefore, the Negro can move in only one direction, the way that leads "toward the realization of complete manhood and equality. . . ." The time is crucial because there are those who would reduce the Negro to a second kind of slavery.[41]

"President Roosevelt . . . has advised us that instead of agitating for our rights, we should apply ourselves to the fulfillment of our duties," he noted. This is not a new philosophy. It was taught by Christ and Joseph Mazzini, the Italian patriot, though their meanings were different from Roosevelt's. It is a man's duty to "support and defend his family and his home . . . and oppose with his life the invader or despoiler of his home." It is his duty to "overthrow the artificial social barriers which intervene and separate him from realizing the highest and best there is within him by freedom of association." It is his duty to pledge allegiance to his country and defend it against foreign invaders. "Tyrants and tyranny everywhere should be attacked and overthrown."[42]

Next he asked the question, "What kind of Negroes do the American people want?" All ten million blacks will remain in America as a factor in politics, education, industry, and wealth. Do the American people want a "voteless Negro," a Negro who "shall not be permitted to participate in the government" which he supports with his money and blood? "Do they want a Negro who shall consent to being set apart as forming a distinct industrial class, permitted to rise no higher than the level of surfs or peasants?" Do they want a Negro who is content to be a social inferior, one who will "avoid friction between the races by consenting to occupy the place to which white men may choose to assign him?" Do they want a Negro who feels he may never stand on equal ground with whites?[43]

The Negro will not be an alien in his home country; will not be eliminated as a political factor; "will not camp forever on the borders of the industrial world"; will be moral; will educate his children; will insist "not only upon voting but being voted for"; will assert himself, "not as a Negro, but as a man"; will not retreat before his enemies; will be faithful to his country; "will consider no task too difficult, no sacrifice too great . . . to emancipate his country from the un-Christ-like feelings of race hatred and the American bondage of prejudice."[44]

He outlined the two current views on the Negro question. "One is that the Negro should stoop to conquer." The other is that he is a man and should not "yield one

"Centennial Oration to William Lloyd Garrison"
given December 11, 1905, at Faneuil Hall, Boston.

syllable of his title to American citizenship." The race has come a long way since Garrison pled their cause before the American people, he said. The Negro has found his place and can speak for himself today. He will not sell his birthright of freedom for a mess of pottage.[45] His voice rose as he looked out at the mass of black faces eager to embrace his dreams: "I feel inspired tonight. The spirits of the champions of freedom hover near. High above the stars, Lincoln and Garrison, Sumner and Phillips, Douglass and Lovejoy, look down to behold their prayers answered, their labors rewarded, and their prophecies fulfilled. . . .They have left us a priceless heritage."[46] He closed by asserting that out of the conflict and differences between the races that separate, "once the tides of immigration have ceased to flow to our shores, this nation will evolve a people who shall be one in purpose, one in spirit, one in destiny, a composite American by the commingling of blood."[47]

The Boston Transcript called it a "fitting close to the two-day celebration . . .that stirred a crowded audience of Negro men and women . . . as no white speaker has been able to stir them throughout the whole series of Garrison addresses at previous meetings yesterday and on Sunday."[48] The Boston Herald of December 12, noted that the applause was so "tremendous," that frequently "the speaker had to pause for several minutes. At its close the scene was indescribable, women wept, men embraced each other. Guests on the platform rushed upon the orator with congratulations, the program was forgotten and only the playing of the band restored order and made it possible to proceed. Many said no better oration had ever been delivered in Faneuil Hall in its whole history."[49] Reverdy noted in *Pilgrimage* that Julia Ward Howe "held [his] hands and caressed them and seemed overcome with emotion and appreciation."[50] The speech was later printed and published by the Boston Suffrage League. On the cover was a picture of the forty-four-year-old pastor with the words underneath: "Rev. Reverdy C. Ransom. Whose Eloquence Rocked the Cradle of Liberty Monday Night with Oration Unsurpassed in Historic Hall."[51]

While admitting that Reverdy was "regarded as one of the ablest and certainly the most eloquent of Negro preachers," on January 3, 1906, *The New York Evening Sun* said his Garrison speech would "be called defiance and a challenge" in the South. Furthermore the Negro has political equality in the North, but it is the majority who decides who should be elected to office. The Negro is in the minority, the article pointed out. When it comes to the "social privileges," if Ransom "means what is called social equality, it will be allowed no more in the North than in the South."[52]

The Christian Recorder wrote a rebuttal to *The Sun* article on January 11. It regretted that the article did not continue "in the same unbiased and intelligent manner with which it began its criticism. . . . It betrays unusual bias and blindness in its treatment of the question of social privileges." By stating that social equality would be allowed neither North nor South, it ignored the facts. Social privilege already existed in the North in terms of "intermarriage between the races" by "sanction of law." While there are millions of Negroes who do not care about the "Southern bug-bear of 'social equality,'" there are thousands "whose taste, like that of the whites, seems inclined in that direction." That there are mixed marriages in the North and always has been a mixing of blood between both races in the South seems to be ignored by the "luminous search light of *The Sun*."[53] This speech was an important milestone in Reverdy's career and marked him as an activist who could sway audiences by his passionate and eloquent delivery.

With acclaim also came censure. According to Reverdy's testimony in *Pilgrimage*, in the spring of 1906, he received an invitation from Principal William H. Council to give the commencement address at the Agricultural and Mechanical College at Huntsville, Alabama. On May 23 he went to the Southern Railroad Ticket Office and was told there would be no trouble "concerning his sleeping car accommodations" on the Epsilon from Washington to Chattanooga. He bought a ticket from Boston straight through to Huntsville. Once aboard the train, he settled in his seat and began to study his speech. At some time or other, he gave one of the porters a pamphlet which had in it his Garrison Centennial speech.[54]

He became aware of a white lady starring at his bag which was covered with stickers from the various foreign countries he had visited. She asked if he were foreign, and he said he had traveled a lot. When she asked if he spoke English, he answered her in French. Paying her no further attention, he went back to his speech. Shortly after, he was pulled from his seat by two white men, William McSween, a lawyer, and Edward Mills, from Newport, Tennessee, both of whom were delegates to the State Convention being held at Nashville. They accused him of bothering the woman, passing himself off as a French count, and giving out subversive literature to the porter. Then they cuffed and kicked Reverdy, told him to get back in the car where the "niggers" sat, and pushed him down the aisles to the Jim Crow car. One of the conductors told him he could return when the two got off at Chattanooga. After the train pulled away from the station at Chattanooga, Reverdy attempted to go back to his original seat. Again he was bodily ejected from the coach, pushed back to the Jim Crow car, and slammed into a seat with his bag thrown on top of him.[55]

News of the incident soon reached Huntsville so that when he arrived there was no one to meet him. A man standing in the station directed him to the colored hotel, supposedly the best in town. Reverdy wrote, "I was sick, sore and exhausted; the odor of the place was so bad, and the bed looked so dirty, I could not, tired as I was, lie upon it. I threw my overcoat across me and sat there with head leaning upon my elbow through the night." The next morning, a Methodist minister was sent for by the hotel managers. After showing Reverdy the headlines of the newspaper which reported what had happened the day before, Reverdy was taken to Normal College and told to wait in one of the cottages. Soon after, representatives from the Alumni Association came and informed him his speech had been canceled. When he asked if it had to do with the train incident, they said they did not care to say. (Later they said the speech was canceled because they did not believe Reverdy was "the right character to be placed before the students.") Although he asked to meet with Professor Council, he never saw him or any other college personnel except the Alumni Committee and a Mr. Charles Stewart. There was nothing left for him to do but to return to Boston. Undoubtedly, on the trip back Reverdy thought of the irony of Council's last letter to him. "Come when you can and leave when you must."[56]

News of the incident spread throughout the country. The southern papers claimed he had tried to pass for a Frenchman (some said German) of high degree and had incensed whites by eating lunch with a white woman in the dining car. He was "forced to come down a notch by the two Newport Citizens, at least he had to hie himself from his luxurious surroundings in the Pullman, forsake the companionship of the whites. . . and take a seat in the Jim Crow section . . . ."[57] Ransom asserted that at no time did he say he was French or German nor had he ever eaten in the dining car with anybody or alone. For breakfast, he had had a cup of coffee in his room.[58]

T. Timothy Fortune, editor of the *New York Age,* and disciple of the Booker T. Washington school, wrote several editorials concerning the incident. In one, he reported that two students had said that Ransom had offered them a nip of whiskey while on the train.[59] Reverdy later learned that Charles Steward, a colored agent of the Associated Press who had been there with the Alumni, had reported to the news media that Ransom had been admitted to Professor's Council's home, "and was so under the influence of liquor that [he] went to bed with [his] boots on, and had to be sent from the grounds."[60] Thus the rumor got started that Reverdy was drunk, and that is why he was not allowed to give his commencement speech.

Booker T. Washington seemed determined not to let the opportunity pass without attacking Reverdy's character. On June 19, 1906, he wrote a letter to T. Thomas Fortune stating, "The scoundrels in Boston are trying to make Ransom out a saint and I see no reason for our lying down while the enemy is constantly at work." He enclosed statements by Council and Charles Steward for Fortune to publish in *The New York Age* which alleged that Ransom had a tendency to become intoxicated. This reputation had followed him in Cleveland, Chicago, and New Bedford, and now in Boston, they said.[61]

Fortune wrote several editorials. In one, after stating that some of Ransom's friends were demanding an investigation, Fortune said: "Every one knows Ransom knows that an investigation is just what he does not want. An investigation might investigate Ransom in Cleveland, or Ransom in Chicago. . . . Ransom has been indulging devotedly in his little nips for fifteen years and ought to be thoroughly braced up by this time." Concerning the report that two white men had ejected him from the car, Fortune said: "Why in the world did not Ransom fight and have his dead body in the car, as he has been advising Afro-Americans in the South to do? It seems to be one thing to give advice in Faneuil Hall and quite another to put in practice in the South."[62]

Most of the people in Boston took Reverdy's side. *The Boston Post* of May 29, 1906, wrote of the "widespread indignation and severe denunciation among the colored citizens of Boston and Cambridge," concerning the false accusations against Ransom. It noted that Ransom was "one of the leading colored men in Boston, and in all movements for the improvement of his people he [had] taken a leading part." *The Boston Herald* reported that Ransom would sue the railway and the Pullman company, claiming that his ticket purchased at Washington, under the interstate commerce law, entitled him to ride any coach.[63] *Alexanders Magazine* thought that Ransom's being ejected from the seat for which he had paid to be "a great crime."[64]

Reverdy's friends, George W. Forbes and Monroe Trotter stood by him. In *The Guardian* Forbes pointed out that the Normal Institute received funds from the legislature of Alabama, and "Mr. Council, the principal, who has never run counter to the southern white estimation of the Negro, undoubtedly did not care to jeopardize his annual state appropriation by entertaining Mr. Ransom at the present time, even though he was his guest by personal invitation." He intimated that many of Ransom's friends felt he had been invited to Alabama to be discredited for his strong stand on Negro rights since Ransom and Council held opposite views. Council's "attitude is that the Negro is not and never can be equal to the white," he concluded.[65] Trotter, as President of the New England Suffrage League, wrote to the editor of *The Globe* that the news dispatch "relative to the maltreatment of Rev. R.C. Ransom, the brilliant pastor of the Charles Street A.M.E. Church . . . which appeared in this morning's issue is entirely erroneous." Mrs. Ransom had told him that she went with her husband to the ticket office and the agent assured both of them he would have no trouble in the sleeping car because of his color. Trotter therefore concluded that it was "altogether untrue that Ransom had gotten his berth under the guise of [being] a Frenchman."[66]

Ransom was convinced that council "did not have the moral courage to permit [him] to speak after the episode on the train." He noted that a few years before when two of his teachers had tried to ride first class on the train, whites had threatened to close the school. "Council did then, what he has always done; he groveled," Reverdy said.[67]

Reverdy's strongest support came from fellow ministers in his district. A Dr. D. A. Graham wrote to the House of Bishops stating that Ransom had been drunk and the church should do something about it. The bishops requested that Bishop Turner hold the New York and New England Conferences. In a review cited in *Pilgrimage,* Turner described the events at the New England Conference (July 5–9, Providence, Rhode Island). When the roll was called, all the pastors passed in terms of their character except Ransom, who was marked by a Rev. C. P. Cole. Cole then proceeded to review the newspaper accounts "and the public confabulations, and the other chit-chat which had attracted no ordinary attention." When he had finished, Ransom spoke in his own defense. During the speech, "men listened and wept, like children, and the writer himself had to use his handkerchief more than once, and after about two hours the doctor was unanimously acquitted and his character passed." Even Dr. Cole voted in favor of Ransom. Ransom was reassigned to Charles Street Church, and the conference passed a resolution denouncing the "dastardly and cowardly" treatment of Ransom. Such action "was a violation of interstate passenger law." It exonerated Ransom and commended "most heartily the brave and manly stand taken by the *Boston Guardian,* the *Voice of the People,* and other race journals, also the fortitude and patience exhibited by [their] Brother Ransom in this crisis."[68] Turner ended the matter by writing: "No one came to accuse or send a scintilla of evidence against him. We have written this somewhat lengthy review to let the slanderers of our church see that there was no disposition to cover, conceal, evade, dodge or compromise, so the church is vindicated and Ransom is acquitted."[69]

On August 5 Bishop Turner wrote Ransom a letter stating that if he wished to squash the rumor of his drinking, he should "take the stump or platform."[70] Evidently Reverdy took his advice. *The New York Age* of August 16 reported sardonically that "Ransom chose to preach at Charles Street A.M.E. Church last night on 'Sobriety, Or How to Keep Sober.'"[71]

Some time after the event was no longer of much interest, Reverdy said he received a letter from Turner stating that "Professor Council says, 'He did you no harm himself, but that those you talked with influenced him to do you harm and he will have no peace of mind until you come to Normal and address the college.'"[72] There is no record of Reverdy ever having gone back to Normal.

The Alabama incident seemed to have added rather than detracted from Ransom's pastorate in Boston. Charles Street's Weekly Bulletin of July 1, 1906, reported that the church was worth $100,000, had paid $1,000 on its mortgage, and had eliminated all floating bills. Reverdy had taken in 124 new members and married sixteen couples.[73] The Ransoms were given a reception and benefit on August 7th to welcome their return for another year and to raise money for their vacation.[74]

During all this controversy, Reverdy was still very much involved in the national civil rights movement. In June of 1905, W. E. B. DuBois had sent out a call "for organized determination and aggressive action on the part of men who believe in Negro Freedom and growth." He asked that a conference be held "to oppose firmly present methods of strangling honest criticism; to organize intelligent and honest Negroes; and to support organs of news and public opinion."[75] In his autobiography, DuBois says that although he was not present when Trotter was arrested for interrupting and heckling Booker T. Washington when he spoke in Boston, "the unfairness of the jail sentence" Trotter received "helped lead him eventually to form the Niagra Movement."[76] Rev. R. R. Wright, who had served as Ransom's assistant pastor in Chicago, had a different version of how the idea of the conference originated. He claimed that Ransom had invited DuBois to Chicago to speak for three days on "The Negro American's Position in America." At the end of the three days, DuBois chose a committee to meet with him at the residence of Charles E. Bentley, dentist. There it was decided that a national organization should be established to fight for the Negro's rights.[77] At any rate, fifty-nine black men from seventeen states signed the call, including Rev. Reverdy Cassius Ransom of Boston.[78] For some reason, Ransom was not present at the first meeting (July 11–13), which marked the beginning of the Niagara Movement, so named by the location of its initial meeting.

Prior to the second meeting at Harpers Ferry, Ransom received an invitation from Frank H. M. Murray, chairman of the Committee on Arrangements, requesting that he speak at the meeting August 17, 1906. He closed the letter by adding, "I am anxious to tell you how I sympathized with you at the time of the Council outrage."[79]

On the platform with Ransom was Frederick Douglass's son, Louis; Richard T. Greener, "who had personal recollections of John Brown"; and a Mrs. Evans, aunt to John Copeland, who was hung with Brown. Mrs. Evans was also sister to Sheridan Leary, "who was killed October 19, 1859, fighting with Brown." Other notables in attendance were W. E. B. DuBois; William M. Trotter; Rev. Anthony Waldron, Baptist minister; and Mary Church Terrell, educator, lecturer.[80]

Ransom titled his address "The Spirit of John Brown," in honor of the man who had been hung when he attacked the United States Arsenal at Harpers Ferry in an attempt to free the slaves. The character of John Brown suited well Ransom's temperament—the martyr who against all odds was determined to fulfill the mission he believed was ordained by the Almighty. Comparing him with David and Moses, who were also commissioned by God to face Goliath and Pharaoh respectively, Reverdy said this "Melchizedek of the modern world" had made Harpers Ferry as classic as Bunker Hill. While Garrison wrote, Beecher preached, Philips pleaded with "silver-toned voice," and Brown performed the DOING OF IT. He became a traitor to his country in order to be true to the slaves, as did Americans became to the British during the Revolutionary War. With the "moral uprightness and strict religious character of the Puritan, as well as his love of liberty and hatred of oppression and tyranny," Brown set out to organize and arm the slaves so they could strike a blow for their freedom.[81]

During Brown's days some Negroes did find freedom by escaping to Canada or to the North, he said. But the Supreme Court made "every white man of the North a detective and an agent of the South" by passing its Fugitive Slave Law. Today Negroes are migrating in large numbers to the North, and though they do have some "sympathetic friends and helpers . . . public opinion no where sustains agitation or action against the conditions that prevail." The way whites deal with the Negro question "is nothing but the old method in a new disguise." Just as was true before the Civil War, when compromises were made which allowed some states to maintain slavery, "today the South is unmolested in its disfranchising constitutions" and Jim Crow policies. The president, Theodore Roosevelt, has been silent; his secretary of state, Taft, who calls the Negro "political children," has not only permitted but endorsed violations of the Constitution.[82]

During the war, Negroes marched and died singing "John Brown's body lies a-moldering in the grave." "The dreams of this dreamer at last found fulfillment as his soul went marching on in the Proclamation of Emancipation, in the Thirteenth . . . Fourteenth and Fifteenth Amendments."[83]

It is indeed, paradoxical that a nation which has erected monuments of marble and bronze to John Brown, Frederick Douglass, William Lloyd Garrison, Charles Sumner and other abolitionists; a nation which proclaims a holiday that all classes, including school children, may decorate with flowers the graves of the men who fought to preserve the union, and to free the slaves, a nation which has enacted into organic law the freedom and political status of a race which has been brought with blood, now sits supinely down, silent and inactive, while the work of the liberators is ignored, while those who fought to destroy the government, REGAIN IN THE HALLS OF CONGRESS THE VICTORIES THEY LOST ON THE FIELD OF BATTLE.[84]

Although the Negro considers the Democratic Party to be their traditional foe, there is little difference between the two parties, he scolded. Republicans in the cabinet and Congress make "the Negro's civil and political rights a matter of barter . . . to secure democratic votes" in the interest of tariff schedules, commerce, or expansion of islands in the Pacific where dark-skinned subjects reside. (No doubt he was referring to American interference in the Philippines.) Again he spoke of the division of the Negro himself: one group "counsels submission to present humiliation"; the other refuses to occupy an inferior place in American life. This group does not believe in "BARTERING ITS MANHOOD FOR THE SAKE OF GAIN." It does not "BELIEVE IN ARTISANS BEING TREATED AS INDUSTRIAL SERFS." Those blacks who fight aggressively are "branded as disturbers of the harmony between the races . . . [but] IN THEM THE SOUL OF JOHN BROWN GOES MARCHING ON."[85]

The reaction to his speech was strong and immediate. J. Max Barbour called it the "most eloquent address [he] had ever listened to. . . . Before he had finished speaking everybody in the house must have felt that John Brown's spirit was with us. Men and women who had attended the New England anti-slavery meeting fifty years ago said that they had witnessed nothing like the enthusiasm in the meeting since the dark days of slavery."[86] In 1935 DuBois was to write: "That speech more than any single other event stirred the great meeting. It led through its inspiration and eloquence to the eventual founding of the National Association for the Advancement of Colored People."[87] The Niagra Movement had two further meetings, in Boston in 1907 and in Oberlin in 1908. DuBois attributed its demise to "internal strain from the dynamic personality of Trotter and [his] own inexperience with organizations."[88]

During the summer of 1906, Atlanta, Georgia, experienced one of the worst race riots that had occurred in America. Within three days, from ten to twelve Negroes were killed, between sixty to seventy wounded, and two whites killed. Gunnar Myrdal called it "more a one-way terrorization than a two way riot."[89] Walter White, who was to become the president of the NAACP, gave a vivid eyewitness account in Langston Hughes's *Fight for Freedom: The Story of the NAACP.*[90]

When Ransom heard about the Atlanta riot, he was incensed. He gave what is perhaps one of the most militant speeches of his ministry at Faneuil Hall, September 28,

1906, titled "The Atlantic Riot: A Philippic on the Atlanta Riot." Early in the speech he said, "If I could frame sentences which could sting like an adder, and hiss and bite like a serpent, they could not enough express my condemnation of the people who performed these lawless deeds." He spoke of Frederick Douglass who had said twenty years ago that "the South was seeking to rob the Negro of the sympathy of the world by branding him as being peculiarly given to assault upon [white] women." Today, public protest against injustice is silent, he lamented. Even some "timorous and time-saving Negroes" who look for approval have joined in "with the vilifiers." He largely blamed the politicians and newspapers for the racial attitudes that prevail. Plain speaking and vigorous action had declined, and the Negro is told that he must give up his constitutional rights in hope that he may regain them at some later time. "When lynched, burned and slaughtered, he is told to keep silent and warned against making any effort at self-defense." Since the Negro can expect no help from the law, "it is his duty to defend himself. . . . If he permits himself to be chased, beaten and slain without resistance, he will be left, deserted and despised."[91]

We have not come to Faneuil Hall to "apologize to a band of murderers . . . to find any palliation for their crimes . . . to give respectful salute to the state militia of Georgia, who have brutally assaulted unoffending Negroes and fraternized with the mob . . ." and who took from them their weapons so they could not defend themselves and families. Negroes are by nature a peaceful people, but if the outrages continue without protection from the authorities, "the Negro will learn, as others have learned, the manufacture and use of that instrument of death which is all muzzle—every part of which is a trigger."[92]

In a more hopeful tone, he said that law and justice in America were not dead. The Atlanta riot has vindicated the wisdom of those men who passed the Fifteenth Amendment. If the country has a will it can find a way to "preserve a republic form of government. . . .Until the Negro has a voice in the choice of city, county, state, and national officials, he will continue to be the victim of injustice and oppression."[93]

He asserted that the South was not the natural home of the Negro. "A man is most at home where he is free." He pleaded with blacks to leave Mississippi "for Vardaman seeks your destruction. . . . Leave the rice swamps of Carolina while Tillman boasts of your destruction and murder in the Senate of the United States." States like Michigan, Ohio, and Illinois could assimilate many Negroes. States like "Wisconsin, Minnesota, Kansas and Nebraska and the far west have millions of sleeping harvests in their soil which await the touch of willing hands."[94]

Heaven does not look upon the Negro with "an approving smile, " he said, if we are silent and inactive while "our women may be insulted and degraded without rebuke, our children stamped with the birth mark of inferiority, our kindness and patience taken as a sign of subjection . . . while we are hunted down and slain like wild beast of prey." He closed by urging Negroes to "throw out [their] anchor and drag the chain until it touches the bottom, resting upon the principles of equality and justice upon which this nation was founded."[95]

In November Reverdy had a welcomed respite from his political activities. He had learned that the African English composer, Samuel Coleridge-Taylor, was touring the United States and had given two recitals at the Pekin Theatre in Chicago. Ever since August of 1901, when Reverdy had visited his London home, he had been trying to get the musician to come to America and give a concert at his church. Coleridge-Taylor had already made a name for himself in the music world with his oratorio trilogy, *Hiawatha's Wedding Feast, The Death of Minnehaha,* and *Hiawatha's Departure,* and in 1905 for "his collection of piano arrangements of African and Afro-American Melodies, *Twenty-four Melodies Transcribed for Piano.*"[96]

On October 2, 1906, Reverdy received a letter from Coleridge-Taylor, which said that his boat would arrive in Boston on Thursday, November 8. He would be available for a concert on either Monday 12, or Tuesday 13. "I suppose you will secure Mr. White as violinist" and Mr. Burleigh as vocalist. He "stands head and shoulders above any one else. He also knows most of my songs." Reverdy was to find a "lady vocalist" as "it would improve the programme immensely."[97]

It was arranged for Coleridge-Taylor to give his concert on November 13 in the Charles Street auditorium, which held about 1,200 people. Reverdy said that some of the society people of Boston wanted it to be held in Symphony Hall, insisting that "it [was] a shame to take a man like Mr. Coleridge-Taylor to that Negro Church down on Charles Street." However, Reverdy prevailed, and it was given at his church. He secured Marjorie Groves, a graduate of Boston Conservatory of Music and the organist at Charles Street Church; Clarence Cameron White, famous violinist; and Harry T. Burleigh, renowned baritone from New York City, to appear with Coleridge-Taylor.[98]

On the night of the performance there was standing room only. "In the midst of this congested condition, Boston society came marching in, gowned in evening clothes, protected by expensive furs and adorned with its best jewelry," Reverdy wrote in *Pilgrimage.* They expected to be seated right away—to get the "immediate attention and deference they thought they would receive." Reverdy let them stand for a while until he felt they had been "punished long enough." Then he had the ushers bring in folding chairs. In addition to representatives of the Conservatory of Music "and the foremost artists and musicians" of the city, some people came all the way from New York for the concert. The church echoed the composer's re-creations of the African and Afro-American heartbeat, and the audience was deeply moved.[99]

Coleridge-Taylor, White, and Burleigh were entertained at dinners, luncheons, and other festivities the few days they remained in Boston.[100] Reverdy was justifiably proud to have been able to present these exceptionally talented men to the city. As he had with Paul Laurence Dunbar, all through his life, Reverdy was to give strong support to Negro artists.

In January of 1907, Reverdy's New Year's message presaged his closing months at Charles Street in Boston. He headed the message "Bon Voyage." The following is an excerpt:

> Again you have launched your ship for a sail across the untried waters of another year; Even now you are well out to sea. You have on board, within the ample store-room of your heart and brain, a cargo of priceless value. Heed the danger signals. No doubt some storms will beat upon you and angry waves arise, but keep your ship in shape to withstand the fury of the fiercest gale. Stick to The Old Chart of the Ages. . . . Then will you forget the perils of the journey as your eyes behold the multitude of friends old and new, waving flags and banners to greet you from THE SHORE OF ANOTHER HAPPY NEW YEAR![101]

During the spring months of 1907, Reverdy's schedule was pleasantly interrupted by the visitation of several A.M.E. clergy members. In *The Christian Recorder* of May 30, 1907, he noted that Rev. A. J. Carey had paid his first visit to Boston. He and Reverdy seemed to have "buried the hatchet" since the Chicago days. While in Boston, Carey gave an address at Charles Street Church which Reverdy said "was strong and made a lasting impression," and which would stead him well in his race for the office of Secretary of the Sunday School Union at the next General Conference. Another visitor was Rev. H.T. Vernon, Registrar of the United States Treasury, who spoke at Charles Street Church on "The Negro in America" and received plaudits from the students of Harvard and Boston Universities.[102] In years to come, Reverdy was not so disposed to be generous in his praise of Vernon.

On May 7, 1907, Reverdy received a letter from Bishop Turner asking him whether there "would be anything in the way, if [he] should desire" to change Reverdy from Charles Street, Boston, to Bethel in New York City. He wondered if Reverdy had "incurred or assumed any responsibilities . . . that would be inconvenient for [Turner] to do so."[103] He followed with another letter on May 27 inferring that in all likelihood he would move Reverdy to New York. He had wanted to make him president of Morris Brown College in Atlanta instead of appointing him to another church, but felt he could not do that without humiliating Flipper and injuring his chances for the Bishopric. (Rev. Joseph Simeon Flipper was President of Morris Brown from 1904–08.)

"If we could pay you a sufficient salary, I would offer you the Deanship of our Theological Department for one year, and then give you the Presidency of the College, for Dr. Flipper must get out," he wrote.[104]

The New England Annual Conference of 1907 was held at Charles Street, Boston. On July 7, Bishop Turner reassigned Reverdy to Charles Street but wrote on the Appointment Certificate "until further orders."[105] A few weeks later, Reverdy finally received his appointment to Bethel, a large church in the Tenderloin District of New York City. After two eventful years in Boston, it was time for Reverdy, Emma, and Reverdy Jr. to pack their bags and head for "The Big Apple."

CHAPTER 5

New York Ministry, 1907–1912

> But God hath chosen the foolish things of the world to confound the wise; and
> God hath chosen the weak things of the world to confound the things which are
> mighty.
>
> 1 Corinthians 1:27, 28

During the 1870s and 1880s New York Negroes, who had settled in Greenwich Village
early in the century, left the area that was being populated rapidly by Italian immigrants.[1] They moved uptown to the Tenderloin and San Juan Districts, West of Broadway and 5th Avenue. Forty-two years later blacks began their trek to Harlem when a
private dwelling near 133rd and 134th Streets was taken over by a black realtor.[2] Bethel's
parsonage on 129th Street in Harlem was "a four family apartment building and the
only house, or building on that street, then, occupied by colored people."[3] This is
where the Ransoms called home in 1907. Harlem was not yet the black Mecca it would
become in the second decade of the century.

The Tenderloin and San Juan Districts were the centers of black activities when
the Ransoms arrived. Most of the black churches were located in those two districts.
As was the custom, they had followed their congregations as they moved uptown and
would follow them later to Harlem.[4] Bethel A.M.E. Church at West 25th Street, between 7th and 8th Avenues in the Tenderloin District, had a membership of 2,500
which grew to 3,000 before Reverdy left.[5] Other churches in the area included Abyssinian Baptist Church (West 40th Street) which would be pastored by Adam Clayton
Powell Sr. in 1908; St. Phillips Protestant Episcopal Church (West 25th Street) where
the more prosperous Negroes went; Union Baptist Church (West 63rd Street); Mother
A.M.E. Zion (West 89th Street); St. Cyprian's Episcopal (San Juan District, peopled
largely by West Indians); St. Marks Methodist Episcopal (West 53rd Street); St.
Benedict the Moor (interracial Catholic church on West 53rd Street); Mount Olive
Baptist (West 53rd Street); and St. James Presbyterian Church (West 51st Street).[6] In
time, Reverdy was to interact with most of these churches and their pastors.

Fifty-third was the most bustling street in the area. Here could be found the colored YWCA and YMCA, the Society of the Sons of New York, the Nail Saloon, Barron Wilkins's Little Savoy, Ike Hine's Place, and the Marshall Brothers' and Maceo Hotels. In addition there were many restaurants where one could mingle with famous jockeys; boxers; actors like the famous duo, Williams and Walker; the writer, James Weldon Johnson; composer, Harry Burleigh; director, Theodore Drury who had founded the colored Opera company; ministers; business persons; and other prominent citizens.[7] There were over two million Negroes in Manhattan or about 2 percent of the population. Over eleven thousand of them were foreign born (mostly from the West Indies).[8] It was an exciting time, but Reverdy soon found that it was also a time of racial unrest. New York could easily explode again as it had during the summer of 1900 when whites went on a rampage after a Negro had killed a policeman. The mob assailed the Negro community, indiscriminately beating, killing, and wounding whomever they found. In most cases, the police aided them in their acts of vengeance.[9]

During Reverdy's first sermon at Bethel, he assured the congregation that he was not only there to pastor the church but also to attend to "the larger life and needs of the city." He recognized that the "moral and social redemption" of Negroes had been left up to the race itself and especially the Negro churches and clergy who must "courageously lead the people to grapple with the work of their rescue and upbuilding." He assured them that he was not the lackey of either the church or state in that he did his own thinking. In terms of civil rights he would "vigorously oppose the enemies and betrayers of the race" and would fight for every right that belonged to the Negro under the Constitution. "He would make his pulpit as large as the varied civic, social, moral and spiritual interests of the people in the community and cooperate with all forces without as well as within the church for the upbuilding of the people."[10]

In keeping with his pledge, Reverdy had an ambitious program planned for Bethel, one that would encompass the entire community. He kept office hours from 10 A.M. to 1 P.M. and from 7:30 P.M. to 9 P.M. every day except Sundays. Because New York had the strange custom of requiring that the pastor rather than couples fill out marriage licenses and send them to the courthouse, Reverdy was sought after by both whites and blacks wanting to unite. He developed the habit of giving the money received for the weddings to Emma. This amounted to over $600 a year, a fair sum for the times. In addition, he officiated at least two funerals per week, all of which were held at night. When the undertakers made up their bills, they always included money for the minister's expenses. If Reverdy knew the family "would have nothing left after the funeral expenses were paid," he gave the money back to the widow or dependent member of the family. Most of the lodges, fraternal organizations, and benevolent societies made it a practice to go to some church for an annual sermon. "By far the most popular choice among the churches for such services was Bethel Church. For eight months in each year there was rarely a Sunday afternoon or Sunday night that did not have a lodge or fraternal organization present to be addressed by the minister." In this way Reverdy was able to recruit new members for Bethel Church.[11]

Not only was Reverdy concerned with his pastorate activities in 1907 at Bethel, but he was looking forward to the 1908 General Conference when he would run for the editorship of *The Christian Recorder*, the church's newspaper. Accordingly, he wrote an article in the A.M.E. *Voice of Missions* announcing his intentions. Next to being a pastor, he felt that the editorship of a paper or magazine was of prime importance. He took this opportunity to answer his detractors who were still referring to the Alabama incident. Admitting that at one time in his life he was not "wholly blameless" in terms of alcohol, he now declared "with all the earnest solemnity of [his] being that the use of intoxicating liquors or any other kind of intoxicant [was] as far from [him] as the throne of God was [from] the gates of hell."[12] (No doubt this was true at the time because Reverdy often went through long periods of reformation.) In the September issue of the same magazine there was an endorsement of Ransom, signed "The Iconoclast." The writer spoke of Ransom's "superb English," compared him to "a Sage," who was "grave," "noble," "dignified," and the "Areopagus" of the A.M.E. Church.[13]

On December 17, 1907, Reverdy returned to Faneuil Hall in Boston to give the Centennial Oration, "John Greenleaf Whittier: Plea for Political Equality." He took this opportunity to rail against opposition to the Fifteenth Amendment, the Southern states who had reversed most of the progress made during Reconstruction, and some of the policies of President Theodore Roosevelt.

He began by affirming that "the muse of poetry has been inspired by no worthier theme, nor tuned the harp of truth to nobler strains than Whittier's *Songs of Freedom*."[14] Now that men like Whittier have helped Negroes to stand on their own feet, it is time for them to speak for themselves "and make a plea for 'Political Equality'," he said. It seemed like yesterday when "black comrades in arms" fought at the side of Theodore Roosevelt in Cuba. And yet during the Brownsville, Texas, Raid in which Negro soldiers were accused of rampaging through a town during a racial incident, Roosevelt had discharged the entire troop, guilty and innocent alike. Reverdy commented:

> If our strenuous President, still holding fresh in his memory this valiant deed [San Juan Hill], sees fit to condemn his saviors on an [unproven] charge, shall the defenders of his helpless victims be branded with cherishing hatred and disloyalty because they resent this action?[15]

For years the Negro has been silent, he continued. Now he asks that he be permitted to speak for himself through the ballot. "Birth, class, rank, title, are artificial distinctions among men and not ordained of God. The first and highest dignity among men is the dignity of manhood." Whoever considers himself to be inferior to anyone else abdicates his manhood. Disloyalty has never been charged against the Negro, for he has been "present at every turning point in the nation's history." Has America forgotten? Tonight the Negroes ask for "the impartial enforcement of the Constitution," he said. The changes in Southern state constitutions and the apathy of the North may keep the Negro down for a while; where the Negro has the franchise, "Political parties may repudiate the planks in their platform framed with a view to capture the Negro vote"; but however much these factors may "disillusion us," they cannot "dishearten us."[16]

He scolded those who use the excuse that the Negro only wants the ballot "to secure political patronage and the spoils of office." Although this may be true of some, both political parties "nominate tickets in which Negroes are almost universally ignored. No state political organization ever gives official recognition to more than one or two Negroes at a time and then for inferior places." The main reach of the Negro is not "office or the emoluments of office," but protection under the law "and the removal of every legal barrier which discriminates against us as a race." History has proven that the Negro will not use the ballot as a means of vengeance, although as any good citizen, he will express his

> resentment of the injustice perpetrated against him and rebuke those in authority who have been untrue to their trust. . . . The day is not far distant when the weight of [the Negroes'] ballots will cause the scales of our civilization to balance in favor of the preservation of our Republican institutions.[17]

The Advocate-Verdict of Harrisburg, Pennsylvania, called the Whittier speech a "masterful and classical oration," and printed it in its December 27 issue.[18]

Meanwhile, the rest of the Ransom family were busy pursuing their own interests. Besides being involved in the young people's groups and the missionary society at Bethel, Emma took an active roll in the YWCA. Having been converted at an early age, Reverdy Jr. was enrolled in New York City College and would soon leave for the seminary at Drew University in Madison, New Jersey. He planned to follow in his father's footsteps and become an A.M.E. minister. Harold was willing to let his brother and father pursue their religious callings. At twenty-five, he was happily married and living in Montclair, New Jersey, in an apartment above a department store of which he was caretaker. He and his wife, Edith, were to have two daughters, Harriet and Elise.[19]

Jervis Anderson in *This Was Harlem* described Ransom of the early 1900s as a "man of fair skin, reddish hair, and a face that was often as stern as a schoolmaster . . . both a minister and one of the radical Negro activists of his time," who hoped "to launch a campaign against—prostitution—a campaign that is reminiscent in some respects of a personal crusade that William Gladstone once conducted in Victorian London."

Anderson admits, however, there is nothing to suggest that Reverdy had the "duality of morality and personal style" that Gladstone had.[20]

Ransom traveled the streets of New York looking for prostitutes whom he might invite to avail themselves of Bethel's services and thereby eventually adopt a different lifestyle. Later he was to take with him his prodigy, Joseph Gomez, a young man who came to New York in 1908 from Trinidad and soon after joined Bethel. Joseph was fascinated by Reverdy, and the two became and remained "Father and Son in the Gospel" throughout their long lives.[21]

Although Reverdy was admired by most of the clergy in New York, as Anderson points out, "the only aspect of [his] ministry that his fellow clergymen deplored was his insistence upon serving as friend and spiritual adviser to black actors and musicians." Most of the ministers looked upon actors and musicians as immoral and would not allow them to join their churches.[22] There were several reasons Reverdy felt a kinship with theatrical people; one was his own propensity toward the dramatic—his ability to create crises and climaxes wherever he found intolerance. Second, his uncle was Sam Lucas, commonly referred to as "The Grand Old Man of the Negro Stage."[23]

Lucas had been born in Washington, Ohio, in 1840. According to James Weldon Johnson, he was "well educated, cultured in his manners, and a neat dresser. He was the sort of man who looks well in a frock-coat." He always carried a cane and wore several diamonds that he was not adverse to pawning when a theatrical company needed funds to get back home after an unsuccessful tour. His career on the stage extended from minstrelsy to the era of the musical comedy in the early 1900s. Later Lucas was to be the first Negro to play Uncle Tom in *Uncle Tom's Cabin* on the stage and in the movies.[24] At the time Reverdy came to New York, Lucas was a member of the original Georgia Minstrels. Reverdy spent many afternoons with his uncle and other actors at the Marshall Hotel on 53rd Street. Before Lucas died, he sent for Reverdy. As Reverdy stood by his bed he said,

> My dear "Nevie," [nephew] I feel like I am going to die. If I do, I believe I shall go to heaven. As soon as I get there, I am going to hunt up Billy Kersands and some other boys of the old Georgia Minstrels, and give one of the best concerts heaven ever heard.[25]

The attitude of the clergy toward the theatre was appalling to Reverdy, who invited entertainers to join Bethel. He was tagged the "Actors' Minister" and was called upon to marry, christen their children, help them out financially, and when the time came, bury them. He knew that most of them "had come from Christian homes, many of them were even the children of clergymen, most of them had been brought up in the atmosphere of the Negro churches in the communities from which they came." To further show his support, Reverdy joined the theatrical club called "The Frogs," which was organized to aid actors in their quest for jobs or to provide funds when they were down on their luck.[26]

On December 24, 1908, Ernest Hogan, an actor friend of Reverdy, wrote an article in *The New York Age* titled "The Church and the Stage." In it, he lamented the alienation between the actor and the church. He asked the church to reevaluate its stand and open its door to theatrical personalities; and, in turn, he requested that the actor adhere to Christian principles.[27] The following month, Reverdy replied to Hogan's article stating it was a shame that the theatre should be crying out to the church instead of the church opening its arms to the actor. He also chastised those ministers who preached against the theatre from their pulpits, but who, when on vacation, were the first to enter the theatre doors. "In our churches," he wrote, "'entertainments' are given. Almost everything is attempted (but with inferior results) that we see acted on the stage." Why then the hypocrisy? he wondered.[28] Much to the consternation of his fellow clergymen, Reverdy continued to speak out for the actor and attend the theatre when there was a performance that interested him. New York had much in the way of drama and musicals to interest him.

Reverdy was one of the 599 delegates to the Twenty-third General Conference that convened in the tidewater city of Norfolk, Virginia, on May 4, 1908. At St. John A.M.E. Church he heard the Quadrennial Sermon delivered by Bishop Evan Tyree, "Choice and Purpose of the Ministry," and the reading of the Episcopal Address by Bishop A. Grant on the second day of the conference. Grant acknowledged that there were "forces at work which threaten[ed] the overthrow of this great temple of freedom (America) . . . [but] the church of God must set her seat of condemnation on all lawlessness and the taking of life without the legal process." Later in the week, the Episcopal Committee recommended the election of three bishops to supervise home districts, one for West Africa, and one for South Africa. On May 14, Edward Wilkinson Lampton, Henry Blanton Parks, and Joseph Simeon Flipper were elected bishops for the home work. In a separate election, John Albert Johnson and William H. Heard were chosen for the African districts.[29]

Another business of interest was a memorial service, during which special honor was paid to Reverdy's friend, mentor, and former bishop, Benjamin W. Arnett, who had died October 8, 1906, at Wilberforce. In his place, Bishop Wesley J. Gaines was assigned to the First Episcopal District that included New York. Two other bishops with whom Reverdy had some acquaintance, Bishop Benjamin T. Tanner and James A. Handy, were retired because of poor health. Reverdy was disappointed in his bid for the editorship of *The Christian Recorder.* The incumbent, H. T. Johnson was re-elected.[30] Reverdy left the conference vowing he would continue to campaign and hoped he would be successful at the next General Conference in Kansas City, Missouri. As it turned out, instead of running for *The Christian Recorder*, by 1912 he had decided to make a bid for *The A.M.E. Church Review*, the church's magazine.

"The lawlessness" Bishop Grant had talked about in his Episcopal Address raged in full force in Springfield, Illinois, that summer. "White mobs invaded black neighborhoods burning, looting and killing." Two blacks were lynched; one was an eighty-four-year-old man. Neither the law nor the government took any action.[31] Other disturbing news was that the Republican Party had carried out Theodore Roosevelt's wishes at their convention and nominated William Howard Taft, Roosevelt's secretary of war, as their candidate for the presidency. This was the same Taft who, as secretary of war, had had a part in Roosevelt's dismissal of some members of the 25th Regiment of black soldiers in Brownsville, Texas. The Democrats again nominated William Jennings Bryan as their candidate. Reverdy had endorsed Roosevelt in the 1904 election as had three of the A.M.E. bishops at the General Conference that year.[32] Nevertheless, in 1908, he had a change of mind about Roosevelt, his chosen successor, and the Republican Party. In a September sermon, he warned his congregation that there was really very little difference between the two parties. Negroes should not vote blindly for the party of Lincoln simply because they had always done so. He was not sure how he would vote, but he just might support the socialist candidate, Eugene V. Debs, even though his friend, W. E. B. DuBois was supporting Bryan and urging other Negroes to do likewise.[33]

In October Reverdy held a political rally at Bethel that almost turned into a riot. The audience cheered the names of Bryan and John B. Foraker (former governor of Ohio and U.S. senator) who had tried to get the black soldiers at Brownsville reinstated. On the other hand, they booed Taft for his part in the Brownsville affair and almost mobbed Fred Moore, editor of *The New York Age* and supporter of Booker T. Washington, who said in effect that no responsible Negro should vote for a Democrat.[34] In the end, Reverdy did vote for Bryan, but to no avail. As it turned out, the corpulent Taft won by 321 electoral votes to Bryan's 162.[35]

December 1908 proved to be a pleasant diversion for the Ransoms. The Wednesday before Christmas, Bethel observed its annual Christmas Tree Celebration sponsored by the Sunday School. After the program, the Ransoms were ushered into the banquet hall for refreshment. On the table was a cake that spelled out "Reverdy Cassius Ransom" in candy letters. Counsellor James L. Curtis, toastmaster, introduced various speakers who paid tribute to the pastor and his wife. At the close of the program, the Ransoms were presented with boxes of groceries that they greatly appreciated because, during the holidays, the parsonage was always filled with in-town and out-of-town guests whom they were expected to feed.[36]

The following spring, Reverdy was asked to come to Albany and address the Joint Hearing before the Senate Committee on Taxation and Retrenchment and the Assembly Excise Committee. The committees were considering the Brackett–Gray Local Option Bill that dealt with the sale of alcohol in New York. On April 14, Reverdy told the assembly that there seemed to be three views on the subject: those who wanted absolute prohibition, those who wanted local option, and those who thought the legislature should come up with some innovative way to regulate rather than prohibit the sale of alcohol. He was in accord with the third view. We have laws regulating marriage, he said. "We say that a man shall have but one wife at a time." We regulate passion that leads to violence. The same should be true when considering men's appetites. You cannot eradicate them, but you can regulate them. Using Ohio as an example, he demonstrated that when tried, neither total prohibition nor local option had worked.[37]

If prohibition or local option were adopted, the illegal sale of alcohol would be confined to the black community as was every other illicit traffic now. The police and administration would close their eyes to what was going on because it was happening in the black community, not the white. Yet, like prostitution, numbers, and other illegal activities, it would be run by whites who would rake in the profits. Blacks would be the sufferers; the responsible and irresponsible Negro would suffer alike since Negroes do not have the option to be mobile. Because of racial practices in housing, they because restricted to certain areas of the city. He concluded:

> I believe from the bottom of my heart that we ought to have upon the statute books of this State a sane law, a law that is not an ultra in relation to public sentiment, a law that could be enforced, where this matter could be regulated and the evils we all complain of . . . abated.[38]

Reverdy made no suggestions as to what kind of law this would be. The address lacks his usual astuteness and clarity, nor is the language persuasive. Perhaps the subject was troublesome to him personally.

When Reverdy first came to New York, he noticed that there were no Negroes on the police force. On the first Sunday in August 1909, after there were several incidents in the Tenderloin between police and Negroes, Reverdy made an appeal in the pulpit for responsible blacks to take a stand against those who insist on disregarding the law. One solution to the problem, he said, would be for Police Chief Edward E. Lee to hire Negroes to service the Negro communities. He asked that ministers and members alike join him in a campaign to petition for Negro policemen, pointing out that cities like Pittsburgh, New Bedford, Newport, and Boston already had black policemen. Crime in their Negro communities had declined as a result.[39] In answer to Reverdy's plea, several business and professional blacks agreed to petition the mayor and Chief Lee. Acting Mayor McGowan met with the group at Mother Zion Church and indicated that he approved of the plan.[40] After stating there was no discrimination in the department, Chief Lee said, "We will never be able to boast of having [Negroes] until members of the race take the examination." For some reason, they will not take the test that is required of all applicants. He claimed that the only two men who had taken it had failed. All those between the ages of twenty-one and thirty who are interested should come down on September 11 and take the examination, he urged.[41]

According to *The Age*, blacks had "been deterred by the belief that life would be made hard for them if they joined the force, and because the Police Commissioners, exercising their options under the Civil Service law, have not appointed of late, those Negroes who passed the examination," this despite the Chief stating there was no discrimination in the hiring of police.[42] Little resulted from the Chief's avowal.

In *Pilgrimage*, Reverdy says that in his fight for Negro policemen "we could elicit no favorable response from any of the men in the Republican Party in New York"; consequently, he and Frank J. Wheaton (lawyer, and active in the Republican Party), James L Curtis (lawyer), and others went to see Charles Murphy, head of Tammany Hall in New York. Murphy told the group that if the Democrats won in the coming municipal election, he would see that Negroes were appointed to the police department. In time, Tammany Hall kept its promise; Reverdy said this "marked the first major break of Negroes away from the support of the Republican Party in New York City."[43]

As a result of the Atlanta and Springfield Riots (1906) and other atrocities against Negroes, Mary White Ovington, a wealthy northern social worker; William English Walling, a liberal southern journalist; and Henry Moskovitz, a Jewish social worker, decided to issue a call for a National Conference. The date of the conference would coincide with the Centennial Celebration of Abraham Lincoln's birth. Oswald Garrison Villard of *The New York Post* wrote the call that invited all "believers of Democracy [to] join in a National Convention for the discussion of present evils, the voicing of protests, and the renewal of the struggle for civil and political liberty" of Negroes. The result was the National Negro Conference in New York City, May 31, 1909.[44] Reverdy was among the three hundred prominent black and white men and women who gathered at the United Charities Building. Many of the Negroes had been members of the Niagara movement, the Afro-American Council, and other organizations designed to secure Negro rights. Booker T. Washington had been asked to support the conference but refused; consequently leaders of the conference went on record as saying that Washington was "too modest in his plans to elevate the colored man. . . . [He] only aims to educate the ignorant Negroes and then let them shift for themselves." Seth Low, former mayor of New York City, Andrew Carnegie, Francis Lynde Stetson, and others who supported Washington also refused to endorse the conference stating that "while they wished to be considered as friendly toward the colored man, they regarded such a conference as merely tending to emphasize the points of offense."[45]

William Hayes Ward, editor of *The Independent* opened the first morning session. After outlining the purpose for the conference, he said that today there is a "readiness to apologize for old wrongs" against the Negro—especially in the South. The basis for the South's subversion of blacks had its roots in "The Types of Mankind," a piece written by Nott and Glidden that attempted to show "the physical and mental inferiority of the Negro."[46] Following Ward's prefatory remarks, Dr. Livingston Farrand, professor of Anthropology at Columbia University, read his paper on "Race Differentiation—Race Characteristic."[47] Then Burt G. Wilder, professor of neurology and vertebrate zoology at Cornell University gave an involved presentation on "The Brain of the American Negro." Because in recent years there had been much discussion of the inferior nature of the Negro brain, Reverdy listened intently at what Wilder had to say.

In the early part of his lengthy paper with its measurement charts and diagrams, Wilder alleged that the average weight of the "obscure" Negro's brain is two ounces lighter than the brain of the average "obscure white," and that more frequently there is a lesser development of the lobes. "But many Negro brains weigh more than the white average, and many white brains weigh less than the Negro average. Some white brains present lateral or ventral depression of the prefrontal lobe, and some Negro brains do not." Therefore, he concluded, as of "yet there has been found no constant feature by which the Negro brain may be certainly distinguished from that of a Caucasian," but both can be distinguished from that of the ape. In other words, there were no known "facts, deductions, or arguments that . . . justify withholding from men of African descent, as such, any civil or political rights or any educational or industrial opportunities that are enjoyed by whites of equal character, intelligence, and property."[48] To support Wilder's argument, in his address, John Dewey, professor of philosophy at Columbia, stated that there was "no inferior race, and the members of a race so-called should each have the same opportunities of social environment and personality as those of a more favored race."[49]

More than likely Reverdy was most interested in remarks given by W. E. B. DuBois, Ida Wells-Barnett, and Bishop Alexander Walters of the A.M.E. Zion Church. DuBois addressed the conference on two separate occasions. In the morning of May 31, he outlined the history of the Negro in politics and industry, assuring his listeners that giving the Negro the franchise had not and would not hinder economic development. "When the Negro casts a free and intelligent vote in the South then and not until then will the Negro problem be settled." In the evening of the second day, he spoke on "Evolution of the Race Problem," again giving historical background from slavery to the twentieth century, and showing the devastating effect racism had had on Negroes and the country as a whole. Against the South's present program of disfranchisement and Jim Crowism that blacks were supposed to accept with a smile, he protested loudly. "The assumption is an outrageous falsehood dictated by selfishness, cowardice and greed, and for the righteousness of my cause and the proof of my assertion, I appeal to one arbitrament and one alone and that is: THE TRUTH."[50] Ida Wells-Barnett spoke about lynching by presenting three facts: "Lynching is color line murder; Crimes against [white] women is the excuse not the cause; [Lynching] is a national crime and requires a national remedy."[51] At the June 1 morning session, Bishop Walters presided and spoke on "Civil and Political Status of the Negro." He closed by criticizing President Taft for the statement in his Inaugural Address in which he said he would not appoint anyone to office if such an appointment would be objectionable to the South.[52] Conspicuously absent from the speaker's platform was Reverdy Cassius Ransom, one of the most eloquent orators for Negro causes. One wonders why?

At the final meeting the evening of June 1, the convention passed a resolution denouncing "the ever-growing oppression of . . . 10,000,000 colored fellow citizens." While agreeing fully with "the prevailing opinion that the transformation of the unskilled colored laborers in industry and agriculture into skilled workers to be *of vital importance*," they demanded that Negroes and all others be given a "free and complete education, whether by city, state, or nation, a grammar school and industrial training for all, and technical, professional and academic education for the most gifted." The underlined words originally read "of great importance to that race." Reverdy asked that it to be amended to read "of first importance." but Walters moved that there be an amendment to the amendment and that it should read "of vital importance." Among the resolutions passed was one that established a committee of forty to investigate the possibilities of a permanent organization to be known as the Committee for the Advancement of the Negro Race. Trotter also proposed a resolution

> deploring any recognition of, or concession to, prejudice or color by the federal government in any office or branch thereof, as well as the presidential declaration on the appointment of colored men to office in the South, contradicting as it does the President's just and admirable utterance against the proposed disfranchisement of the colored voters of Maryland.

He also proposed that lynching be made a federal crime.[53]

In reviewing the conference, a reporter for the *Evening Post* commented that "perhaps never before in the history of the negro movement has there been such an intelligent presentation of papers and addresses by negro men and women."[54] A year later at the second meeting the organization was incorporated under the laws of New York State and became officially known as the National Association for the Advancement of Colored People (NAACP). Its first president was Moorfield Storey, a renowned Boston lawyer; William English Walling was chairman of the executive committee. W. E. B. DuBois became director of publicity and research, and eight of the original members of the Niagara movement were on the board of directors.[55]

While Reverdy was involved in his many crusades, Emma had her own battles. In 1907, when the Colored Young Women's Christian Association was still located on 53rd Street, she was asked to be the chairman of the board of management. A year later the Metropolitan Board, which included such people as Mrs. Fellow Morgan, Mrs. John D. Rockefeller Jr., and Mrs. Dwight Morrow, launched a campaign to raise $1,000,000 for the expansion of the organization. Of that amount, Grace Dodge, chairman, offered Emma $10,000 for the Colored Women's Branch. Emma informed her she could raise that much herself and that she would not consider accepting any amount less that $100,000. Emma's committee began to seek a suitable location in Harlem for a colored "Y" because so many Negroes were beginning to move there. They found a place on 7th Avenue near West 136th Street. Immediately, white property owners began to protest, and the Metropolitan Board was about to acquiesce to their demands. When Emma accused Grace Dodge and her board of their "un-Christlike and cowardly attitude," Dodge suggested that they get on their knees and pray. "This they did, Mrs. Ransom doing the praying and Miss Dodge doing the crying." The result was that Emma got her $100,000 and permission to purchase the building her committee had chosen. In appreciation for her efforts, they called it "The Emma Ransom House." At the cornerstone-laying ceremonies, along with the Metropolitan Board members, former president Theodore Roosevelt attended and insisted that he stand near Emma when the reporters took pictures.[56]

During Thanksgiving 1909, Reverdy gave his annual sermon, this time from the subject "The American Tower of Babel or the Confusion of Tongues." At one point in his sermon, he referred to the confusion of tongues between Booker T. Washington and W. E. B. DuBois. Washington says "Eschew Politics"; DuBois says "vote." Washington emphasizes "vocational training which shall be chiefly industrial." DuBois "insists upon no special brand but the largest opportunity for that which is highest and most liberal." These opposing attitudes were best illustrated by Washington's National Negro Business League and DuBois's Niagara movement and in Washington's autobiography *Up from Slavery* and DuBois's *The Souls of Black Folk.*[57]

There is also a confusion of tongues between the Constitution of the United States and the Supreme Court that does not seem to understand or to interpret the Constitution when it comes to Negroes, Reverdy said. There is a confusion of tongues between the former president, Theodore Roosevelt, and the present Mr. Taft.

Whatever may be our attitude as to [Roosevelt's] conduct with reference to the Brownsville Affair, [he] stood unequivocally for a square deal, for the open door of opportunity, and for an equal chance for all men; while on the other hand. . . . [Taft] has gone out of his way to make public proclamation of his intention to appoint no Negroes to Federal offices in communities where such appointments are displeasing to the white people.[58]

There is a confusion of tongues among scientists. Some try to show the inferiority of the Negro by the measurement of his brain; others say the size and shape of the brain has nothing to do with intellectual capacity. There is confusion in the pulpits. When the church is not hesitant or incoherent, it is dumb when it comes to the questions of lynching and other injustices, he asserted.[59]

"Our confusion will grow more confusing until we as a nation comprehend the fact that the ethics of Jesus, as set down in the New Testament, is not an iridescent dream." Jesus sees from the Tower of Babel scattered groups of people returning, having learned that despite all differences of speech, the two words they have in common is "MAN and BROTHER." They then will set about building a civilization "animated by a common purpose . . . peace, happiness and the common good of all."[60]

On December 2, 1909, once again Reverdy was invited to speak at Faneuil Hall in Boston. This time he was to give an oration celebrating the fiftieth anniversary of the hanging of John Brown. Reverdy's speech was the third during an all-day celebration, and "was by far the longest one."[61] Though not trying to make a demigod of Brown, Reverdy did point out some of the similarities between Brown's fate and that of Christ with whom millions today reach forth to "enter into communion with by celebrating his death and suffering." Tonight, he said, "we hail John Brown as a man sent from God to lift up the flood gates that have long restrained waters of liberty . . . and permit the nation to stand forth purified by a new baptism of freedom." In order to attack "tyranny . . . assault must be directed against the very citadel of power." Often martyrdom is necessary. This is what John Brown was at Harpers Ferry, a martyr.[62]

Reverdy criticized Taft. He said he would not "charge the President with the betrayal of the trust of a confiding people," but would remind him that he could not have been nominated for his office "without votes of these black Republicans whose claim he now frankly disallows." The direction of the Republican Party could be summed up by the suggestion of Senator Shelby M. Cullom of Illinois that the Negro be disfranchised in order for the party "to win the support of southern congressmen and presidential electors, to keep the Republican Party in power." The next step would be the repeal of the Fifteenth Amendment, Reverdy predicted. The Negro should use every weapon at his command to fight for his rights—"the pen, the printing press, the pulpit, the rostrum, the court, right of petition to Congress and state legislatures," the education of his children as men, the saving of the money he earns "to buy one hundred cents' worth of equal treatment"; the freeing of himself "from the bondage of party thraldom."[63]

The year 1910 was unusually busy for the Ransoms. During the year, Reverdy Jr. was ordained by Bishop J. H. Jones as an itinerate elder and joined the New Jersey Conference.[64] In January, Reverdy Sr. held a series of revivals and took in many converts. Emma invited Mary Church Terrell, February 14, to give an address on Abraham Lincoln to over six hundred people at Bethel. Terrell had met Reverdy when she was a student at Oberlin College. When she graduated, she taught in Washington, D.C., and then was elected a School Board member. In 1892, she married Robert Herberton Terrell who later became a municipal court judge. After forming the Colored Women's League in Washington to fight for suffrage and other women's rights, she helped to merge several Negro women's organizations into what became the National Association of Colored Women in 1898 and served as its first president. Terrell was torn between the philosophies of Booker T. Washington and W. E. B. DuBois. Although she had worked with Washington to prevent DuBois from becoming assistant superintendent of public schools in Washington, she often criticized Washington "for his dialect stories and accommodationist policies." During the 1909 National Negro Conference, she was appointed to the committee of forty that laid the groundwork for the NAACP.[65]

Standing on the podium at Bethel behind an assortment of American flag, Terrell told her audience she was proud that the illiteracy of the American Negro had decreased by 47 percent over the past few years. She urged them to "be loyal to one another, and to support all praiseworthy business enterprises launched by members of the race." She emphasized the importance of Negroes going into business for themselves and giving support to all kinds of educational institutions, which included liberal arts and industrial schools.[66]

On March 10, there appeared an article in *The New York Age* severely criticizing DuBois for his alleged attack on Booker T. Washington while speaking in Boston the first week of March. The article reflected the conservative tone of its editor, Fred R. Moore, an ardent Washington supporter. It stated "that the majority of [DuBois's] hearers did not coincide with what he said was shown by the silence and frigid manner in which his utterances were received by the few present." He quoted a passage from the *Boston Post:* "It must be disquieting to the true friends of the Negro to see such a growing breach between Professor W. E. B. DuBois and Booker T. Washington." Each has his place in the development of the race. "DuBois, the most eloquent and cultured of his race" teaches the highest type at Atlanta University; and Washington, "the most energetic man of affairs and ablest executive, builds up character and the power to do useful work" at Tuskegee. The *Post* denounced DuBois for calling

Washington "The political dictator of the Negro race." Washington had done too much for Tuskegee and his race to "be set down as a boss. All of DuBois's learning has not imparted half as much of value," the writer concluded.[67]

Despite Emma's disavowal of Washington's accommodationist policies, she invited him to speak at Bethel on behalf of the YWCA later that month. Both she and Reverdy believed that his views should be heard so that people could make up their own minds about his validity. A large audience heard Washington say that he intended to give an old speech. Every time he attempted to give a new speech, it did not go over as well. Besides he would have to be brief because he had to catch a train going south. He praised the work of the "Y" and assured them they did not need new speeches after the one Mrs. Ransom had given prior to his.[68] (Emma had introduced him.)

The speech seemed disconnected. He noted that the race crisis was shifting to the North, and the North was about to experience tremendously large problems. It was up to people like those in the audience to see that Negroes set the right examples. Most of them had come from the South just as he had; he had no patience with people who were ashamed of where they had come from or of their race. Negroes in the North had a double responsibility, to set a good example where they were and to be a credit to Negroes in the South. Girls in the North had some advantages. They could attend good high schools and colleges, but when they graduated, the opportunities for jobs were seldom there. In the South, there were more opportunities for jobs, particularly if one had training in a practical vocation. He inferred that the South was the best place for Negroes to live. If they were properly trained they could find jobs, own land, could open their own businesses, and make a contribution to the region. When this happened, all the freedoms they now sought would automatically be given them.[69] As Washington had warned, the speech was brief and covered no new ground. After having been exposed to the passionate sermons and orations of Reverdy, the listeners must have found Washington rather tame.

To further demonstrate his interest in journalism, in April, Reverdy joined Charles F. Taylor in becoming associate editor of the *Original Rights Magazine*, published by Charles Lincoln in the Central Building, Room 42–44, at 25 West 42nd Street. The editor, Charles Lenz, was the chairman of the executive committee of the Original Rights Society, whose preamble stated that the organization took its inspiration from the Declaration of Independence and the Constitution. It aimed "to forward intelligence in all social, economic and political affairs" and to maintain all "truly democratic institutions."[70]

The *Original Rights Magazine* was the society's mouthpiece. Its aims were also social and political in nature, and it did not advocate "party fanaticisms with blind obedience to the dictates of [political] bosses." It believed in "absolute separation of Church and State," "self-government for cities," "the solution of the Negro question," effective public education in all sections of the country, the regulation of immigration to the exclusion of "undesirable elements," a solution to the problem of alcohol "in a common-sense manner, and all those questions relating to labor and the great social problems now before the people."[71] The statement about alcohol is reminiscent of Reverdy's speech before the Senate and Assembly Committees in 1908.

Unfortunately only two issues of the magazine remain, and they have in them two articles by Ransom, "The Bad Negro," dealing with a lynching that occurred in Kansas City, and "The Reno Prize Fight,"[72] which can also be found in Reverdy's *Pilgrimage* and *The Spirit of Freedom and Justice* and in Anthony B. Pinn's *Making the Gospel Plain*.

On the first Sunday in June, Reverdy had preached about the upcoming fight between the Negro heavyweight champion, Jack Johnson, and his challenger, white Jim Jeffries. The match was to be held in Reno, Nevada, on July 4, 1910. In his sermon, Reverdy expressed his amazement that many of the white ministers and their alliances were attempting to have the fight stopped because they disapproved of a black man waging a battle against a white man. On the other hand, they had never protested the lynching and burning of blacks by whites in America. Could a prizefight be more revolting than these acts? he wondered. Many people felt that Jeffries was fighting to defend "White Supremacy." Reverdy, however, did not believe that Johnson was trying to maintain the championship for the Negro race, but to "hold it and defend it against all comers." Should boxing be a contest to show racial superiority? If so, did Americans believe whites should be matched only against other whites; or should boxing be a contest "of merit and efficiency," regardless of race? he asked.[73]

In his essay, "The Reno Prize Fight," Reverdy described the match as a contest between the "sleek, ebony athlete," Jack Johnson, and the "grizzly white gladiator," Jim Jeffries. He said more space had been given in the newspapers to this fight than the return of Roosevelt from his African hunt. What was the fight really about? "Some said for money; most said it was to demonstrate the superiority of the white over the black race." To Reverdy it was more revealing as a

> psychological study of the American people in their attitude toward the Negro than all the outgivings of Edward Gardner Murphy, Booker T. Washington, Albert Bushnell Hart, W. E. B. DuBois, Ray Stannard Baker and their like combined . . . FROM OUR VIEW POINT THIS COUNTRY HAS NOT WITNESSED FOR YEARS, IF EVER, A GREATER EXHIBITION OF MOCK CHRISTIANITY, SHAM MORALITY AND DOWNRIGHT HYPOCRISY THAN THIS PRIZE FIGHT HAS BROUGHT TO LIGHT. Rev. Thomas Dixon's *The Clansman*, which depicts the Negro as a beast, has been allowed to be played in movie houses all over the country, while pictures of the fight have been forbidden in the Philippines, India, South Africa and South America, on the ground of their demoralizing or brutalizing influence.

The real reason they have been prohibited, Reverdy postulated, is the belief of many whites that the darker people of the world "might go restive and could not be held so firmly in leash after they had witnessed the spectacle of a white man being defeated by a black man in a contest of brute strength, endurance and skill."[74]

The only positive lesson that was taught by the fight, said Reverdy, was that if the Negro could succeed in the boxing ring, he should be allowed to show his ability in "larger fields of activity," the factory, mill, arts, industry, commerce, and trade and thereby become more productive, "a safer political quantity and a better and stronger citizen to bear and share the burdens and responsibilities of the state."[75]

In July, Reverdy became embroiled in an A.M.E. controversy in which he supported Bishop Joseph Simeon Flipper who refused to attend the Bishops Council that met at Wilberforce in 1910. In a letter to the council, Flipper listed as his reasons for his absence: there was no fixed order of business at the meetings, and

> the Council is possessed of no legal authority, in the bounds of the Church, by reason of the fact that all the bishops are equals, and not even a majority vote of these equals can have any restraining power upon any bishop, whatever might be his official acts.

In other words, the council could only act in an advisory capacity.[76]

Reverdy believed the council should be able to do something other than "consider and advise." It should be empowered to act; otherwise its yearly meetings were an unnecessary expense to the church and had no significant purpose. He also proposed that the bishops be rotated on a regular basis so that their Episcopal districts did not become little kingdoms. Rotation would infuse new life into the church. The bishopric is manmade; the influences that go into a bishop's election are "more human than divine," he said. When the ministers understand that they do not "serve under" the bishops, "but with them, then will our church reap the benefits of the highest and best that each is able to contribute for the good of all." He suggested that the 1912 General Conference outline some guidelines for the council and clearly define its power. Reverdy also took to task the church publications that often would not print dissenting views. "When matters vital to the church are being agitated and discussed," the church papers are where all sides of an issue should be voiced, he insisted. This statement presaged his own policies when he became editor.[77] On August 4, he followed up these opinions with an article in *The Christian Recorder* titled "Let the Bishops Rotate."[78]

January of 1911 found Reverdy back in Boston, this time at Park Street Church where he delivered a Centennial Oration Plea for Charles Sumner, a senator from Massachusetts and an ardent abolitionist who, for his views against slavery, was assaulted by Representative Preston Brooks from South Carolina. The assault left him partly crippled.[79] Reverdy called Sumner's "eloquence lofty," "the form of his periods chaste and beautiful, but the power of his logic as terrible as Justice." After outlining Sumner's brilliant career that included his memorable speeches "The Crime Against Kansas" and "The Barbarism of Slavery," Reverdy again took the opportunity to talk about the importance of the franchise for Negroes. He urged his audience not to be for parties, "but for men." In both parties, he said, there were men who are "willing to concede to us the rights which are now denied." Better still, blacks could unite with the Socialist Party, as did "the Negroes of Oklahoma in the last election." Near the end of his speech, he indirectly criticized Booker T. Washington when he asked: "*Is any one so bereft of reason as to believe that the South has driven the Negro from political power so that he might devote himself to industry and the acquisition of power and wealth?*" (The italics are Ransom's) Nevertheless, he said, this is the argument of the "'so called friends of the Negro, and those Negroes who are most tolerated and subsidized."[80]

In March of 1911, Booker T. Washington was arrested for trespassing. While allegedly trying to find the whereabouts of Daniel C. Smith, white auditor of Tuskegee Institute, he was physically assaulted by Albert Ulrich, who accused him of attempting to rob the apartment building at 111–2 West 63rd Street and of bothering his wife. When Washington was able to identity himself, the police released him from jail.[81] *The New York Age* reported that he was seriously hurt and under the care of a doctor in a room at the Hotel Manhattan.[82] In *Pilgrimage*, Reverdy writes that Washington gave this account of the episode: It was after dark and Mr. Washington got no further than the vestibule "which contained name plates and room numbers of the occupants." Not knowing exactly which apartment Mr. Logan was in, he began to push several buttons. (Washington was trying to find a Mr. Logan, the treasurer of Tuskegee, rather than Mr. Smith according to this account.) "An irate husband, whose call bell he had been ringing came down and pounced upon him." Washington ran. The man pursued him, caught him, and beat him. A policeman arrested Washington rather than his assailant. Reverdy said that when Washington was released, instead of going to the home of his friends, Charles W. Anderson, Internal Revenue Agent, or Fred R. Moore, editor of *The New York Age*, he came to Ransom's home covered with bandages and tapes.[83]

Reverdy was persuaded by Washington's friends to allow a mass meeting to be held at Bethel in protest of the treatment Washington had received. The meeting convened the last Sunday afternoon in March. Reverdy opened by stating: "[H]e thought it fit that those who stood for the highest and best in the life of the colored people in New York should express confidence in the personal worth and honor" of Washington. *The New York Age* reported that "Almost every speaker expressed the opinion that the brutal attack made on Booker T. Washington had done more to bring the race together than any other incident in many years." President Taft received praise for a letter he had written Washington in support of him; a resolution was passed by the assemblage "deploring the assault and promising to stand by him." Speakers included Charles W. Anderson who chaired the meeting; Rev. Adam Clayton Powell Sr. of Abyssinia Baptist Church; Bishop W. Derrick of the A.M.E. Church; Rev. W. H. Brooks, counsellors James L. Curtis and Wilford H. Smith; and Fred R. Moore. Bishop Alexander Walters of the A.M.E. Zion Church sent a letter saying he regretted he could not attend because of a previous engagement, but that he supported the mass meeting.[84] Oswald Garrison Villard of the NAACP, who also had been invited, declined to come because, alleged Ransom, he could not speak for Washington's character.[85]

Washington's case was heard before a jury who could not bring in a verdict. There was no retrial, "hence until this day, so far as the courts are concerned, the case remains undecided."[86] Ulrich was acquitted of assault by three judges, two for and one against.[87] In retrospect, Reverdy's opinion of Washington seemed to have softened, for he concluded later:

> Whether Mr. Washington was innocent or guilty, I think the overwhelming majority of Americans believe that Mr. Washington was too great a man and rendered too large a service, not only to members of his own race, but to his country, to be further humiliated and challenged.[88]

On May 18 at the Ninety-first Session of the New York Annual Conference, Reverdy was elected delegate to the Twenty-fourth General Conference of the A.M.E. Church to be held in Kansas City, May 6, 1912. His certificate of election was signed by his bishop, Wesley J. Gaines, and the secretary of the conference, Rev. Walton Mason.[89] He fully intended to run for the editorship of *The A.M.E. Church Review* and set out to make his desires known throughout the Connection through articles, letters, and visitations to other districts.

Meanwhile, in mid-August, incensed by the burning of a Negro in Coatesville, Pennsylvania, by a white mob, Reverdy preached a burning sermon on lynching. He received several letters praising him for speaking out against such atrocities. In one letter, William Pickett of Pickett and Miller law firm in Brooklyn said he felt impelled to send a note congratulating Reverdy on his "clear perception of the unfortunate situation of [his] race in its relation to the people of this country. Yours appears to be one of the few voices raised in protest against the Booker T. Washington theory of abject submission to any and all humiliation and oppression," he said. President Taft should

> suspend his well-meaning efforts to advance peace among the great powers, and endeavor to bring about a condition leading to peace in Georgia, Mississippi and

Texas. His abandonment of the rights of the African race to the franchise in the South, clearly denotes the superficiality of his claim of interest in the real welfare of the race.[90]

A second letter came from a Mr. Parker of Nail and Parker Realtors in New York City. Parker stated he had read Reverdy's address pertaining to the burning at Coatesville and thought it to be "one of the best addresses he had ever read" coming from an American pastor. The speech reminded him of Garrison's addresses during the abolitionist period, and he was surprised that a white paper would publish it. He hoped he could read many more because the church had "remained silent too long on this issue."[91]

A third letter came from J. E. Spingarn, president of the New York Branch of the NAACP. It read as follows:

I congratulate you on your utterances last Sunday, which have just been called to my attention. If I understand you correctly, you advise your race, not to make reprisal against their wrongs, but to make manly preparation for defence and honor. It is a just message. There are no such things as the Rights of Man; there are only the Fights of Man. If your race wishes to achieve "rights" it must prepare itself to win them by agitation and struggle, and to retain them after they are won by vigilant and incessant perserverance.[92]

In October of 1911, Emma and Reverdy bade farewell to Joseph Gomez, who was leaving to attend Payne Theological Seminary at Wilberforce University. They would miss the Sunday dinners Gomez had shared with them at the parsonage and the companionship he had provided when Reverdy walked through the Tenderloin talking to the people and extending invitations to Bethel's many services. It was Reverdy who had convinced Joseph to abandon his thoughts of a law or medical career and pursue the ministry. The A.M.E. Church was badly in need of young, bright ministers, and he had no doubt Joseph would be worthy of his calling. With Reverdy's coaxing, the New York Conference had granted Joseph a four-year scholarship to the seminary. The money was not much, but if he supplemented it by working on the campus, he could make it through. The Ransoms had given him luggage as a going-away present and, entrusting him in God's care, had reluctantly watch him leave.[93]

Alterations seemed to be the rule during the winter of 1911. Reverdy married Reverdy Jr. to Aida Stewart of Cambridge, Massachusetts, on Christmas evening at Bethel, New York.[94] The church was packed with members and friends of various persuasions, professions, and races. Reverdy and Emma hoped the couple would find the kind of happiness they had known in their marriage. Little did they dream that Reverdy would be married on two other occasions and give them two sets of grandchildren. With the wedding over, Reverdy could concentrate on the upcoming General Conference and his bid for editorship of *The A.M.E. Church Review.*

On May 6, 1912, the Twenty-fourth General Conference of the A.M.E. Church convened at Allen Chapel Church in Kansas City, Missouri, with 579 delegates in attendance. After Bishop Turner called the conference to order, Bishop C. T. Shaffer gave the Quadrennial Address, "Glorifying God or Worship Acceptable to the Infinite." The evening session was devoted to welcoming addresses from the governor of Missouri, Herbert S. Hadley; Darius A. Brown, mayor of Kansas City; and other dignitaries.[95]

The morning of the second day, Bishop C. S. Smith read the Episcopal Address. Among the recommendations made by the bishops was that the Centennial Celebration of the A.M.E. Church be held at the 1916 General Conference in Mother Bethel, Philadelphia. They also requested that four bishops be elected to take the place of those who had died during the Quadrennial. The four newly elected bishops were John Hurst, William David Chappelle, Joshua Henry Jones, and James Mayer Connor. Afterward, Bishop Turner read his Historiographer's Report and confessed that he should not have asked to be appointed historiographer at the last General Conference because of his declining years. As Bishop C. S. Smith commented in his *The History of the A.M.E. Church*, Turner was not temperamentally suited for it. "He practically accomplished nothing as Historiographer."[96] Reverdy was to remember Turner's words in his late years when he was relieved of a district and given the job of historiographer.

The evening of the ninth day, Booker T. Washington addressed the conference. Part of what he said was:

> No class of people should be more interested in the plans and work of our Negro Church organization than the capitalists, the captains of industry, those who directly or indirectly employ Negro labor. Nothing pays as well in producing efficient labor as Christianity.

He stated further that his was "not a selfish plea to the Church." He wanted to see "the Negro saved for his own sake in order that the white race which surrounds him may be saved."[97] Ransom's reaction to the speech has not been recorded, but he must have flinched at the overall premise of the speech.

The day before the election of general officers, Ransom presented "The Mission of the Religious Press." Among the points he made were that "the religious press must be free and incorruptible and in so far as human frailty will permit, unbiased." It should be "absolutely divorced from partisan politics, dealing with principles rather than parties, and giving its influence to those men and measures that make for the most enlightened and beneficent statesmanship and policies of government." It should be "more than a mouthpiece of public opinion" in that it should "educate, influence and guide public opinion in the right direction." It should deal "with the great international and world questions of peace and war, arbitration, colonization and the exploitation and government of the backward people of the earth." A.M.E. Church publications must "uphold the ideals, and maintain the principles for which we stand. . . . stimulate activities and record and publish our accomplishments to the world. They are the guardians of our heritage."[98]

> The audience is assembled, the stage is set; we now await the rising curtain to reveal in the foreground the black Garrisonian journalist who will make good this solemn declaration: "I am in earnest. I will not equivocate. I will not excuse. I will not retreat a single inch—*And I will be heard.*"[99]

The election of general officers was interrupted on several occasions by the transaction of other controversial business, so Reverdy had to wait to see what his fate would be in terms of his editorship. Before the election, the Committee on Connectional Periodicals read its report in which it recommended that *The A.M.E. Church Review* have an editor and manager who shall be one in the same.[100] When the balloting was finally over, Reverdy had beaten his closest opponent, Dr. C. V. Roman, a prominent Canadian, and became editor of *The A.M.E. Church Review*. The date was May 17.[101] He had set for himself an almost impossible mission, but he looked forward to the challenge.

On April 27, he was slightly amused to receive W. E. B. DuBois's terse compliment.

My dear Dr. Ransom:

Let me congratulate you upon your election to the Editorship of the Review. It is about time you had a new picture taken, and I should like a copy of [it for] the *Crisis*.

Very sincerely yours,
W. E. B. DuBois[102]

CHAPTER 6

Ransom the Editor, 1912–1916

In the beginning was the word.
John 1:1

The New York Age called Reverdy's rise to the editorship of *The A.M.E. Church Review* "signal."[1] The *A.M.E. Magazine*, predecessor of *The Review*, had been created in 1841, but only existed for seven years. In 1876, wanting once more to promote the literary skills of Negroes and give them a voice in the affairs of the Church and nation, Benjamin T. Tanner said, "Let [the] General Conference but give us a 'Quarterly,' and we will show some folks what we really can do." It rankled him that only a few articles by Negroes occasionally appeared in white journals. By 1880, Tanner had the support of Henry McNeal Turner. Turner's endorsement went a long way in getting the church to consider the possibilities of a journal.[2]

The *A.M.E. Church Review*, therefore, was founded in 1883 by Benjamin T. Tanner, then editor of *The Christian Recorder*. After presenting *The Review* to the 1884 General Conference, he became its first editor and remained in the post until he was elected bishop in 1888. L. C. Coppin succeeded him as editor. H. T. Kealing, a layman of Texas, followed Coppin in 1896 but died in office; and Dr. C. V. Roman was appointed by the Publication Board to finished Kealing's term.[3]

Roman went to the 1912 General Conference expecting to be elected for four more years. In *Pilgrimage*, Reverdy describes him as "a noted physician, and a teacher . . . [who] had small respect for the scholastic equipment and literary ability of Negro preachers and did not take seriously [Ransom's] competition with him for the editorship of the Review."[4] Nevertheless, in light of Reverdy's many articles, sermons, and printed orations and his popularity among the clergy, Reverdy had little difficulty winning the position. He thanked Roman for making the election unanimous "before the votes were counted"; and he acknowledged that "throughout the entire contest [Roman] showed himself to be genteel, high-minded, square."[5]

For twenty-eight years, the *Review* had been housed in Philadelphia, Pennsylvania. When Kealing became editor, "on his own initiative," he had moved it to Nashville,

Reverdy C. Ransom, editor of the *A.M.E. Church Review,*
1912–24.

Tennessee. To give credence to the move, at the 1908 General Conference, the Committee on Church Periodicals successfully introduced a resolution to keep the *Review* in Nashville. When Reverdy took over the editorship, he moved the magazine back to Philadelphia (631 Pine Street). He stated his reasons. The resolution passed in 1908 had no enacting clause "repealing the law of our Book of Discipline which places the *Review* under the Board of Publication of our Book Concern located at Philadelphia." The bishops and ministers with whom he had spoken did not object to it being returned to Philadelphia. In fact, many had advised him to do so. His home was near Philadelphia, and, therefore, its proximity would eliminate the need for the church to rent a house for him. He believed he could produce a better magazine in Philadelphia where he had access to the best public libraries, "freedom of contact with the best literary currents, as well as with men of thought, and the molders of public opinion." Most of the magazines of influence in America were housed on the Atlantic seaboard, he reasoned.[6]

In the editorial section of his first edition, Reverdy said that although established by the denomination, *The A.M.E. Church Review* was never intended to be so narrow in its aims and purposes as to devote itself chiefly to the service of its religious household. . . . Its aim was and is to provide a medium of expression for the best thought of Negro scholarship in every department of knowledge.

In order to make sure the quality remained high, the *Review* would deal chiefly with "*potential literature*," and would not publish "commonplace essays on hackneyed or profitless themes." Topics would range from politics to religion, science, social science, civil rights, the theatre, other art forms including an occasional poem, and so forth.[7] Under Reverdy's editorship, the *Review* was as varied in its subject matter as was DuBois's *Crisis*.

Reverdy appointed Dr. George Edmund Haynes as associate editor of the department of social science. He had been the first black to receive his Ph.D. from Columbia University, was professor of social science at Fisk University, and director of the National League on Urban Conditions. Reverdy and Haynes "were alike in their concerns about race and both were basic believers in the power of Christianity and the church to bring about racial and social change."[8] George W. Forbes became literary reviewer and, in addition, wrote his own column titled "Within the Sphere of Letters." Other divisions in the magazine were a quarterly survey that covered international as well as national issues and a homiletic section, headed by Dr. J. T. S. White, aimed at helping ministers structure their sermons. (Dr. White, who was from Texas, had also run for the editorship of the *Review* at the last General Conference.) Unfortunately, he was to write for only two issues before his untimely death.[9] Frequent contributors to the journal included: Charles S. Chestnutt, novelist and short story writer, from Cleveland, Ohio; Timothy T. Fortune, founder of *The New York Age*; Richard T. Greener, diplomat; Alice M. Dunbar, wife of the late poet, Paul Laurence Dunbar; William S. Scarborough, scholar and president of Wilberforce University; Bishop Alexander Walters of the A.M.E. Zion Church; Oswald G. Villard of the NAACP; and Rev. R. R. Wright of the A.M.E. Church.

The July issue of 1912 reflected Reverdy's interest in the political scene. Many articles were devoted to the presidential race between the Democratic candidate, Woodrow Wilson; the Republican, William Howard Taft; and former president Theodore Roosevelt. Once again Negroes found themselves in a quandary as to which of these three candidates was the least of the evils. They recalled both Roosevelt and Taft's involvement in the Brownsville incident. Taft had angered blacks further by stating that he would not appoint any Negro to federal office in the South if the community objected. On the other hand, if Wilson were elected, he would be the first southern president since the Civil War and, as *The New York Age* reminded its readers, had "most of the prejudices of the narrowest type of Southern white people against Negroes."[10] He had served as president of Princeton University, 1902–1910, the only university in the North to exclude Negroes. "Moreover, as governor of New Jersey, 1911–1912, his 'Progressivism' did not embrace the Negro."[11]

Although Taft had been Roosevelt's choice for president in 1908, they had became bitter rivals in 1911 when Taft sued U.S. Steel for buying the Tennessee Coal and Iron Company, an acquisition Roosevelt had approved when he was president. Taft "accused Roosevelt of undermining the conservative tradition in the country and [he] began working to undercut the influence of the Progressive Republicans" by campaigning against Progressive senatorial candidates in 1910 and setting up antiprogressive organizations throughout the country. Roosevelt decided to depose Taft at first by seeking a third term on the Republican ticket.[12]

Reverdy carefully watched as the political drama moved toward a climax. On the eve of the Republican National Convention, June 17, he was in Chicago at Bethel Church speaking before a large Negro audience. "We are about to witness the climax of one of the bitterest as well as one of the most spectacular contests ever waged within the ranks of the Republican Party," he said. He warned that anyone who thought that the convention would bring to blacks "political millennium [was] doomed to a rude and speedy disillusionment." He understood that as a race, Negroes were divided and confused. "We have trusted too long in a sycophantic, compromising, and time-serving leadership while our liberties have been invaded and our rights annulled." Prejudice against blacks, however, was not confined to the United States but was a global problem "wherever the white man has gone to proclaim his over-lordship of the black or dark-skinned people." Reverdy used Cuba as an example and said he was categorically against "any American intervention in Cuba whose object is to set up a white man's government on that island." He would prefer to see all Negro soldiers dishonorable discharged than "to see them follow the flag of [America] bearing arms to crush the aspirations of brown men in the Philippines or black men in Cuba [who want] free and equal participation in all the affairs of their own government," as do Negroes in America.[13]

Negroes could not expect the nominee of the Republican Party, whoever he might be, to put to rest the specter of slavery or the injustice that accrued after its demise. All we can do now, he said, "is to give our support to the man who will set his face most strongly" against injustice. He then examined the two leading Republican candidates, Taft and Roosevelt. Besides agreeing not to appoint Negroes in the South to office, Taft had said, "The Negro should be held in tutelage to the white people of the South," and "The Negro youth of this country should be educated in a different manner from the whites." No man with such a philosophy should gain the support of Negroes, Reverdy reasoned. Roosevelt, on the other hand, made a grievous mistake in the Brownsville Affair. "It is the one black spot in his record so far as the Negroes are concerned." However, before and since, "he has stood for justice and a square deal to the Negro." Nominate and elect Roosevelt, and if he does not do well in the next four years, the party will "repudiate him."[14]

Although some Negroes have turned to the Democratic Party, hoping their defection from the Republican Party might make it return to its original promises, "the Democratic Party is today as of old, controlled by southern sentiment, which is in favor of injustice to the Negro and would today, if it had the power, repeal the Fifteenth Amendment, as it has already nullified it." He closed by saying, if the Republican Party makes William Howard Taft its standard bearer, "they can under no circumstance count upon our support."[15]

When Reverdy said some Negroes had turned to the Democratic Party, he was undoubtedly thinking of Bishop Alexander Walters, president of the Colored Democratic League, and W. E. B. DuBois, whom Walters had persuaded to support Wilson. Walters had gotten from Wilson a statement that said "I want to assure [Negroes] if I should become President of the United States they may count upon me for absolute fair dealing, for everything by which I could assist in advancing the interests of their race in the United States." Encouraged by Wilson's promises, DuBois resigned from the Socialist Party so he could vote for Wilson. Impressed by Wilson's scholarliness and gentility, DuBois used the *Crisis* to promote his candidacy.[16] In the December issue, after once again reiterating the wrongs done by both Taft and Roosevelt to the Negro race, he told why he had voted for Wilson: "First, we faced desperate alternatives, and secondly, Mr. Wilson's personality gives us hope that reactionary Southern sentiment will not control him." He repeated the statements Wilson had made to Walters but also cautioned that "it would take, on Mr. Wilson's part, more than good will—it will demand active determination to know and receive the truth, to get at the sources of Negro public opinion and sympathize with wrongs that only Negroes know."[17]

As Reverdy had promised, the *Review* gave equal coverage to different points of view. James L. Curtis, New York lawyer, who would later be appointed U.S. Minister to Liberia by Wilson, wrote an article titled "Side Lights on the Baltimore Democratic National Convention." He said the large number of Negro delegates at the June 25–July 2 convention proved that Negroes were beginning to pull away from the Republican Party. Colored Americans are "convinced . . . that all white Republicans are not his genuine friends nor all white Democrats his real enemies." Curtis quoted a member of the Democratic National Committee who said the colored delegates admitted that most that had been done in the past *for* the race had been done by Republicans, and most *against* had been done by the Democrats. However, now "since the [Republican] entente cordiale with representative Southern Democrats, as evidenced" by Taft's behavior, it is a good policy for Negroes "to play the same game, and 'beat the Republican Party to it' by courting the friendship of the Democratic Party, without regard to section."[18]

Reverdy admitted that Curtis had at present "prepared the best case . . . for the Democratic Party" but found his article "vulnerable at too many vital points." In reply to George C. Ellis's article concerning the Republican Party, Reverdy acknowledged that many Negroes would attempt to fight within the party "to win it back to the paths which, in faithlessness, it has forsaken" rather than desert it, but "if the new political movement, headed by Col. Roosevelt will give the Negroes a 'square deal,' then Negroes in great numbers will meet them on the square."[19] However, at the 1912 Republican Convention, Taft, who had control of the party machine, won the nomination. Feeling betrayed, the Progressive Republicans formed a new party, referred to also as the Bull Moose Party, with Theodore Roosevelt as their candidate. Using the slogan "New Nationalism," Roosevelt advocated a "national approach to the country's affairs . . . efficiency in government and society," with social justice for women, children, and workers.[20]

In reference to church news, on the frontispiece of the July issue of the *Review* was a picture of the new bishops elected at Kansas City and an article in the Editorial section by Ransom, "The Psychology of a General Conference," in which he quoted Bishop Thomas B. Neely of the Methodist Episcopal Church. Neely had called the past M.E. General Conference "an impulsive body," filled with young people who knew little about Methodism and its traditions. Reverdy pointed out that many delegates had described the A.M.E. General Conference in the same manner. The "pessimists" had cried "too many young men—new delegates unacquainted with our laws and traditions." These people forget that they were once young, he scolded. Some of the bishops and ministers at Kansas City "proclaim[ed] against the 'impulsive action' 'hasty legislation' and 'lack of deliberation.'" He reminded his readers that "the creation of the work in South Africa was due to this so-called 'impulsive action,'" and that some of the most valuable departments and laws of the Church were "the result of 'hasty legislation.'"[21] In the same section of the magazine, Reverdy wrote on one his favorite subjects, ecumenicalism: the efforts of the A.M.E., A.M.E. Zion, and Colored Methodist Episcopal Churches to prepare for denominational union, efforts that continued for many years but never came to fruition in his lifetime.[22]

The subscribers to the *Review* seemed to be impressed with Reverdy's first issue. Bishop Evans Tyree, who had become the prelate of the First Episcopal District (New York) replacing the deceased Bishop Gaines wrote: "I have read every word in the issue of the Review that marks your beginning, and I regard it as a very instructive one." Even though he knew little about politics, he had enjoyed all the articles pertaining to it.[23]

The October issue of the *Review* included a rather detailed biographical sketch of Ira Aldridge, the black Shakespearean actor, by former chaplain, T. B. Steward, and an article honoring Samuel Coleridge-Taylor by R. R. Wright Jr. Coleridge-Taylor, the composer, had died of pneumonia September 1, 1912, at his home in Thorntonheath, England. Wright wrote that in losing the musician, "the race [had] suffered a severe blow, quite equal to that suffered from the loss of the late Paul Laurence Dunbar, the poet."[24] Reverdy, who had spent time in Coleridge-Taylor's home and had presented him in concert at Charles Street in Boston, must have keenly felt the loss of this musical giant much as he had felt the loss of his friend, Dunbar.

One of the most interesting articles in the October edition was titled "Proportion of Mulattoes in the Negro Population of the United States: Preliminary Thirteenth Census Statistics Issued by the Census Bureau." According to the bureau, in 1910 there were 9,827,763 Negroes in the United States, of whom 20 percent were mulattoes.[25] Reverdy stressed that the mulattoes were not merely "Dry Statistics" but "constitute a living, breathing, human document." Some of these "people without an identity" have swung back and forth between races; others pass over to the white race; the mass of them prefer to stay with their black relatives. To those whites who fear that the growing number of mulattoes may eventually Africanize this country, "these bleaching millions may be heaven sent messengers . . . [ushering] in the . . . dawn of the realization of human brotherhood on these shores."[26] Was he advocating intermarriage as a solution to the race problem, or simply stating that mulattoes were proof that such intermixing was not as disastrous as many whites believed? Considering his strong pride in his own black blood, one must conclude that he meant the latter.

Because the presidential election had not taken place yet and all the conventions were over, there was still great interest in the three leading candidates. In Taft's attempt to further "woo" the South, the platform of the Republican Party for 1912 omitted the "Rights of the Negro" that had been included in the 1908 plank. Instead there was no direct reference to Negroes at all.[27] The editor of *The New York Age*, Fred R. Moore, included an article in the *Review*, "The Republican Party and the Negro," in which he still insisted that Taft was "one of the best equipped and sanest and safest of the ten Republicans who have occupied the White House from Lincoln to Taft."[28] Curtis wrote a follow-up article to the one he had submitted in July, attempting to urge blacks to support Wilson and the Democratic Party[29]; Reverdy included an editorial, "Hunting Big Game Out of Africa." He had completely reversed his opinion of Roosevelt and now viewed Roosevelt's proposals "as monstrous, unpatriotic, unjust and politically immoral."[30] What had occurred to alter Reverdy's strong endorsement of Roosevelt? At the Progressive Party's Convention, Roosevelt had approved of the practice that the "all-black contingents from the Deep South" should not be seated on the grounds, "they were not representative of their constituent communities," but all whites should be seated and also Negroes from the North.[31]

For the first time, Northern Negroes are being arrayed against Southern Negroes, Reverdy wrote. The Northern Negro is asked to "join in a movement that openly proclaims the exclusion of his Southern brother." Roosevelt has fallen "from the lofty summit of 'political and social justice,' to grovel in the dust before race exclusion and discrimination." Unfortunately, there are some Negroes in the South who "blindly consent to their own further political degradation; while in the North are Negroes of light and leading, who re-echo his wicked logic and support his proposal for political serfdom." Negroes today, like Roosevelt, are hunting for big game—but the game they want is "complete realization of equal political and social justice and they will not be diverted in their quest by Mr. Roosevelt's dishonorable decoy."[32]

The actions of Roosevelt further strengthened Bishop Walters's and DuBois's position and no doubt were responsible for some Negroes switching to Wilson; however, after the Progressive Party Convention, Ransom did not express his support for any of the candidates, and it is not certain how he voted. He may even have voted for Eugene Debs, the Socialist candidate, as he had often threatened to do.

The January 1913 *Review* was a Jubilee edition marking the fiftieth anniversary of the "physical freedom of the Negro." On the frontispiece was a sketch of Frederick Douglass, inscribed "The noblest slave that ever God set free," followed by a lead article, "Reminiscences of the Proclamation of Emancipation," by Bishop Henry M. Turner. Other articles on the anniversary theme included: "The Negro Soldier's Contribution in the Wars of the U.S." by Rev. W. Spencer Carpenter; "A Message for the Next Fifty Years" by Oswald Garrison Villard, grandson of William Lloyd Garrison and editor of the *New York Evening Post*; "Some Glimpses of Ante Bellum Negro Literature" by Chaplain T. G. Steward (retired); "The Negro on the American Stage" by Lester A. Walton; "The Aftermath" by Bishop Alexander Walters; and the only essay in response to a Jubilee Essay Contest, "Fifty Years of Freedom," written by fourteen-year-old Laura Mackey from New York City.[33]

Booker T. Washington submitted an article on "Industrial Education and Negro Progress," which reiterated his gospel of industrial education. Education, "if it is to be of any permanent value to the race, must take some account of the practical interest of the people, must connect in some way with the common, ordinary, daily life of people," he wrote. "Directly or indirectly, [industrial schools] have encouraged people to buy lands, to build and own their own homes, to go forward in the matters of industry and trade, and to put brains and thought and conscience into the affairs of every-day life." Near the end of the article, he again said that the only kind of agitation that could win respect and help from others is that "which shows to the world that we have the strength and the courage and the disposition to help ourselves."[34]

While agreeing in part to what Washington had written, in an editorial, Reverdy made veiled reference to the loopholes in Washington's thesis:

> For more than a score of years there has been at work an insidious influence, under the guise of philanthropy, to fix the Negro in a place of permanent inferiority. He is to be educated along the lines which will make him a better servant; he is to

be free to buy land and own homes (provided his "white neighbors" do not object to his presence in that vicinity) and work independently upon the soil; he may apply himself to trades and work at a minimum wage in the South and in the North work not at all, if the Labor Union objects; he may have a bank account, but it will not buy him comfort or convenience in travel, or entrance to places of entertainment, or that make for the culture of intellect or the higher elevation of the spirit; he may own land, but his broad acres give him no voice in the laws under which he is taxed or in the choice of the men who are to administer them, neither do they give him equal standing in the courts, nor protection from the violence and fury of the mob.[35]

In the same editorial, he answered Villard's article in which Villard said Negroes should get together and join in numbers those organizations that are formed to "assert their rights. . . . And [they should lay] aside all differences that a united front may be shown to all the race's enemies."[36] Reverdy agreed, but added: Those Negroes who seek to gain favor by "bartering the rights of the race for the honors of office or the gain of gold" must be spurned as well as those whites who pretend to be philanthropists, great friends of the Negro, but who cannot be found when "their personal or partisan ends [have] been served."[37]

In June 1913 Emma and Reverdy traveled to Wilberforce to attend the graduation exercises where Bishop C. S. Smith delivered the commencement address. Speaking on "The Noachian Curse," Smith denied the charge that because Ham had looked on his father Noah's naked body, he was fated to be a servant to his brothers all his life. As a result, blacks, who were alleged by whites to be akin to the swarthy Ham, were also to be servants all their lives. Smith argued convincingly that history did not bear out this myth.[38] In describing how Smith's speech was received, Reverdy noted that "the great audience, composed mostly of young people, students, was entirely unprepared for his outgivings, nor did they, with many of their elders, grasp its audacious significance." On the other hand, he applauded Smith for his "critical discussion of a much-abused text." He admitted that while "some of the Church fathers who had fixed the standards of doctrines" were Africans, the "Americans of African descent have not written a new chapter in theology or Biblical criticism in 300 years— had not given their concept of God." Reverdy hoped that

in some of our theological schools, some original thinker and investigator will soon appear to teach the ministers of the next generation how to boldly challenge the men of religion who have been torturing the word of God into a vehicle to voice a divine authority for the practice of race and color discrimination.[39]

While in Wilberforce, the Ransoms were pleased to learn that their "Son in the Gospel," Joseph Gomez, was doing well in his seminary studies and would graduate the following year. They had to hurry back to New York and, therefore, did not get to meet Joseph's fiancée, Hazel Thompson of Toledo. Another year would pass before they would meet her.

"In obedience to a vision of God," during August 1913, Reverdy and Emma conceived the idea of starting a mission in the Tenderloin. They called it Simon of Cyrene after the black man who had carried the cross for Jesus on his way to Calvary. The mission would serve the derelicts and underclass people whom society of both races seemed to have forgotten. They rented a store on West 37th Street between 8th and 9th Avenues, a few doors from a gambling hall. Reverdy assured the proprietor that he would not interfere with his business because "the regularly constituted authorities deal with such things"; however, if he saw young people frequenting the hall, he would try to have the place closed down.[40]

The Ransoms moved into an apartment at 341 West 36th Street so they could have "daily contact with the people there." (In *Pilgrimage*, Reverdy says they moved on 38th, but letters found during this period are addressed to the 36th Street address.) Because the *Review* came out quarterly with Emma's help, Reverdy felt he had plenty of time to run the mission. To those critics who said he had been elected to edit the magazine only, he answered that he did not care what other general officers of the church did with their nights and Sundays, but he chose to spend his at the mission. "The Church gives us a salary for the performance of the duties of our position, and we count it an honor and have great joy in serving [the mission] without pay or the acceptance of pecuniary reward from the hand of any one," he wrote in the October 1913 *Review*. The Negro population in New York was equal to or larger than it was in such cities as Baltimore, Chicago, Pittsburgh, Atlanta, St. Louis, and so forth and yet there was only one A.M.E. Church in New York (Bethel that had moved to Harlem). It was the Ransoms' purpose to "establish, on permanent foundations, a church in that section of the city which is most neglected, and which is being abandoned by the larger organization [A.M.E. Church], but for years to come will hold a Negro population of many thousands." Rev. Benjamin Arnett, pastor of Bethel, objected to Reverdy opening the mission because he feared it would hamper his work and take away from his membership. To allay his apprehensions, Reverdy refused to take in members from his church or any other church. He was, however, "joined by about thirty devout people to whom [his] type of service appealed."[41]

In the *Review*, he responded to critics of the mission by asking, What is going to happen to the so called "Bad Negroes?" those whom the middle class have abandoned? Because American Christianity had left the moral and spiritual uplift of Negroes in their own hands, "Shall we sit smug and comfortable in our large churches?" His solution involved the bringing together of "the Negro who is up and the Negro who is down, the Negro who is good and the Negro who is bad, the Negro who is intelligent and the Negro who is ignorant . . . until each stands uplifted . . . animated with unity of purpose to face a growing national attitude" that would reduce them to "a position of inferiority."[42]

In soliciting members, Reverdy and Emma said nothing to them about religion. With little fanfare, they opened the mission officially on September 4. They "visited the sick, the saloons, the houses of prostitution, the gambling joints and all other places [they] could find that had never known the friendly touch, or the personal interest from people connected with the churches." Learning that the prostitutes had money one day and were broke the next, they got them to stock a storeroom in the back of the mission with food. During the winter months, those who needed food "could come day or night and have their wants supplied from the stock of things they had laid up before hand." The people in the neighborhood came to love and trust the Ransoms. They knew they could count on them in all kinds of circumstances. Reverdy developed a relationship with the captain of the police precinct, and the two worked together for the benefit of the community. This meant that Reverdy's responsibilities were doubled. He was "frequently called from the police station at all hours of the night to come and look after a prisoner whom they were willing to parole in [his custody]."[43]

The mission in no way diminished the quality of Reverdy's editing of the *Review*. For example, he received a letter from his old friend, Chaplain George W. Prioleaux, complimenting him on the magazine. He had met Prioleaux when he pastored St. John, Cleveland. Prioleaux was originally from South Carolina and had paid his way through college by mending shoes. At one time Bishop Payne had made him a presiding elder in the North Ohio Conference. He was the first Negro to serve as chaplain to an integrated garrison; in 1895 President Grover Cleveland appointed him to the 9th Calvary with the rank of captain.[44] At the time of the letter, April 27, 1914, he was fifty-seven years old and stationed at Douglas, Arizona. He wrote Reverdy to renew his subscription and he congratulated the "Old Man," as he affectionately called Reverdy, for the quality of the magazine. "I knew that you could do it, with the able assistance of Mrs. Emma," he said. Reverdy's editorials were "sources of help . . . and inspiration" that he could not put down until he had finished all of them. He congratulated Emma on the work she was doing in the New York YWCA and hoped "God would give her the strength to carry out her plans and [her] work for the uplift of [Negro] young women." He had decided to stay in the service because returning to the pastorate at his age with all its responsibilities would make "an old man of him in two years." He closed by asking where Reverdy C. Jr., "Pepin," was. (He nicknamed Reverdy Jr. "Pepin" because, unable to pronounce Prioleaux's name, Reverdy Jr. had called him "Pepin."[45])

On June 18, 1914, Reverdy and Emma made their annual trip to Wilberforce to attend graduation. It was a trek they always looked forward to. They loved the wooded groves and hidden springs that would someday be their home, but this visit had special significance for them. Joseph Gomez had completed his courses at Payne Seminary with honors, was to be ordained an elder, assigned to his first charge in Bermuda, and married to Hazel Thompson, all on the same day. At 2 P.M., the simple wedding ceremony was performed on the campus by George F. Woodson, dean of the seminary. The Ransoms immediately fell in love with the tiny bride who looked up at her new husband with such seriousness. They were a miniature couple, like the figures on a wedding cake. Hazel was only a little shorter than Joseph who never stood more than 5'4". Reverdy felt now he had the daughter he had always wanted, and he called Hazel "Daughter" throughout his life.[46]

After graduation, Joseph left for New York where he was to catch the boat for Bermuda. Because he did not have enough money initially to take Hazel to New York with him, the Ransoms and Joseph's uncle, James Richardson, gave him the money to send for her. When Hazel arrived, the Ransoms escorted the couple around the city and introduced them to the members of Simon of Cyrene. They were impressed with the mission and the work that was being done for the community. All too soon, it was time for them to board the ship for Bermuda. Being uncertain of what they would encounter in Bermuda, they said lengthy good-byes to the Ransoms and Uncle James. They knew it would be some time before they would meet again. [47]

On August 11, 1914, the Ransoms sent out an open letter announcing the first anniversary ceremony of the mission that was to be held in Bryant Hall on 6th Avenue near 42nd Street on September 4.[48] With the assistance of people in the Tenderloin and other interested New Yorkers, the Ransoms had been able to put into practice Reverdy's concept of the social gospel. Those few years at the mission remained for them some of the most fulfilling of their lives.

By June 1915 the *New York Age* was able to report that the New York Annual Conference had officially recognized Simon of Cyrene as a part of the conference and Connection and had appointed the church a full-time pastor. Between 1913 and 1915, its membership had grown from thirty to 114.[49] Reverdy says in *Pilgrimage* he stayed at the mission until 1924. It can be assumed, therefore, that he continued to be involved in some capacity with it until his election to the bishopric.

Meanwhile, subscribers to the *Review* grew in number. In the summer of 1914, Reverdy could report that the magazine had "2,500 bona fide subscribers." His wish was that each person who got the magazine would convince one other person to do likewise. If this happened there would be five thousand on the mailing list, and the magazine could become a bimonthly.[50] In the next issue, he promised to publish the names of ministers and other persons who submitted the names of one or more subscribers.[50]

Because the General Conference would convene in two years and aspirants for the bishopric would soon begin their campaigning, in July Reverdy wrote two editorials in the *Review* concerning the bishops of the A.M.E. Church. "The Negro Bishops and Their Opportunity For Race Leadership" was Reverdy's reminder that bishops were "no more restrained from considering the interests of the people that lie beyond their ecclesiastical boundary than Dr. Washington from dealing with the interests of his people that lie outside the surveyor's chart of Tuskegee Institute." The areas they should investigate were health of the Negro, conditions of public schools, and industrial exploitation. The spread of diseases and the high death rate among Negroes reflect the "unhygienic conditions in which they are forced to live," he wrote. The bishops should be engaged in seeing that the free public schools are improved, particularly in the South, where little money is spent by the state for Negro schools. They should warn their people against "commercial frauds and fakes and get-rich-quick schemes."[51]

Under the heading of "Bishop Timber," he warned that the section of the country where the candidate for the bishopric comes from or his nativity should not be an issue. At present, there are men from the South who only want to serve in the South, and men in the North who only want to serve in the North. "A man who cannot stand on his feet and measure up to the responsibilities in any section of the Church is not fit to be a bishop at all," he declared. In describing the most-fit bishop, he used the extended metaphor of wood. When we select bishops to support the weight of denominational and national responsibilities, he said:

> give us that which is neither bent, knotty nor crooked; give us neither saplings nor that which is decayed; but give us the seasoned oaks that have defied the storms, the summer drought and the winters blast, deep rooted in knowledge, in wisdom and the love of God.[52]

The *Review* reflected the Negro's general disappointment in President Wilson's administration. As Reverdy had predicted, it reflected his Southern background and prejudices. In the 1912 election, Walters had led some very influential blacks away from the Republican and Progressive Parties to support Wilson based on his promise of justice for all races. Despite these promises, Wilson had dismissed "wholesale" Negro federal officers and civil service employees and had agreed to a policy of segregation. In addition, bills had been introduced in the Democratic Congress "forbidding intermarriage and calling for the repeal of the Fifteenth Amendment."[53] When Oswald G. Villard of the NAACP proposed that a National Race Commission be formed to study race relations, "Wilson rejected the idea because he feared he might lose southern Democratic votes in Congress." Not since the Civil War had "southern views on race dominated the nation's capitol."[54]

In an editorial, Reverdy asked, "What Will Bishop Walters Do Now?" Will he continue to support the Democratic Party?[55] Reverdy did not have long to wait. Walters
answered Ransom's question in the October 1914 issue of the *Review*. In a letter to the
editor, he said he had joined the Democratic Party because it dominates the South
and the largest number of Negroes lives in the South. It seemed to him that something had to be done to change the Negro's political condition in that part of the country. Because the Republican Party had abandoned the Negro, "an alignment with the
Democratic Party was the best way out of the difficulty." Perhaps if the northern and
western Democrats supported blacks, they might be able to influence the South. In
terms of segregation in government departments, it had begun under Roosevelt's administration and had continued under Taft's as had the dismissals of Negro government employees. He then listed a number of people who had been dismissed by the
Taft administration. He did not excuse Wilson's behavior, but he was going "to continue to urge the President to keep his promises." He would also continue to "advise
the black man to divide his vote, and support the men who have proven themselves to
be friends" regardless to their party affiliation. If none of these things worked, he
would advise Negroes to organize their own party, and "where it is feasible . . . to put
Negro candidates in the field of municipal, county, state and congressional offices."[56]

According to DuBois in *Dusk to Dawn*, when Walters visited Wilson at the White
House in 1915, "Wilson asked him, 'By the way what about that letter I wrote to you
during the campaign? I do not seem to remember it.' When Walter handed the letter
to Wilson, 'the President forgot to return it.'"[57] Along with the forgotten letter went
his forgotten promises. By 1917, Walters was saying that Wilson's "New Freedom [was]
all for the white man and little for the Negro."[58]

Reverdy kept his promise to inform his readers of events that were vital to their
well-being. In another editorial in the July 1914 issue, Reverdy quoted at length the
hearings of the Committee on Reform in Civil Service that had met March 6, 1914, to
determine whether clerks and employees in the service should be segregated. He
quoted James B. Aswell, representative from Louisiana, as saying:

> The Almighty by the stamp of color decreed that the Caucasian race should oc-
> cupy positions of authority and control the destinies of this country. . . . It is un-
> just to a member of this inferior race to put him in positions of authority over the
> Caucasian. By inheritance he is a misfit when in authority even over his own race.

Reverdy also printed the testimony of Archibald H. Grimke who had asked the committee not to separate the colored people in government service from the whites. This
would humiliate them. "Here they are in the service. They have proved themselves to
be faithful and efficient, and this bill separates them, and separation always mean

inequality." At the end of his account of the hearings, Reverdy said, "Segregation is the spirit of slavery profaning the sacred altar of freedom. It should be scourged and cast forth into the outer darkness from which it came."[59]

As was the customs of most General Officers in the A.M.E. Church, not only did Reverdy attend graduations during 1914, but he spent a great deal of time visiting the various Annual Conferences. He attended the Chicago Conference and came to admire Bishop Benjamin F. Lee's financial innovations. All reports relating to money were given to the board of finance outside of the "conference proper" so that no minister stood in front of the delegates and read his report "either with a sense of elation or failure" as had been the custom and was still the custom in most conferences. At the Kansas Conference in Atchison led by Bishop H. B. Parks, Reverdy was amazed to see how the conference took on the responsibilities of the Connectional Preachers' Home at Colorado Springs (not supported by the Connection, but the Fifth District); the Douglas Hospital in Kansas City, Kansas; and Western University at Quindaro, Kansas. Despite the tremendous burden, most of the ministers reported "substantial sums for the support of these [A.M.E.] institutions" without complaint.[60]

While in Kentucky at the Louisville Conference, Reverdy took time out to visit the "splendidly equipped YMCA and two branches of the public library set aside for 'colored people.'" While admiring the progress of the institutions, he deplored the segregation that seemed "an odd note" in terms of racial harmony.[61]

He also visited the Tennessee Conference at Murfreesboro, the Central Tennessee Conference at Dickson, and then went on to Nashville as a guest of Dr. J. W. Sexton. His opponent for the editorship of the *Review* at the 1912 General Conference, Dr. C. V. Roman, gave him a tour of Meharry Medical College and took him to the Bible Class of over seventy members that he taught on Sunday mornings at St. Paul's A.M.E. Church. While in Nashville, Reverdy also visited the new A.M.E. Sunday School Union Building. He felt it was not only a monument to Ira T. Bryant, its director, but to the entire Connection. It was so well equipped that he believed it could do "not only all the printing of the A.M.E. Church," but all the other Negro churches as well.[62]

In Oklahoma he became aware that it still bore the marks of its "primeval state and territorial days." He was sure that A.M.E.s did not know of the many difficulties experienced by the people who tried to maintain the church's influence in the state. Nevertheless, Bishop W. D. Chappell showed "a masterly grasp of the situation" there and in Arkansas. Reverdy visited Shorter College in Little Rock and met Dr. William Byrd, its president. At Jonesboro, he was asked to speak Sunday afternoon in the Opera House. Strangely enough, the whites occupied the balcony while the Negroes sat on the main floor. After Little Rock, he visited the North Georgia Conference where he was welcomed warm-heartedly by Bishop Joseph S. Flipper who was successful in persuading more people to subscribe to the *Review*. His last stop was Corsicana, Texas.

There he visited the Northeast Conference where his friend, Bishop C. S. Smith, supervised. Under his direction, over $30,000 had been raised for Paul Quinn College, the A.M.E. College in Waco.[63]

Reverdy concluded from his trip that there was no North or South where the Negro was concerned. "The large migration of our people from the South, particularly into the great cities of the North, and the prevailing conditions which have linked us all to one common fate, seem to be causing the people as a whole to cherish the same aspirations and ideals," he wrote.[64]

As mentioned in an earlier chapter of the book, the October 1914 issue of the *Review* was largely devoted to the memory of Paul Laurence Dunbar. Alice M. Dunbar, the poet's wife, wrote the lead article, "The Poet and His Song," in which she told "in what manner the great phenomena of Nature [had] impressed him as exemplified in his poetry." Like Reverdy, she disagreed with Howells who seemed to have preferred Dunbar's dialect poems. She believed, "they were to him side issues of his work, the overflowing of a life apart from his dearest dreams" that he expressed in his pure English verse.[65] W. S. Scarborough called him "Poet Laureate of the Negro Race," in his article. He marveled that "this young Negro should take what has heretofore been the white man's own distinctive art, equal and surpass in it." He recalled the unveiling of a monument in Dunbar's honor on June 26, 1909, in Dayton, Ohio. The monument was located "in harmony with the poet's expressed wish [in his poem 'Death's Song'] under a willow, near a pool of water and not beyond the noises of the road."[66] The issue also included a chronological bibliography of Dunbar's works.[67]

While the *Review* was progressing steadily, events on the international scene presaged dark days for Europe. Archduke Franz Ferdinand, heir to the Austro-Hungarian throne, had been assassinated at Sarajevo on June 28, 1914. A few weeks later Germany, Turkey, and Austria-Hungary were at war with England, France, and Russia. World War I had begun. In an editorial Reverdy stated he did not believe the assassination was the cause of the conflict but "only a fuse that fired a continental mine." The cause was

> commercial rivalry and jealousy between England and Germany; the long cherished revenge of France over the lost provinces of Alsace and Lorraine which were taken from her by Germany in the Franco-Prussian War of 1870, and the race antagonisms of the Teutonic and Slavic races.

He found it ironic that Austria, where Catholicism was so strong, and Germany, which gave birth to the Protestant Reformation, should be the main cause of the present crisis. Had Christianity failed? he asked. His answer to his own question was "No." The people had failed Christianity. "Let the dominant peoples of the world, as they sit by the smoldering embers of broken kingdoms and depopulated nations, read again the decree of the Almighty: 'The nation and the kingdom that will not serve God shall perish,'" he wrote.[68] Little did he realize that despite Wilson's efforts to keep America out of the war, many Negroes would once again join in the fight to keep the country safe for a Democracy that, up to now, had excluded them.

In an editorial in January 1915, Reverdy reported that the National Independent Equal Rights League of which Ransom was a member had first visited President Wilson in 1913 after his inauguration and had come away believing that he would support Negro rights. Not satisfied with his performance, they visited him again on November 12, 1914. Spokesman for the group this time was William Monroe Trotter of Boston, secretary of the league and a Democrat who had supported Wilson. The delegation had come to renew their protest and appeal to Wilson to "entirely abolish segregation of Afro-American employees in the executive department." After citing specific examples of segregation in terms of dressing rooms, eating facilities, working stations, and bathrooms in departments like the Treasury, State, Navy, Post Office, the Bureau of Engraving and Printing, and the Marine Hospital Service Building, they said they had come as "full-fledged American citizens, absolutely equal with all others, to demand . . . equal rights under the Constitution." Wilson was particularly offended by what he called "the bad manners of the chairman."

> Trotter insisted that he spoke in measured words and with deliberation, positiveness and directness, looking President Wilson squarely in the eye, with the thought only that [he] had a difficult task to refute a masterful piece of sophistry on the spur of the moment, and that there was a great responsibility resting upon [him] to refute [Wilson], point by point, successfully.[69]

On December 11 Reverdy had sent a letter to the city editor of the *New York Age*, stating that at Bethel A.M.E. Church, located at 132nd Street near Lenox Avenue, there would be a public meeting of the National Independent Equal Rights League, December 15, 1914. The purposes of the meeting, he said, were "to endorse the action of the committee composed of members of this body which recently called upon President Wilson to protest against the segregation of Colored employees in the departments of the government, and to pass suitable resolutions." Speakers at the meeting were to be Rev. Byron W. Gunner of Hillburn, New York, national president of the League; Rev. W. H. Brooks, pastor of St. Marks M.E. Church, New York; Rev. Adam Clayton Powell, Sr., pastor of Abyssinian Baptist Church, New York; and Reverdy C. Ransom, editor of the *A.M.E. Review*. [70] No copy of Reverdy's speech exists, but in light of his January 1915 editorial describing the meeting between Wilson and the National Independent Equal Rights League, his passionate objection to the president's response is quite evident.

He entitles this satirical editorial "The Ape That speaks Like A Man" and refers to

Wilson's behavior as a "current illness, serious in nature and permanent in character." Eminent specialists as Doctor W. K. Vardaman of Mississippi and other racists
had assured Wilson that "his violent contact with the Nation's Stumbling Block on
the 12th of November . . . when a delegation of Negroes representing the National
Independent Equal Rights League called upon him, was the best thing that could possibly have happened to the 'block.'" Reverdy warned, the president fails to remember
that the career of Daniel Webster was destroyed by contact with the sharp corners of
the nation's stumbling block that rent asunder the country for four bloody years of
Civil War. The Negro entertains grave fears for the president's recovery. His tempera-
ture had shot up to 106 when he came into personal contact with the "Human problem . . . the straight and clean-cut issue of equal and undiscriminating treatment of
all its citizens by the government."[71]

Russia was often called "the Bear that walks like a man," he wrote. It may be that
"the Americans of African descent have at last supplied the 'missing link' . . . by giving
us the 'Ape that talks like a man,' for have we not variously classified this species of
American as 'nigger,' 'darkey,' 'coon,' 'monkey,' 'Ape'?" At this point, Reverdy quoted
verbatim the logical, factual testimony and appeal of the delegation when they visited Wilson. At the conclusion of the quote, he exclaimed, "Shades of Jefferson Davis,
defend us! When in the memory of Presidents, Confederate or otherwise, did ever the
'grinning,' 'good-natured,' 'patient,' 'non-resistant creature,' so address a Chief Executive" who only a few months ago had promised that should he become president,
Negroes "could count on [him] for fair dealing." Reverdy said he believed Wilson became upset with Trotter because he did not come in "with shuffling gait, cringing, hat
in hand; but standing erect like a man," speaking in tones like a man. Since the meeting, the president had "been seeing things."[72]

In another editorial, George W. Forbes followed Reverdy's article in which he quoted
the reactions of newspapers throughout the country. Most of the white papers regretted the behavior of Trotter and called him a troublemaker but were almost unanimous in saying the president should rescind the order to segregate governmental
workers because they had worked together before and there had been no friction. For
instance, Forbes quoted the *Courier-Journal,* a leading Southern paper, as approving
the President's "calling down the impudent Negro who acted as spokesman for the
committee . . . [but] the segregation order should be revoked." Others wrote that friction only came about when McAdoo, the president's son-in-law, "began his Jim-Crow
proceedings in the Treasury Department."[73]

All the meetings and protests proved to be fruitless. Wilson and his administration continued its practice of racism and segregation in the nation's capitol. Only the
impending war would divert the attention of blacks from job discrimination in Washington to another area—segregation in the armed forces.

In the same edition of the *Review,* Reverdy wrote of his concerns about the church's preoccupation with expansion before making sure the departments already established were strong. He compared the missionary policy of the church to that of America's commercial policy in foreign affairs. While fighting for European markets, American had neglected rich markets at her doorstep to the south. Likewise, the church continues to put forth ineffectual "puny efforts" in West and South Africa, while more than twenty million blacks need their assistance in the United States, Cuba, the West Indies, and Central and South America, he said. When the Spanish-American War was over, the church missed its opportunity to enter Cuba and Puerto Rico, and she was now losing ground in Haiti. The A.M.E. Church does not support sufficiently her schools and colleges right here in the United States, he wrote. In addition, interest in publishing has expanded beyond the support given by the clergy and laity. Of the three church papers (*The Christian Recorder, Southern and Western Christian Recorders*), the A.M.E. *Church Review,* and the *Voice of Missions* "not one of them is mechanically, either in dress or form, highly creditable to a Church that wears the title, 'great.'" Why? Because although the church has over a half-million members, not more than thirty thousand subscribe to the papers, despite the fact that the bishops have required each minister to take at least two of the publications. The church does not need anymore "born leaders of men," but men who "are capable of developing the rich fields that lie beneath our already far-reaching cords lengthened almost to the breaking point."[74]

On February 24, 1915, Amanda Smith, the evangelist whom Reverdy had had preach at his churches in Cleveland and Chicago, died at Sebring, Florida, at the age of seventy-eight. In the April issue of the *Review,* two pieces were written in her honor, one by Julia A Savage titled "The Last Days of Sister Amanda Smith," and the other an editorial by Reverdy. He told how there had been thirteen children in her family, seven who were born slaves, and how her father bought first his wife's freedom then the children's, "one by one, until all were free." At the time of Amanda's death, only one sister remained. As a young woman, she had become an evangelist; then in 1883, by invitation of Lady Somerset, she left for England to give temperance speeches for the Women's Christian Temperance Union for three months. Instead, she stayed for twelve years lecturing in England, Ireland, Scotland, India, Japan, and Africa. When she returned home she founded the Amanda Smith Orphan Home by investing $10,000 of her life's savings. Reverdy had been a member of her board of managers. He said, "The thing which, above all others, distinguished her was heart power—spiritual life. . . . She was a clear-visioned prophetess, who saw the deliverance of her race from proscription and persecution as clearly as she did its emancipation from slavery." She was not of the "censorious, factious, holier-than-thou kind . . . temperance, social purity, holiness, the rescue and care of neglected children . . . this was her richest legacy to her race."[75]

In the same issue, Reverdy also quoted a news item. By a vote of 228 to 60 on January 11, the House had passed a bill prohibiting intermarriage between whites and Negroes in the District of Columbia. Any mixed couple entering the city would be liable to prosecution. Persons who contracted such a marriage were to be fined between $1,000 and $5,000 and be imprisoned for between six months to a year. All such marriages would be considered null and void. Anyone who had one-eighth Negro blood was considered to be a Negro.[76]

Reverdy remarked sarcastically:

> We count ourselves happy in this move of the U.S. Congress to disentangle and legally define our veri-colored racial identity. But African sunshine is a powerful resolvent, which has a sly way of revealing, even to the thirtieth degree, the rich pigment it has held in solution.

This law, however, would have little effect on Caucasian men as long as they were allowed to "insult black womanhood as a half human thing by day and fondle it in his arms as a thing of joy by night." He quoted the *New York Sun* as saying that whether the law to prevent such marriages was wise or humane was debatable. But there could be

> no doubt as to the abomination of a statute which would render null and void a marriage, contracted legally elsewhere, as soon as the couple entered the District and would render them liable to pains and penalties for continuing to live in the marriage state.[77]

Reverdy had strong words for Senator William E. Borah of Idaho who had delivered a speech before the U.S. Senate stating that the mistreatment of American citizens in Mexico by Mexicans (several had been killed) was because Mexicans did not believe that America protected its own citizens. The "flag which will not protect its people is a dirty rag," he said. It was rumored that Senator Borah would be the next Republican candidate for president of the United States; Reverdy felt Senator Borah's statement did not ring true on the race question.

> We will have none of him. He was one of four lonesome Republican Senators to vote for the bill to exclude Negro immigrants from the United States. The race would gain nothing by changing from Wilson the Segregationalist to Borah the Exclusionist.

Borah could only be taken seriously when he was as much concerned for the protection of Americans at home as those abroad.[78]

In the editorial that followed, Reverdy saluted the "Serbians" who requested that the public and press from here on use a "b" instead of a "v" when referring to them because the "v" was "highly offensive . . . suggesting a false derivation from the Latin root." Likewise, he said, Negroes in the United States continually request that the press and public use a capital "N" when referring to them "because the 'n' is highly offensive to their people, suggesting not a false derivation from roots, Latin or otherwise, but an attempt to dehumanize them by placing them in the same class with a horse, cat or dog." Some of the metropolitan papers even used "coon," "darkey," "negro," interchangeably, he said.[79]

In reference to the Mondell resolution that proposed a constitutional amendment to give women the right to vote, Reverdy quoted the segregationist Representative Dies of Texas as saying he was opposed to such a resolution "because it would thrust the ballot into the hands of millions of Negro women in the South." Although the South had constantly stripped the Negro man of his right to vote, with the Negro woman it would be different, said Reverdy, because they are more courageous than the men. In the day that women get the vote, he predicted "the enfranchised Negro women voters will bring back vigorously the long-departed sceptre of political influence and power."[80]

Reverdy was careful only to choose for his magazine those articles that had substance and were well written, particularly those dealing with the race question. One such article in the April 1915 issue was "An Edgefield Idyll—South Carolina Reminiscence" by Richard Theodore Greener. Greener, a graduate of Harvard, had been professor of metaphysics and logic at the University of South Carolina (1873–77), teacher of law and then dean of the law school at Howard University (1879–80), and first U.S. Consul to Vladivostok, Russia. He was decorated by the Chinese government "for his role in famine relief in the wake of the Boxer Rebellion." Dismissed from his post on charges that were never substantiated, he returned to Chicago in 1906. He was a strong advocate of individualism and, therefore, believed in the migration of Negroes to another country or a separate state where they could have political and economic power. Although he did attend the second Niagara movement meeting, he never joined either the DuBois or Booker T. Washington groups. He seemed, however, to side more with DuBois.[81]

Greener's article in the *Review* dealt with the disfranchisement of Negro voters at the South Carolina Constitutional Convention in 1890 and was a backward glance at the supposedly idyllic town of Edgefield where so many racist acts were committed as Reconstruction gradually diminished and Negroes lost all political power.[82] In an editorial Reverdy praised the article and referred to Greener as a gentleman and scholar who at seventy-one years "sits in the afterglow of his brilliant career, clear-visioned, with voice and pen employed potentially in the higher things of mind and spirit." As secretary of the Grant Monument Association in New York, it was Greener who had chosen the simple but unique mausoleum on Morningside Heights in New York City.[83] Although Reverdy did not embrace all of Greener's philosophies, he admired his individualism and rich intellect and seemed to understand more than others that Greener's personality and regard for privacy prevented him from assuming more of a leadership position. There were times when he, like Greener, preferred his books and thoughts to the company of others.

The July 1915 issue of the *Review* had a "new dress," as Reverdy described it. It was larger, more "in harmony with that of the standard magazines" of the period, and provided more room for illustrations. It had a "face of type and form of page which [he] believed would prove more restful to the eyes."[84] The frontispiece carried a cameo picture of the deceased Bishop Henry McNeal Turner. He had died of a massive stroke on May 8 in Windsor, Ontario, on his way to an Annual Conference. Ironically, he had gotten his wish, not to die on American soil because of "its denial of citizenship rights to blacks." His body was transported to Atlanta, Georgia, where over 25,000 people viewed his body as it lay in state. He was buried in South View Cemetery on May 19.[85]

George W. Forbes, in "Within the Sphere of Letters," called Bishop Turner "the Grandest Old Roman of Them All" who, whether in church matters or civil rights, "was always fearless and forceful."[86] Reverdy referred to him as an "uncommon man," who had come on the stage when the most burning questions—slavery, emancipation, war, and freedom—were in the forefront. In all of these, Turner "played a leading role." He appealed to "the popular imagination" because "he said and did so many things that were dramatic and picturesque, and because he so boldly expressed and sought to realize the long-restrained aspirations and ideals of the great silent mass." Reverdy recognized Turner's contributions in the fight against lynchings, mob violence, unjust court decisions, and Jim Crow laws. No one had done more to create in newly freed blacks "self-confidence and the spirit of independent denominational life than he did." There would not be another Turner nor should there be. What was needed today were men who were uniquely fitted to meet contemporary issues as Turner had been to meet the issues of his day. Reverdy wished Bishop Benjamin F. Lee, who would take Turner's place as senior bishop, best wishes in his new responsibility. Near the end of the article, he defined the role of a bishop as "more than a holy man," but also a person of "broad culture and refinement, of liberal education and breadth of vision."[87] He hoped the Church would take these qualities into consideration when they elected new bishops in 1916.

The article "Boston's Fight against the Slanderous Play" and Ransom's editorial "The Birth of Race vs. 'The Birth of a Nation'" described the controversy the movie had caused in Boston, New York, and elsewhere. In the first article, the writer (name unlisted) outlined the events that began in Boston in April when *Birth of a Nation* was to open at the Tremont Theatre for the summer. Attempts were made by Butler R. Wilson, Moorfield Storey, and Mott Hallowell of the NAACP and James Monroe Trotter of the Equal Rights League to have the movie banned. During a picket of the theatre, Trotter and Rev. Arron Puller were arrested. The Board of Censors, however, would not revoke the license of *Birth of a Nation*.[88] Reverdy was glad that "the falsification of history and insidious appeals to passion and race prejudice" in the movie had "met a peremptory challenge at every turn." These protests were proof that Negroes still have friends among whites who were willing to fight for and with them and that the black race can and will unite in their fight against a common foe. Such plagues as this movie might be necessary to bring back those "elements of the race who are seeking to stand apart, or flee from it, save when they may secure some honor or emolument by their identification with it." In referring to the Negro's progress in the few years since slavery, he wrote: "Against the 'Birth of a Nation' we present the encouraging and inspiring spectacle of 'The Birth of a Race.'"[89]

On October 11, Reverdy received the following letter from Greener that reveals much about the personality of the man, his esteem for Ransom, and his attitude toward Booker T. Washington. It is also symbolic of the passing of an era.

> R.T.G. 5237 Ellis Ave., Chicago, Ill.
> Oct. 11, 1925
>
> My dear Ransom:
>
> I have just been clearing up the debris of my desk and have uncovered the enclosed two letters and an extract from an English Magazine, now two years old, all which I thought I had sent before my eastern trip.
>
> Perhaps I was so ashamed of crude, and rattling pens, I may have recopied them. The article contains a point, which shows a weak place, in the South's armor, through which we can make a break, and at any rate show disloyalty. Do you get the *Negro Farmer?* If not, you must. I am following up his editorials which are unique, and so strong and have so much good sense, "ginger" in them that they bode no assurance of his long continuance, in the Tuskegee camp, where just the reverse is true of the tracks from the bear's cave . . . 'No backward tracks'—most tracks of 'talented' inmates are said *always to lead back home* [Most criticism of Washington from his followers got back to him.]
>
> I have in mind for your Jan. number, an article on not, "A New Coon in Town," but "A New Prophet in Israel," with quotations from the prophet, Isaac Fisher. *This is between us, even if you accept my offer.* I am pleased with your number in general, but especially with your brave editorials on Church polity—and Forbes' excellent work. I am sending a copy of the article of Mrs. Hammond which I commented on. How about my subscription? Is it not near due or over-due.
>
> Hastily yrs. R. T. G.[90]

The October *Review* carried a picture on the frontispiece of Greener, and a lead article by him titled "Russia's Financial Position During the Russo-Japanese War—How She Builds Railroads." In it he told how the Great Siberian Transcontinental Railroad and the late Prince Khilkofff's "brilliant, experienced management" had prepared Russia for the war in 1904.[91] In addition there appeared the article sent to Reverdy by Greener with quotes from Mrs. L. D. Hammond's speech before the graduating class of Atlanta University. She had made a strong appeal for the elimination of hostility between whites and blacks who profess to be Christians. Blacks cannot love only their own race, she had said. Even haters love their own. As Christians, we are to love others into being loveable and in that way build, not just for one race, but for the race of man.[92]

Several articles in the edition had to do with the disturbances in Haiti. On July 28, President Vilbraum Gilliaum Sam was assassinated, and Americans occupied the capitol, Port-au-Prince, without any protest from the populace. During the revolution, headed by Dr. Rosolvo Bobo, hundreds of people were killed and decapitated, including the governor and president. The pride in the accomplishment of Toussaint L'Ouverture, Dessaline, Pation, Colombo, and Geffrad had suffered a dire setback. Many of the newspapers, including the *Boston Transcript*, wanted to know if America felt justified in intervening in Haiti when it had not intervened in Mexico that has been "in a perpetual state of anarchy for a half dozen years." Haiti's revolution was "a little above two months old."[93]

Reverdy lamented the eclipse of "the fairest pearl of the sea" (Haiti). While he did not object to a friendly nation going in to restore order, he assigned ulterior motives to America's interest in Haiti. He believed the United States wanted to "exploit the people and the resources. . . . President Woodrow Wilson's dilatory attitude toward Mexico is in poor contrast with the violent haste with which he sent armed forces into the harbors of Haiti," he said. He agreed that something drastic had to be done given the situation, but he "protested against the extinction of its sovereignty." He knew the white American too well. It was a matter of history that he had subjugated and coerced "all dark-hued humanity not subject to his will." Instead of the Haitians' using the sword against each other for "personal aggrandizement," they should "unsheathe the rusty sword of Toussaint . . . who used it against the enemies of liberty and freedom." He did not agree with those Negroes who said Haiti should be an American protectorate. A commission of American Negroes acting as representatives of the Haitian government "means only that if they fail to coincide with the prevailing American idea, their council would be ignored."[94]

In another editorial Reverdy turned his attention to "Ecclesiastical Imperialism," quoting frequently from Bishop Payne who spoke against overexpansion of the Church at home and abroad. Once again Reverdy pointed out how the Church has multiplied the number of missions, schools, and colleges to the extent that she is unable to equip them properly, much less to "adequately provide for their maintenance." On the Boards of Trustees of the schools there are "too many men all of one size. Each one is as large and as wise as the other, or thinks himself so to be." He suggested that we readjust our school management to meet the conditions of foundations who are able and willing to help financially. In terms of missions, in West Africa, the church cannot compete with the other denominations that are there. The money could better be spent on teachers and ministers at home and in other nearby places. Instead of fulfilling Payne's dream of mission work in Haiti, the church has "now become a part of the ruin of that unhappy isle." In the West Indies, the church should maintain what it has, but not try to expand by opening new churches that she can ill afford.[95]

At 4:15 Sunday morning, November 14, 1915, Booker T. Washington died at "The Oaks," his home in Tuskegee. He had carried out his "off-expressed wish when he said: 'I was born in the South; I have lived in the South and I expect to die and be buried in the South." On Tuesday, he was carried to Institute Chapel where he lay in state until Wednesday, the day of his funeral. Service was conducted by Chaplain John W. Whittaker and Dean G. L. Imes of the Phelp's Hall Bible School. The Tuskegee choir gave a moving rendition of the spiritual "We Shall Walk Through the Valley and Shadow of Death in Peace." On order of Mayor E. W. Thompson of Tuskegee, all businesses were closed during the funeral.[96]

The January 1916 *Review* carried Washington's article "The Mission Work of the Negro Church" written before his death. He had postulated, there is "no other place in which the Negro race can to better advantage begin to learn the lessons of self-direction and self-control than in the Negro Church."[97] In his memory, the issue also carried an article by George W. Forbes, "The Passing of Booker T. Washington," and an editorial by Reverdy; both men had opposed many of Washington's theories. Forbes wrote, "The coming of Booker T. Washington . . . with his Atlanta speech in this very same year of Douglass' death, was due more to the changed order of things than to the chance of a speech." Washington was not the creator of his age, but rather the expression of that age during which technical education and applied science at home and abroad were being hailed. Tuskegee Institute was a testament to his life's work. However, while his success "was monumental and beyond praise, his method of winning a hearing was not so universally approved." When he was criticized, he often blamed his people for their shortcomings rather than those who had wronged them. His libel suits against the *Guardian* management, the controversy in the Afro-American Council, and the protest at the Boston meeting at Zion Church had caused Washington to modify somewhat the way he stated his doctrine. There could be no doubt that his real doctrine of the need for industrial training for most Negroes was incontestable from the start. Industrial education classes in the colleges and universities of both America and Europe prove "the world-wide influence of this mighty apostle of industrial education." He and Douglass had similar aims, but the expression of those aims was in direct opposition. Douglass

> challenged your highest sense of justice . . . and aroused you to a sense of duty by his great mastery of human emotions. Washington summoned your calmer judgment. He asked you whether the whole question at issue was not unnecessary, or if it could not be better adjusted by returning to fundamentals.

After having praised and censored Washington, Forbes concluded: "No one can deny that his career was without parallel either at home or abroad."[98]

In his editorial, Ransom admitted that he was not one of Washington's disciples. "Yet like men of all the ages, I bathe in the sun and applaud the man who is earnestness on fire," he wrote. Like other critics of Washington, Reverdy would approach the subject with "great consideration and restraint." He called Washington a product of the times, "the high priest of the subordination of his race to the spirit of a materialistic age," as were Rockefeller and the Carnegies with their gospel of houses, land, and money. For Washington these things had to come before blacks' insistence on rights and absolute equality. He tried to show both races "the way out"; Negroes through industrial education and land-ownership, and whites by friendly cooperation. If this were done, the Negro would become the South's "greatest industrial asset. . . . His influence did more to restrain both races from releasing the rising tides of race antipathy than any other." How long the path of "least resistance" will be followed in the midst of "growing civic consciousness and material strength," he could not say. "But the mightiest hand that has laid hold of both races in the last thirty years, to lead them out, was the hand of BOOKER T. WASHINGTON."[99]

After four years as editor of the *The A.M.E. Church Review*, Reverdy was witnessing the passing of an era. The Negro's disillusionment with America's political leaders, the inevitability of the country being drawn into the war, the death of Washington, the growing influence of DuBois and other more radical leaders were creating *A New Negro*, as Alain Locke would define the race. Within a few years, the Negro Renaissance would burst forth, artistically expressing a new militancy, racial pride, and identification with Africa. Through his *Review*, Reverdy became a significant and powerful voice in this awakening.

CHAPTER 7

From Editor to Bishop, 1916–1924

> But the liberal deviseth liberal things; and by liberal things shall he stand.
> Isaiah 32:8

At the same time the Allies in Europe were engaged in a deadly encounter for survival and Wilson was running for a second term with the slogan "He kept us out of the war," the A.M.E. Church convened its Twenty-fifth General Conference at Mother Bethel in Philadelphia, May 3–21, 1916. "The galleries [were] packed with lay members, some of whom had made a pilgrimage from points as far distant as Texas and Oklahoma, Canada, Africa and the Isles of the Sea." They had come to visit "the birthplace of African Methodism and participate in the celebration of its centennial."[1] Reverdy was one of the twelve general officers who joined with the other 585 delegates, not only to celebrate, but to deliberate Church policy and the condition of the race. Benjamin F. Lee, who had replaced the deceased H. M. Turner as senior bishop, called the conference to order; and the delegates settled down to hear Bishop H. B. Parks deliver the Quadrennial Sermon from the timely subject, "The Miracle of Continuance."[2]

On the morning of the second day, Bishop L. J. Coppin read the Episcopal Address affirming how fitting it was for the conference to be held at Mother Bethel because the name Bethel had come down to A.M.E.s "with curious legend and sacred traditions." This spot, he continued, has been "hallowed by the prayers and tears of those who fought the legal battles which followed the first attempt to throw off the yoke of ecclesiastical bondage," from the Methodist Church. Being here causes us to "breathe anew the spirit which actuated our fathers and mothers and nerved them to undertake [the task that] less heroic souls would have considered impossible."[3] Among the recommendations contained in the Episcopal Address that had particular relevance for Reverdy was that the publishing house should remain in Philadelphia and "be as originally intended, a Book Concern."[4]

After the reading of the Episcopal Address, the bishops, general officers, college presidents, and deans led the delegates to the tomb of Richard Allen. As they filed by silently, they laid flowers on the sarcophagus until it became sepulchred beneath a mound of flowers.[5] That evening at the public reception, the Conference was welcomed by Pennsylvania Governor Martin G. Brumbaugh and Mayor Thomas B. Smith of Philadelphia.[6]

Tuesday, May 16, Reverdy and Joseph Gomez spent time together discussing Gomez's experiences at Shelly Bay, Bermuda, his first pastorate. That evening the two men went to the Convention Center to see the pageant, "The Star of Ethiopia," put on by the Horizon Guild under the management of W. E. B. DuBois. Over one thousand participants from various denominations, civic organizations, clubs, and fraternal organizations dramatized this review of Negro history. Its purpose was to offset D. W. Griffith's movie, *Birth of a Nation*, which distorted the Negro character and depicted him as a primitive barbarian.[7] Both of the men found the spectacle to be highly moving and expertly produced.

Returning to political matters on May 18, the Conference elected W. W. Beckett and I. N. Ross as bishops on the second ballot.[8] Ross had been pastor of the Church in Oberlin when Reverdy was a student there thirty years before, and Reverdy had taught in his Sunday School. Reverdy said at that time Ross's charge was considered to be the "starvation appointment of the conference." Now by reason of his "natural abilities and intrinsic worth," Ross had risen to the highest position the Church could offer.[9]

After defeating his closest competitor, Professor C. G. Garrett, Reverdy was again elected editor of *The A.M.E. Church Review* the next day. He was to admit later that Garrett had "caught him napping," by amassing quite a few votes. Reverdy had been so confident that the Church would reward him for a job well done "that [he] forgot to follow [his] grandmother's advice— 'Son, remember it is always dangerous to be safe.'"[10]

Reverdy and Emma returned home satisfied that some positive things had occurred at the Conference. The only negative factor in evidence was that of "sectionalism," the South against the North. A church that is both national and international cannot afford to allow sectionalism to play a part in its elections, he warned. Nevertheless, "amid much noise and confusion the Conference never permitted itself to be stampeded, and, if at times it seemed to lose its head, it never lost its temper."[11]

Frequently the NAACP *Crisis* and *The A.M.E. Church Review* worked together on important issues and were sold as a package deal. Both journals highly publicized the hideous practices of lynching. To assist the NAACP in its antilynching financial drive, the July 1916 *Review* carried an article and graphic pictures by Roy Nash of the lynching and burning of Jesse Washington, a Negro, from Waco, Texas. Within forty-eight hours of the burning, the NAACP had sent a special investigator to the city who reported that on May 15 with fifteen hundred spectators crowded in the courtroom and over two thousand waiting outside, the jury found Washington guilty of rape and murder. Before the judge could pronounce sentence, the crowd took Jesse out of the courtroom, put a chain in his mouth so he would not choke too soon, and hung him.

"When the boy's clothes had been cut up and distributed as souvenirs there were not enough pieces to go around, so somebody cut off an ear for his keepsake." According to the *Waco Times Herald,* "fingers, ears, pieces of clothing, toes and other parts of the Negro's body were cut off by members of the mob that had crowded to the scene." Over ten thousand people watched as they set Jesse's body on fire. Later, some boys lassoed what was left of the corpse and dragged it all over town. The NAACP was soliciting $10,000 so it could send a lobby to Washington to persuade Congress that an antilynch law was essential. The *Review* announced that contributions were to be sent to Oswald Garrison Villard, treasurer of the NAACP. Reverdy was incensed by this rape that was a flagrant disregard for law and for human dignity. He hoped that those who read the article would contribute generously to the NAACP Fund.[12]

To demonstrate the A.M.E. Church's abhorrence of lynching, Reverdy included in the *Review* a resolution that had been adopted by the 1916 General Conference in the form of a letter to "Mr. President and Members of the United States Congress." The letter emphasized the "growing spirit of mob violence and disregard for Constitutional law" of which the Negro was usually the victim. It strongly urged Congress to pass a law "making lynching a federal Crime."[13]

In the October 1916 *Review,* Reverdy again turned his attention to the upcoming presidential contest. As had been predicted the Democrats had chosen Woodrow Wilson for a second term, and the Republicans, "needing somebody who would draw Bull Moose Progressives back into the fold," turned to Justice Charles Evans Hughes who had made a progressive record as governor of New York from 1907 to 1910.[14] Reverdy titled one of his editorials "The Old Black Mule," the same mule on which the Republican Party had ridden to power for forty years. "Now that the Republican Party is seeking to regain political ascendancy," he wrote, it was trying to win the progressive and independent votes and to "find the old black mule—the Negro vote—standing hitched where it left him tied." What should the Old Black Mule do now? His answer was: "Let him kick, refusing to be saddled, bridled and mounted politically until approached in the proper spirit, and until there is open an avowed assurance of just and liberal treatment."[15] To Reverdy's regret, Wilson's promises of peace and progressivism brought him victory in the November election by nine million popular votes to Hughes's 8.5 million.[16]

Politics was not the only subject occupying Reverdy attention in 1916. Sometime during the year, he and John R. Hawkins compiled and edited a *Handbook of the A.M.E. Church* that carried general information about the various districts and churches. It was published by the A.M.E. Sunday School Union in Nashville.[17] In September Reverdy took time from his writing to lecture at West Virginia State College located a few miles from Charleston. Afterward he attended the small West Virginia Annual Conference where

Bishop C. T. Shaffer presided. Reverdy noted that "the rough topography" of the state, "and the strenuous industrial life of its people called for a ministry of virile and rugged type." He concluded that those ministers who were interested in social Christianity, as he was, would find it to be "a most inviting field." On November 15, he attended the North Carolina Conference where Bishop J. A. Johnson dealt with men and measures "in a straight forward manner, sometimes to the point of bluntness." Nevertheless, Kitrell, the A.M.E. college there, was thriving under his leadership, and its debts were about to be liquidated. Although Reverdy had wanted to attend three of the annual conferences in South Carolina, he was able to attend only the one in Lancaster where the ministers had criticized the business management of the *Review.* He explained to the ministers that the irregularities in the subscriptions were not the fault of the magazine but of their conference publication representative.[18]

While visiting the South Georgia Conference at Fitzgerald, Reverdy was apprised of the "great unrest among the people in Georgia" that resulted in a large migration. The bishop of the district, Joseph S. Flipper, was openly advising the people to go north if "better industrial opportunities were offered." Because of the number of people moving and, consequently, the loss of church membership, Bishop Flipper transferred seventeen ministers from the Southwest Georgia Conference and nine from the South Georgia Conference to northern churches. Reverdy's experiences at the various southern conferences gave him a better understanding of the changes blacks were experiencing and helped him determine the future focus of his journal. Much of his January 1917 issue would deal with the great Negro exodus from the South.[19]

Sometime during the year, the Ransoms had bought a home in Oceanport, New Jersey, as well as maintained a residence in New York City. Reverdy called Oceanport "a little village of about five hundred inhabitants." Six years later, he was to describe his village by the sea in poetic terms:

> It lies diagonally back of Sandy Hook, is in front of Pleasure Bay and is a suburb of Long Branch, New Jersey. Through it winds the waters of the beautiful Shrewsbury River, teeming with fish, eels, crabs and clams. In Spring time the mating robins sing in the maples and cherry trees beneath the window. . . . Winter is no less beautiful than summer here. The ice carnivals for those who indulge in the sport of skating are quite as joyous as bathing on the beaches in Summer time. Winter and Summer, the glorious music of the ever changing sea is always there, while at night the rustle of the tides, sometimes like the movement of Autumn leaves, or the wind blowing through a forest of pines, wafts one to sleep in a lullaby soft and gentle as that of a mother to the babe upon her breast.[20]

Among Reverdy's papers kept by his third wife, Georgia Myrtle Teal, was a journal. It has entries for January 1, 1917–February 7 and then skips to July 2–13.[21] The

Reverdy (*standing at center*) with other A.M.E. ministers, ca. 1917. To his left is Bishop John Hurst.

journal reflects the rather quiet, homey life the Ransoms pursued at Oceanport, interrupted only by Reverdy's frequent speaking engagements away. Because it also gives insight into their personalities, the journal has been quoted rather extensively.

Reverdy referred to the house in Oceanport as a cottage, but a picture of the structure shows it to be a large rambling farmhouse with a porch that extends around the structure. On the grounds, the Ransoms raised vegetables, horses, fowl, and pigs. Both he and Emma seemed to have had an affinity for country living.[22]

Many of the early entries of the journal have to do with the inclement weather that, while poetically beautiful, had its inconveniences. January 1, 1917, was the coldest day ever recorded, Reverdy wrote, thirteen degrees below zero. The entire water system in the house, including the pump, was frozen. On his fifty-seventh birthday, January 4, Reverdy spent a quiet day writing letters while his wife worked at thawing the pump. For dinner, Emma cooked a special meal, as she always did on his birthday; this time she prepared a goose. Reverdy, who insisted on ceremony for special occasions, dressed in a new suit. On January 5 he regretted the delay in getting out the *Review,* noting that only part of the proofs had been read. The weather was moderate, and he was pleased to have received a ton of oats, pig and horse feed. On Sunday the weather was pleasant and, as was their custom, the Ransoms went to the A.M.E. Church in nearby Long Branch. Overnight the rain changed to sleet and made walking almost impossible. Nevertheless, Reverdy bought two guineas at five cents each, worked on the horse's mange [probably mane] and, in the evening, prepared to go to Philadelphia to see about the *Review*.[23]

January 8 found him first in New York visiting friends on West 35th Street, then leaving New York at 5 P.M. for Philadelphia. The next day was spent reading proofs at the unheated *Review* office and soliciting a promise from the printers that the publication would be out by January 19. Arriving at Long Branch at 8:33 A.M. he traveled back to Oceanport, reassured that the magazine would soon be ready for distribution.[24]

On January 11 Emma went to New York for the annual meeting of the YWCA. (Throughout her life, she continued to be active in that organization.) Reverdy spent the day mailing ninety-seven copies of his editorials to A.M.E.Z., C.M.E., and A.M.E. officials.[25] In these editorials he credited "lynching, terrorism, oppression, robbery, deception and fraud in business transaction, meager and inadequate school facilities, unjust application of the laws and lack of protection by the courts, the delay of political and civil rights," plus the promises of higher-paying jobs in the North as the chief causes of the exodus of Negroes from the South. The war in Europe had opened opportunities in the large northern industrial centers; but the responsibility for the social, moral, and spiritual welfare of these migrants (most of whom had come from rural areas) will rest with the churches, he said.[26]

In the evening Reverdy's neighbors, a Dr. Rankin and his granddaughters, came by in the evening and reported that the severe wind storm the night before had blown down the doctor's large cedar tree. On Sunday, January 13, despite the bitter cold and strong wind, Emma and Reverdy went to New York where he preached (probably at Simon of Cyrene) in the afternoon. After eating dinner at the church, they returned on the 8:30 train only to learn that one of their neighbors, Mrs. Johnson, had died of pneumonia. Reverdy conducted her funeral on Wednesday at her house and then buried her in the Long Branch church cemetery. The rest of the week was spent entertaining guests who were treated to Emma's special duck dinner on Sunday.[27]

On January 22, Reverdy drove through a severe snowstorm to Long Branch where he bought a calf from a Mr. Bullock for $25—$10 on account, $15 due. (It is interesting how precisely Reverdy records his spendings.) Three days later, he returned to Philadelphia only to find that the *Review* had "not been collected [collated] for binding," because Dr. R. R. Wright was home sick with "facial paralysis on his left side." Reverdy did not think his condition was serious. He left for Norfolk, Virginia, at 11.25 P.M. The train crossed the Chesapeake Bay, and from his upper berth he could see heavy fields of ice. But the weather in Norfolk was mild. He stayed in the parsonage with his friend, Rev. S. S. Morris. Reverdy spent the day walking about the city watching crowds of sailors who reminded him that America might soon be drawn into the war. On Sunday, January 27, Reverdy spoke at the 11 A.M. service under the auspices of St. John's

Brotherhood on the subject "The Mind of Christ" and on "Boundaries of Liberty" at the 7:30 P.M. service. There was only a "fair sized audience" due to the overcast and chilly weather. He was paid $25 for his participation. At 5 P.M. Reverdy left by boat for Philadelphia so he could work on the *Review* until it was time for him to catch the train to Boston. While in Boston he visited Clarence White, the famous musician, and the editors, Forbes and Trotter. He spoke for a real estate concern at St. Paul Baptist Church and received a compensation of $36. At midnight he left for New York.[28]

Reverdy stayed in New York until 4 P.M. and then caught a train for New Brunswick to fulfill another speaking engagement. He arrived back in Oceanport about noon the next day. In the evening, Emma went to New York, leaving Jerry (last name unknown) and Reverdy to fend for themselves, and Reverdy to do the cooking. On February 2, when Emma returned, the first installment of the January *Review* had arrived. The following day, Reverdy preached for the Bridge Street Church in Brooklyn, New York, which was celebrating its 100th anniversary. His subject was "The Beauty of God." The next day was spent in Manhattan, conferring with John M. Royal whose United Civic League was urging Reverdy to run for congress from the 21st District in New York. Reverdy's only written comment was, "We shall see."[29]

Back in Oceanport, the thermometer read four below zero. Emma was not well, and the two spent most of the time sitting by the fire. February 6, Reverdy writes that he made "tentative arrangements with a brother Robinson to farm [the] place. Advanced him $3. Weather moderating." Reverdy describes the next day as bright and warm causing the melting snow to turn to slush. He found many frozen potatoes in the cellar. That afternoon, he bought one half-ton of coal and fifty pounds of grain.[30] Because this is the last entry until July, it would seem that Reverdy and Emma were preparing to leave Oceanport until summer.

Despite Wilson's campaign promise to keep America out of the war, on March 10, 1917, his cabinet "unanimously endorsed a declaration of war and the following day the president called a special session of Congress." As Reverdy had suspected, the sinking of five American merchant vessels by German submarines made it impossible for the country to remain a nonparticipant. After the Senate passed the war resolution, 82 to 6, and the House, 373 to 50, on Good Friday, April 6, Wilson signed the document. The Selective Service Act of May 18, 1917, dictated that all men between twenty-one and thirty (later eighteen to forty) must register for service.[31] Negroes supposed that this included them. If so, in what capacity? Would the army remain segregated, and the Negro soldier be used only in service jobs? Many asked should the Negro have to beg to participate in a war where he might be killed, or return only to encounter the same racist policies? At first, Negro volunteers were only allowed in the four black regiments already established. When the draft began, senators like James K. Vardaman of Mississippi wanted them exempt from the army altogether. The government finally decided that Negroes should be allowed to join the armed forces but must be trained in separate units.[32]

The April issue of the *Review* made clear Reverdy's stand. In "One Country and One Flag," he urged Negroes to defend their country.

> Let those Negroes who are reluctant to follow the flag in case of war, because in time of peace it has not afforded them full protection with equality of opportunity, remember that while under the American flag we were held as slaves, under it we were also made free men and citizens, clothed with a constitutional liberty beyond that enjoyed by the people of any other country.

Americans have one common fate and must together uphold the flag, he said, until "all distinctions of race and color shall be lost in a common patriotism and fraternity."[33] Like Reverdy, W. E. B. DuBois also supported the war effort. He wrote in the *Crisis:* "Let us, while this war lasts, forget our special grievances and close our ranks shoulder to shoulder with our white fellow citizens and the allied nations that are fighting for democracy."[34] Both men grudgingly accepted the segregated Negro officers training school set up by the military in Des Moines, Iowa. They reasoned that if a separate school was the only way Negroes could become officers, it should be established and supported.[35]

In May, Reverdy traveled to Atlanta a few days after a great fire had swept the city destroying about seventy-five blocks, including the homes of black middle-class property owners and A.M.E. leaders. Morris Brown, the A.M.E. college, had been lucky. Only the hospital attached to it had been destroyed. Reverdy had come to examine the damage, hear Bishop John Hurst deliver the Baccalaureate Sermon, and to address the literary societies. He chose as his subject "The Measure of a Man," declaring that civilization should have one standard of measurement and one ideal for everyone. All except the most noble and best standards should be discarded. At the commencement exercises, he and Bishop Hurst received honorary doctor of law degrees. From Atlanta, Reverdy went to Durham to deliver the graduation address at Whitted Grammar School, staying at the home of W. G. Pearson, the principal. To Reverdy, Durham was "a shining example, in many respects, of the height of substantial attainment reached by the race." Pearson took him to the North Carolina Mutual and Provident Association, the largest Negro life insurance company in the world. In Durham, there was also a substantial bank owned and operated by Negroes.[36]

June 1 found Reverdy in Columbia, South Carolina, where he preached the baccalaureate sermon at Allen University. Dr. R. W. Mance, a personal friend, was serving his first year as president. In time, Mance would be elected secretary treasurer of the A.M.E. Church. In all of his travels, Reverdy enjoyed visiting the church's colleges most. He understood their importance, particularly in light of the discrimination so prevalent in most white universities. He found it ironic that "in its effort to fill its quota of [college trained] colored young men for the officers training camp at Des Moines, Iowa . . . South Carolina presented the paradox of spending only $1.90 a year for the education of colored youth." John A. Gregg, distinguished president of Edward Waters College, delivered the address to the literary societies at Allen from the theme "Twentieth Century Ideals." Reverdy found the address to be "scholarly and inspiring."[37] Though the two men were different in style and personality, he and Gregg would develop strong bonds of friendship. Whereas Gregg was quiet and deliberate, Ransom was fiery and passionate. Nevertheless, both were highly intelligent and loved to delve beneath the surface of an idea.

From South Carolina, Reverdy traveled to Wilberforce. Despite its large enrollment this year, only 100 students stayed for commencement. Most had gone, either to enlist in the armed forces or to work in the war industry. Chicago was well represented among the dignitaries by Bishop L. J. Coppin, who preached the baccalaureate sermon; Dr. A. J. Carey, who delivered the address celebrating the quartocentennial of Payne Seminary; the Honorable Richard T. Greener, who gave the commencement address; and Dr. Daniel H. Williams, who dedicated the new campus Tawawa Hospital.[38] Williams spoke of the significant pioneer efforts in Negro Church life and education expended by the A.M.E. Church and its influence in the establishment of Provident Hospital in Chicago, "the first colored hospital and training school in the United States." He noted that in 1917 there were now ninety-five colored hospitals in the United States. He hoped that Tawawa Hospital would "add renewed vigor to the awakening of Negro leadership in medicine and for the very highest forms of professional and research service for the social advance of [the] race."[39]

On June 3 Reverdy attended a memorial sponsored by the NAACP in honor of the late Senator Joseph B. Foraker at Emery Auditorium in Cincinnati, Ohio. Reverdy had first heard Foraker speak at Wilberforce when he was a student. Now Reverdy and Gilchrist Steward of New York were asked to be guest speakers for the occasion. Reverdy based his speech on remarks given by the senator in 1901 at the Ohio State Republican Convention.

> Constituted authority must find a way to stop disfranchisement and lynching, or the government will deserve to lose support of a race that has shed its blood for our flag in every war and upon almost every field where it has waved.

When Reverdy finished applying Foraker's sentiments to the present status of blacks now serving their country, the assemblage of over three thousand gave him a standing ovation. He spent the last week of June in Chicago. On the tenth he preached at Bethel, which was filled to capacity, and at night at the Institutional Church "to an audience that over-flowed to the galleries."[40]

Reverdy and his stepfather, George Warner Ransom,
ca. 1916. Courtesy Ruth Ransom, Xenia, Ohio.

In his Oceanport journal, Reverdy writes that on July 2 he borrowed from the Citizens
National Bank $150 for three months. He does not indicate the purpose of the loan,
but it may have helped to take care of his father's medical expenses. Evidently, his
father had been ill for some time. On July 8, Reverdy received word from his mother
that George W. Ransom, the only father he had ever known, had died at 5 A.M. at the
age of seventy-five. Reverdy left at once for Cambridge, Ohio, to comfort Harriet and
attend the funeral on July 7. On July 8, Reverdy took over the Ransom account at the
Cambridge Building and Loan Company ($250) so he could settle his father's debts.
Funeral expenses came to $132.85. Of that amount, Reverdy paid H. M. Stephens, the
undertaker, $100 on account, and gave the remainder to his mother. The funeral bal-
ance was to be paid by August 20. After making sure his mother was all right, he

returned to Oceanport and Emma, July 11. In the very last journal entry, Reverdy says he "paid Jerry in full up to July 7." This would seem to indicate that Jerry was a farm-hand rather than a relative. No further information about Jerry is available.[41]

Reverdy's editorials in the *Review* continued to reflect his concern for the Southern Negroes who were migrating to urban centers. He felt that the bishops of the A.M.E., A.M.E.Z., and C.M.E. denominations were "letting slip from them one of the greatest opportunities" ever presented by allowing the National League on Urban Conditions and other philanthropic agencies to provide more assistance to these migrants than the Negro churches. He pleaded with the three denominations to "look beyond the boundaries of your Episcopal Districts; look beyond the boundaries of your denominations, and behold the crying needs of your people and your opportunities for co-operation in the work of the kingdom of God." If ever there was a need for a collective institutional approach to religion and a social gospel, it is during these war years with its radical changes and human needs.[42]

In the late summer and early fall of 1917, Reverdy was disturbed to learn of two of the bloodiest race riots to date in the United States. In East St. Louis in late summer, "white strikers [employed in] war work killed and mobbed Negro workingmen." One hundred and twenty-three Negroes were killed; six hundred were driven from their burning homes. Nine white men were imprisoned for five-to-fifteen years; eleven white men, imprisoned for one year; eighteen white men, fined; and ten colored men, imprisoned for fourteen years. That September, Negroes in the 25th Infantry stationed in Houston, "goaded and insulted, by white citizens and officials, suddenly went wild and 'shot up' the town." Thirteen of the soldiers were sentenced to be hung, forty one to life in prison for the deaths of eighteen whites; forty others, imprisoned. According to the NAACP, "The Negro soldiers, desperate over the brutalities of the Houston police and the taunts and insults of white civilians," had exploded and retaliated for the injustices they had experienced. Negroes all over the country felt that the punishments were too harsh, and the NAACP continued to fight for their cause. Nevertheless, before Christmas the thirteen soldiers were hung. That same year, in other parts of the country, forty-seven Negroes had been lynched without a trial. Given the inequity of American justice, many called the punishment of the thirteen Negro soldiers "a legal lynching."[43]

Reverdy did not feel that the "Court Martial which tried them and [the] government which stood back of it, however just the decision, acted in . . . an impartial manner." Punishment for crimes should be the same for all people. The riot, he said, was not the "result of undisciplined [colored] men." The citizens of Houston had warned the government not to send the Negro troops to that city. "On their arrival they were subjected to insult, humiliation and assault by police officials and others." Reverdy did not doubt that the East St. Louis "massacre"... had had "its effect on their already burning sense of injustice and outrage." In addition, there had been several instances where black citizens had been shot down in cold blood by white soldiers. To his knowledge, not one had been court-martialed or punished. Second, in the Houston case there was no announcement of the verdict. It seems the military board acted independently, and the condemned men were never given a chance to appeal to the War Department before they were hung. This might have made a difference because the War Department appeared to be making an effort to "give a square deal" to colored soldiers. One positive step was the appointment of Emmett J. Scott (a Negro) as advisor to Secretary of War Baker on matters relating to Negro soldiers. Reverdy believed he would be instrumental in getting fairer treatment for black soldiers.[44]

In 1918, Reverdy decided to accept the United Civic League's invitation to run as an independent candidate for congress representing New York's Twenty-first District. The league had been organized by John M. Royall in 1913 for the purpose of launching "an aggressive campaign for civic justice and elective representation" for Negroes. Until that time the late Bishop W. B. Derrick, Charles W. Anderson, and Bishop Alexander Walters had been considered the political leaders of the race. The Twenty-first Congressional District included Harlem, where approximately 120,000 Negroes lived. At first, the United Civic League went to the Republican Party and asked that Ransom become their candidate. Given the splendid record black soldiers were making abroad and at home in the war industries and

> since the unexpired Congressional term... was but for a few months, [the League] felt that the Republican organization would see the wisdom of making the concession, thus heartening the people at home and sending a thrill of hope to the race throughout the nation.

The Republican Party refused until they realized that the league would nominate Ransom as an independent and, therefore, take votes away from the Republican candidate. Seeking to placate Ransom and the League, the convention gave him a complimentary vote. Charles W. Anderson and Gilchrist Steward nominated Ransom, who received twenty-six votes. Meanwhile, on the same night at the Palace Casino, led by the United Civic League, more than five hundred people, including women who now had the right to vote in New York state, nominated Ransom for congress as an independent. They determined to petition for the necessary signatures so his name could appear on the ballot. [45]

From the beginning, there were those who attempted to persuade Reverdy not to run. In *Pilgrimage*, he relates how Johnny Lyons (campaign manager for the Republican candidate, John A. Bolles) promised to send Ransom to the state senate if he dropped out of the race. When Ransom turned him down, he offered to give him five thousand dollars. "To this [Ransom] replied, 'I can neither be bluffed, bribed, or bought.'"[46]

Most of the New York newspapers took an interest in the race. The *New York Sun*, of February 27, reported that the contest promised to be lively if Ransom stayed in the race. Bolles was praying that Ransom would drop out, but the Democratic candidate, Jerome F. Donovan, was "holding his breath for fear something [would] happen to put Ransom out." Many Republicans felt that Tammany Hall was behind Ransom. Although Ransom had not yet filed a petition, he did speak as a candidate at the Women Suffrage meeting, and the League was sending out letters headed "On to Washington." Ransom had little chance of winning the race, but his running "might mean the defeat of the Republican Candidate," the reporter concluded.[47] The same day the *New York Post* reported that although most Negroes belonged to the Republican Party, "colored voters [had] decided to bolt the nomination of John A. Bolles and to run in his place the Rev. Reverdy C. Ransom."[48]

The *New York Post* asked Ransom what he would do if elected to Congress. He sent a statement that he also repeated in the April *Review.* First he would support "every just proposal designed to enable the nation to throw the full strength of all its resources into the war" until its goals were realized. He considered his candidacy to be "a challenge and a test, to the just and righteous decision" that caused the nation to send its soldiers to the battlefields of Europe— "to the end that all free peoples shall control their own government." His election would permit twelve million Negroes "to become articulate in the legislative halls of the government." In Congress, he would resist any "suppression" or "compromise" on questions relating "to political and social justice." He would uphold the Constitution and all its amendments. He would not "stress the race question by flaunting in the foreground its many irritating features," but he would strive to make lynching a federal crime because the states refused to prosecute the offenders. Whether elected or not, he and others of his group would stand "ucompromisingly for justice to all classes, races and sexes."[49]

The former actress and suffragette Kathrine Clemmons (now Mrs. Howard Gould) was so impressed by his statement that she came to Harlem to speak at Mother Zion Church on 136th Street in support of Reverdy's candidacy. She told her two-thousand listeners that they must go to the polls, vote for Ransom, and not let whites "beguile them" into doing otherwise. Not to cast a vote for him would brand them traitors to their race. The election of Ransom would go a long way toward creating a better democracy, and the Negro voter should attempt to break up the solid South and bring "more enlightenment and political privileges to the Negroes there." Later she was to tell reporters that she knew Ransom "would be the last man to stand for disruptive theories of racial equality," but that as a member of Congress he would "give expression to a protest against injustice to his race in which the best of the white race could join with the . . . Negroes of the country."[50] One wonders what she meant by "disruptive theories of racial equality," and how she interpreted Ransom's insistence of social justice.

In order to appear on the printed ballot, Ransom was required to have 2,245 signatures of registered voters. The League turned in over 2,600 names. James W. Adams, a Republican, petitioned Justice Erlanger of the New York Supreme Court to throw out Ransom's petition "on the ground that many of the signatures were not signed by the men whose names they purport to be." On March 1 Justice Erlanger ruled:

> I think from the proof as it has been presented up to this stage of the trial, that there is sufficient [evidence] to justify the granting of this motion to strike out the petition of the Rev. Dr. Ransom, and the motion to strike out the certificate and not to print the name is granted, solely upon the ground that the number of signatures required by law have not been furnished.

But he did acquit Ransom of "any attempt or effort to infringe or violate the law." Ransom addressed the court, thanking the justice for his "spirit of fairness," but regretted "that those who have had charge of the matter for my interests," he said, "have come short through reasons that have been brought to the surface in the midst of these investigations."[51] It seems, in their attempt to elect Ransom, some League members had used unorthodox means to secure signatures on the petition. Nevertheless, Ransom decided to continue to run and asked his followers to write in his name on the ballot at the election March 5.[52]

From the start, Reverdy's ten-day campaign was seriously handicapped by lack of funds and organization. He reported that the only voluntary contributions came from Bishop John Hurst of the South Florida A.M.E. Conference, Bishop W. H. Heard, Dr. J. W. Rankin, and Miss Elizabeth C. Carter of New Bedford, Massachusetts.[53] Nevertheless on March 5 nearly thirteen hundred people wrote Ransom's name on the ballot, all of which were thrown out as void except 465 because the election official alleged there were errors in "marking the ballot or mistakes in writing [Ransom's] name."[54]

Although he did not win the election, Reverdy's running had served "to awaken Negroes in the North . . . to strike for the same things" he had attempted by making a run for Congress. In addition, it alerted the Republican Party in New York that "they may not hope for success in the Congressional Elections next fall without giving respectful consideration to [the Negro's] just demand." Finally, it had driven "a wedge into the gnarled and hitherto unsplitable political oak of New York which will open a way for Negro voters to have representative voice in their government."[55]

In the July 1918 issue of *Crisis,* W. E. B. DuBois focused his attention on the war. In an article, "Close Ranks" he stated that the Negro had "no ordinary interest in the outcome" of the War. German power would mean death to "the aspirations of Negroes and all darker races for equality." He urged that Negroes "forget their special grievances and close ranks shoulder to shoulder with [their] white fellow citizens and allied nations."[56] Reverdy commented on the article in the editorial section of the October 1918 *Review.* Close ranks, he said, "on the battlefields of Europe against the brutal aggression of a common foe." But he also insisted that we "stand up and fight with relentless determination [at home] the same spirit of tyranny and oppression which our brave boys are facing abroad." This would include standing with President Wilson and Moorfield Storey of the NAACP "against lynching and all forms of lawlessness."[57] (In late July, Wilson had finally come out against mob violence although he never used the word "Negro.") In terms of "sinking" minor differences until the war ended, Reverdy said that Negroes would stop protesting when prohibition advocates, women's suffragettes, and organized labor are willing to wait until after the war.[57]

Reverdy devoted his January 1919 issue of the *Review* to the contributions of Negroes serving in the armed forces. In the lead article, "Facts Concerning the Activities of the Negro in Work of the World War," the reader was supplied with data from Emmett J. Scott, special assistant to the secretary of war. He reported that as of October 1918, 400,000 Negroes were in the military. They had entered the war with four regiments, the 9th and 10th Calvary and the 24th and 25th Infantry of the regular army. "In the National Guard (as it was formerly known) made up of units from several states . . . the race also had about 10,000." When the first draft had come in 1917, 737,628 registered, 8 percent of the nation's total registration. Although there had been few commissioned officers in the original Army, the highest in rank being Col. Charles Young of Ohio, now there were more than fourteen hundred Negro officers. Among the Negro schools listed under the Student Army Training Corps were Howard, Lincoln, Fisk, Atlanta, Morehouse, Wiley, Talladega, Virginia Union, Wilberforce Universities, and Meharry Medical School. Under this program, young men eighteen years and over who wanted a college education could study military science and tactics along with their academic courses. In July of 1918, the two-thousand colored nurses who had registered with the Red Cross "would be accepted for service in the army."[58]

Another article in the January *Review,* a reprint of a report by Ralph W. Tyler, special war correspondent on the staff of General Pershing, told of the heroic exploits of Negroes in Verdun, No Man's Land, Belleau Woods, Chateau-Thierry, Soissons, the Vesle, Argonne, Champagne, and other areas in France. Tyler reported that "the French folk liked the colored boys, and felt highly honored at the way [they] learned the French language."[59] A third article by Imogene Burch outlined the activity of colored women in industry, noting not only their contributions in factories, but also in "brick yards, lumber yards, [on] railroads," and how they cleaned taxis, handled freight, and did other heavy forms of labor.[60]

Following the signing of the armistice in November 1918, Woodrow Wilson's arrived in Paris in December to the applause of millions who believed his presence at the Peace Conference would ensure a lasting peace.[61] In a January editorial, Reverdy had his own views concerning the possibility of such a peace. "Amid the din of the pandemonium" that accompanied the announcement that an "armistice had been arranged and peace was in sight," he lamented that Negroes could not rejoice with other Americans because of old wounds before the war, and the injustices during the war that often led to violence. Although whites in America and Europe might fight over blacks, they would never fight for them, he said. He could not cry "Peace" when there was no "Peace" and there would be none until peace was accompanied with justice, righteousness, and brotherhood at home as well as abroad.[62]

The year 1919 was a nadir for Negroes in the United States. Race riots broke out in Longview, Texas; Washington, D.C.; Chicago, Illinois (38 dead, 537 injured); Knoxville, Tennessee; Omaha, Nebraska. Negroes fought back. Seventy-six Negroes were lynched, "the highest annual figure in eleven years."[63] Reverdy said 1919 marked the passing of "old things." The riots illustrated that the Negro had come a long way in the past three hundred years.

From the naked, helpless barbarian he then was, from the helpless shackled slave he remained for two hundred fifty years, from the cringing, hunted victim of the night-rider, the Ku Klux, the lyncher and the mob, he has been for more than fifty years, we find him at last fearlessly facing the mob and courageously defending his life, his home, his children and his wife. "Old things have passed away."[64]

Negro soldiers returned from the war with new attitudes. Having been treated with respect abroad, especially in France, they were determined not to return to their old status in America. As Reverdy put it:

Never again can these men be awed by a man simply because he has a white face, or is armed with a gun, or menacingly threatens them with superior numbers. All of these conditions they have met and triumphantly overcome by repeatedly vanquishing the best drilled soldiers in the world.[65]

W. E. B. DuBois warned in the *Crisis* that despite the contributions of Negroes in the war, America still lynches, disfranchises, encourages ignorance, steals from Negroes, and insults them. "We return," he wrote. "We return from Fighting. We return fighting. Make way for Democracy! We saved it in France, and by the Great Jehovah, we will save it in the United States of America, or know the reason why."[66] Seemingly he was having second thoughts about his "Close Ranks" article. So objectionable did the

Justice Department find DuBois's remarks that it called for an investigation of the NAACP and its publication.[67] No doubt, it also had reason to keep its eye on the editor of the *A.M.E. Review* as well.

⟁

As of January, the *Review* was no longer printed and published in Philadelphia by the A.M.E. Publishing House on Pine Street. Instead, it had moved its offices to Nashville, the home of the A.M.E. Sunday School Union. All communications relating to the business of the *Review* were to be addressed to the editor's home office in Oceanport, New Jersey. The change, Reverdy wrote, was "justified by more prompt and satisfactory service to [the] subscribers, as well as in economics connected with the business administration of this office."[68] After Reverdy's strong urgings to have the journal moved to Philadelphia in 1912, one wonders if these were the only reasons for his reversal. Perhaps it also had to do with the inadequate facilities in Philadelphia and/ or his decision to run for the bishopric at the 1920 General Conference where he would need southern support if he were to be successful. His friends, including Joseph Gomez and John Gregg, had strongly urged him to run. He decided to acquiesce but said later that he had "no strong aspiration, or desire to become a Bishop" at the time. He would have preferred to have been elected secretary of missions.[69]

In May, Emma and Reverdy traveled again to Wilberforce for the commencement exercises. The Address was delivered by Emmett J. Scott, who, after paying tribute to the founders, outlined the essentials that "must make for a judicious and permanent readjustment between the New Negro and the New Nation."[70] (The term *New Negro* would be heard repeatedly throughout the 1920s. In 1922, Reverdy himself wrote a poem titled "The New Negro.") During the week, Reverdy was elected president of the Wilberforce Alumni Association. As president, his aims were to urge people to remember Wilberforce when drawing up their wills, to raise $25,000 on Founders Day, to work toward the erection of an alumni building that could also be used for administrative offices, and to guard the spiritual, intellectual, business, educational, and administrative policies of the school.[71]

Although not mentioning his own candidacy for the bishopric, Reverdy wrote an interesting editorial in the January 1920 *Review* in which he described the kind of men who should be elected. Above all, they should give "full proof of their ministry. Not politics, or statesmanship, or scholarship, or the ability to raise or acquire money—but men who have sufficient grasp upon [all] these things, along with consecration to God" are fitted for the office. Following the war, the church does not need men to "wrestle flesh and blood," but to wrestle "the great social, civic, and moral questions of the new age." The same should apply to the general officers of the church.[72] In another editorial, he gave his opinion concerning preaching styles needed by those who lead. There were two opposing styles, he said, one that "creates a sensation" and one that is "sensational preaching." The later is "cheap and vulgar" and aimed at notoriety . . . void of conviction, coherence dignity, or poise." Although it may "draw," it cannot "hold." The former, on the other hand, creates a sensation because of "its boldness and strength of its position in defiantly assailing entrenched evil and wickedness. . . . Its strength is righteousness and truth . . . and its purpose always lofty and unselfish."[73]

In April, Reverdy learned there was friction between the university (College of Liberal Arts run by the church) and the Normal Department (run by the state of Ohio) at Wilberforce. Allegedly the state was trying to duplicate the curriculum of the university by broadening the Normal Department's education program from a two-year Normal Tract to a four-year program. It was also alleged that the state wanted to buy the school from the church because the university was having financial difficulties. In order to help solve some of its problems, the church planned to raise $100,000 by June commencement, wrote Reverdy. He hailed the successful efforts of Bishop Joshua H. Jones, president of the University Trustee Board, and those of President W. S. Scarborough to lead the university through this difficult period. Little did Reverdy surmise that this was just the beginning of the fight that would emerge between the state and the university—a fight in which he would be inextricably involved as bishop of Ohio.[74]

Reverdy was basically in favor of the organic union of the three Negro Methodist bodies, the c.m.e., a.m.e., and a.m.e.z. denominations. But in October 1919, he raised some serious questions. One was whether or not the three bodies had the "same spirit." "Do they hold the same strong convictions as to the place their race should occupy in the industrial, social and political life of the nation as a whole?" He did not believe the Colored Methodists were conceived in the a.m.e. spirit because it had "remained in tutelage to the [white] Methodist Episcopal Church South." The a.m.e. Zion Church was more similar in spirit and background to the a.m.e.s. Reverdy felt that if the three organizations could not unite "to fight to a finish the great battle for racial equality and manhood, it is far better now that each should keep its separate path." The a.m.e. Church has always been in politics—has stood not only for the "right to vote, but also to be voted for," and has never had the spirit of "compromise or subserviency," he said.[75] There were many Negroes who took issue with Reverdy for raising these questions and accused him of being against organic union.

The April 1920 *Review* carried an editorial by Bishop L. J. Coppin in which Coppin recalled that in 1916 the three Negro Methodist bodies had met in council and had drawn up articles of agreement to be sent to the various General Conferences for approval. If ratified they were to be handed down to the Annual Conferences and churches for sanction and, hopefully, lead to organic union. The c.m.e. Church had held its General Conference in 1918 and had ratified the articles. Now it was up to the a.m.e.z. and a.m.e. Churches to ratify the agreements at their 1920 General Conferences. The reasons Coppin gave for supporting unification were: to prevent overlapping of efforts that cause a "useless and burdensome expenditure of funds" and to add the strength of these more than two million Christians to the fight for civil, political, religious and social justice.[76]

In the same issue, Reverdy answered his critics concerning his views on organic union. He refused to withdraw anything he had said before because such a serious proposal as unification should be examined from every angle. Although he had always favored union, he still maintained, "if the union is to hold, then it should be at least able to stand the preliminary test of inter-denominational cooperation." Such a union had to be fortified "by preliminary steps in order to make it a union of strength rather than one tied with a rope of sand woven from the threads of popular enthusiasm."[77] This undoubtedly included the examination of the other denominations' stands on equal rights. He was as determined as ever that the church could not separate religion from the day-to-day life struggles of the people.

With these and other serious issues to be decided, the Twenty-sixth Quadrennial Session of the General Conference of the A.M.E. Church met May 3–18, 1920 in St. Louis, Missouri, at the Colisseum on Jefferson and Washington Streets. During the Welcoming Evening Service of the first day, Reverdy addressed the conference on the subject "The Coming Vision." He used as his text the cry of Habakkuk who asked Jehovah how long he would have to witness violence, strife, and contention before receiving an answer. God replied . . . "the vision is yet for an appointed time, but at the end it shall speak, and not lie: though it tarry, wait for it; because it will surely come, it will not tarry."[78]

After reviewing various periods throughout history when people had asked the same question of God, Reverdy spoke of Negroes who were still enduring violence and injustice. They had listened for God's answer during slavery, lynchings, and dehumanizing Jim Crowism. Despite these debilitating experiences, blacks must continue to hold on to the vision. "If the vision, tarry, wait for it," Ransom said, but waiting for the vision did not mean inaction. It meant developing the church, the home, the school, and acquiring knowledge in all the arts and sciences of the modern world. "God must have people who are prepared to go with him in spirit, as well as in the things of the mind, in carrying out his divinely ordered programme for humanity." In the closing moments of the speech, he turned to the vision of a unified Christianity that he said did not involve only the bringing together of black denominations or even black and white churches. Christianity must adopt a larger vision. "Its mission is not to save black men, or white men, or yellow men, but men—all men everywhere."[79]

On the fourth day, the Committee on Organic Union read its report and recommended that the A.M.E. Church adopt the Articles of Organic Union. After some attempts to table the motion, the conference voted in favor of the articles after which the congregation sang "The Church Is Moving On." On the fifth day, a telegram arrived from the A.M.E. Zion Church's General Conference announcing that it had endorsed the Articles of Organic Union, 378 for and five against.[80] It would seem the issue had been decided. No one predicted the opposition that would arise when the articles were presented to the various Annual Conferences and churches.

Another significant event of the conference was the presence of Congressman L. C. Dyer, the author of the Anti-Lynching Bill now before Congress. He brought words of welcome to the delegates and said he would continue to fight for justice for the colored people of the United States. The conference passed a resolution thanking him and promised to stand by him and pray for him through all of his efforts for the Negro race. They also asked that he use his influence to withdraw all American military occupation troops from Haiti.[81]

The Committee on the State of the Country reported that the League of Nations as proposed by President Woodrow Wilson was "unwise" and "unsafe."

> Had the Senate adopted the plan, our country would be placed at the mercy of foreign powers, and the world wide conquest, and victory won . . . on the battlefield of France would have forever held the heads of our veterans down in shame and disgrace.

They praised the Honorable Henry Cabot Lodge for his leadership in opposition to the League of Nations.[82]

Of the resolutions passed, the most significant was the one calling for the appointment of a special committee of three bishops and one representative from each Episcopal District to lay before congress and the Republican Party "certain conditions, complaints and demands for adjustment of difficulties, under which [Negroes] suffered." The demands stated that there should be: one or more representatives from the A.M.E. Church on the Committee that framed the party's platform, a National antilynching law, remedial legislation to ensure the franchise for all citizens, abolition of "Jim Crow" cars, "the granting of identical accommodations on Railroad Cars, Common Carriers, Waiting Rooms, etc.," legislation to prevent segregation in all federal services—civil or military—and legislation to prevent or punish mob violence. [83]

The Episcopal Committee recommended that five new bishops be elected. Joseph Gomez was a member of that committee and had from the very beginning of the conference campaigned vigorously for Ransom and John A. Gregg. Reverdy had introduced Gomez to Gregg and highly recommended Gregg as candidate for the bishopric.[84] He held out little hope for his own election because, unlike most of the other candidates, he had "no campaign manager, no steering committee, no headquarters," and had spent no money.[85]

On May 13 the election was held. William. D. Johnson of the Southwest Georgia Conference and A. J. Carey of the Chicago Conference were elected on the first ballot. Reverdy had received 146 votes, Gregg, 115; Gregg decided to drop out of the race. On the second ballot, W. Sampson Brooks was elected. This time Reverdy received 182 votes. On the third ballot, the contest was among William. T. Vernon of the West Tennessee Conference; William A. Fountain, president of Morris Brown College; and Reverdy C. Ransom.[86] Vernon and Reverdy had addressed the conference the night before the election. In *Pilgrimage*, Reverdy, who had never had much respect for Vernon's apologetic attitude toward whites, described Vernon's presentation as "oratorial acrobatics" which had "grotesque appeal."[87]

At the beginning of the third ballot, Vernon was ahead, but Reverdy was leading Fountain "almost two to one." Then the clerk stopped reading the name of "Ransom." When it was over, Vernon and Fountain became the fourth and fifth new bishops.[88] Once again the south had stood firm and had elected all southern men, with the exception of Carey from Chicago. In *Pilgrimage*, Reverdy said the clerk later told people that Ransom had been elected, but he had "read Fountain in."[89] In years to come, the church would finally modernize its voting methods, thereby eliminating all successful efforts to fix elections. Reverdy lamented that though the balloting for bishops was always preceded by prayer, instead of prayer prevailing, combinations and organizations prevailed, accompanied by political machines, campaign methods, primaries, and headquarters "induced to win delegates whose high moral sense [have] already been perverted by being schooled in these decadent methods."[90]

Reverdy experienced a sense of accomplishment when on May 15 he was reelected editor of the *The A.M.E. Church Review*, winning 354 of the 548 votes cast. Eight other men had aspired for the position and had received a sprinkling of votes, but Reverdy had won a sizeable majority.[91] He did not take badly his defeat in the bishopric race because his "heart was not set on becoming a bishop." Nevertheless, his supporters were disappointed, notably Joseph Gomez, who felt that Ransom and Gregg were the most qualified of the candidates. "It was a difficult lesson for him that the deserving do not always prevail."[92]

In summarizing the actions taken at the General Conference, the one that Reverdy most regretted was the overwhelming decision of the church not to give women the vote in church affairs. On careful investigation, he learned the overriding reason for this rejection was the fear that because women were in the majority, if allowed to vote, few men would be elected delegates to the General Conference. As a dissenter, Reverdy wrote:

> the church had nothing to fear but all things good to be hoped for by the accession to membership in the General Conference of . . . representative women who . . . compose the character, intelligence and consecration which is the salt of the Church today and its hope in the future.[93]

Two other important pieces of legislation of which he did approve was the adoption of the "Hawkins Plan" that required that 20 percent of the Dollar Money raised by the churches be sent from the Annual Conferences directly to the financial secretary so he could assist superannuated preachers, widows, and orphans. The other was the "20th Century Financial Drive" that would raise $5,000,000 in the next five years for the improvement of education, missions, evangelism, and social service.[94]

In the October 1920 issue of the *Review*, Reverdy took notice of the convention held in New York on August 15 by West Indian Marcus Garvey and his Universal Negro Improvement Association (UNIA) and African Communities League. During the convention, the group had issued a Declaration of Rights for Negro People of the World that, as Reverdy said, was "bold enough to make the late A.M.E. Bishop Henry McNeal appear like a mild conservative." Garvey had a tremendous grassroots following with his Back-to-Africa movement, his colorful Black Cross Nurses, Black Legions, Black Star Line, and his own bright uniform and plumed helmet in which he paraded through the streets of large metropolitan cities. Outstanding among the UNIA's fifty-four statements of rights were: the freedom of all black men, women, and children throughout the world as citizens of Africa, the motherland; that "no Black shall engage himself in battle for an alien race without first obtaining the consent of the Black peoples of the world"; a condemnation of those nations who "by open aggression or secret scheme have seized territories and exhaustible natural wealth of Africa"; the observance of August 31 every year as an international holiday for blacks.[95]

Reverdy's reaction to the declaration was that "entirely apart from the question of an endorsement of the scheme, we welcome the Declaration as an encouraging awakening." He noted that at the end of World War I, DuBois had organized in Paris the Pan-African Congress and had been awarded the Spingarn Medal by the NAACP for this feat. However, "Nothing quite so militant as this 'Bill of Rights' [had] ever issued from a body composed of the rank and file of Negroes." Some would receive it as a joke, he guessed, others as "harmless oratory." But he was sure Great Britain would pay strict attention because the declaration's "chief significance . . . [was] to arouse and inspire black people throughout the world to preserve their national and territorial inheritance in Africa, and take a place of racial respect and independence among the free and liberty-loving people of the world."[96] Instead of moving to Africa, the Afro-American's job was to address itself to building the structure of the spiritual, social, and intellectual life of the people and to see to it that Africans were saved from "'Christian civilization'—a civilization which through the centuries has been unable to save itself from destructive wars, from greed for alien territory, the cruel oppression of the weak and the lust of power."[97]

Although Negroes like Ransom and DuBois in all honesty could never embrace Garvey's Back-to-Africa movement that branded some middle-class, intellectual Negro leaders as traitors (especially if they were light skinned), Reverdy was aware of the importance of Garvey's ability to attract the masses and inspire in them race pride. As an organizer of the NAACP, DuBois would not be welcome in Garvey's ranks. According to Garvey's son:

> Marcus Garvey poured contempt on those Black organizations that existed on the philanthropy of white liberals. . . . They had not been created by the sacrifice and dedication of their own people and, as they were manipulated by the whites who financed them, were practically useless in the cause of African redemption and race uplift.[98]

Because the A.M.E. Church had been created by the "sacrifice and dedication" of Negroes, Garvey had to take another line of criticism when referring to it. The A.M.E. Church's doctrine was based on that of the white Methodists and therefore was not an African religion. He proposed instead the African Orthodox Church, rooted in African principles, with an African Catechism (written by Bishop Alexander McGuire originally from Antigua), a black God, and a black Christ.[99] No doubt he applauded the late Bishop Turner who had said: "We have as much right biblically and otherwise to believe that God is a Negro, as you buckra or white people have to believe that God is a fine looking, symmetrical and ornamental white man."[100] George W. Forbes wrote in the *Review* three years later when Garvey was imprisoned for allegedly using the mail to defraud:

> His great talent, restless energy and marvelous magnetism deserved a better fate. We never saw in his scheme anything other than arrant charlatanism, but his ability to draw the masses together and build up in them a confidence in a leader of their own was at least something.[101]

As usual, the *Review* took special note of the 1920 presidential campaign and elections. George W. Forbes wrote of his disappointment in the unethical methods the Democrats used to promote their candidate, Governor James M. Cox of Ohio. Allegedly Professor W. E. Chancellor of the College of Wooster in Wooster, Ohio, had put out a circular claiming that the Republican candidate, Warren G. Harding, had Negro blood in that "the grandmother on his father's side was a colored woman named Mary Ann Dixon." The newspapers argued the merits of this rumor, and some of the Cox supporters said that the Republicans had put out this story "as an election trick so as to come back in injured innocence with a horrified denial!"[102] Nevertheless, the tactic did not succeed. Harding won by 404 electoral votes to Cox's 117.

In the April 1921 *Review*, Forbes highlighted several important cultural milestones involving blacks. Henry O. Tanner, the painter son of the late Bishop Tanner, who had moved to Paris because of racism in America, had returned to America on January 22.

He presented his first Boston art exhibition at the Vose Gallery. Among his ten paintings displayed were: "Les Fetes de Morts, "The Flight into Egypt," "Moonlight in Tangier," "The Home of Jeanne d'Arc," and "The Holy Women." In February, Bert Williams had appeared in *Broadway Brevities* at the Waldron Casino and the Shubert in Boston. Finally, after having been snubbed by members of the Drama League, Charles Gilpin, who played the title role in Eugene O'Neil's *The Emperor Jones*, had been honored at the league's banquet on March 7 in New York City.[103] The progress of these gifted artists must have given Reverdy a great deal of pleasure, especially Tanner whose exhibit he had been privileged to attend.

Reverdy had other reasons to be proud in 1921. After delivering the commencement address to the graduating class at Shorter College, Little Rock, Arkansas, where Rev. Sherman L. Green was president, he visited Joseph Gomez at Bethel in Detroit. He called Gomez "one of the forward-looking young men whose life we believe ourselves to have touched vitally at certain turning points in his career." He spoke of how at the young age of thirty-one, Gomez was preaching to overflowing congregations and leading his members to "erect a new building on a commanding site which has been purchased at a cost of $40,000." While in Detroit, Reverdy also visited Bishop C. S. Smith, who in his "methodical and scientific manner" was writing the history of the A.M.E. Church. From Detroit, Reverdy traveled to Dallas, Texas, to celebrate the emancipation of the slaves in Texas at the State Fair Grounds. (Traditionally the celebration—called Juneteenth—is held on June 19 when the Negroes of Texas first got the news they were freed, but in 1921 it fell on Sunday and so was celebrated the next day.) Reverdy had been invited to address the crowd of over twenty thousand. He said he spoke through an amplifier "and like a grown-up child with a new toy . . . may have spoken too long, if not too loud." Later that summer, Reverdy delivered an address to the Teachers Summer School at the Ministers Conference at Hampton Institute where about six hundred teachers from all over the south gathered.[104]

The October *Review* was noticeably smaller than other issues. In the front, Reverdy wrote an announcement explaining why. He had mailed Ira T. Bryant, head of the Sunday School Union in Nashville, the literary section of the *Review* and a long article entitled "The Menace of the Ku Klux Klan." Reverdy's "return address was plainly written on the package, which was sent 'first class.'" Bryant never received the packages, and the Post Office Department could not seem to trace its whereabouts.[105] To Reverdy there was no mystery as to what had happened to the envelope. It had been absconded with what had been a great deal of material expressing opposition to the racist KKK.

The most interesting editorial that did appear was "The Quadrilateral View of the Attitude and Outlook for Negroes Throughout the World" by Reverdy Ransom. As stated previously, Reverdy was an avid reader. Throughout his life, he kept scrapbooks of articles that highlighted important events. Consequently, subscribers to the *Review* benefited from this practice in that he frequently quoted from newspapers, essays, letters, and books that offered the pros and cons of an issue. It would be highly unlikely that anyone could read the *Review* and conclude that blacks were always of one opinion anymore than any other group of people.

The four views cited in "The Quadrilateral View" were those of the Pan-African Congress, the Universal Negro Improvement Association, Garvey himself, and Kelly Miller of Howard University. The reprint of two cablegrams sent to the American press from DuBois's Pan-African Congress in Paris made clear the organization's disapproval of Marcus Garvey's program. In answer to these cablegrams, Dr. W. H. Ferris, literary editor of the *Negro World*, official organ of the UNIA, said he saw neither "Pan" nor "African" in the Pan-African Congress that seemed to be made up largely of American and Frenchmen who preferred allegiance to their own countries rather than to Africa. He also had harsh words for DuBois who "while not showing the Negro's creative, constructive and original force in modern civilization . . . pre-eminently shows the Negro's ability to absorb civilization on the side of dress, manners, and morals as well as on the side of scholarship and literary style." Garvey called for "one united race, with the grand and glorious object . . . of a free and redeemed Africa." Kelly Miller's views coincided more with Reverdy's. He advocated that blacks fight for their rights in America. "Any individual or group of individuals who are willing to accept without protest less than the fullness of the stature of American citizenship is not fit material for the new order of things now about to be ushered in."[106]

In the same issue, Reverdy applauded the nonviolent, noncooperation protest of Gandhi in his effort to free India from British rule. Reverdy found the "spiritual weapon" used by Gandhi to be "intensely practical." The success of the Mahatma would be determined by time, but to Reverdy, his movement marked the doom "of British or rather Western imperialism."[107] Afro-Americans would employ many of Gandhi's methods during the 1960s. Unfortunately, Reverdy would not be alive to participate.

In January 1922, once again Reverdy published an article on "The Menace of the Ku Klux Klan." This time the mail was not tampered with. However, he was unable to duplicate the data used in the original, but he was able to find other facts in the *New York World.* He traced the organizing of the new Klan to October 26, 1915, in Atlanta, Georgia, by William Joseph Simmons. It was supposed to be a revival or rebirth of the old KKK of Reconstruction days that also had as its slogan "White Supremacy." The new Klan was anti-Catholic, anti-alien, and anti-Jew as well as anti-Negro. After going into detail about its recruitment program, the results of its activities, and recent steps being taken to curb its progress, Reverdy concluded that nothing had been done until the Klan included groups other than Negroes in its hate program. Now *The New York World* and other influential journals are beginning "to expose its evil menace and un-American spirit." Reverdy pledged that African Americans would be glad to unite with Jews, Catholics, aliens, and "all other patriotic Americans in ridding our country of the Invisible Empire of greed, hate, lawlessness and masked terrorism."[108]

At the winter Bishops' Council meeting held in Montgomery, Alabama, Reverdy, "in cooperation with Bishop C. S. Smith and Prof. John R. Hawkins, was authorized to prepare a Year Book" that would be revised annually and contain "general and statistical information in regard to churches and religion, education and schools, social betterment activities, inter-racial activities, health and sanitation, wealth (including land ownership), homes, business, thrift and saving, historical events, noteworthy achievements." Reverdy said such a book would be a great service not only to the A.M.E. Church, but to "the general public of the religious world."[109] He was to continue to provide such a book for many years to come, sometimes with others and sometimes by himself. The Year Book was a valuable accomplishment for its time.

In April there appeared in the *Review* one of Reverdy's strongest visions of an informed and inspired Church. In "The Teaching Church," the final paragraph of the editorial carried these words:

> We want a church where ignorance cannot breed, nor superstition hide; a church where innocent credulity cannot be bent to selfish ends; where narrowness and selfishness cannot command a hearing; a church where greed, bigotry, and power shrink from the light of heaven-born, high instructed men who walk with Jesus in redemptive paths. A Church like this calls for enlightened men who know their problems in the cause they serve.[110]

Reverdy also hoped that the General Conference of 1924 would see the already highly effective Women's Mite Missionary Society and the Women's Home and Foreign Missionary Society united into one strong organization. In addition, he urged that much attention be paid to the office of secretary of missions that he believed to be the "biggest position which the A.M.E. Church has in its power to bestow upon any one."[111] Perhaps at this time Reverdy still had hopes of being elected to that office even though his strongest supporters wanted him to run again for the bishopric.

In the April 1922 *Review,* Reverdy mourned the passing of Col. Charles Young on January 8, 1922, in Lagos. Young had been a West Point graduate and the highest ranked military officer of his race. As did many other Negroes, Reverdy believed the army had retired him at the beginning of World War I to keep from sending him to France with the rank of General. Nevertheless, Young was kept on the payroll with the same salary as those on active duty; ironically, at the end of the war, he was again called to actively serve in Africa.[112]

The Review also noted the passing of Egbert Austin Williams (Bert Williams) on March 4, 1922. Reverdy took to task the *New York Herald* reporter who said that in death Bert Williams "leaves no successor among the members of his own race." Of all the Negro comedians, "none has attained the unique eminence of Williams. . . . The task of carrying on the work of the blackface funny man will hereafter be the white comedian's burden." Reverdy felt this was a "good illustration of that cock-sureness of mind exercised by white men when they come to consider black people in relation to the highest standards of excellence." He mentioned other Negroes who had contributed greatly to the arts: Ira Aldridge, the Shakespearean actor; Charles Gilpin of *Emperor Jones* fame; in art, Edmonia Lewis and Meta Warwick; in music, Samuel Coleridge-Taylor; in poetry, Paul Laurence Dunbar; his uncle, Sam Lucas who, "as a comedian, was as great before the theatre going public of his generation, and was our first great writer of popular songs." He noted that theatrical manager, Daniel Frohman, at Lucas's funeral had called him a "gentleman" who "never indulged in a vulgar joke or sally, and has done more to keep the American stage clean than any other actor of his day." There would be many successors to Williams. Reverdy predicted the day would come when the white man would no longer "prescribe the role the Negro would portray on stage." In "every activity of life, more and more . . . the curtain will continue to rise upon new scenes in which a dark-skinned American will enact the leading role."[113]

With interest, Reverdy followed the progress of Dyer's Anti-Lynching Bill and the NAACP's lobbying of Congress for its passage. In 1919, Leonidas C. Dyer, a Republican congressman from East St. Louis, had introduced his bill. Surprisingly, it was passed by an almost two-thirds majority in the House, January 26, 1922. But when it reached the Senate, it was "buried by southern Democrats and northern Republicans." The main argument against the bill was that it "transferred local police power to the federal government."[114]

Reverdy wrote an editorial, "Lawless American True to Form in Its Defeat of the Dyer Anti-Lynching Bill," in which he noted that although the government was going to great lengths to see that the Eighteenth Amendment (prohibition) was enforced, it continued to allow violations of the Fifteenth Amendment. The repeated disfranchisement of the Negro by Southern states, in turn, gave the "lynchers license and free reign." The blame for the defeat of the Dyer Bill could not be put completely on the southern Democrats, he wrote. But the Republican majority, "Senators whose weak-kneed, or hypocritical surrender caused the Dyer Bill to fail, bear the greater measure." Even If the bill had been enacted, however, he doubted whether "a supine nation which has long permitted disfranchisement [of the Negro] would have bestirred itself to enforce its provisions." He applauded the NAACP and its continuous "pitiless publicity," graphically depicting the horrors of lynching, and hoped such publicity would continue. He forewarned that "the forces of law and order . . . even the government itself, will reap in blood and wild political and social disorders, the lawlessness and crime now being openly practiced with Negroes as the unprotected victims."[115]

In April, Reverdy dedicated his lead editorial to Bishop Benjamin T. Tanner, the founder of the A.M.E. *Review*, who had died in Philadelphia, January 14, 1923. In many of the volumes of the *Review*, his "words of light and wisdom" are embalmed and treasured; "but what is perhaps better still, the atmosphere he created, the literary form and standards he made from the very beginning, have never been absent from the pages of this journal under all the editors who have succeeded him," Reverdy wrote. Tanner had been retired by the General Conference in May 1908 and yet lived beyond nearly all those who "influenced the vote leading to his retirement." Reverdy hoped "that our retired Bishops will in the future be invited and urged to continue active as lecturers at our colleges and seminaries, in reviewing books, and in writing, at least, works of autobiography and reminiscence."[116] It was as if he were predicting his own retirement in 1952.

In another editorial, Reverdy mourned the death of Charles Spencer Smith who had written the definitive *History of the African Methodist Episcopal Church 1856–1922*, and who had founded the A.M.E. Sunday School Union. Reverdy acknowledged Smith as one of the great orators of his time but admitted "neither his temperament nor ambition permitted him to find a settled place, or a sustained career in the regular ranks of the pastorate." He was an asset to the bishopric in "his interest and activity in large public questions and in great civic, political, social and religious movements." During Reconstruction, he had been a congressman in the Alabama state legislature. Reverdy recalled that the late Frederick Douglass confessed that Smith "was the only man who ever embarrassed him in debate."[117]

The July 1923 *Review* celebrated the fortieth anniversary of the journal with a lead article by Bishop L. J. Coppin in which he complimented the journal

> for its pioneer work and for its faithful and efficient service in higher journalism, and for the opportunity it still extends to our writers to get before the public that which is noblest and best in what we have accomplished as a people.[118]

In Reverdy's editorial, he called the review a "literature of protest and aspiration" and noted that it was needed now even more than it had been in Tanner's day. How else was the world to learn how the Negro felt about discrimination? he asked. How else was the race to be "rallied, strengthened and inspired" except by giving voice to its aspirations and ideals through a vehicle like the *Review*? "There is no more valuable archive of the mental and spiritual unfolding of the mind and soul of the Negro than that which is treasured up in the preceding thirty-nine volumes of the A.M.E. *Review*." [119]

In January Reverdy wrote what turned out to be his farewell editorial, titled "Three Quadrenniums of the A.M.E. *Review*," in which he summed up what he had tried to do and the problems he encountered and made some suggestions for the next editor. He had endeavored to "take the literary soundings as well as the altitudes of Negro thought and scholarship," he said, "to portray the trend, the scope and quality of this thought." He lamented the "shallowness, the false pretense, and down right laziness" of some men with degrees whose offerings (articles sent in) were neither correct nor neat. He expressed gratitude for the work of George W. Forbes who reported the literary life of blacks and Dr. G. W. Henderson of Wilberforce who had headed the Department of Homiletics and furnished outstanding articles. He hoped that whoever aspired to be his successor would not take the "duties and responsibilities" of the position lightly and run the paper merely as a sideline to other unrelated jobs. The journal was never meant to be a newspaper; it was not intended for the magnification of personalities or to be "a broadcasting station for the common place achievement of men in the ordinary pursuit of their line of duty." Instead, it offered "a medium of expression for the best thought of the race"; therefore, the editor must also be alert to new talent and "encourage every exhibition of promise." In addition, he must be well read and have "sound, firm and clear" convictions, not only in matters of the Church but the "people as a whole." He admitted that the *Review* had never shown a profit. Each year it lost a few hundred dollars "through dishonest agents or other persons entrusted with the transmission of funds." Even if this had not been true, the journal still would not show a profit. Because there is no great hunger for "solid and informing reading matter," it is up to the editor to keep "the standard high and seek to create an appetite. The *A.M.E. Church Review* is a measure of our standards of value in the realm of the mind and spirit," he wrote.[120]

It is to his credit that Reverdy did not promote his candidacy for the bishopric in his editorials, nor did he use the *Review* to directly further his personal ambitions. He did, however, frequently define what kind of leadership the A.M.E. Church needed that included an educated, intelligent, and spiritual ministry. Certainly his pastoral record, civic involvement, and numerous articles and editorials demonstrated his high intelligence and his dedication to the church even though, at times, his ideas seemed unorthodox to the traditionalist. Reverdy had decided to abandon the idea of secretary of missions and make a run for the bishopric again with his friend John A. Gregg who now served as president of Wilberforce University. A few weeks before the conference, Reverdy visited his mother in Cambridge, Ohio. She had not been well for the past two years. He asked her if she were praying for his success. She said, "No, I have already prayed for you, and God has answered my prayer. He let His glory shine round about. When you are elected, let me know."[121]

On May 5, 1924, Emma and Reverdy arrived at the Jefferson County Armory in Louisville, Kentucky, for the Twenty-seventh Quadrennial Session of the General Conference. After Bishop Benjamin Lee opened the conference, John Hurst preached the Quadrennial Sermon from the subject "The Glories of the Eternal King." In one part of the sermon, he stressed the inferior role women had had to play throughout the ages and said the modern church "welcomes her in the administration of holy things and accords her voice in her legislative assembly. Why not the African Methodist Episcopal Church and why may it not be done now?" On the third day, the women took up Lee's cry for representation by parading with banners through the auditorium. Both Emma and Hazel Gomez participated in the demonstrations, and Reverdy and Joseph applauded them loudly.[122]

During the conference, Reverdy passed out several small flyers containing thoughts for every day of the conference. He called them "The Leaf." Number 1, dated May 6, was meant to unify the delegates. It read:

We are all here.

Neither enemies without, nor foes within, shall be able to disrupt or divide the A.M.E. Church established by the Fathers upon the foundation of Jesus Christ.

We may differ, but we are not divided. Our brain is clear and our heart is warm.

Right here on the floor of this General Conference, we shall not lack Decision, Action and Capacity, to put over a program that shall meet the needs of our people and serve the high demands of the kingdom of God.

The Lord of hosts is with us; the God of Jacob is our refuge.[123]

In the afternoon session of May 7, Reverdy presented his Quadrennial Report for *The A.M.E. Church Review*. After giving the historical background and noting that it was the oldest magazine in the United States published by African Americans, he spoke of its importance in that it was "unsubsidized and uncontrolled by white churchmen." Today there are three or four other journals "which appeal to a larger audience and which specialize in certain forms of agitation," but the *Review* has held its own with the best of them, he said. It has been circulated in every state in the union, in Canada, South America, the West Indies, and West and South Africa. At first he had wanted to make the *Review* a monthly but soon learned that it was best as a quarterly if the quality and character of the magazine were to be maintained. He listed the number of present subscribers as 1,980. During the Quadrennium, the magazine has netted $12,904.36; expenses were $12,585.03, credit $319.33.[124]

On May 13 the election of bishops was held. The number of votes cast on the first ballot was 766; votes necessary for election, 384. At the close of the first ballot, the leaders were A. L. Gaines of Baltimore, Maryland, with 272 votes; John A. Gregg with 240; Reverdy C. Ransom with 224.[125] The three men had promised to support each other's candidacies and did so throughout the election. In *Pilgrimage*, Reverdy states that of the three, he and Gregg had the most obstacles to overcome. First, they were from the north in a church largely dominated by southerners. Second, Bishop Joshua H. Jones, who presided over the Third District, had not allowed Gregg, president of Wilberforce, freedom to travel in behalf of his candidacy and withheld his salary until Gregg was almost out of funds. In addition, Jones had a personal dislike for Reverdy and would not welcome him at any of his Annual Conferences, only allowing him to speak on matters pertaining to *The A.M.E. Church Review.*[126]

Because no one had received a majority on the first ballot, a second ballot was needed. At the end of the voting, Gaines received 366 votes of the 735 cast and was declared elected. Gregg had received 345, Ransom 340.[127] According to Reverdy, after the second ballot, some of the southern delegates tried to get an adjournment so they could "reform their lines and shut out" Ransom and Gregg. Reverdy told the presiding Bishop Chappelle what was happening; Chappelle replied, "Get off the platform! There will be no adjournment until you are elected."[128] As Chappelle had promised, there was no adjournment; on the third ballot. Ransom and Gregg were elected with 479 and 475 votes, respectively. At the conclusion of fifteen straight hours of voting, Gaines, Ransom, and Gregg became the forty-seventh, forty-eighth, and forty-ninth bishops of the African Methodist Episcopal Church.[129]

The new bishops were ordained Sunday, May 18. Gaines was the first to be consecrated by Bishops Benjamin F. Lee and A. J. Carey. As was customary, the three men were presented for ordination by several minister friends from different districts. Reverdy C. Ransom's presenters, led by Joseph Gomez of the Michigan Conference, were Rev. H. K. Spearman of the New Jersey Conference, Rev. W. T. Pope of the Central Arkansas Conference, Rev. A. D. Avery of the North Carolina Conference, and I. G. Duncan of the Central Alabama Conference. He was consecrated by Bishops J. Albert Johnson and I. N. Ross. One of Gregg's presenters was Rev. Francis M. Gow of the Cape Colony Conference (South Africa), who was later to become the first bishop from South Africa. Bishops W. D. Johnson and W. A. Fountain were Gregg's consecrators. Near the end of the service, Bishop W. Sampson Brooks presented each with a Bible, and Bishop W. T. Vernon accorded the sacrament.[130] The occasion was marked by its dignity and solemnity.

At the afternoon session of May 19, the Episcopal Committee read the assignments of the Bishops. Gaines was sent to the Thirteenth Episcopal District (Louisiana, North and Central Louisiana, South America, the West Indies, and the Virgin Island Annual Conferences); Gregg to the Seventeenth Episcopal District (South Africa, Cape Colony, Transvaal, Orange River, Zambezi, Natal, and the Basutoland Annual Conferences); and Ransom to the Fourteenth Episcopal District (Kentucky, West Kentucky, Tennessee, and East and West Tennessee Annual Conferences).[131] "Despite [his] wide and varied experience," and his sixty-three years, Reverdy felt like a "novice." He knew he would have to learn how to be a bishop.[132]

Early Episcopal Districts, 1924–1932

For every tree is known by his own fruit. For of thorns men do not gather figs,
nor of a bramble bush gather they grapes.
Luke 6:44

Reverdy had been elected bishop in the middle of the Negro Renaissance, that period
between 1920–1929 characterized by the flowering of black arts and culture. "The New
Negro," succinctly defined in 1925 by Alain Locke, had arrived "vibrant" and "with a
new psychology."[1] As early as 1923, Reverdy had written a poem on the subject describing the Negro of the 1920s as both "new" and as "old as the forests primeval . . . crystallized by the heat of Oriental suns" standing "dauntless" and "unafraid." His theme of
the race's spiritual leadership emerges once again in this poem. The Negro, as "the last
reserve of God on earth," would "rule the world with peace" and "love" Reverdy wrote.[2]

Always a champion of black artists, Reverdy had lived to see Paul Laurence Dunbar
reexamined, and writers like Claude McKay, Charles W. Chesnutt, Countee Cullen,
Jean Toomer, and Langston Hughes find recognition in such magazines as the NAACP's
Crisis, the Urban League's *Opportunity*, and *Ebony and Topaz*. A few like Hughes even
received sponsorships from white philanthropists who found it fashionable to frequent Harlem, hobnob with Negro writers, and foot the bill for their publications
during the 1920s.[3] This romance, however, Reverdy knew would be short lived.

Although he would often return to his New York and Oceanport homes, Reverdy's
assignment to the Fourteenth Episcopal District in 1924 took him south where Negroes had been leaving in numbers for northern urban centers like Harlem, the South
Side of Chicago, Central Avenue in Cleveland, and the Black Bottom in Detroit. Between 1910 and 1920, the South had lost 323,000 Negroes and by 1930 would lose
another 615,000 or 8.2 percent of the black population.[4] Still there were enough Negroes left to maintain a sizable A.M.E. Church in the region.

Reverdy and Emma settled in the Episcopal Residence on Eighth Avenue South in
Nashville, Tennessee, where once again Emma fashioned a home. Soon it became a

popular meeting place for the ministers of Tennessee and Kentucky and visitors from other districts who attended the various Annual Conferences or came to meet the popular new bishop and his wife.

The beginnings of the A.M.E. Church in Tennessee had been fraught with danger. Dr. R. R. Wright Jr. described the ministers who established churches there between 1863–1868 as:

> men of valor who braved the insults and abuse of enemies of the Church and even ran the gauntlet of the Ku Klux in order to plant the African Methodist banner on the mountains, hill-tops and [in the] valleys of Tennessee.

Despite these perils, the churches grew so rapidly that in 1868 the General Conference recommended Tennessee be divided into two Conferences, the Tennessee and West Tennessee. The continued growth of the district resulted in the establishment of the East Tennessee Conference in 1899 under the leadership of Bishop Benjamin T. Tanner.[5] Reverdy's superintendency included all three of these Annual Conferences.

In *Pilgrimage*, Reverdy said that in 1924 he found the conditions in Tennessee to be "turbulent. Bishop A. J. Carey had presided over this district the previous quadrennium and had left it in a storm." There existed the Carey and anti-Carey factions and the Bryant (Ira T. Bryant, head of the A.M.E. Sunday School Union) and anti-Bryant factions. Reverdy was warned by some of the clergy that he had better join the anti-Bryant faction; however, he was determined to join no faction even though it might cause him friction with some of his fellow bishops. Bryant was in opposition to a number of the bishops whom he alleged had abused their power and had been less than honest in handling the finances of the church. Nevertheless, the bishops had to acknowledge that Bryant had developed the Sunday School Union in Nashville "into a plant worth more than a quarter of a million dollars" where he did a "substantial" printing business. In addition, he launched a crusade to help "underpaid pastors, retired ministers, widows and orphans of ministers."[6] Though outwardly Reverdy took no side, it is obvious from his description of Bryant's accomplishments and his own tendency to champion the underdog that he was sympathetic to Bryant.

Reverdy described the spirit of the people of Tennessee as "narrow" and conservative. They "could not bring themselves to do anything in a large way." For instance Turner College, housed in an old factory building in Shelbyville, Tennessee, was in a deplorable state.[7] Established by Bishop Henry M. Turner in October 1885, it had initially been a private school started by local people. Turner appointed the minister of the A.M.E. Church in Shelbyville as principal of a program that included a high school and an institute. Before long it became known as Turner College, though it never reached the status of a four-year institution.[8]

When Reverdy arrived, he learned that many of the churches only gave "lip service" to Turner rather than financial aid. He attempted to rally the district behind the college by reminding them it bore the name of Bishop Turner and should be a worthy monument to him.[9] Later Reverdy suggested the school drop its "primary grades and establish the school strongly as a junior college and normal school."[10] When it became obvious the rally had not succeeded and the contributions barely took care of the necessities, Reverdy set about liquidating the property in spite of the protests of many of the people. The liquidation was finalized later by Bishop Albert Johnson.[11] It was always Reverdy's contention that the A.M.E. Church should concentrate its efforts on schools like Wilberforce and Morris Brown in Atlanta and close those small institutions that drained the church's coffers and offered little in the way of scholarship. Quality to him was always of more import than quantity. Selling this idea to the church, however, would be difficult because no district wanted to give up the prestige of having a college under its jurisdiction.

In Nashville were Fisk University and Meharry Medical and Dental Schools, prominent black institutions of higher learning that were not affiliated with the A.M.E. Church. Reverdy observed that:

> So far as easing friction between the races [these schools presented] more of a potential, political and social powder keg, requiring the president and teachers to be constantly alert, lest some student, refusing surrender to Jim Crow, light the spark for a city-wide explosion.

Reverdy was saddened to see on the streets of Nashville "the cream of [Negro] young manhood and womanhood kowtowing, sidestepping and easing their way along the color line" despite their professional attainments and degrees.[12]

On the other hand, from the beginning of his appointment to the Fourteenth District, Reverdy found Kentucky to be "a congenial field to supervise." Perhaps, he decided, this was because "slavery [had] touched Kentucky more lightly than it [had] her southern sister states" and because of the influence Cassius M. Clay had had on the area.[13] In 1880 at Richmond, Kentucky, Bishop J. P. Campbell had divided Kentucky into two Annual Conferences, Kentucky and West Kentucky. The latter had grown "from a small organization to be the rival of the mother conference" by the time Reverdy arrived.[14] The people he remembered most during his four years there were the capable Reverends George David and F. W. Frazier and Belle Jackson whom he called "the Matriarch of Lexington and the blue grass country."[15]

An event of import during Reverdy's tenure in Tennessee was the famous "Monkey Trial" of John T. Scopes in Dayton, Tennessee, which began on July 3, 1925 after the legislature had outlawed the teaching of Darwin's theory of evolution in public schools and colleges.[16] Reverdy watched with interest the arguments of fundamentalist William Jennings Bryan, who sided with the prosecution, and the sharp-witted agnostic, Clarence Darrow, lawyer for the defense. Through the years, Reverdy was to study the brilliant career of Darrow and wonder how he himself would have fared if he had followed his early desire to become a lawyer back in Cambridge, Ohio.

Reverdy's Kentucky Annual Conference of 1925 reflected the Negro's concerns about evolution, lynching, and the growing boldness of the KKK. In terms of evolution, the Committee on the State of the Church reported that there was no conflict between science and religion. The church had nothing to fear from the theory that was still being studied and "elaborated in Universities." Its aim was to study the process of creation. "Some of the brightest minds are Christian evolutionists," it stated. The report by the Committee on the State of the Church included a strong reaction to the Klan's presence in Washington, D.C., in March.

> The spectacle of this organization which would take the law into its unholy hands, invading our national capital and parading down Pennsylvania Avenue, under the glare of the dome of the building in which our laws are made, is one that calls for the most severe condemnation.

There had, however been some decrease in lynchings. "The records show that while in 1914 there were 52 lynchings and only 14 preventions, in 1924 there were only 16 lynchings and 45 preventions. Thirteen states now have anti-lynching laws."[17] Reverdy felt there could be no celebration until there were no lynchings and the federal government passed antilynching laws.

On December 27 of the same year, Reverdy delivered an address to the Fiftieth Annual Grand Chapter Convention of the Kappa Alpha Psi Fraternity in New York City from the topic "Future Influence of Negro Scholarship in America." He spoke first of African Americans as being "joint heirs" with Anglo-Saxons in that they "spoke the same language, worshipped God in identical articles of religious faith, and without a single betrayal . . . sustained their country with a common loyalty and patriotism." Their aspirations and hopes lie in America and not in Africa. Although they have not had direct influence in American statesmanship, literature, the arts, sciences, and philosophies, their "indirect influence has been immense," he said. They have stood "as the crucial test of the spirit of freedom and liberty that lies back of all [of America's] legal enactments, moral standards and spiritual attainment."[18]

Black leaders in the early years were largely uneducated and untrained, but today there are many trained men and women in all fields so that leading scholars no longer "debate the question of the Negro's natural and inherent inferiority," he affirmed.

The black man has, to date, gained and absorbed the information given to him by professors in some of the most prestigious universities in the country. But unlike the Japanese, he has not yet "put the imprint of [his] spirit and racial characteristics and aspirations" on that knowledge. The Negro has the opportunity not only to illuminate and guide his own race, but to liberate the "spirit" and strengthen the moral purpose of whites in America.[19]

He posed several questions. What direction will Negro scholarship take when confronted by Bolshevism, by capital and labor, by racism and segregation even in some of the departments of the federal government? Will these black scholars with their degrees "come to the moral, social, political and spiritual rescue of their white countrymen and seek to deliver them from an attitude which menaces our own nation and the future peace of the world?" No learning can reach a high level until it becomes spiritualized, he said. Despite the excellent educational opportunities this country offers its citizens, there is still "banditry, crime, moral laxity and general disrespect for law. . . . In the highest and best sense, the black people are the only free people in the United States today." They are not fettered by tradition, bound by prejudice. They hold no "animosity" nor "contempt for their white fellow citizens."[20]

The intelligencia of the race then must not now resort to violence against the KKK but must elevate the fight to a higher plane "where intelligence and character may meet it in a decisive battle of brains."

> When its thinkers have voiced its highest thought, and its artists have painted their golden dreams, when its poets have given wings to the heart and spirit of the race, and its musicians have enabled them to sing as they fly; when its scientists, philosophers and saints erect a monumental throne to Peace, Justice, in the name of the American people [we can then] invite the white men of Europe, the brown men of Asia, and the black men of Africa . . . to share with us the victories we have won, the triumphs we have wrought in agony of soul, the freedom of our minds, the liberation of our spirits.[21]

Reverdy had altered considerably his youthful belief in "an eye for an eye." The responsibilities of the bishopric and the lessons of Gandhi had revealed to him that violent retaliation in the name of justice only delayed the day of reconciliation. This newer philosophy was more in tune with his thesis that God had brought the Negro to these shores to become the spiritual conscience of America. Through nonviolent protest, love, morality, and intelligence, he must melt the cement heart of the white racists. This was the task of the old/new Negro. Through the years, Reverdy Ransom was to be categorized in many ways: radical, social gospeler, reformer, prophet, and seer. Indeed, he was all of these things; but most of all, he was spiritual. As Bishop Joseph Gomez was to say in his eulogy of Ransom in 1959, "He was spiritually sensitive; he felt deepest because he suffered most," often because of his own frailties. Nevertheless, he was "ever sure of God and His redeeming presence."[22] It was this quality more than any other that attracted people to him and made him a powerful spiritual leader.

⟅⟆

In 1926, Reverdy was still concerned with the "ecclesiastical oligarchy" of the bishopric in the A.M.E. Church and felt there should be more checks and balances. To this effect, he submitted to *The Southern Christian Recorder* in December an article titled "Shall We Have Eighteen Ecclesiastical Principalities or a Connectional Church?" One of the solutions he offered was the rotation of bishops on a regular basis. He pointed out that for several Quadrennials many bishops had presided over the same district where they had first been assigned. Others were only assigned to sections of the country in which they were born; consequently, they had never experienced a different locale. He objected to the long tenure of bishops in one district because "it breeds sycophants, and sets up a brood of little ecclesiastical satraps who, for their own personal aims, seek to solidify and strengthen the power of the reigning ecclesiastical prince." This could be seen in the makeup of the Episcopal Committee composed of seventy-two clergy and laypersons from the various districts. Most had been appointed to ensure that the present bishop would be reassigned to his district. The remedy, he wrote, was for the laymen to assert themselves by placing people on the Episcopal Committee who owned "their own souls."[23]

So strongly did Reverdy feel about this matter that the following year he submitted several more articles on the subject. In the final one, he broached the subject of graft and dishonesty among the prelates, stating that bishops who become rich "in the service of the Gospel ministry, [have] disgraced [their] calling and stand dishonored in the sight of God."[24] R. R. Wright Jr., editor of *The Christian Recorder,* argued against Reverdy's plan to rotate the bishops. He said there was no sensible reason for any bishop to have to move every year, "or every four, five, or six years" because neither the Bible, nor the discipline made such demands.[25] Ransom's views not only rankled Wright Jr. but did not make Ransom popular among many of his fellow bishops. He would pay the price for his candidness at the next General Conference.

At the West Kentucky Conference in October, 1927, Reverdy announced that *The Spirit of Freedom and Justice*, a book of his orations and speeches, had been published in 1926 by the Sunday School Union in Nashville and was now on sale for two dollars.[26] In his introduction to the book, he explained that it had always been his desire to put together such a volume, and that for the past twenty-five years, people from all over the country had requested that he do so. He apologized for the absence of some speeches. "The fact is, some of my most ambitious efforts have never been written, and most of their substance has gone from me beyond recall," he said. Among those speeches included were tributes to famous personalities like William Lloyd Garrison, John Brown, John Greenleaf Whittier, Wendall Phillips, Charles Sumner, and Abraham Lincoln and topical essays such as "Crossing the Color Line" and "The Atlanta Riot."[27] At the same West Kentucky Conference, Reverdy was reunited with Joseph Gomez who came to visit his mentor, attend conferences, and help Reverdy celebrate his fortieth year in the ministry. During the afternoon session of October 6, Reverdy introduced him to the delegates as a young minister for whom he had the greatest respect. Joseph had built the largest church in the Connection, Greater Bethel Detroit, and for his efforts had been moved unfairly to Ebenezer Detroit by a vindictive Bishop Vernon. Reverdy remarked "the time was fast approaching when they [young ministers like Gomez] would have to [walk in] the steps of the fathers of the church and carry on the great work of the same, because they were sons of the morning." In return, Gomez commended Ransom "whom the 14th Episcopal District admired for his greatness as man and father to all who came to him for advice." It was his prayer and that of the district that Ransom might "live long to lead on the church of God."[28]

On October 25, 1927, Emma and Reverdy celebrated their fortieth wedding anniversary at the Episcopal Residence in Nashville that was decorated with palms and multihued roses. Friends, family, ministers, and laity from all over came to pay tribute, including Drs. J. G. Robinson and R. R. Wright of Philadelphia; Revs. S. S. Morris and G. W. Allen; Mrs. Evans Tyree; President and Mrs. Thomas E. Jones of Fisk University; Professor C. Fry of New York City; Dr. T. Ellis of Manchester, England; President and Mrs. W. J. Hale of A and I State College; and President and Mrs. E. E. Wittenburg of Turner College. In addition, hundreds of letters and telegrams of congratulations poured into the residence. Emma was draped in a black velvet gown trimmed with silver lace and pearls; Reverdy "as elegant as ever" wore his black tux that accented his lean, stately form. A friend (unidentified) paid the following tribute to the couple:

> Your voyage has been long and eventful, crowded with great . . . opportunities for usefulness, wisely and ably used, and brilliant in achievements, far reaching in their influence. Such a career is only given to the gifted and fortunate few. You have been friends of the young, the lowly and unfortunate; yours has been the clarion voice speaking in trumpet tones for the rights of your people. You have been courageous when others have been faint hearted, brave when others have been cowardly.[29]

On November 2, 1927, Reverdy received news that his mother, Harriet Ransom, had died of an "organic heart disease" in her home on Batey Avenue in Cambridge, Ohio. Through the years, he had kept close touch with her, and she had visited him in the various parsonages where he lived. She and Emma also had a warm relationship. The Ransoms traveled to Cambridge to attend her funeral that was held more than likely in the A.M.E. Church. (No record of the funeral can be found.) Afterwards she was interred in Northwood Cemetery, not far from her home.[30] Reverdy would sorely miss her; she had always been there when he needed her, particularly through the formative years when he was trying to decide his calling. At each turn in his career, she encouraged him to give his best and let God take care of the rest. Her faith in him was unwavering, no matter how heated the controversy surrounding him. After all, he had been "let down from the skies," she "always firmly maintained."[31]

Despite his grief, Reverdy had to get on with his life and turn to pressing church matters. The spirit of reform prior to the General Conference was strong among the ministers, laymen of the church, and Reverdy, the only Bishop who openly supported the movement. George Singleton in his *The Romance of African Methodism* describes the districts in 1928 as "little episcopal principalities" where many bishops abused their power. The situation came to a head at the Bishops Council meeting in Birmingham, Alabama, in February. Reverdy delivered a sermon, taking his text from 1 Timothy 3:15, "The Church of the living God, pillar ground and the truth." In it, he dealt specifically with the abuse of power, including the "burdensome assessments" put on the churches and the dictatorial acts practiced by the leaders. He warned that "The clock is wound up so tight, that if you give it just one more turn, something will snap." Although the ministers and laymen present applauded the sermon, Reverdy's fellow bishops (particularly John Hurst of South Carolina) censured him harshly.[32]

It was this sermon that prompted several ministers to meet after the service and plan "definite action for the forthcoming General Conference to remove the Bishops and get relief for the pastors and people." Among those present were Revs. D. Ormande Walker, E. A. Adams, George A. Singleton, John Harmon, A. D. Avery, W. T. Pope, S.H.V. Gumbs, and J. W. McDade. Later they were joined by A. J. Wilson, L. L. Berry, and Joseph Gomez, who was to compose and read a resolution expressing their determinations at the next General Conference in Chicago. The group decided the vote to move the bishops had to be taken by secret ballot so that no one would be intimidated. Second, it had to be read on a day when the presiding bishop was sympathetic to their cause. They finally settled on Bishop John Albert Johnson who agreed to allow the resolution to be read on the day he was in charge.[33]

The Twenty-eighth General Conference of the A.M.E. Church opened at the Armory of the Eighth Regiment of the National Guards in Chicago, Illinois, May 7, 1928. Reverdy described the opening as a "most unseemly spectacle" for a religious convention. The host bishop, A. J. Carey, who was also Commissioner of Police for the city of Chicago, was accompanied by a police band of "blasting horns, trumpets and drums" and a platoon of policemen who went about "frisking some of the delegates to see if they carried a gun. Detectives in plain clothes, sat, or stood at the steps leading to the platform where the bishops presided." Reverdy was stopped by a policeman, but he brushed past him and took his seat.[34]

Bishop William Decker Johnson of the Tenth Episcopal District (Texas) delivered the Quadrennial Sermon from the theme "The Church, Her Support, Her Strength, Her Beauty, and Her Work." After referring to several definitions of "church" as given by reknown religious figures, he concluded that the real church is identified and known by its spirit and life. It has and needs no other credentials. It is the "miracle of the ages . . . the mightiest influence for right known to man." Following the sermon, the holy sacrament was administered by Bishops Hurst, Jones, Carey, Gaines, and Ransom.[35]

On the third day, Bishop Joshua H. Jones read the lengthy Episcopal Address on behalf of all the bishops. There were so many pages that several other bishops had to assist in the reading. Among the recommendations given at the close were: that members of the Women's Home and Foreign Missionary and the Parent Mite Missionary Societies be made delegates of the General Conference and be allowed to sit in the ensuing General Conference; that a special hour be set aside to discuss the organic union of Methodist bodies; that four bishops be elected; that lynching and segregation in public highways, public carriers, and civil institutions be protested; that Negroes continue to struggle for economic justice; that there be thoughtful, high-minded use of the franchise in all elections.[36]

As planned, on the afternoon of May 10 Presiding Bishop John Albert Johnson called Joseph Gomez to come to the platform to read his resolution. After giving a brief background of Methodism in general and the African Methodist Episcopal Church in particular, Gomez said, "the time has come to decentralize the District, and connectionalize the Church"; therefore he resolved that the Episcopal Committee be instructed to change all bishops who had served in one district for two or more quadrenniums.[37] When he had finished, there was stunned silence. Then pandemonium ensued. Bishop Johnson recognized Rev. J. W. Walker of North Carolina who seconded the motion. He was "a portly man, slightly round-shouldered, dark skinned, clean shaven, with a shrill, keen voice" that rang through the hall. Delegates tried to get to the floor microphones, and the bishops on the platform protested loudly to no avail. As a part of the strategy agreed on by the reformers, "Rev. H. Y. Tookes made the motion that the Gomez Resolution be tabled" and that the motion to table be taken by secret ballot. He knew that when the motion to table had failed, the original resolution would also have to be taken by secret ballot. Bishop Joseph S. Flipper arose angrily and stated:

We have submitted the assignment of the bishops to the Episcopal Committee as a matter of convenience, and the Conference has no right to instruct the Episcopal Committee, in reference to the assignment of a bishop; if you do, I tell you the bishops will assign themselves at the General Conference.

In order to bring the meeting back to order, Bishop Johnson called for the vote as to whether the resolution should be tabled. The result was 263 for, 569 against. Then followed the vote on the original Gomez resolution. It passed by 641 to 203. The bishops would all be moved to other Episcopal Districts.[38]

According to George Singleton, after the vote, the militant editor of the Philadelphia *New Era*, Rev. V. C. Monk, brought out placards and banners that said "Emancipation Day has Come" and "Move them All!" "For a brief moment the sign painters did a lucrative business. . . . Such a move had never been made in the history of the Church. Bishop Johnson was the hero."[39]

In *Pilgrimage*, Reverdy relates that after the vote, Bishop A. J. Carey asked him to meet with him. Carey tried to convince Reverdy to use his influence to have him reassigned to the Fourth District that included Chicago. In return, he would see that Reverdy was assigned to the First District (New York). Although ministers from the First had approached Reverdy about coming there, he knew that his senior, Bishop John A. Johnson, wanted the district. After seeing Reverdy was not interested in the First, Carey offered him the Second District. Reverdy rebuffed him in rather caustic language. Although the bishops were moved to other districts, they had a measure of success in the end. Those "who objected to the action of the Conference in regard to their removal gained control of a majority of the Episcopal Committee." According to Reverdy, they met at the home of A. J. Carey and made up the list of bishop assignments. Because the law stated that the General Conference could not change the assignments of the Episcopal Committee, the delegates had to accept their determinations.[40]

Sunday, May 13, of the conference was especially busy for Reverdy. In the morning he preached at Institutional, the church he had founded when he pastored in Chicago. He participated in the afternoon memorial service held in honor of A.M.E.s who had died during the Quadrennial. Among the deceased bishops were B. F. Lee, L. J. Coppin, W. D. Chappelle, W. W. Beckett, I. N. Ross, and J. M. Connor. Reverdy had chosen to speak on the life of Bishop Ross. He said that although Ross did not have "exceptional abilities as a financier or a church-builder . . . he had what gifted people possessed, 'The Divine Gift.'" He was "converted, soul and body. To hear Ross preach was to hear the Gospel on fire."[41]

The following day, the conference listened to the report of the Joint Commission on Organic Union between the A.M.E. and A.M.E.Z. Churches. The commission suggested that the two denominations be merged under the name of the United Methodist Episcopal Church. Outlines for the redistricting and property rights of the two denominations were offered. Before the report could be adopted, Bishops Flipper, Parks, and Ransom and Rev. J. T. Thompson of Florida objected to the elimination of the word "African" from the name of the new organization. It was not until the next day that the resolution to adopt the Commission's report was accepted.[42] Reverdy had always been for union, but he strongly felt that to omit the word "African" was to lose the rich heritage and minimize the unique justification for the founding of these two Methodist bodies.

On May 17, the election of the bishops was held. Robert Alexander Grant, Sherman Lawrence Greene, George Benjamin Young, and Monroe Hortensius Davis were chosen. When the assignments were read a few days later, Carey had been sent to the Fourth as he had desired.[43] For their part in the Gomez resolution, Bishop John A. Johnson was sent to Kentucky and Tennessee, and Reverdy was sent to the Thirteenth (Louisiana).[44] The conference had separated Louisiana from Mississippi and made it into an Episcopal District with only three Annual Conferences and a small mission conference. (In *Pilgrimage*, Ransom said there were three conferences, but his printed stationery lists four: the Louisiana, North Louisiana, Central Louisiana, and Southwest Louisiana.) Reverdy noted that Johnson's assignment that was a demotion, "wounded his pride and broke his spirit."[45] In his *Romance,* Singleton said that the last time he saw Johnson at the General Conference, he had tried to console him. Johnson merely answered, "Singleton, I have learned to go wherever the Church sends me."[46] Johnson died that same year.

Along with his interest in church politics in 1928, Reverdy was actively involved in the presidential election of 1928. The Republicans had chosen as their candidate Herbert Hoover, a "Protestant, a dry, and an old stock American who stood for efficiency and individualism." His Democratic opponent, Alfred E. Smith, governor of New York, was Catholic, against prohibition, and aligned with Tammany Hall in New York.[47] Because of "the lily-white issue in the South, the hysteria and hypocrisy in regard to the eighteenth amendment, the attitude of the Republican party toward the fourteenth and fifteenth amendments, and the open-arm welcome given by the Republican party to the Ku Klux Klan," the Smith for President Colored League of New York had been formed.[48]

As chairman of the Speaker's Bureau of the Smith for President Colored League of New York, Reverdy addressed large audiences at Trinity and Bethel A.M.E. Churches in Baltimore, Maryland, the last Sunday in August. "He disclaimed any attempt to mix church and politics, explaining the work of the League will not be done from the pulpits." He said he believed he was the only A.M.E. prelate or minister to openly "support Smith's candidacy and the attitude of the Negroes of the country toward it."[49]

Early in the campaign, James A. Farley had sent for Reverdy to come to the Democratic headquarters in New York and requested that he use his influence to contact as many Negroes as possible on behalf of Smith. When Farley asked him how much he would charge, Reverdy answered, "Nothing. . . . You pay the actual expenses connected with the work, that is all I ask." For his support of Smith, Reverdy was soundly denounced by white and black Republicans as a traitor who had sold out to the Democratic Party; this did not deter him.[50]

At one of the meetings at a Harlem casino, Reverdy asked the controversial Father Divine to attend. Divine was a evangelist who had gathered around him masses of poor people to whom he was "God." He opened up several "Heavens" in which he fed, housed, clothed, and employed his flock before and especially during the Great Depression years. In return they gave him what few earthly possessions they had and, most of all, their allegiance.[51] Although the more traditional ministers considered him to be a charlatan and cultist, Reverdy recognized that, like Marcus Garvey, Divine had tremendous appeal. In addition, Divine fed and gave dignity to many Negroes who may not have survived without his intervention. At the Harlem meeting he was accompanied by two hundred of his "angels" (followers). When he had finished speaking, Reverdy said the casino resounded with applause, and his "angels" cried, "Peace, it is wonderful!"[52] No doubt Reverdy again received severe criticism by some blacks and whites for inviting Divine.

Reverdy disagreed with those ministers who called the Eighteenth Amendment (prohibition) a moral question without recognizing the "immorality resulting from it." Instead, they should suggest some other kind of regulation that would be more effective. "All the clergy of the country cannot put a bone-dry law on a wet people, a law that is un-American." Now was the time for Negroes to emancipate themselves from the Republican Party. Seventy-five percent of the Negro population live in the South and yet in fifty years the Republican Party has done nothing to liberate them politically, he said.[53] Once again Dr. R. R. Wright of the *Christian Recorder* disagreed with Ransom and felt Negroes should remain loyal to the Republican Party.[54]

To Reverdy's dismay, Hoover won by over six million votes, riding in on the country's economic prosperity under Republican rule and American's unwarranted fear of a papal takeover if a Catholic became president. Not until John F. Kennedy's election in 1960 was a Catholic to win the presidency. Nevertheless, Smith had brought about a change in the Democratic Party. He had won a majority of the votes in "the nation's twelve largest cities," which were composed of a new Democratic electorate: Catholics, Jews, Irish and Italians, Poles and Greeks.[55]

Traveling back and forth from New York and New Jersey to Louisiana in 1929, Emma came down with a serious case of pneumonia. Reverdy was careful to write down the recipe for her cure:

1 pound flaxseed meal, a few drops of turpentine, 5 or 6 large onions cut up and braised in lard, 1 package of hops. Moisten all with vinegar and make 2 poultices—heat in oven or a pan and apply until patient improves, constantly reheating them.[56]

Having reached the age of sixty-eight, he also wrote her a poem titled "After 42 Years." It began by referring to the early years when Emma's "bright eyes and raven hair" had held him enthralled. Now in "the ripe bloom of love's unfolded glow, Gray hair and sober eyes hold [him]. In the years long sped . . . comes the ebbing tide . . . that leads to union of the shoreless deep of recognition in immortality."[57] He still held the same deep affection for her he had had when they first met in Ohio, and he never doubted she would be up and about soon. If anyone were to die, surely God would take him first. Emma did recover and lived for many more years. Little did he dream he would outlive her by sixteen years.

In Louisiana Reverdy found Lampton College, another inept little school that was a financial burden on the district and of little educational value. He soon closed it and encouraged the people instead to support Campbell College, a more substantial school in Jackson, Mississippi. After only two years in Louisiana, "Providence" intervened lifting the "punishment" given to Reverdy by the bishops at the General Conference in Chicago. Bishop John Hurst, whom Reverdy alleged had "chosen his assignment to South Carolina," died. The Bishops Council appointed Reverdy to succeed him as prelate of the Seventh District as well as to keep his original assignment in Louisiana. Now, instead of only four Annual Conferences, he suddenly found himself bishop of two Episcopal Districts and ten Annual Conferences.[58]

When Emma and Reverdy moved into the Episcopal Residence at 2323 Taylor Street in Columbia, South Carolina, America was in the early stages of the Great Depression. Hoover's election promise of continued prosperity had been thwarted by the abrupt decline of the stock market in October 1929. It was to last "for ten years, dominating every aspect of American life during the thirties" and changing the political climate from Republican to Democratic domination.[59] Reverdy would soon see the Negro's allegiance dramatically switch from the party of Lincoln to that of Franklin D. Roosevelt and the New Deal.

In his autobiography, Reverdy noted that in 1930 half of the population of South Carolina was Negro, "most of whom [were] agricultural and industrial workers." Actually most were sharecroppers, and whites subsisted "largely by the fruits of the labor of their Negro employees." In his fading memory (he was eighty-nine when *Pilgrimage* was published), Reverdy wrote that the Depression did not seem to paralyze the state as badly as it did other sections of the country. People were able to "produce at least enough food for their basic needs."[60] Nevertheless, the total cash income from livestock and crop sales for South Carolina farmers dropped from $129,910,000 in

1929 to $44,428,000 in 1932, a decline of 66 percent. Funds for colored public schools that had never been equal to funds for white schools, "declined drastically: the average expenditure per pupil in attendance dropped almost 30 percent between 1930 and 1932." Even though there was some improvement "as the Depression wore on, things were fairly bleak throughout the decade."[61]

South Carolina blacks were churchgoers. Fifty-five percent were Baptist, 41 percent Methodist (A.M.E., A.M.E.Z, C.M.E.), and "the remaining 4 percent Presbyterians or Episcopalians. Only 170 were Catholic."[62] The founding of the A.M.E. Church in Charleston paralleled the founding of Bethel A.M.E. Church in Philadelphia by Richard Allen. In the early 1800s, the white Methodist Churches of Charleston, South Carolina, permitted Negroes to participate in their Sunday services. In addition, blacks were encouraged to conduct their own Quarterly Conferences, trials, and other business. In 1815, this independence was suddenly taken away. Not only were their affairs controlled entirely by whites, but on Sundays they were removed from the main floor of the sanctuary and made to occupy seats in the galleries. Led by Rev. Morris Brown in 1820, blacks decided to build their own African Church at Hanover and Reid Streets in spite of the opposition from the white Methodists and the city. Learning of Richard Allen's African Methodist Episcopal Church, Morris Brown traveled to the Philadelphia Annual Conference where he was ordained by Allen. Soon afterward, the African Church of Charleston became a part of the African Methodist Episcopal Church.[63]

Prompted by negative editorials describing the African services as noisy and conducted by ignorant, vicious people, the city of Charleston razed the church in 1820. Nevertheless, blacks managed to find other places to worship until 1822 when Denmark Vesey, a slave, led a rebellion against the slaveholders and alarmed the entire white population. All assemblies held by Negroes were banned. The African Church had to go underground until the close of the Civil War when Bishop Payne returned to Charleston, his hometown. (He had escaped a possible lynching in 1835.) Payne called a Quarterly Conference May 13, 1865, at Zion Presbyterian Church.[64] He organized the South Carolina Annual Conference of the A.M.E. Church that had grown into six Conferences by the time Reverdy arrived: The South Carolina Conference (organized in 1865), the Columbia Conference (1879), the Northeast South Carolina Conference (1892), Piedmont South Carolina Conference (1909), Palmetto South Carolina Conference, and the Central South Carolina Conference (1911).[65]

Allen University in Charleston, the second oldest of the A.M.E. schools (Wilberforce was the oldest), had been established in December 1880 by Bishop W. F. Dickerson with J. C. Waters as its first president. The current president, David H. Sims, was a graduate of Georgia State College, Oberlin Theological Seminary, and the University of Chicago and a candidate for the bishopric. Despite the Depression,

A.M.E.S not only liberally supported their church in South Carolina but gave over $60,000 a year for the support Allen.[66]

"The history of Black Carolina evolves around central themes of repression and powerlessness and the effort to overcome or adapt to those conditions."[67] This was the first time Emma and Reverdy had lived in the deep South. Used to the more subtle prejudice of the North, they must have found the blatant racism of South Carolina unsettling. The Negroes' way of dealing with it at times seemed less aggressive, perhaps because they feared life-threatening reprisals. Having no other outlet, often blacks turned their frustration and hostility on one another rather than the offending whites. The Ransoms soon recognized the class schism between the people of the Piedmont section who were more independent than "those radiating from Charleston." Charleston blacks referred to the people of Piedmont as "Up Country Niggers."[68]

Reverdy was also fascinated by the "strange ideas about occult influences and practices" held by many black South Carolinians.[69] Influenced by the African tribal practices of the Gullahs off the coast of South Carolina and Georgia:

> like religious belief, magic prevailed in a new setting because it held such a firm grip on the mind, helped one to cope with the unknown, and provided some sense of protection in a threatening world. . . . More a secret practice than a social one it said, "My will be done," rather than "Thy will be done."[70]

Being a student of the effects of assimilation, it must have been of special interest to Reverdy to study these people, many of whom were offspring of the Gullahs and who maintained their customs and lingual ties. For them it seemed a simple matter to unite African magic with Christian miracles and morality, thereby assuring themselves double protection.

On March 6, 1930, Reverdy took time out from his Episcopal duties to deliver an address on Crispus Attucks at the Metropolitan Opera House in Philadelphia. Affirming that "every good gift has been brought with blood" of martyrs, he listed one such martyr, black Crispus Attucks, the first man to die in the Revolutionary War. Since then, blacks have given their lives in every war to date, including the Civil War, he said. During World War I, when some two hundred thousand Negroes were sent to France, "there they were compelled to work and fight under abject and humiliating conditions, so far as most of their white officers were concerned"; however two of them were first to receive the Croix de Guerre from a grateful French government. Negroes have continually had to beg for the right to fight in what turned out to be a segregated armed forces. Reverdy warned:

> In any future war, if Negroes do not refuse to enlist and fight under our flag, except under exactly the same conditions of rank, assignment to duty, promotion, honor and reward, as are accorded to their white fellow citizens, they shall deserve all the insult, humiliation and contempt that may be visited upon them.[71]

Evidently Reverdy regretted having urged Negroes to fight in World War I given the prejudice they endured in camp and abroad and the race riots that erupted when they returned home.

He expressed his reservations about the present London naval conference conducted allegedly to reduce naval armaments in the interest of international peace. European nations are interested mainly in peace for economic reasons; but most of all "the menace of the dark-skinned world, developed and united, is ever in the background of every conference among the white nations to establish international peace among themselves."[72]

Since the days of Attucks, Negroes have become more educated, own more property, and "they can capture every stronghold of prejudice and opposition that would obstruct their progress and achievement." The white man yields nothing, through either sympathy or love, persuasion of logic or sanctity of his religious creeds, except in the face of aggression. Negroes must, therefore, honor martyrs like Crispus Attucks by

> emulating in the paths of peace the virtues they displayed in war—by aggressively fighting for rights, by agitating to arouse and stir, by uniting and solidifying every gain we get. We have not yet begun to fight. So far we have only skirmished. In the coming years when fifty million Negroes advance to the charge in ranks that cannot be broken, Americans black and white, shall lead the way for all the people of the earth to Equality, Brotherhood in the paths of peace.[73]

The Ransoms were happy in the Seventh District and seemed well liked by the people. According to a special A.M.E. issue of *The Palmetto Leader,* Reverdy was "the bishop who [had] brought peace and good will to the A.M.E. Church in South Carolina," and Emma was "a true type of womanhood . . . a cultured and refined character, a gifted speaker. To know her is to love her, for she is an ideal Bishop's wife," the editor wrote.[74]

Always willing to encourage the Negro press, Reverdy advised the members of his district to "make the *Leader* survive and prosper by support[ing] it with their patronage as well as with their praise." Although the paper was inter-denominational, at Reverdy's request the February 1932 issue carried the names and addresses of ministers and lay delegates to the upcoming General Conference and endorsements of the leading candidates for the bishopric and general officers.[75]

Reverdy's supervision in South Carolina was almost spoiled just prior to the 1932

General Conference when some of the "Trustees of Allen University [wanted] to file charges against D. H. Sims, [the] president with the view of dismissing him." Reverdy was able to persuade them not to take such action because "it would embarrass the school, and the entire State for us to wash our dirty linen, and take it up to Cleveland and hang it out to dry before the eyes of the whole convention," he advised. It would be better to wait until after the Conference and then conduct a thorough investigation of the charges.[76] As it turned out, the conference had more than its share of dirty linen to wash without the addition of charges against Sims.

The Twenty-ninth A.M.E. General Conference convened in Cleveland, Ohio, between May 2–16 in the decadent Woodland Community Center on Forty-sixth and Woodland Avenues. The imbedded dirt on the windows and in the frescoes did little to lift the angry mood of the eight hundred delegates, most of whom were still deep in the throes of the Depression. It "opened on a current of deep emotion and with material prepared for explosive and tragic scenes."[77] The laymen had come insisting to be granted representation on the powerful Episcopal Committee that determined how many new bishops should be elected, to which district a bishop should be appointed, and which bishops should be retired, suspended, or unfrocked.[78]

Before the conference had ended, Bishop Vernon was suspended for four years for mishandling funds; Bishop Joshua H. Jones for the alleged misappropriation of funds; the laymen received equal representation on the Episcopal Committee; and Noah Williams of St. Louis, David Sims, president of Allen University in South Carolina, and Henry Y. Tookes of Florida were the newly elected bishops. All three were from the South. Dr. R. R. Wright of Philadelphia who had been a top contender during the first three ballots was defeated.[79] Sectionalism had reared its ugly head again.

Reverdy had never liked Vernon and accused him of "lacking the spirit of brotherly kindness, impartiality and straight-forwardness in business." When the Episcopal Committee recommended his suspension, the presiding bishop, H. B. Parks lost control of the Conference that became "boisterous and stormy." The delegates refused to listen to Vernon's appeal or the defense of his friends and supporters. When he was finally allowed to say a few words, he had little effect on the outcome. The motion to suspend was carried. "With head slightly bowed, Bishop Vernon left the platform."[80] In retrospect Reverdy wrote in *Pilgrimage*:

> Now that he has been removed from our midst, under the seal of the silence of the grave, where bitterness and rancor can have no place, we cannot know how much and how far he was guilty of all the things that doubtless were greatly magnified by passion and resentment.[81]

Reverdy was presiding at the time the Episcopal Committee brought in a guilty verdict for Bishop Joshua H. Jones. According to Ransom, what followed was "the wildest

The welcoming entrance to Tawawa Chimney Corner, Wilberforce, Ohio.

scene of disorder, confusion, and threatened violence." Mob psychology ruled, and Jones was not allowed to present his books and records to clear himself. "Thus the curtain was lowered on the official life of one of the most dynamic and forceful men that has ever presided over the administration of affairs in the A.M.E. Church," Reverdy wrote. Within a year, Jones was dead, and it was found that he had not been guilty. His estate was able to collect over $10,000 due him by Wilberforce University and the First District.[82]

When the assignments of the bishops was read, Reverdy had been appointed to the Third Episcopal District that encompassed the Pittsburgh, Ohio, North Ohio, South Ohio, Pennsylvania, and West Virginia Annual Conferences. Even before the General Conference, delegates from Ohio had asked him to come to their district, but he told them he had promised he would return to South Carolina. He suggested they ask Bishop John Gregg instead. Ohio persisted, and Reverdy was able to persuade delegates from South Carolina that Bishop Noah W. Williams would serve them well.[83]

Providence seemed to have decreed that the Ransoms spend their autumn years in Ohio. Despite the old saying, they knew they *could* go home again. In many ways, the Third District was a prize. Most important, it contained a highly educated and progressive clergy. On the negative side, however, Wilberforce University was in dire debt. It owed back pay to its professors, and its treasury was practically empty. Welcoming the challenge and wanting to give something back to his old alma mater, Emma and Reverdy left for Wilberforce where they would live in Bishop Arnett's old house, Tawawa Chimney Corner, for the remaining years of their lives. These would prove to be the most important and controversial years of Reverdy's bishopric.

CHAPTER 9

The Third District and Wilberforce, 1932–1940

When I consider thy heavens, the work of thy finger, the moon and the stars,
which thou hast ordained; what is man, that thou art mindful of him?
  Psalm 8:3–4

Emma and Reverdy moved to Wilberforce in May 1932 when nature was beginning to
sport its vernal hues. As it turned out, Ohio was to be their final home. Soon they were
comfortably nestled at Tawawa Chimney Corner, the residence built by the late Bishop
Arnett and former home of Maj. W. T. Anderson. To A.M.E.s, it was a historic landmark.

Tawawa Chimney was a large, two-story, white frame structure that sat back from
the main road. In front of the tree-lined walkway leading to the house was an arch
that read "Tawawa Chimney Corner." The wide front porch enticed callers to pause
before entering the house. Looking through the door one could see a steep staircase
leading to the second floor and a long hallway that formed a "T" at the rear. Upon
entering the house, to the left was Reverdy's library with its large desk, executive chair,
inviting fireplace, and numerous bookshelves. Behind the library was the hall, a bath-
room, the back stairs, and a kitchen that opened onto a porch. Adjacent to the library
to the right were a sizable living room, a music room, a hall, and stairs that led to a full
basement. Next there was a dining room with decorative stained-glass windows
through which the sun cast colorful images. It was used daily by the family and by the
many ministers, wives, and other friends who came to visit and were invited to stay
for a meal. Having once dined at Tawawa, people always spoke of the warm hospital-
ity and succulent fare supervised by Emma and hosted by the Sage. Behind the dining
room was a solarium that never seemed to be adequately heated in winter but was
surprisingly cool during the humid Ohio summers, perhaps because of the trees that
surrounded it. Under the solarium was a four-car garage that accommodated relatives when they visited. Being first and foremost a man who delighted in an extended
family, Ransom was happiest when his family surrounded him. He watched with
amusement as Emma chased her brood of grandchildren through the long halls of
Tawawa. She and Reverdy were at once strict and indulgent, depending on the seriousness of the infraction. Of the two, Reverdy tended to be more lenient.

After walking up the long staircase to the second floor, Reverdy liked to relax with a book in the large sitting room that ran almost the length of the house. Right and left of the sitting room were six bedrooms. In the master bedroom right center, Emma and Reverdy slept in a specially made king-sized bed that had been designed to accommodate Reverdy's height. There were ample windows throughout the house so that wherever they were they could look out on wooded glens and springs.

The Ransoms supported Wilberforce University not only financially but by recruiting students. It was important that blacks learn about their heritage and about other blacks from all sections of America, Africa, South America, and the Caribbean. They encouraged nine of their grandchildren to live in Wilberforce and attend the university. Reverdy III, Stewart, Paul, Louis, Harriet, Elise, Emma, Madeline, and Josephine were students at one time or another and most graduated. All shared their grandparents' love for Tawawa Chimney Corner and the campus.[1]

The aesthetic beauty of Tawawa Chimney and the campus, however, did not lessen the many problems facing Reverdy when he arrived. Besides the Depression that affected the A.M.E. Church and the university's finances, was the growing friction between the two main divisions of the school, the Combined Normal and Industrial Department and the College of Liberal Arts, referred to respectively as the "State Side" and the "Church Side."

A relationship between the State of Ohio and the university had been initiated March 1887 when an act of the Ohio legislature established a Combined Normal and Industrial (CN&I) Department at Wilberforce University. There were two boards of trustees, the church's and the state's. Initially on the state board there was equal representation, three members appointed by the state and three by the church. In time the church's representation on the state board was lessened, and the university president's authority over the CN&I was superseded by a state-appointed superintendent.[2] The church had always regarded the CN&I as a department of the university. A report compiled by the Committee on Study of State Relations at Wilberforce University in 1947 still maintained the sponsors of the bill in 1887 "had as their primary aim that of helping a worthy institution carry out its objectives more effectively." The state had no a desire "to control the University, to operate a separate institution, to compete with the University in any way, not even to exert undue control over the CN&I department."[3]

Gradually the state saw the CN&I as a separate department *at* Wilberforce. By 1910 the superintendent, W. A. Joiner, had begun pushing for less emphasis on industrial education and more on teachers' training in the department. The church board and President William S. Scarborough felt Joiner was infringing on the educational program of the university.[4] As a compromise in 1929, the "clock hour" came into being. It stipulated that courses in secondary education and high school were to be taught by the CN&I department. In exchange, on a per student "clock hour" basis, the state was to pay the tuition for students who needed general education courses taught by the university. Despite the compromise, there was still an undercurrent of ill will between the state and church.[5]

There had been many changes since Reverdy had been a student in 1881. The state had poured a good deal of money into the Combined Normal and Industrial Department. Among the new buildings it had erected were Howells Hall for the Department of Printing (1900); Arnett Hall, a women's dormitory (1905); Galloway Hall, named for the president of the CN&I's board of trustees (1906); Mitchell Hall, a senior women's dormitory (1910); Tawawa Hospital (1916); Bundy Hall that housed the commercial and normal departments and the administrators of the CN&I Department (1917); and the Mechanics Arts building. On the "Church Side," there was Carnegie Library, donated by Andrew Carnegie (erected 1907); Kezia Emery Hall, donated by Miss E. J. Emery in honor of her mother (1913); and Shorter Hall that had been destroyed by fire a second time and rebuilt. It had dormitories for four hundred students, twenty-six classrooms, and an auditorium that accommodated two thousand.[6]

When Reverdy arrived, the president of Wilberforce was Gilbert H. Jones, son of Bishop Joshua H. Jones, who had just been suspended at the 1932 General Conference for allegedly misappropriating funds. Joshua had been president of Wilberforce from 1900–1908, and later had been responsible for the rebuilding of Shorter Hall. Gilbert became president in 1924, when his father, as bishop of the Third District, was president of the university board of trustees. During Gilbert's second term (1924–32), Bishop Jones had been moved to the First District but still had power as vice president of the university board and as member of the executive committee.[7] Although Reverdy had a great deal of respect for Gilbert as a scholar and educator, he knew that Bishop Jones had dictated many of the university's policies and greatly influenced his son. "Under the chaotic conditions of the school finances," Reverdy said he "could not, as chairman of the Trustee Board of the University, possibly go forward with Gilbert as president." The trustees agreed with Reverdy.[8] In light of Bishop Jones's suspension and the power he had wielded at Wilberforce during Gilbert's presidency, there must have been a great deal of pressure on Reverdy and the board to dismiss Bishop Jones's son.

As early as 1928, Reverdy had received correspondence from faculty and administration about the conditions at Wilberforce. George W. Henderson, an employee at the university, had written: "nothing but a revolution—a change from top to bottom can save us from ruin." Large portions of the faculty's salaries have not been paid in two years. "The quality and spirit of the student body is not as good as it has been and, the thinking students, have no confidence in the morality or wisdom of the faculty," he lamented. "The old Wilberforce, the child of great faith and high ideals is gone." It had departed when John Gregg left as president, he said. In addition, one of the presiding elders had told him that the churches in the Third District "were spiritually dead—Where we once got thousands for education we now can hardly get hundreds." Henderson believed the only cure was a "change of administration, both of the school and of the district."[9]

In mid-May, Reverdy had written Charles H. Wesley, dean of the Graduate School at Howard University in Washington, D.C., asking if he were interested in the presidency. Frederick A. McGinnis, in his *A History and an Interpretation of Wilberforce University,* noted that Wesley "had much to recommend him for the position. He was tall, handsome, and an unusually versatile and effective public speaker." He had received his bachelor's degree from Fisk University, his master's from Yale, his doctorate from Harvard and had years of teaching and administrative experience. In 1928, Wilberforce had awarded him an honorary degree. He was an A.M.E. minister, had been a presiding elder of the Baltimore Conference for a few years, and had run for the bishopric twice, including at the last General Conference, but had not been elected.[10] In reply to his question concerning Wesley's interest in the presidency, Reverdy received handwritten letters from Wesley dated May 24 and June 3, 11, and 15. These letters have been quoted at length because of their relevance to the crisis that developed later between the university and the State of Ohio and Wesley's part in that crisis. The following is the opening paragraph from the letter of May 24:

My dear Bishop Ransom:

Your letter has been received and I have been giving its contents earnest and prayerful consideration. Both Dr. Hawkins [Financial Secretary of the A.M.E. Church] and Bishop Davis had conveyed to me your messages and have talked with me concerning their own opinions, all of which were most favorable to my acceptance of this connection with Wilberforce University. While I was at Cleveland several persons spoke to me of this also, urging that I consider the matter. My reply has been the only tactful thing to say, and that was that Wilberforce had a President, and that I could not indicate my point of view until there was actually a vacancy. Accordingly, I would say that I shall be glad to consider the proposal, because I consider it is an opportunity for me to render the Church, the University and the Race a service. If there is a vacancy created there, quite aside from the consideration of it as a stepping-stone to the bishopric but as a challenge in itself to larger service, and other things being equal, I shall accept the Presidency if elected by the Board.[11]

(It is interesting that Wesley saw the presidency as a stepping-stone to the bishopric as did some others who had or would assume the position.) The rest of the letter was concerned with several questions. "Is the salary to be $6,000 as reported and is it to be regularly paid?" "How much of the control of the university's future rests in the hands of Bishop Jones through loans, endorsements or notes or mortgages?" "Is it possible to interest the State of Ohio more largely in Wilberforce?" "Will the President have a house or will he be compelled to secure and furnish his own home?" "What is to become of the present President?" "What are the present sources of income for the University?" Wesley indicated that Dr. Hawkins had suggested it would not be wise for him to come to Wilberforce on June 7 when the board would be deliberating, "but to hold [himself] in readiness to come so as to be there on June 8th a.m." If he were to be called by long distance when the board's decision had been made, "it would not seem as though he was seeking a place and endeavoring to put a man out of his job."[12]

Reverdy's reply to Wesley's letter, unfortunately, no longer exists. Nevertheless, he received a second letter from Wesley on June 3, 1932, thanking him for his letter and enclosing a resume. "Am interested, I assure you and will await your call," Wesley wrote. He would come to Wilberforce as soon as he was contacted. After receiving other letters from Ohio, he said he felt that there was "sentiment for a change without doubt."[13]

The Annual Meeting of the board of trustees was held on Monday, June 6, 1932. Bishop Heard (former bishop of the Third District and president of the university board of trustees since 1928) indicated that he had called the annual meeting one day early so that "the business of his administration might be completed and the leadership of the session turned over to Bishop R. C. Ransom, who by his assignment to the Third Episcopal District would become president of the board." After Reverdy was formally introduced, Ransom told the board he hoped to establish a "New Deal" at the university, and though he had great admiration for Gilbert Jones, because "he would be charged with the responsibility for the success or failure of the school," he asked that they appoint a new president. That afternoon, Gilbert Jones resigned, and the board voted to offer the position to Charles H. Wesley.[14] Congratulations from all over the country came to Reverdy concerning Wesley's appointment. Most papers echoed the sentiments of *The Palmetto Leader,* that congratulated Wilberforce "for having secured such a gentlemanly and scholarly, withal, experienced educator . . . as its head.[15]

On June 11, 1932, after Wesley had been contacted by the board, he sent another letter to Reverdy in which he quoted W. E. B. DuBois:

"I have known Wilberforce since I taught there in 1894-6 and have followed conditions fairly carefully:

"1. The President of Wilberforce has practically no support and no income, except the unreliable contributions of the Church. Wilberforce University is really supported by the State of Ohio and the power of the State of Ohio is in the hands of the Superintendent of the 'Combined Normal and Industrial Department' at Wilberforce University. This State Department owns all the best buildings and pays a large proportion of the salaries and expenses of upkeep of Wilberforce University. Unless, therefore, your appointment combines the two offices, you are going to be in an impossible position.

"2. Wilberforce and its State Department are inextricably combined. There is no way of separating them today, without a major operation which would practically mean death. The Church exercises power over the State Department by its right of representation on the State Board and by its political power through the State. This political power, however, is modified by the attitude of the Baptists who must be placated and represented on the Board. The State is angry and disgusted at the way in which things are run at Wilberforce but it is between the devil and the deep sea. If it abolishes the State Department it offends Colored people and alarms white Ohio which does not want Negro students in Ohio State University and other white colleges. On the other hand, if the State supports and increases its support of the Department at Wilberforce, its money is wasted and stolen. It does not know which way to jump." [DuBois] closes with "I put these statements before you in order that you may act with your eyes open. I am sure that they all can be substantiated."[16]

Wesley felt DuBois had made an accurate assessment of the situation and wanted to know if the two positions, president and superintendent, could not be combined. However, he understood the difficulty because an act of the legislature stated that "no sectarian influence, direction or control in the management" of the CN&I Department should exist. He urged that Reverdy meet with the governor and see what could be done "in the interest of a unity in operation." He further stated that the Baptist were busy trying to push a man from West Virginia as their candidate for superintendent of the CN&I. Wesley thought it was important that the A.M.E.s get behind their own candidate, preferable Professor Howard Gregg, an A.M.E., former dean of Morris Brown College in Atlanta and the Agricultural and Mechanic College at Orangebury, South Carolina, and now professor of education at Howard University. Wesley said his acceptance of the presidency depended on who would be the new superintendent of the CN&I and whether he would be provided with a house for himself and family. "I look to you to help me in reaching solutions in these last two matter," he closed.[17]

In his June 15 letter to Reverdy, Wesley again was urging that the offices of the president and superintendent be combined. "Then with the State back of our program, there is no doubt of success," he affirmed. [From the beginning, he welcomed the State's intervention.] He hoped he would see Reverdy at the New York and Baltimore Annual Conferences. If not, he looked forward to meeting with him on June 24.[18]

The excitement of having Wesley assume the presidency was short lived. As president of the university board, Reverdy had his first major setback on July 4 when he received Wesley's resignation after only thirty days in office. Wesley listed "the interest and welfare of his family as weighty considerations . . . [and] an uncertain income and support, the lack of a home for the president and the prospect of an inadequate one as a result of the financial condition." He assured Reverdy that the indebtedness of a quarter of a million dollars of the college "would not have deterred [him] as a single factor."[19]

> At first, I was challenged by the call to Wilberforce University—the oldest school founded by our race group. The challenge which the school makes through its history, its opportunity and its racial appeal is indisputable. But each of us must decide this matter in the light of his own personal views, abilities and experiences, and his largest service to the group. I believe that I can be of larger service in the field of Historical Scholarship, in which I have had intensive training, rather than in the administration of the work which comes within the province of the President of Wilberforce University. The failure of our effort to unify the administration by combining the offices of President of the University and Superintendent of the Combined Normal and Industrial Department at Wilberforce was an obstacle to our progress as a unified educational plant, and may continue an unfortunate division between State and Church.[20]

He hoped his resignation would not cause Reverdy "personal or official embarrassment," and wished for him God's "blessing and guidance."[21]

Evidently, DuBois had had an impact on Wesley's decision. Reverdy believed that the "mountain of debt . . . and the challenging conditions that surrounded it" were the major causes of Wesley's resignation. His leaving "was to us a disconcerting blow and made our confusion more confused," he wrote.[22]

The board met and offered the position of acting president to. R. R. Wright Jr., editor of *The Christian Recorder,* who like Wesley had unsuccessfully run for the bishopric. Although he and Reverdy did not always see eye to eye, they had remained friends ever since Wright Jr. had served as Reverdy's assistant pastor at the Institutional A.M.E. Church in Chicago in the early 1900s. His credentials were as impressive as Wesley's. He had received his A.B. from Georgia State College, his B.D. and A.M. from the University of Chicago, his Ph.D. from the University of Pennsylvania; had done additional study at the Universities of Berlin and Leipzig in Germany; and was the author of several scholarly works.[23] Both Reverdy and Frederick A. McGinnis (dean of the College of Liberal Arts and vice president), agreed that Wright Jr. was the right person at the right time. McGinnis described him as "agreeable, analytic, thoughtful, shrewd in business dealings, and a great worker at whatever he undertook." His attitude toward the State, however, was "conciliatory." "In this manner he established harmonious relations with the CN&I department that continued for the most part throughout his administration." One of his first acts was to rehire Gilbert H. Jones, who became dean of the College of Education.[24]

Wright Jr. was aware of the friction between the teachers in the CN&I and those on the "Church Side." The institution owed the church employees some "sixty thousand dollars" in back pay, while the state teachers received their pay on time and, therefore, thought themselves superior. Nevertheless, Wright Jr. noted the "Church Side" "had a majority of the best trained and experienced teachers."[25] Reverdy acknowledged that Wright Jr. was able to "get the finances under control, strengthen the faculty, build up the enrollment of students, and above all, restore confidence."[26]

⤜

Meanwhile Reverdy had to begin his Annual Conferences. An examination of his first Pittsburgh Annual Conference at Park Place, Homestead, Pennsylvania, October 12–16, 1932, establishes the procedures and style he would adopt during his leadership of the Third District. His focus at Homestead was on the rebuilding of the district's support of Wilberforce University. On the first day, following communion, he told the delegates:

> With its quarter of a million dollars of indebtedness . . . what we need is not money but the confidence of the people. With the confidence of the people restored, there will be found the solution to many of our problems.

Eight hundred students are now in attendance at Wilberforce, and though some are low in funds, Ransom said, none would be turned away.[27] Later he presented Emma to the conference with Mrs. Howard Gregg, wife of the superintendent of the CN&I department.[28] (Reverdy had taken Wesley's advice and pushed for the election of Gregg as superintendent.)

During the evening program dedicated to education, Superintendent Howard Gregg addressed the conference. He prefaced his remarks by first congratulating the district for its new leadership. "Bishop Ransom is not only a national figure; he is known internationally for his great worth. We are glad beyond expression to have him as our leader at Wilberforce," he said. In his plea for financial support of the University, he reminded them that white people were now expecting Negroes to support their own institutions; therefore, they should "strain every nerve, stress every point, and by all means refuse to sacrifice our boys and girls on the altar of [the] Depression."[29]

R. R. Wright Jr., acting president of Wilberforce, followed Gregg. He related how the legislature of South Carolina had passed a law designed to stop the education of Negroes. "Whatever may be the condition of my people, I do not care what Congress or what Legislature may pass laws, they cannot stop the progress of the black people in this country, for God Almighty is leading on," he said. He pointed to the half million Negroes in the North who wanted to send their children to a Negro university so they could have freedom of expression, "and I am one of those Negroes. . . . We lack power because Negroes have been educated wrong. I want to see a group of Negroes here in this institution [Wilberforce] who will believe in the ability and the integrity of the Negro." He recalled the four most important teachers in his life. "One taught me how to think, another taught me how to study, another how to apply, and another how to aspire; and that is why I am at Wilberforce today," he concluded.[30]

Reverdy's conferences were noted for their spirituality as well as civic, economic, and political concerns. This one was no exception. He tapped his foot and clapped his hands as the hymns, anthems, Negro spirituals, and gospel songs were sung by visiting church choirs and the congregation. The delegates seemed spellbound by his words that were delivered with intelligence, poetry, and drama. Before every major decision, he quoted from the great philosophers and from the Bible. For instance, at the Sunday afternoon closing session, before reading the ministerial appointments, he turned to Acts 20:22–24. Slowly he read:

> And now behold, I go bound in the spirit unto Jerusalem not knowing the things that shall befall me there: Save that the Holy Ghost witnesseth in every city, saying that bonds and afflictions abide me. But none of these things move me.

He knew that some of the ministers would be displeased with their church assignments and some of the churches would not get the minister they wanted. He had prayed over the appointments as he always did and had tried to match the right church with the right minister whenever possible. When he completed the scripture, he looked up at his ministers and assured them that wherever they went there would not be all afflictions, all losses, all bonds; "there are joys and compensations. Brother ministers, believe in me. We want to make African Methodism count." When he read the appointments, the ministers sang, "I'll Go Where You Want Me to Go," convinced at least for the moment they should go willingly where God, through the bishop, had sent them.[31] Certainly in his lifetime, Reverdy had been sent to less desirable churches, but with God's help he had made the best of the situation and as a result had grown and had helped those churches grow. He expected no less of his ministers.

In 1932, again Reverdy became involved in the presidential election. The Republicans had met in Chicago in mid-June, renominated Herbert Hoover for president, and chose Charles Curtis as his running mate. The Democrats, also convening in Chicago that month, nominated Franklin Delano Roosevelt, governor of New York, and John Nance Garner as his running mate. The contrasting mood of the two conventions was an indication of the outcome. The Republican proceedings reflected the fatalism of the Depression and seemed "apathetic and dreary"; the Democrats were "confident."[32]

As a registered Democrat and chairman of the National Colored Citizens Roosevelt for President Committee, on October 21, 1932, Reverdy spoke at a political meeting in Springfield, Ohio. He accused Hoover and his postmaster general, Walter F. Brown, of eliminating the "Negro from a prominent place in the Party Councils in the South" and denying seats to "'Blacks and Tans' from Mississippi, South Carolina and Louisiana" at the Republican National Convention in favor of all "Lily White" delegates. In contrast, Franklin D. Roosevelt represented the progressive, liberal platform of the Democratic Party. "The background, the training, the achievement and the character of Governor Roosevelt inspire confidence to revive our spirits and restore health to our sinking economic heart," he said. Because 95 percent of Negroes belong to the laboring class; for them, it is no longer a question of North or South, white or black, but one of economics. Roosevelt's program gives "the strongest pledge and brightest hope of National economic revival and stability."[33]

In the November issue of *Crisis*, Reverdy again expressed his reasons for supporting Roosevelt. He reminded blacks that Hoover had "never taken a whole hearted stand for the political recognition of the Negro voters who have supported him and his party." Although the "capitalistic system" dominates both political parties, the Democrat is "closer to the great body of the common people than is the Republican.... An uprising of Negro voters against Mr. Hoover and his party, would free our spirits equally as much as Mr. Lincoln's Proclamation freed our bodies," he wrote.[34]

In 1934, Reverdy asked a small group of ministers from different denominations to meet in Washington, D.C., to organize The Fraternal Council of Negro Churches (FCNC). Although most of those present already belonged to the Federal Council of Churches of Christ in America, they were aware that that organization "could not bring its full influence to bear upon many questions that were vital to the Negro and other minority groups."[35]

> The original purpose of the [Fraternal Council of Negro Churches] was to promote a higher religious tone among Negro churches and to consolidate opinion and effort in the attempt to secure a fuller share of economic, political and social enjoyment for a suffering minority.[36]

Reverdy delivered an address at the second annual meeting of the Fraternal Council of Negro Churches in Cleveland, Ohio, August 21, 1935. African Americans have adopted "every creed and form of religion" and just followed "the divergent paths ... of white fellow Christians," he said. These divisions have made Negroes "almost helpless to defend [themselves] in the social, industrial, and political frame work of American society." Because religion is their most powerful weapon, the FCNC seeks to become a rallying point for fearless action in behalf of the interests of our people where religious beliefs and denominational interests and ambitions shall not be permitted to enter to divide our councils, and where partisan and political divisions shall have no place.

Among the issues the organization must address are the need for a federal law against lynching, defense of "the fundamental issues involved in the case against the Scottsboro Boys and Angelo Herndon . . . the economic injustice against cotton farmers in the South and rank discrimination against industrial workers in the North" by both business and organized labor. So far the Negro press seems to be "bearing the brunt of the battle," he said.[37]

Turning again to his theme of the church's involvement, he admonished, if the black church is to survive, it has to offer youth something other than a home in heaven. The hour is at hand when the Negro church should unite to fearlessly challenge the faithless stewardship of American Christianity by submitting it to the test of political, social, and economic justice. It must accept no peace "on the basis of submission, compromise, or surrender." If the FCNC followed these guidelines, it would not only serve Negroes but all oppressed people.[38]

Memorial Day, 1935, found Reverdy in Cincinnati, Ohio, giving a memorial address under the auspices of the Peace Heroes Memorial Society. Instead of honoring war veterans, he paid tribute to heroes of peace, those "plain people who, unnoticed, quietly followed the ordinary pursuits of life in the paths of peace" and saved the life of another person. "The artificial distinctions of wealth, race, class, and creed were all erased in the revealing light of a crisis that called for instant decision and action." Unlike Biblical heroes such as Sampson, Deborah, Gideon, and Beniah, these heroes did not lose their lives; "they found them through the glorious deeds that translated them into immortality."[39]

On May 6, 1936, Emma and Reverdy attended the Thirtieth General Conference of the A.M.E. Church at the Palace Casino on Thea Street and 8th Avenue in New York City. In *Romance*, George Singleton describes Reverdy's participation in the opening service: "After devotions the Quadrennial Sermon was delivered by the very popular Bishop Reverdy Cassius Ransom. His tall, Indian-like . . . stringy, gaunt, and lean [form], filled the pulpit. Immediately there was close attention to his shrill, musical voice." Reverdy took his text from Exodus 14:15: "And the Lord said unto Moses, Wherefore criest thou unto me? Speak unto the children of Israel, that they go forward." Because he was not to deliver a lecture or a formal address, but a sermon, he said, he would deal with religion, emphasizing "the revelation of God, through Jesus Christ, His Son." And because his was a Quadrennial Sermon, he must look forward as well as backward, hence the title, "The Church That Will Survive."[40]

The A.M.E. Church, if it is to survive, cannot live on the accomplishments of pioneers, but must "furnish our own redeemers and prophets . . . to go forth and walk with the timeless and ageless God." He predicted in the coming days of this conference there will be those who will cry, "They are trying to wreck or destroy the Church. Let everything remain as it is." Regardless, there are changes that have to be made, he said. For example, the church should close all but two or three of its colleges and one theological seminary and see that those schools are of the highest quality and are financially supported. In foreign missions, the church is using the same methods it used forty years ago and should upgrade its programs. Consideration of the union of the three great bodies of Negro Methodism should be revived and pursued "until it becomes an accomplished fact. If we cannot achieve denominational union, the day of united action along business, commercial, civic, and political lines seems far distant."[41]

When the A.M.E. Church was first founded, its members were looking merely for religious freedom and independence. There are many other questions to address today, he said. For instance, do we have a program that will attract the youth? "I see little hope for the survival of the A.M.E. Church, or any other distinctly religious Negro denomination, if we do not so apply the Gospel of Christ as to make it a vital force in the life of society," he warned. The church that will survive is "one that knows neither race, color, nor nationality . . . wealth, class, nor station, but only the dignity and sacredness of our common humanity." The world cares little about the deliberations of this General Conference. To them it is just another Negro Church body, legislating and voting on things that concern it. "But once let us take up, in the name of a just and righteous God, the conditions that confront our people in this country; and the newspapers and every other public influence will immediately spring to attention."[42]

As Paul had said, the church that shall survive must "become all things to all people, in the sense of being flexible enough to minister to the actual conditions that confront it at a given time." The church that shall survive must be "prophetic . . . must proclaim liberty to the captive . . .with authority of a Divine justice that will not rest until every fetter of injustice and oppression is broken."[43] Reverdy's social gospel had lost none of its vigor; the delegates were on their feet clapping, crying, and shouting "Amen" when he finished.

At one of the sessions Reverdy read a letter from President Franklin D. Roosevelt in which the president complimented the A.M.E. Church for its pioneer work in education, its large membership, and money it had raised in the last twenty-four years. The following day, R. R. Wright Jr. was elected bishop on the third ballot; Joseph Gomez, who had been running third, withdrew. Reverdy assured him he had run well and that there would be other opportunities. After all Reverdy had had to wait until he was sixty-three to be elected. On the fourth ballot, E. J. Howard became the second new bishop. Other important events involved the controversial defeat of Ira T. Bryant by E. C. Selby for secretary-treasurer of the Sunday School Union, the tabling of the recommendation that women be ordained, and the rejection of the resolution that laymen on the Episcopal Committee be allowed to be on the Judiciary Committee that tried bishops. A few days later, when the appointments of the bishops were read by the Episcopal Committee, Reverdy had been returned to the Third, as his district had requested, and had been made historiographer.[44]

At one session, Reverdy had announced the publication of his book, *The Negro the Hope or the Despair of Christianity*. The ninety-eight-page volume was dedicated to the memory of the late Jane Addams of Hull House and the late William Monroe Trotter of *The Boston Guardian*. It contained addresses and articles on the Negro family, church, school, pulpit, economic and industrial plight, freedom, share in culture and good will, the race problem in a Christian state, Crispus Attucks (an earlier speech), and a forecast of the future for the Negro in the United States. The title piece was an address Reverdy had delivered at the Century of Progress Exhibition in Chicago at one of the sessions of the Fellowship of Faith. The book posed the question, "Who shall lead us away from the divisions of Nationalism and Race?" Our statesmen and religious leaders have proven to be impotent.

> Let the national and international builders plan and labor as they will, they can build no temple of "peace on earth," until the black man, who is their "stumbling [block] and rock of offense," is given his rejected place in the corner stone of the Temple of Human Brotherhood.

The language throughout the book is so militant for its time that R. R. Wright Jr. felt obliged to write on the jacket: "Those who know the conditions surrounding the Negro in America will not think the author unfair when they read the strong language he employs to take to task our derelict Christian organization." He hoped such language would "call the leaders to a greater sense of their duty." The book sold for $1.50 and was distributed throughout the Connection and country.[45]

Committee reports and resolutions at the General Conference reflected the optimism of Reverdy and other A.M.E.s despite the Depression. The Committee on the State of the Country applauded Roosevelt's New Deal. More people were working. "The huge relief programs as provided by the administration [had] taken sufficient care of the needy." Homes and farms have been financed and modernized under the Federal Housing Administration and Farm Loan Cooperation; and the banking system had been made secure. "If congress passed social security and unemployment insurance, we may be assured of an early return to prosperity, especially when we consider the Cash Bonus to be paid to World War Veterans in the near future," the committee concluded.[46]

A resolution concerning Wilberforce University asked that August 30, the eightieth anniversary of the school, be set aside as General Educational Rally Day. Fifty percent of the amount raised should go to Wilberforce, the rest to the other A.M.E. schools. This would liquidate most of the educational debts. Wilberforce should become the outstanding university for the Connection, and a board of trustees representing every conference should be appointed so that all A.M.E.s would be vitally connected with it. All the other schools should become feeders to Wilberforce. There should be one main seminary, Payne Theological Seminary. Only students who have had two years of college should be admitted. This would upgrade the seminary and reclaim some of our students who attend elsewhere.[47] These suggestions were sound, and more than likely Reverdy endorsed most of them, except the part pertaining to the expansion of the board of trustees at Wilberforce. This would make an already top-heavy board more unwieldy.

A second resolution of which Reverdy totally approved called attention to the "present low estate into which the 9th and 10th Calvary Regiments and the 24th and 25th Infantry Regiments have fallen." Therefore the congress, president, and American press were advised that "these four Negro regiments should be restored to all of their former numbers, prestige and assignments to duty. And that under the new and extended military program we have such additional units as our past loyalty and our present increased numbers justly warrant." It was further resolved: that telegrams be sent to the majority leaders of the Senate and House of Representatives and to the president asking them to endorse the Costigan–Wagner Bill or a similar bill aimed at outlawing lynching; and that the Conference endorse and urge the passing of the bill introduced by Congressman Arthur W. Mitchell, "for providing a pension of $2,500 and a suitable gold medal to commemorate the services rendered by Matthew A. Henson, in accompanying Admiral Perry on his polar expedition."[48]

Because R. R. Wright Jr. was now a bishop, Reverdy's first task when he returned to Wilberforce was to select a new president. After much deliberation, the Board of Trustees offered the position to Rev. D. Ormonde Walker, pastor of St. James in Cleveland. Although his academic credentials could not match either Wesley's or Wright's, he was a "go getter," a fund raiser, and a dynamic speaker. At St. James where he had pastored from 1926–1936, he had decreased the indebtedness from $76,000 to $15,000. The St. James Literary Forum founded by him was one of the most prestigious organizations of its kind in the city and was attended by Negroes and whites of all persuasions and political affiliations. It met every Sunday at 4 P.M. and was a "platform for free and unhampered discussion of all questions affecting the welfare of human beings," locally and internationally.[49] Walker and his wife, Eva Emma, had one daughter, Deon Yvonne, who was later to become the president of Wilberforce. In *Bishops of the A.M.E. Church*, Wright considered Walker to be "one of the best thinkers of the

Church" and described him as "outspoken," a man who "could not be diplomatic but [who] gained his objectives by aggressive action."[50]

Reverdy recalled in his autobiography that:

> Walker had much to offer, not only by way of scholastic training, but [had] a vigorous, dynamic personality; had sufficient aptitude [and] understanding to meet and cope with the many complex situations confronting him. He began with a firm hand where Bishop Wright left off, so there was no lost momentum in the progress of the school.[51]

Like Ransom, Walker was a Democrat. "As far back as the eighteen nineties, Wilberforce had been one of the seats of Republican Party power and influence." Walker's political affiliations were to get him in trouble a few years later.[52]

At the Pittsburgh Conference held at Brown's Chapel September 23–27, 1936, Wilberforce University was well represented. On Friday evening during Young People's Night Reverdy asked D. Ormonde Walker to speak to the delegates. He began by saying that Wilberforce University was the greatest investment the A.M.E. Church had ever made, and it represented "the first emancipation of the mind of the black man in America." It was therefore essential that the church spiritually and financially support the university. Walker's plea was followed Sunday afternoon by Charles S. Spivey Sr., dean of Payne Seminary, who quoted Richard Allen as having said, "any philosophy, any person or group of persons who took away from the other the responsibility of doing for themselves, also took away from them the privilege of living." He had believed that it "was far better for a Negro to worship God under a tree, in a blacksmith shop, in a hole even, if he planted that tree, built that ship or dug that hole for himself." Spivey warned that "any religion that is not educational is dangerous, and any education that is not religious is more so. . . . If the Negro Church is to serve its day, it must have preachers who are fully qualified to lead the people." Payne Seminary was training tomorrow's ministers and deserved to be supported. When Spivey had finished, Reverdy took donations for the Student Loan Program, encouraging everyone to give liberally.[53]

After Walker's appointment to the presidency, Reverdy's next task was to fill the pulpit vacated by Walker at St. James, the most prestigious church in Cleveland and second largest in the district. Some time in June, he called Joseph Gomez in St. Louis and offered the position to him. After much consideration, Gomez agreed to come to St. James and "serve under one who had been through the years [his] father in the ministry, and [had] made the largest single contribution to [his] success."[54] When the ministerial appointments were read at the North Ohio Conference on October 4, Reverdy announced, "Joseph Gomez, St. James A.M.E. Church." No one was surprised because Reverdy had had Gomez participate throughout the conference, and everyone

A Third District Ohio Annual Conference, ca. 1938. *Seated, beginning third from left:* Bishop Ransom and wife, Emma, and Bishop Sherman L. Greene and wife, Pinkie. *Second row center:* Joseph Gomez, pastor St. James A.M.E. Church, Cleveland.

knew of their close relationship.[55] The inscription written in the copy of *The Negro the Hope or the Despair of Christianity* Reverdy gave to Gomez sums up his feelings. "Achievement through merit and service mark the ministerial career of Dr. Joseph Gomez. But I sound the deeper note of Love that binds me to him as his devoted friend."[56]

During the conference, Ransom told of some "scurrilous letters that had been scattered throughout the state, undoubtedly because he was a Democrat" and the man he had appointed as president of Wilberforce also happened to be a Democratic. "I am a Democrat," he said, "and it's nobody's business." He warned that people were trying once more to drag politics into the affairs of the university, particularly the Republicans who, in the past, had been supported by Mitchell, Joshua Jones, Scarborough, Gilbert Jones, and Arnett when they were in power. Ransom said it was *he* who had taken Wilberforce out of politics. After all, the men he had recommended for the board of trustees were all Republicans.[57] Though Reverdy probably believed what he said, it is hard to imagine that his politics played no part in his selections. Certainly his appointment of Republican trustees showed political savvy in light of his presidential choice.

On March 18, 1937, D. Ormonde Beaconsfield Walker was formally inaugurated as president of Wilberforce University. The dignitaries marched across the green and gold into Shorter Auditorium to the strains of "Mach de Tannhauser" played on the massive pipe organ by Anna Mae Terry, professor in the department of music. First came Walker, then the presidents of both boards of trustees, the recipients of honorary degrees, the trustees, delegates from Ohio government departments and from forty-one prestigious institutions like Yale, Princeton, Howard, Moorehouse, and Boston, and representatives from Ohio colleges and universities. Last came the Wilberforce alumni chapters, the faculty, and the senior class.[58]

After Reverdy opened the ceremony, the audience joined in singing "Lift Every Voice and Sing," by James Weldon Johnson, a song that had become the "Negro National Anthem." Whenever and wherever it was played, Negroes would rise to their feet and sing with reverence, particularly the verse that began, "God of our Weary years, God of our silent tears." The installation ceremonies were performed by Bishops Andrew Gregg and Ransom and James Alexander Owen, chairman of the state board of trustees. At the end of the ceremony, Reverdy pronounced the Installation Charge:

> The things most valuable and sacred here are the standards, the traditions, the high ideals, and spirit of Wilberforce. These are beyond price. . . . They must not be surrendered for any consideration whatsoever. . . . Wilberforce University is both the morning star and the hope in the realm of higher education for Negroes in America and throughout the world.[59]

In his inaugural address, Walker echoed Reverdy's words. "Wilberforce has her place, deep-rooted in the life of America, a place definitely set by the records of the past, and an indicated future bright with hope." She was the first college established by Negroes and has carried out the fundamental purposes of a university by preserving, transmitting, enlarging, and creating knowledge as evidenced by the 4,689 graduates "who have given of themselves to the enrichment of society." Although there is no such thing as "Negro education," there is a "Negro science of society, a Negro religion, a Negro church, a Negro home, and a Negro people, all of which need study and interpretation." This is why a university like Wilberforce is so important to Negro students. "The right to educate should not be left entirely to the state. . . . Mass education may be necessary in a civilization of mass production, but leaders are never provided in masses." The Negro school must have a broad and in-depth program that prepares its youth for life conditions. He chastised the CN&I department for deviating from its purpose to provide vocational guidance to its students. "Step by step these provisions are being systematically set aside." While the world needs scientists, teachers, artists, doctors, and lawyers, it also needs plumbers, carpenters, farmer, cooks, and electricians. Wilberforce has the opportunity to provide both.[60]

In the South, Negroes are exploited and denied fundamental rights including the right to vote and be voted for. However most of the "institutions of learning for Negroes are . . . blind to these conditions, and no attempt is being made to explain or to correct these inequalities." It is the duty of Negro institutions

> to point out with candor and without fear the existence of these inequalities. . . . Better have these Negro schools closed, protesting for the right, than to have them open and acquiescent in the wrong. Schools for Negroes must set the current of thought moving into the streams of Negro life.[61]

Among those areas Wilberforce must emphasize are the social sciences, "because the natural sciences have led us into strange paths" that have not secured happiness; history and government; the arts, particularly music, a field in which the Negro is uniquely gifted; religion that "to some may be an opiate, but to the Negro . . . is a sustaining force which has kept him alive in the darkest hours of his suffering." Wilberforce may not have the most costly buildings, the best equipped laboratories, but

> if a school is to be judged by the service its graduates render to society, then Wilberforce has an enviable place in American life. . . . The sense of possession, that is owned and controlled by black men gives a measure of pride that perhaps cannot be felt on any other campus in the world.[62]

⤙

Early in July, Emma and Reverdy sailed on a French liner to participate in the World Council of Churches held in England and to get a much-needed rest. They had been married for fifty years, and Reverdy wanted this trip to be a present for Emma. Several of the ministers had traveled with them to New York to wish them bon voyage and to shower the couple with presents. Although there is no record of their reactions to the conference itself, there is a handwritten letter at sea from Reverdy to Joseph Gomez on July 7, 1937. Evidently, both he and Emma were enjoying the solitude and warmth of each other's company.

> My Dear Bro. Gomez: While many were kind, nobody was quite so gracious and cordial as were you in helping speed our departure. I shall ever treasure the many tokens of your whole hearted kindness & good will. So far, the sea has been calm. Both of us well, eating and sleeping abundantly. We hope to land at Plymouth on Sunday. Mrs. Ransom joins in love to you, your wife and the girls.[63]

They returned in September to attend the Fifty-sixth North Ohio Annual Conference in Akron, Ohio, September 29–October 3, 1937. The first day Reverdy announced that he had been appointed to the Parole Board of the State of Ohio by Governor Martin L. Davy. "It is great for one of our group to be on that Board," he said. "There were three judges endorsed for the position, and one man was endorsed by the newspaper, and it is he [who] has made the greatest contention for the position. No one knows what Governor Davy has suffered for making [my] appointment." He hoped by serving on the board he might be able to open the way for other Negro appointments. A minister cannot fully serve his people, he said, by only standing in the pulpit but must be involved in all areas affecting the lives of his congregation. Next he spoke of church politics. Several people had come to him saying "that the appointment of Rev. Jos. Gomez to St. James Church in Cleveland was a stroke of politics." He had chosen Gomez because he had the stature to successfully succeed D. Ormonde Walker. He also hoped the appointment would help Gomez's election to the bishopric because the A.M.E. Church was badly in need of men of his leadership quality.[64]

As was the custom, the president of Wilberforce spoke on Youth Night. When Walker had finished, he received enthusiastic approval, especially from those members who were alumni of the university. "The provocation of that yelling . . . I have seen the like before [at] Harvard University—old gray headed men jumping and yelling when struck by the spirit of their Alma Mater," he said. "If you want your children to lead in this complex civilization, send them to Wilberforce. If you want them to be just servile followers, send them anywhere else. Wilberforce belongs to God, for God Almighty founded it." As a follow-up, on the last day of the conference, Emma Ransom asked for donations for students who were in need of financial assistance.[65] So strong was her belief in the efficacy of education, she made a life project of raising money for indigent Negro students to attend Wilberforce, and after her death Reverdy established the Emma Ransom Memorial Fund for the same purpose.

When Reverdy read the appointments, his son, Reverdy C. Ransom Jr., had been made presiding elder of the Cleveland District. No one seemed to object because C. J. Powell, Reverdy Jr.'s predecessor, had been appointed presiding elder of the Columbus District. The conference ended amicably with the delegates expressing affection and high esteem for their leader.[66] This admiration between district and bishop was to be repeated time and again. At every General Conference between 1932–1948 (when he was eighty-seven), the district petitioned the Church to send him back to the Third. He, who had initially objected to a bishop staying too long in one district, was to remain in the Third for sixteen years. The name Reverdy Cassius Ransom became synonymous with Ohio, and Wilberforce University; he was appropriately titled "Sage of Tawawa Chimney Corner." He presided over his domain with grace. The old house was always filled with ministers, students, and friends, sometimes around the clock.

In addition to Reverdy and Reverdy Jr., it seemed for a while there would be a line of A.M.E. ministers in the Ransom family. At the Ohio Conference in Zanesville the following year, Reverdy C. Ransom III, grandson of the bishop, was recommended by the Second Year Studies Committee to become a traveling deacon. "After satisfactorily answering the disciplinary Question, [he] was received into the Conference" and

Emma and Reverdy's fiftieth wedding anniversary, October 25, 1937, at Tawawa Chimney Corner. *Left to right:* Reverdy C. Ransom III, Joanna Ransom, Hallie Ransom, D. O. Walker (president of Wilberforce University), Eva Emma Walker, Ella Thomas, unidentified, Reverdy C. Ransom, Emma, unidentified, Sadie Anderson, Alice Muntz, Mary Scott, T. D. Scott, and Reverdy C. Ransom Jr.

was ordained traveling deacon by his grandfather.[67] However, none of the children or grandchildren reached the stature of Reverdy Sr. in the ministry or the A.M.E. Church.

At Tawawa Chimney Corner on October 25 from 7 P.M. to 10 P.M., the Third Episcopal District celebrated Emma and Reverdy's golden wedding anniversary. In addition to the guests, the Ransom family was well represented. Reverdy Jr.; Harold George (from Montclair, New Jersey); grandsons Reverdy III, an instructor of religion at Wilberforce; Stewart Ransom, a student at Wilberforce; Paul Ransom; and granddaughters Emma, Harriet, Elise, and Madeline attended. The program had been planned by Georgia Myrtle Teal, dean of Women. To the strains of Lohengrin's "Wedding March," Reverdy, in his usual black tux, Emma, in a gown of gold lace, and Sadie Anderson of Cleveland acting as matron of honor, led the way to an altar decorated with fifty golden lighted candles intermingled with autumn leaves and yellow flowers. During the ceremony, President Walker talked about the sanctity of marriage as soft music played in the background. Afterward, Reverdy and Emma expressed their appreciation for the guests who had come from Ohio, Pennsylvania, and other states. Reverdy read a poem he had written to Emma; then everyone adjourned to the dining room for refreshments.[68] It was a simple but tasteful occasion enriched by the deep affection of the couple who had been through so much together.

In addition to his regular work in the district and the university, Reverdy established the Tawawa School of Religion and Seminar where ministers gathered on the campus in the summer to study and discuss religious and philosophical topics. With James H. Robinson, dean of the College of Liberal Arts, Reverdy compiled and edited the *Year Book of Negro Churches*, a massive undertaking that they hoped to complete by the 1940 General Conference. (During his life he was to compile five year books, two of the A.M.E. Church in 1918 and 1922–23 and three books of Negro Churches in 1935–36, 1939–40, and 1948–49.) He also found that his responsibilities as a member of the Ohio Parole Board demanded more time than he had anticipated. He had been given an office in the Wyandotte Building in Columbus, Ohio, where he had access to a stenographer and typist. The Parole Board supervised the Ohio State Penitentiary at Columbus, the Boys' Reformatory at Mansfield, the Women's Prison at Marysville, the London Prison Farm, and some smaller prison camps around the state.[69]

At his Annual Conferences in 1937, Reverdy had revealed some alarming statistics concerning Negroes who were serving terms in the penal institutions of Ohio. Of the 8,400 men between the ages of eighteen and thirty imprisoned at Mansfield, Columbus, and London Farm, one third were Negroes. Of the three hundred women at Marysville, 50 percent were Negroes. "Although Negroes constitute only ten percent of the population of Ohio . . . they produce one third of the criminals of the state of Ohio," he said. Thirty percent came from Cleveland, the next highest from Hamilton County, Columbus, and Dayton. Only about 2 percent of these prisoners had been born in Ohio. Obviously, those who had migrated into the State, mostly from the South, had not been able to make the adjustment.[70]

During his first year on the board, there were three members besides himself, two former judges and a lawyer. In *Pilgrimage,* Reverdy recounts how the other members always deferred to him whenever a Negro came up for parole. Finally he asked them how they would feel if he turned to them every time a white prisoner came before the board? "As I understand it, we do not consider people who come before us in regard to whether they are white or black, but without prejudice or favor, we hear and decide each case on its merits." He discovered that many of the Negroes were in prison for minor offenses "and had simply been railroaded to prison, because their rights had not been protected by the procurement of proper defense counsel." Some men were held for "stealing chickens, hogs," and so on, for longer terms than men who had embezzled thousands of dollars from banks. Reverdy said he used to toss all night following a parole decision, wondering if he had done the right thing. He was against capital punishment but found that because he had sworn to uphold the law, he was compelled to yield on some few occasions.[71]

Never in my life did I receive greater relief than when the counter currents of politics relieved me from serving as a member of the board, but I shall always be thankful that the fair-mindedness of Governor Martin L. Davy made it possible for me to be the first of my race to enter the door of service on the Ohio Board of Pardon and Parole.[72]

(He served on the board from 1937–41.)

Realizing that at the age of seventy-seven Reverdy often became fatigued conducting his Annual Conferences, younger bishops came to assist him from time to time. Often Bishop Davis was at his side; but at the Pittsburgh Conference in Washington, Pennsylvania (September 20–24, 1938), Bishop David Sims took Davis's place. In addressing the conference, Sims expressed his gratitude for the "undying influence Bishop and Mrs. Ransom had exerted in his own life." Reverdy has been "engaged in making men," he said. "He has . . . an innumerable number of sons and daughters in whose memories he will live on, even long after he has left these services."[73] Reverdy was never too tired, however, to lead his ministers by persuasion and by dramatizing his own colorful experiences that often paralleled their own. For instance at the North Ohio Conference September 28–October 2, 1938, when he wanted financial support for St. James, "he spoke feelingly about the calamity" that had befallen Joseph Gomez just when he was having such an auspicious beginning in Cleveland. St. James had burned to the ground on January 2 as a result of faulty wiring, and Gomez and his members were waging a massive fund-raising campaign. After Reverdy described the fire in graphic terms, especially how the firemen's hoses kept springing leaks, and praised Gomez and his loyal members for their sacrifices, the delegates made liberal pledges for the rebuilding of St. James.[74]

Next Reverdy reminisced about his own posterity. Although he loved all people, he said, certain churches had been closest to his heart. Among the churches he had not wanted to leave was St. John, Cleveland, "but Bishop Arnett, with some friendly expressions" moved him from Cleveland and sent "Mrs. Ransom and [him] to the church of [his] choice in Chicago." He had been doing well in Boston when Bishop Turner sent him to New York. "I have a tender spot in my heart for Altoona, Pa.," he said, "for it was there in my early ministry that I took Mrs. Ransom as a bride, and it was there that my first baby died." He then read a letter from the church at Altoona requesting that the bishop return their pastor O. H. McGowan to them. McGowan had asked to be transferred to the North Ohio Conference, and Reverdy had written his transfer. After listening to the letter and Reverdy's remembrances of Altoona,

McGowan rose from his seat and said, "Bishop if it be your will, in God's Name, I will return to Altoona." Reverdy tore up his transfer and sent him back to Altoona.[75]

Reverdy had a special way with women. At one time during the Pittsburgh Conference, the missionaries were squabbling among themselves about some procedure. Reverdy told the conference that he felt Pittsburgh undoubtedly had the best group of women in the district. Then he turned to the women and admonished them to be sweet to each other, "loving, forbearing. I want you to turn a new page today and begin a new chapter and give to your work a devotion, a consecration, a loyalty that shall not be excelled." The controversy ended as quickly as it had begun.[76]

At Wilberforce, Walker brought about many needed changes. He made several physical improvements including completing the enlargement of the library:

> He unified the office of the registrar so that records of both church and state controlled units were filed in one office, reduced the heavy indebtedness to half its original size, and introduced a tenure system for teachers which the church board adopted but the state board would not.

Most important, he "got the institution [conditionally] accredited by the North Central Association in 1939 with a Committee of Review for annual visitation appointed by the Association."[77] Nevertheless, the *Minutes of the University Board of Trustees for March 1939* indicate that he was encountering some opposition from the state legislature and from the Ohio press because of his political pronouncements from the pulpit. It seemed his problems began when the Democratic governor, Martin L. Davey, was replaced by Republican John Bricker.

During the Tuesday evening session of the trustee board, Bishop John A. Gregg read a letter he had been asked to draft to Governor John W. Bricker of Ohio.

> Honorable Sir:

> In the midst of our Annual Session of the Board of Trustees of Wilberforce University, we were deeply concerned this afternoon when there was brought to our attention a release sent out by the Associated Press to-day to the effect that you were in favor of a Ripper Bill concerning the representation of Wilberforce University on the Board of Trustees of the Combined, Normal and Industrial Department. [This bill would reduce the number of church members on the State Board— Six would be appointed by the Governor and only 3 by the University.] According to the paper, your attitude is based upon the alleged political activity of Dr. D. O. Walker, the president of Wilberforce University. In our opinion your attitude does a grave injustice to the university, and the large number of citizens who have loyally supported you and the party you represent.

For sixty years the presidents of Wilberforce University have exercised and ex-pressed their political convictions up to now without challenge or criticism. The trustees and responsible management of Wilberforce are absolutely free from par-tisan, political activity, and have never put the sanction of the university upon the political activities of anyone connected with the school. But as loyal Americans we cannot deny the right of anybody to the free expression of his political conviction. We have carefully weighed all statements and arguments and considered their ef-fect upon the administration of affairs at Wilberforce University. We are happy to report that in spite of the many obstacles that have been placed in the way, the university is in better condition than it has ever been in its history. We note with pride the growth and development of our institution. . . . We deplore the actions of any person or persons who would permit their personal or political differences with Pres. Walker to cause them to so forget the best interest of our people as to strike at a great institution and to seek to cripple it to get even with the president.

We, therefore, this twenty first day of March, 1939, reaffirm our confidence in the Chairman of the Trustee Board, Rt. Rev. Reverdy C. Ransom, D.D., and our most efficient and courteous President, D. O. Walker.[78]

Later in the meeting, Georgia Myrtle Teal, dean of women, and a group representing the student body requested that they be allowed to speak to the trustees. Upset by the negative articles in the media concerning their president, the students read letters affirming their support of Walker. Even stronger support came from the Committee on President's Report, expressly commending Walker for insisting that the "institution remain forever under the direction of the African Methodist Episcopal Church. . . . The valiant attempt by the President to connect the State department with the Uni-versity spiritually as well as physically is worthy of commendation." The report also supported Walker's suggestion that there be emphasis on student quality more than quantity and felt his retirement provisions for teachers and administrators had much merit. Before the meeting adjourned, the entire report was unanimously approved by the board.[79]

On April 13, 1939, Bricker replied to Bishop Gregg's March 21 letter concerning Walker:

Nobody can object to political activity by anyone except that the law prevents it on the part of Civil Service employees. Personally I believe the same restriction might well run to State-supported educational institutions, but since it is not the law, it is none of my business. Whenever one is treated as I was by the president of Wilber-force in his vicious efforts to discredit me personally without any foundation of fact for his statements, it goes beyond legitimate political activity of any public citizen let alone the president of a state university.[80]

It was obvious that there was no love lost between Bricker and Walker. The governor had begun to cast his long shadow and that of his legislature over the president. The results were pedictable to everyone but Walker.

At the North Ohio Conference at St. John Cleveland, October 18–22, 1939, Bishop Sims was at Reverdy's side. Referring to his health, Reverdy told the conference, "the task pulls at my strength, and my resources are limited. If you only have a little bit of money in the bank, you can only draw out a little," he quipped. He recalled how in his younger days, he had helped the older bishops just as Sims was doing now. Because this was the last North Ohio Conference before the Quadrennial, as in the past four years, the bishop and the district endorsed Rev. J. A. Allen of the American Bible Society and Joseph Gomez of St. James, Cleveland, for the bishopric and George Singleton for editor of the *Christian Recorder*.[81] The District's wishes were only partially fulfilled. At the 1940 General Conference in Detroit, Michigan, May 1–15, Allen was elected bishop, but Gomez, who had to spent much of his time rebuilding St. James rather than campaigning, was not elected and dropped out after the third ballot to support Allen.[82]

Reverdy was able to announce at the General Conference that the 1939–40 edition of the *Year Book of Negro Churches* compiled and edited by him and James H. Robinson, acting dean of the College of Liberal Arts at Wilberforce University, had been published and was ready for distribution. The 219-page book was to become a valuable resource for historians and other scholars. For instance it gave the world population by races; distribution and number of black people; religions of the world; denominations and sects among Negroes not listed in the 1926 census of religious bodies, including their leaders, number of churches, membership, and periodicals; and information on the Fraternal Council of Negro Churches that Reverdy had founded, its affiliates and officers. (Bishop L. W. Kyles of North Carolina was current president.) No doubt Emma had assisted in the section on the "YWCA Work Among Negro Girls and Women." In terms of education, the book recorded that 161 Negroes had received Ph.D.s since 1876 and listed, by name, those for 1937–1939. It gave a chronology of the Negro press, journals, and magazines from 1827–1890, sketches of Negro editors, then listed current Negro newspapers by states. There was also a section on "The Negro and Fine Arts" and the "Negro in Sports." Almost as a reminder that all was not well in America despite a great amount of progress, the book ended with statistics on "Lynchings."[83] Many delegates purchased copies and praised Reverdy and James Robinson for their labor.

The General Conference had been a difficult one. Reverdy was disappointed his special friend, Mary McLeod Bethune, had not been able to attend, but she had written him that she was in Johns Hopkins Hospital and would be there for two months for "restoration" and a "much needed rest." In addition to being a renowned educator, she was now director of the Division of Negro Affairs for the National Youth Administration and a member of Roosevelt's "Black Cabinet," an unofficial group who advised the president on affairs having to do with Negroes. Her presence and words would have meant a great deal to the delegates.[84] In addition, Reverdy was amazed that the conference had voted to table the ordination of women; however, he was satisfied that his *Year Book* was well received and that he had been returned to Ohio and could continue his involvement with Wilberforce University. Nevertheless, he became aware of an undercurrent of growing dissatisfaction with D. Ormonde Walker. As had Bricker and Republican state legislators, some A.M.E. Church members were becoming wary of Walker's political assertiveness, especially when it might mean the loss of state funds for the university. Reverdy would have to make difficult choices in the coming year, some of which he would come to regret. He and Emma left the conference with uneasy feelings about the future of Wilberforce University.

In July, Reverdy was invited to give the invocation that began the second day of the Democratic National Convention in Chicago. He prayed that the delegates would outline a platform that would allow all people "to walk with dignity and self respect in every path of . . . American life." He asked God to bless the president "whose vision and initiative so wisely guide our nation today." Although Americans were not homogeneous in "race, religion, color, and creed," he said, they were in ideals and aspirations, and in the American way of life. "God grant that those who can not be thus assimilated remain forever alien."[85]

CHAPTER 10

The Wilberforce Dilemma and Sims Trial, 1940–1947

The night is far spent, the day is at hand; let us therefore cast off the works of darkness, and let us put on the armor of light.

Romans 13:12

The 1940s would prove to be a stressful decade for America. For Reverdy, Wilberforce University, the African Methodist Episcopal Church, and the Negro soldier, it was especially difficult. Reverdy would face personal losses, vindictive attacks on his character, and strenuous tests of his stamina and leadership. Wilberforce University and the Bishops Council would be split into two factions that almost destroy them both. The A.M.E. Church would find itself at its most abject in esteem and spiritual leadership. As if this were not enough, throughout 1940–1941, the United States was steadily being drawn into global conflict.

By April 1940 Hitler had captured Denmark and Norway and, on May 10, split the English and French armies. Deprived of British help, France was defeated. If England also fell, America would be in great danger. Roosevelt answered German aggression by giving warships to England in exchange for the right of the United States "to build air and naval bases on eight British possessions in the Western Hemisphere." Though the American public was divided between isolationism and interventionism, before long, most agreed that Hitler must be stopped.[1]

As chairman of the A.M.E. Bureau of Research and Publicity, in February 1941 Reverdy published a bulletin in which he made clear his position on the war and that of the A.M.E. Church. Under the caption "We Do Not Bless War, But We Do Uphold Our National Self-Preservation," he said:

> When the ideals of our American Democracy are being challenged, and religious freedom is being menaced by the threat of a "New World order" we have no other choice but to call upon the members of our Church and race to contribute in every way possible to support the program of our government for National defense.[2]

He was aware, however, of the fight that would have to be waged on the home front to gain equality for blacks in the armed forces.

In the midst of impending crises, the Ransoms found a retreat. During the summer of 1941, Hallie Q. Brown, who had always felt a close kinship to the Ransoms, sold them her cottage in Woodland Park, Michigan, for one dollar.[3] In actuality it was her gift. Woodland was a resort that had been inhabited by blacks in the 1920s. Those who found big-city life oppressive, especially migrants from the South, stayed all year round. Woodland was eighteen miles from Idlewild, the more fashionable resort where the Negro upper-middle class and rich gathered in the summer. Having been denied access to white resorts, they bought their own playground some ninety miles north of Grand Rapids. Of the two sites, Woodland had the larger lake and a wooded area inhabited by deer. Hunters came in abundance during the fall. Fishermen trolled the lake in summer looking for perch, blue gill, and catfish. In winter, they pitched their tents and cut holes in the ice, hoping to equal their summer catch.

The Ransoms had often been Brown's guests at Woodland. They loved the small cottage that sat at the top of a hill, shadowed by oak trees and looking down on a silver lake. While resting in his newly acquired summer home, in July Reverdy received a letter from President Roosevelt appointing him member of the Volunteer Participation Committee in the Office of Civilian Defense. Reverdy became one of forty-five Civil Defense Citizens and was assigned to the Fifth Corps that included Ohio, Kentucky, Indiana, and parts of West Virginia.[4] After accepting the appointment, a telegram came from F. J. LaGuardia, mayor of New York City and U.S. director of civilian defense, congratulating him and inviting him to attend the first meeting at the White House, July 24. Included was an invitation to attend a luncheon hosted by Eleanor Roosevelt.[5] Reverdy's reactions to the meeting are not recorded, but one can imagine the honor he felt resulting from his appointment and his luncheon with the First Lady.

At Wilberforce, the situation between Walker and both boards of trustees had reached a crisis. Throughout his administration, "Dr. Walker insisted that he was both de jure and de facto president of the state as well as church units." This had never "sat well" with the state board. As stated in the previous chapter, his real trouble began when Martin L. Davey, Ohio's Democratic governor, was replaced by Republican John Bricker whom Walker openly opposed in the pulpit. Bricker began calling for Walker's dismissal. The Gillespie Bill, passed May 25, 1939, had given Bricker the power to appoint six of the nine members of the state board. Of the remaining, two were appointed by the university, and the president of the university was an ex officio member. The act became known as the Ripper Bill, "because it provided for the appointment of a new set of trustees apparently on a strictly political basis."[6] A second act passed by the Ohio legislature in May 1941,

> raised the status of the Combined Normal and Industrial Department to that of the College of Education and Industrial Arts at Wilberforce University. By this time the church board had been led to believe that an open breach between the church and state-supported units could not be avoided unless they selected a new President.[7]

In *Pilgrimage*, Reverdy recalled that "President Walker made bad matters worse by recommending to the trustees the dismissal of five professors all at the same time." If they were not dismissed, he threatened to resign. Reluctantly, the Board granted Walker's request. Immediately rumors went out that the professors were fired because they were Republicans.[8] Harry D. Smith wrote to Governor Bricker that Walker had been nasty to those faculty members who were Republicans. "If word can be delivered to Bishop Ransom that Walker as president is objectionable to our state administration, I am sure Walker would not be reelected this coming June as president," he concluded. Bricker and other Republican officials who disliked Walker cried "political martyrdom." At the June Board meeting, a motion was made to dismiss Walker but was lost by 10–11. The state board continued to put pressure on the university to fire Walker by threatening to withhold state funds.[9] Reverdy said there was "so much bitterness on the part of the Ohio State Republican machine, we felt at the time we must call for Dr. Walker's dismissal." Many believed the church was not financially secure enough to make a complete break with the state. As a result, "we vacated the presidency of one of the most capable presidents Wilberforce University ever had. In the light of what followed, I think now it would have been better had we stood our guns," Reverdy lamented.[10] Throughout his final years Reverdy was to say this was one of the most serious mistakes of his bishopric. Always before he had followed his own dictates no matter how unpopular they might have been. This time he had listened to those who advised him to take what they believed was a safe course.

An angry Walker predicted to a *Call and Post* reporter that the North Central Association would withdraw the university's accreditation because of the way he had been treated. He accused the CN&I board of trustees of being one of the most politically minded ever appointed by a governor and held Bricker largely responsible for his firing:

> I shall expose his hypocrisy on every platform available to me in the state of Ohio and shall do everything in my power to retire him from public life. His action shows that he is not interested in the welfare of Negroes, and resents any Negro speaking to him on a basis of equality.[11]

Once again, Bishop R. R. Wright Jr. was appointed interim president. Meanwhile, following the suggestions of the Special Committee of the North Central Association, a joint executive board composed of three members from the church and three from the state board was created. It had the power "to consider and pass upon such matters as [were] referred to it by the respective boards." It recommended Charles H. Wesley for president, and his appointment "was approved by all members of both the church and state boards." Furthermore, at the end of his short period as interim president, R. R. Wright Jr. joined the joint executive board and recommended Wesley to be his successor.[12] This time Wesley accepted and became the "first president of Wilberforce ever elected [by both boards] to preside over the State Department, as well as, the Department of Liberal Arts." The selection was "made on the basis of Dean Wesley's demonstrated ability as an educator and administrator" and that he pledged "to steer clear of church and state politics."[13] Forgotten was Wesley's departure in 1941 after only a few weeks in office. At fifty years old, he was still handsome and a family man who was well connected in high society. He had been married to Louise Johnson Wesley since 1915, and the couple had two daughters, Louise and Charlotte.[14] For a while, at least, it seemed to Reverdy that most of the problems at Wilberforce had been solved and he could expend more of his energies in the District; however, soon there were distractions of a global nature.

The United States was attacked by the Japanese at Pearl Harbor on December 7, 1941, and Roosevelt declared war on Japan the following day. On December 11, Germany and Italy declared war on the United States.[15] The year before, Walter White of the NAACP; A. Phillip Randolph, founder and president of the Brotherhood of Sleeping Car Porters; and T. Arnold Hill of the Urban League had submitted a seven-point program to Roosevelt that would eliminate segregation in the armed forces. The NAACP lobbied Congress to amend the Selective Service Act so that Negroes could be inducted without discrimination. "In the spring of 1941, NAACP attorneys met in Washington to plan legal action against the various racial restrictions in both the civilian and military phases of the defense program," but after Pearl Harbor they backed off and supported the government in its war efforts.[16] Nevertheless, A. Phillip Randolph planned to march on Washington to force an end to discrimination in the service and industry. To prevent the march, Roosevelt created the Fair Employment Practices Committee (FEPC) banning discrimination in war industries.[17]

Reverdy had a personal reason to be concerned about the war. It would mean that his grandson, Louis, would have to go to the army. In 1937, when Louisville, Kentucky, experienced a devastating flood, Louis's father, Reverdy Jr., had brought him to Tawawa Chimney to live with his grandparents and finish his education. The Ransoms had grown fond of him, and he repaid their kindness by chauffeuring them to Annual Conferences and taking care of their physical needs.[18]

On June 11, 1942, Wilberforce University held its Seventy-ninth Commencement in Jones Memorial Chapel. Noticeably few male students attended. Many had already left for the service. The original list of guests receiving honorary degrees was long and diverse, perhaps in an attempt to appease both sides of the Walker controversy. Among recipients of the Doctor of Laws were John William Bricker, governor of Ohio; Rev. Joseph Gomez, pastor of St. James A.M.E. Church, Cleveland; Bland L. Stradley, dean of the College of Liberal Arts, Ohio State University, Columbus, Ohio; Republican Ray E. Hughes, member of the Civil Service Commission, Columbus, Ohio, and the State Board of Trustees at Wilberforce; and D. Ormande Walker, former president of Wilberforce University, now minister of Bethel A.M.E. Church, Buffalo, New York.[19] According to the *Wilberforce University Bulletin*, when Governor Bricker and Ray E. Hughes learned that Walker was to receive an honorary degree, they threatened to boycott the commencement unless Walker's name was withdrawn.

> The church leaders told Dr. Walker that he would not be given the degree even tho his name was on the program and that he could get it by the back door by going to the business manager's office after the exercises, which, of course, he refused.[20]

Three months after the commencement, the North Ohio Conference met at St. James, Cleveland. Bishop Frank Madison Reid was on hand to assist Reverdy. The report of the Committee on the State of the Country reflected the conference's concerns about the war. It concluded that:

> if the seeds for future wars are not to be sown and if we are really engaged in this war to rid the world of Nazi philosophy of life, these freedoms [speech, worship, from want, fear] must become a reality for twelve million Negroes of America and for the 300 million people of India and for all the people of the earth.[21]

At the evening session of the first day, Reverdy introduced Wesley to the conference who said that Wilberforce had more students now than she had ever had. He declared that the university is:

> through with politics and henceforth will be purely educational. We want Wilberforce to be a free university, independent in its thinking and administration. We want to promote the kind of education which will develop self-respect among Negroes, that will remove the psychological subordination of Negroes to white people.

When Negroes are able to free their minds, many whites will sympathize and cooperate with them, he said.[22]

In early March, the bishops' council met in Nashville, Tennessee. Their major concern was the treatment of Negroes in the armed forces. The church leaders had from the very beginning asked their people to support the government and the war effort and put aside, for the time being, their personal frustrations with the racial situation. The result had been blatant Jim Crowism in the army and navy, on the bases and in the towns. German prisoners of war were often treated better than Negro soldiers. In the southern states of America, the prisoners were allowed to enter the front doors of restaurants while the Negro soldiers guarding them were sent to the kitchens. Reverdy joined the bishops in issuing a strong proclamation that made clear that although it was the duty of all citizens to fight against any ideology that threatened democracy, the Negro's duty did not end there. "It is neither unpatriotic nor disloyal to vigorously protest with every legal weapon at our command, to fight exclusion from any branch of the armed service of the war effort on the ground of race or color." The fight for equality at home had to go hand and hand with the fight abroad. No longer would the bishops ask Negroes to put their demands on hold.[23]

The Third District decided to give a testimonial celebration for the Ransoms at St. Paul A.M.E Church in Columbus, Ohio, Thursday noon, March 25, 1943. However, Emma, who had been seriously ill, was confined to her bed, and Reverdy had to receive the accolades alone. The *Cleveland Call and Post* reported that "the aged Bishop who still is extremely active sat [through] two sessions of celebration, afternoon and evening, before some 200 cheerful church folk." The reporter called the celebration "unprecedented" and "most momentous." Although there were supposed to be only eight guests to speak for seven minutes, so many wanted to express their appreciation to Ransom, that both sessions had to be extended.[24]

During the noon program over which Joseph Gomez presided, Sadie B. Anderson, president of the Third District Missionary Society, and Christine S. Smith, president of the Connectional Missionary Society, praised the absent Emma for her faithful service to missions, the YWCA, the A.M.E. Church, and to her husband. Governor John W. Bricker and James A. Farley, special assistant to Roosevelt, talked about Ransom's accomplishments as "Citizen of State and Country"; Bishop R. R. Wright called Ransom "Civic Leader and champion of the Negro Church"; Bishop Frank M. Reid referred to him as "Organizer" in whose footsteps no one would ever be able to walk; George Singleton of *The Christian Recorder* acclaimed Reverdy as "Champion of his race and of the young people of the nation." Most impressive were Bishop Robert Jones of the Methodist Church who said Ransom was "the only bishop to fight the problems of the race from the pulpit" and Dean Charles Spivey from Payne Seminary who listed Ransom's five talents, the greatest being that of a prophet.[25]

Reverdy acknowledged these tributes by reading 2 Corinthians 12 in which Paul speaks of his vision of a Christlike man who was "caught up to the third heaven."

Feeling somewhat embarrassed and unworthy of the lavish praise given him by the speakers, Reverdy emphasized the verse that said "of such [a] one will I glory; yet of myself I will not glory, but in mine infirmities." He wished Emma had been there by his side, but he knew she would want him to express her deep appreciation and love. Wiping his eyes, he turned away and took his seat. It was Ransom at his best.[26]

Sometime in April the Ransoms received an invitation to attend an appreciation celebration for the Gomezes at St. James, Cleveland, to be held May 10. Uncertain of their ability to be present because of Emma's failing health, Reverdy wrote on April 26 to Mae Basey, organizer of the affair: "I am glad to have your invitation to the appreciation to be extended to Dr. and Mrs. Gomez. You honor yourselves in honoring them. He has done a monumental work in Cleveland; there is no one here can rival his outstanding ability and achievements."[27]

Emma and Reverdy left Tawawa Chimney Corner by car for Cleveland, May 9, 1943. Evidently, Emma was feeling well enough to attend the celebration. Afterward they spent a pleasant evening at the parsonage talking over old times with the Gomezes and then went to bed early because Emma complained again of not feeling well. The next morning when Reverdy attempted to wake her, he found she could neither speak nor move. He summoned the Gomezes who immediately called the doctor. Emma had had a stroke. An ambulance carried her back to Wilberforce where she died at the age of seventy-nine after fifty-six years of marriage.[28] Reverdy was eighty-two years old and had never dreamed he would outlive her. Together they had met adversity and fulfillment with the same passion and had been blessed with two sons, eleven grandchildren, and fourteen great grandchildren.

In *Pilgrimage*, Reverdy describes his grief:

> We were each a part of the other. When she went away and left me solitary in the agony of my heartbroken loneliness and pain, the light of life burned low and all the stars were dead. In my grief I prayed in my bed, I prayed beside her grave, until in the darkness, by faith, I touched the right hand of God, who lifted me up and gave me strength to stand and walk the few shortening steps that lead into the eternal silence beyond which the day dawns and the shadows flee away.[29]

Funeral services were held at Jones Memorial Chapel in Shorter Hall, May 18 at 11 A.M. with Bishop Frank M. Reid presiding and Bishop Noah W. Williams delivering the eulogy. Grandsons Reverdy Ransom III, Stewart L. Ransom, Paul Swain Ransom, and Louis Albert Ransom lifted the body into the limousine that carried it to Massie Creek Cemetery, a few miles outside of Wilberforce, where Emma was interred and where other Ransoms would be laid to rest.[30] Friends expressed their appreciation for the life of Emma Ransom and their grief for the void she would leave. For weeks, Reverdy could be seen lumbering through Tawawa Chimney Corner as if he would soon join Emma. Though eventually his strong spirit prevailed, he knew, as did his friends, that nothing would be the same without Emma. That period of his life was over, and he had to go on.

≈

Reverdy was able to attend the Bishops' Council in Birmingham, Alabama, February 17, 1944. The Bishops reported that A.M.E.s throughout the United States were "buying government bonds, supporting the Red Cross and enlisting in the Armed Services and war production industries, in so far as they [were] not barred on account of color and or race." Reverdy presented a report on the progress of the Third Episcopal District. He was able to confirm that the district was never more prosperous. Many of the churches had paid off their mortgages. Significant changes had been made under the administration of President Wesley at Wilberforce including an invitation to membership in the Inter-University Council of Ohio; selection and utilization of the institution by the War Department for the Army Specialized Training Program; the launching of the Wilberforce Centenary Campaign in 1944 to liquidate the university mortgage; and the granting of an appropriation by the State of Ohio for the College of Education and Industrial Arts of $1,042,000 for 1942–1944. There had been rumors that some of the ministers and bishops in other districts wanted to retire Reverdy at the next General Conference. To counter this move, Reverdy ended his report: "I am not weary of well-doing; neither am I yearning to put off the harness of activity, but await, along with the rest of you, the guidance of God as to the course of our united action."[31]

The Thirty-second Quadrennial Session of the A.M.E. General Conference met in Philadelphia, Pennsylvania, from May 3–14, 1944. It must have seemed strange for Reverdy to attend his first General Conference without Emma, especially when the assembly sang the hymn that opened all General Conferences, "And Are We Yet Alive?" At the first evening session, Governor Edward F. Martin of Pennsylvania welcomed the conference stating that "the Negro had proven his loyalty and devotion to America in every way, and therefore must not be denied equal opportunities for education, health, security of life and property—the God-given opportunities guaranteed by the American Constitution." He was followed by Judge Vincent Carroll of the Common Pleas Court who pleaded for "the unity of races into one great American Nation, with the Negro fully recognized as a first class citizen." Then Mayor Bernard Samuel of Philadelphia "urged the Negro race to continue to press forward in the spirit of Richard Allen, despite any and all handicaps."[32]

Reverdy presided on the second day. If any had doubts of his ability to be effective at the age of eighty-three, those doubts were soon dispelled. One of his first rulings had to do with Bishop Wright's challenge concerning representation of a foreign delegate on the Episcopal Committee. Reverdy reminded Wright, "It was the unanimous decision of the Bishops in Council that representatives may be chosen for Foreign Fields with the approval of the Bishop from whose territory the representative was selected." He therefore ruled that "the entire matter of the challenge was out of order." At the evening session, the conference listened to an address by Dr. E. Stanley Jones, world missionary. Jones spoke on "Some Solutions to the Race Problems," in which he "sought to explode the theory of racial superiority." The following day, the delegates were graced by the presence of Eleanor Roosevelt who "delivered a stirring and widely humanitarian address." Both Jones and Roosevelt were favorite personalities of Reverdy and were well received by the conference.[33]

Reverdy attended the Memorial Services May 7 during the Sunday afternoon session. Only one bishop, two bishops' wives, and several ministers had died during the Quadrennial. Bishop M. H. Davis delivered the eulogy for Bishop Edward J. Howard; Minnie L. Gaines and Hazel Gomez for Emma Ransom; and Helen A. Williams for Celia A. Gregg.[34] Reverdy was moved by the tribute paid to Emma and warmly thanked the women.

Throughout the conference, Reverdy had worked hard for the election of Joseph Gomez to the bishopric that he felt was long overdue. During the first two ballots he was optimistic that Gomez would be elected. After the first ballot those receiving the most votes were George W. Baber with 427, Gomez with 287, L. H. Hemmingway with 233, and John H. Clayborn with 210. After the second ballot, it was Baber 671, Gomez 443, Clayborn 368, and Hemmingway 316. During the third ballot alleged discrepancies were found, and voting was delayed for an hour. There was much speculation about what happened during that time. As expected, Baber was elected at the end of the third ballot with 915, but Clayborn, who had run fourth during the first and third ballots, was miraculously elected on the fourth with 962 votes.[35] Some said the votes were tampered with in Clayborn's favor, hence the delay in the voting after the third. Other said that the South used the hour to pool resources and make sure a Southerner was elected. Still others alleged that Southerners went through the delegation saying Gomez was a foreigner, a West Indian, and should not be elected.[36] Whatever the truth, there were angry and hurt feelings. Baber was considered to be an exemplary leader, but Clayborn was suspect. (A few years later, he would be unfrocked by the church.) Reverdy was furious. He knew that his friend had been cheated and found it difficult to console him. But there would be another day. The church could not afford to ignore one of its strongest pastors, he reasoned. Nevertheless, that did not compensate for the bad faith demonstrated by the election.

As a result of the law concerning the retirement of bishops being changed, Reverdy was sent back to the Third District for another four years, and once again he returned to Tawawa Chimney Corner. Georgia Myrtle Teal, dean of women, had taken a special interest in the welfare of Reverdy after Emma's death. Opinions concerning her motives were divided. Those who were opposed to the relationship found her to be manipulative; and as dean, she was not always popular with the students. But Reverdy had been used to the close companionship of a wife and found little joy in fending for himself at the age of eighty-three. Myrtle was not Emma, but she was able to fill some of his lonely hours. He found her to be attractive and intelligent, and she spoke with a genteel southern accent. Even though she was much younger (forty-four years old) than he, and Emma had only been dead about fifteen months, some family members and close friends accepted the impending marriage because now he would have someone to take care of him.

In *Pilgrimage,* Reverdy explains their relationship:

> There came a time, at the end of more than four score years, when I sat in my home, solitary and bereft, because the prop that had sustained me through the years had been forever removed and the light that had cheered and brightened my days blended with the unfading light of heaven. But life always has its compensations. It was not romance, but Reality that brought light, comfort and love into my days. It was not a flash of light that blinded, but the light of a gentle personality that brought comfort to my life and made it luminous in the lengthening days.[37]

At Wilberforce, the romance between the university board and Charles Wesley was about to come to an end. Through a series of interoffice communications, Reverdy, representing the university, and Wesley, alleged spokesman for the state, began to wage what seemed on the outside to be a gentleman's war of semantics. Actually, it turned out to be a deadly battle. On June 15, the Trustees of the College of Education and Industrial Arts met and passed the following recommendations, most of which seemed to Reverdy to have come from Wesley: dismissal of the assistant registrar; dismissal of the dean of men and dean of women; transfer of R. R. Wright III to the College of Education and Industrial Arts; and placement of the book store, the large dining-hall, and cafeteria under the supervision of Miss Edwards.[38] According to the *University Bulletin,* there were no charges against the dean of women, except that she had been a strong supporter of Walker. Allegedly under orders from Governor Bricker, Ray E. Hughes, chairman of the state board, had attempted to fire Dean Teal as early as 1939 but had been unsuccessful.[39]

On June 19 following the state trustee board meeting, Reverdy wrote a letter to Wesley in which he accused: "Both your printed recommendations and your open alignments are obviously with the State Trustees. It would appear that you had, beforehand, full knowledge of what they intended to do." He reminded Wesley that the state trustees had "no authority or power to dismiss the assistant registrar," thereby putting the registrar's office entirely under their control. This he believed would adversely affect the College of Liberal Arts. Second, "the State Board of Trustees [had] no authority whatever to arrogate to itself the disposition of ... the Dean of Men and the Dean of Women without the advice and consent of the University Trustees," and replace them with a counselor of men and women. In Dean Teal's case, she had been hired by both the state and church.

> Her contract began on the 1st of September, eleven years ago, therefore she [was] entitled to her salary from the time of her attempted dismissal until September 1st, 1944. R.R. Wright III had been hired by the University Trustees as a leave replacement for Prof. Points; consequently, it was up to the Executive Committee to make the adjustment, not the State Board. As to the bookstore, it had been set up by the University, "but there was mutual agreement" concerning its operation. Although it might be a good thing for all concerned to place it and the dining-hall and cafeteria under Miss Edwards, there are "vital things that were not touched upon in the recent meeting of the [State] Trustee Board."[40]

In his concluding paragraphs, Reverdy expressed his dissatisfaction with the president's recommendations as they related to the Department of Liberal Arts. It seemed to him that Wesley's general attitude and the movements he was making were aimed at placing everything "vital under the control and authority of the President of the University and of the State Board of Trustees." Perhaps he was not aware that "a part of the present attitude of some of the State Trustees [had] implications that are political" and went all the way back to the dismissal of former president, D. Ormonde Walker. Personally, Reverdy avowed not "to be a party toward making Wilberforce University one of the boroughs of either the Republican or the Democratic Party." He said he had tried to be Wesley's friend and had permitted nobody "to plot, to plan, or to unfavorably criticize" him or his administration. Wesley should not be supersensitive if people did not always agree with him, he counseled. "I am for you, but not to the submersion of the attitude and actions you have taken or may take." He signed it "Very cordially and sincerely yours."[41]

Wesley replied in a seven-page letter. He said he had endeavored to be president to both colleges but recognized the difficulties as expressed in DuBois's 1940 Commencement Address in which DuBois affirmed there must be one head to this institution. "Anything else spells friction, lost effort, and eventual disaster." Wesley then quoted the report of the North Central Association that in 1941 said that the relationship between the two boards had grown worse and suggested that there be effected a mutually satisfactory plan of cooperation in the control of the university. Recently the association commended the university for the establishment of the joint executive committee of both boards.[42]

Wesley denied having any beforehand knowledge of the recent decisions made by the state board of trustees "except immediately prior to the meeting when four members of the State board met [him] in front of Shorter Hall and he rode with them to the meeting." Had he known their recommendations beforehand he would have shared them with Ransom. He said he had no interest in politics, attended no political meetings, made no political speeches, nor had friends in all political parties. To underscore his impartiality, he boasted of the money he had raised to reduce the mortgage of the university for which he wanted no credit. On the other hand, he minimized the support that came from the A.M.E. districts through the efforts of Ransom.

> I have tried to "sell" Wilberforce University to the people of the State and as far as possible of the nation. I believe that we have had success in this respect. . . . I hope that I may have the fine privilege, which has been mine times before, to talk with you concerning these matters, and in the light of your letter and my reply, lay the basis for the continuance of our personal friendship and my long admiration for you as a person and a public leader.[43]

Ransom realized he was up against a smooth, clever opponent, who would bridge no opposition. He not only suspected that Wesley was in league with the state board but was also poisoning the minds of the North Central Conference so that it seemed all the problems at Wilberforce were solely caused by the university board and its chairman.

What he did not know was that he had opposition within his own family that would have far-reaching consequences. Louis had written him a letter from the front supporting his grandfather in his new relationship with Teal. Both he and his wife Ruth wished the couple well. (Louis had married Ruth in 1943.) On the other hand, Reverdy III, his other grandson, was bitterly against the relationship. In August, he took personal letters from his grandfather's drawer written by Myrtle and published them in a bulletin entitled "Uncovering the Facts," using as a slogan "Money and Power are the Root of all Evil." He distributed it throughout the Wilberforce community and in other key places.[44] The campus was buzzing, and the phones constantly ringing throughout the community.

Reverdy Sr. had been vacationing at Woodland Park when he received a copy of the published letters. They were not only damaging because of their affectionate expressions, but because Myrtle was highly critical of the Wesley administration and the state board. Her tone tended to give credence to those who had found her to be manipulative and believed she desired to influence Reverdy. She made several suggestions in terms of school policy. [45] In addition, she had worked out a brief to send to each of the executive members "defending the present Dean of Women [herself] and showing the need for a Dean of Women at Wilberforce University" though she was not interested in the position. There should be "a Dean of Women at Wilberforce

University the same as at all of the other leading colleges in the country. . . . And I have proof that Wesley is a liar when he says changing the term Dean to Councilor is in keeping with the more modern practices in Educational policies," she wrote.[46] In her letter dated July 9 she said Reverdy seemed as though he "had lost some . . . determination to stand [his] grounds . . . and let the state trustees and Wesley know that [he was] going to take a stand." She thought Reverdy must have decided to compromise rather than have them "put things back the way they were in order to give me a chance to resign. Now my dear this not only makes you a weakling but it gives the public a feeling that I am incompetent and [don't] deserve the job." Wesley and the state board had not only insulted her, she said, "and damaged [her] professional status" but because she was to be his wife, they had grossly insulted him as well.[47]

Her obvious dislike for Reverdy III was revealed in her accusation that he was working with Wesley against Reverdy Sr. and in her insistence that she would not come to Woodland until he had left. She said he was determined to run their business, and the only way Reverdy could prevent that was to "clear him away . . . and keep him out of everything in the school setup as well as the district." She accused Reverdy III of saying he was with Wesley because his grandfather "wouldn't live long and he [Reverdy III] had to think about his future by joining up with younger man . . . who could help him." Myrtle felt that Reverdy Sr. was blind when it came to his grandson.

> I know too that time is so short and soon you will have me to depend on forever and I have faith in you and know that whatever comes into our lives in the future to make unpleasantness will be readily removed.[48]

Reverdy III had caused his grandfather a great deal of pain by publishing these letters, but being compassionate and understanding human weakness, in time, Reverdy forgave him. Myrtle never did, no matter how much Reverdy tried to persuade her.

Myrtle's letters also revealed that she was busy making repairs on Tawawa Chimney Corner so that Reverdy would be comfortable when they were married. She was solicitous of his health and well-being and looked forward to their union. She hoped he would allow her the same freedom to redo the house as he had given Emma.[49]

During the latter part of July, she visited him at Woodland Park, and they were issued a marriage license on July 27 by the county clerk of the Probate Court of Newago County in White Cloud, Michigan, a few miles from the cottage. They were married sometime in August, and around August 29 took a honeymoon Caribbean cruise.[50] Although this gave them a brief respite from campus and district matters, their problems with Reverdy III were not over.

In June of 1944, the university had granted Reverdy III a leave of absence with pay to study for an advanced degree at Yale. Appalled by his unprofessional behavior of releasing Myrtle's letters for publication, in October the board rescinded the leave

Bishop Reverdy C. Ransom and his new wife, Georgia Myrtle Teal
Ransom, 1946.

and pay at a time when Wesley was at convocation. In retaliation, Reverdy III wrote to
John D. Russell, secretary of the North Central Association of Colleges and Secondary Schools, charging that the trustees (not the president) "of Wilberforce are failing
to operate the institution according to North Central standards . . . and have failed to
recognize in any respect the authority of its President . . . so a teacher has no rights or
protection." Russell wrote Wesley stating:

> In view of the fact that the situation described by Professor Ransom seems to indi-
> cate an undesirable form of control through the Board of Trustees of Wilberforce
> University, I should like to have you submit for our information a statement giving
> your version of the situation.

In addition, Russell requested a statement from Bishop Reverdy C. Ransom, chairman of the board of trustees. Both statements were to arrive in time for the board of
review meeting on December 8.[51]

Wesley answered Russell by quoting from board minutes. He said that on June 6, 1944, the Committee on Teachers had granted Reverdy III a sabbatical for 1944–1945 to complete his Ph.D. and appropriated $100 a month to help with his expenses. On October 10, while Wesley was attending a university convocation, the board met again and on a motion by Bishop John Gregg, seconded by Rev. D. V. Kyle, the leave and all conditions precedent were unanimously rescinded. Wesley said when he finally arrived, no one told him what had taken place until the meeting was over. Nevertheless, he did not believe any further investigation was needed. Because it was largely a family matter, the university should not be drawn into it.

> While I would not have recommended or agreed to the summary dismissal of Professor Ransom's leave with pay, I would have recommended his return to the University be not approved and I am going to give him notice of the same, in accordance with tenure regulations.[52]

Reverdy's statement to Russell was in the form of a lengthy letter. He reiterated how Reverdy III had come into possession illegally of correspondence between two school officials, himself and the dean of women, who were about to be married. These letters were distributed widely. Even after publishing the letters, Reverdy III "continued to issue public statements." The reason for his grandson's behavior was that he objected to the proposed marriage and wanted to thwart it. Failing to do this he sought to discredit his grandfather and Teal. As a result, the board had decided to rescind his paid leave because of his "unethical and unprofessional conduct."[53] Reverdy was greatly grieved. Reverdy III had been his favorite grandson; Emma had fussed over him and admittedly spoiled him. In fact, the Ransoms had practically raised and educated him. Around 1940–1941, Reverdy had built a house next door to Tawawa Chimney for his grandson, his second wife Lillian, and their children. They had a key to Tawawa and access to anything they might need.[54] "I had the highest expectation of him and made my greatest sacrifices for him and his failure to live up to these expectations is, to me, a life time disappointment," Reverdy wrote.[55]

In terms of the board's failure to respect the authority of the president and to operate the institution according to North Central standards, Reverdy reminded Russell that the president receives his authority from the Board of Trustees and "for the first two years of his two and a half year tenure we gave him almost unlimited authority . . . with the assumption that his education and experience fitted him" to do the job. All personnel had been appointed by his recommendation, and all educational policies adopted by his recommendation. "In these things, in matters of finance and general administration we followed him implicitly." In recent months, the board had decided they had better review his recommendations with greater scrutiny. Such a decision, it seemed to Reverdy, would be made by any university concerning any president in the light of experience. As long as the president and the board could get together and solve their problems, he trusted they should have no disposition to criticize each other to the public and to such august body as the North Central Association.[56] Reverdy had been told that Wesley had criticized the university board in general and him in particular to the North Central Association.

By the time the Board of Review of the Commission on Colleges and Universities met in December, they had the statements of Wesley and Ransom. In a letter to Wesley dated December 19, Russell reminded Wesley that the accreditation of Wilberforce "has been questioned on several instances in recent years because of an unsound administrative situation." He had hoped that that situation had been cleared up. The dismissal by the board of a faculty member (Reverdy III) without the recommendation from the president and without the president being present was particularly disturbing; consequently, "the Board of Review voted to appoint a special committee to make an investigation at Wilberforce University, to determine whether a complete survey is needed as a basis for continuing the institution on the accredited list." All traveling expenses of the committee were to be paid by the university. Russell closed by saying he hoped "conditions would be entirely cleared up before the visit of the committee."[57]

By April 5 Russell was able to report that his board had met and had voted to continue the accreditation of Wilberforce. However, "The board further voted to appoint an investigating committee which [would] visit Wilberforce University next autumn and make a report to the Board of Review not later than December 1, 1945." The board considered unsound the control of the university through two different boards. Russell made it clear that these decisions were no reflection on Wesley's administration. In fact, he wrote, Wesley's leadership:

> was the single point of strength that warranted the continuation of the school's accreditation. Our complaint is exclusively against the kind of control exercised by the Boards of Trustees and certain members of the Boards, a control which at times apparently ignores the leadership of the President of the University. Unless the Boards can act as a unit and unless they are willing to entrust executive direction of the University to competent administrators, we do not see how we can continue the accreditation of the University.[58]

Obviously Wesley had impressed Russell and other members of the commission. He allegedly had done little to encourage the commission to note the worthwhile efforts of the university and its board. In addition, the commissioners did not seem to know the reason for the university's disenchantment with Wesley. "The Wilberforce Dilemma: A Critical and Objective Evaluation of Dr. Wesley's Administration" included in the *Wilberforce University Bulletin* in 1948 is an attempt by several faculty members, students, alumni, and prominent members of the Board of Trustees to look at both sides of the question in retrospect. Although highly critical of Wesley, it does list as his accomplishments improvement of "the external relationship of the institution . . . both among the colored and white public." In other words, he was a first-rate public relations president. "He succeeded in securing large appropriations from the State of Ohio for postwar buildings for the College of Education and Industrial Arts." He helped to spearhead the drive to reduce the mortgage along with the three supporting A.M.E. districts who paid the major portion, although he took most of the credit. He improved relations between the president and the state, an "achievement for any Wilberforce president . . . and boasted on many occasion that his word was law in so far as that board was concerned." Under his administration the university and its College of Education and Industrial Arts were accredited by the American Association of Teachers Colleges and was "accepted as a member of the Inter-University Council of Ohio," a natural follow-up to the accreditation granted by the North Central Association under Walker's administration.[59]

Besides his dismissal of the deans of men and of women, the *Bulletin* accused Wesley of instituting a summer school in which he adopted two policies "which were academically unsound and unjustifiable." He required that all faculty members teach in the summer school regardless to other commitments they may have had. The summer school was on a cooperative basis that meant the institution was not going to underwrite any salaries. For six weeks' work (each class met two hours a day for five days) teachers received about $200 for the entire session. Some students were allowed to enroll for four five-hour courses and could receive twenty quarter-hour credits for six weeks' work. Some took "three laboratory courses requiring longer periods which could not possibly be covered in a day of twenty-four hours." Wesley was accused of "never being firm on any of his policies, and the faculty and student body soon learned that he yielded readily to pressure." Time and again, the calendar was changed in the middle of the school year— "granting a holiday here, extending Christmas vacation there, cutting down the length of the term during a session under the pretext of a so-called accelerated program." The faculty learned that the best way to get along was to vote in the affirmative for any recommendation the president wished passed.[60]

According to *The Bulletin*, one of the faculty committees appointed by Wesley reported that during the academic year many students were permitted to enroll for twenty quarter hours of credit against faculty ruling, some for even twenty-five hours. There were several cases where a student's average grade was D, but when he or she reached the senior year he or she suddenly had all As so as to meet the minimum requirement of C for graduation. Wesley tabled the report for two years and then appointed another committee to do the same job. Students who were not qualified for admission were given special permission by the president through the chairman of the "Admission Committee" who bypassed the wishes of members of his committee. There were many duplications of courses and "top-sided curricular programs." For instance the College of Education and Industrial Arts had the following divisions: General Educational Theory, Elementary Teacher Education, Secondary Teacher Education, Special Subjects in Education, and Applied Arts. The first three had only one department each, and the first with its one department had no enrollment at any time. In addition, instead of giving academic guidance to the faculty, Wesley was said to spend much of his time off the campus lecturing, not in the interest of the University, but for personal gain. He rarely met with the faculty of the College of Liberal Arts.[61]

The concluding pages of the *Bulletin* said that faculty members refused to follow him because he "talked of great ideals but practiced none of them and never took a public stand on any local controversy except for his own selfish end." He would tell the faculty:

> that it is a shame to have white men of the North Central Association tell us how to run the institution when. . . they really know nothing of our problems and for that reason we should get rid of the special committee appointed to check on us each year. And as soon as he succeeds in this, he goes to other white men in the state house behind our backs and does everything he can to destroy Wilberforce University instead of trying to save her.[62]

The *Bulletin* wrote:

> There is no question in the minds of those who are familiar with Dr. Wesley's five years of laissez faire administration of the affairs at Wilberforce that he proved himself weak as well as vain and mainly interested in his own advancement. . . . Ever since his arrival on campus, he leaned rather heavily toward the state board which had ample funds and which accepted his leadership without question.[63]

In later years, Reverdy said often it had been a mistake from the beginning for the church to allow the state to establish a department at Wilberforce with its separate board of trustees, its unlimited funds and resources. The church and state differed in their views of Negro education. It had also been a mistake to hire Wesley a second time. In his early letters, Wesley always seemed to be more interested in the state's input, and Reverdy concluded that Wesley's loyalty was to himself and the highest bidder. To Reverdy he lacked the spirit of Payne, Arnett, Scarborough, and Walker who loved the A.M.E. Church and the school it had created from sheer faith. Reverdy suspected, as did many other Negroes, that the state's intentions at first had been philanthropic. It wished to help a struggling church school succeed in its attempt to educate its people. At the same time, it would supplement the liberal arts program with practical, mechanical, industrial, and domestic training. However, as its department grew, and it poured more and more money into it, it altered its purpose, said

Reverdy. It would build an all-Negro state school at Wilberforce so blacks who wanted to attend Ohio State University could be directed instead to Wilberforce. Wesley, no doubt, had initially wanted to develop a great A.M.E. school, but when he sensed the prestige and power that would come to him as president of a state school, he was willing to change allegiance.[64] Both sides played politics to reach their ends and as a result almost destroyed Wilberforce.

While facing the crisis at Wilberforce, Reverdy was asked by the senior bishop, W. A. Fountain, to preside at the trial of Bishop George Edward Curry for maladministration. The trial was to be held in Tulsa, Oklahoma, March 14, 1946 at 11 A.M.[65] In *Pilgrimage,* Reverdy says that Curry was "a victim of circumstances," and had really done no more than some of his colleagues. Nevertheless, A.M.E. members were determined to bring law and order back to the church by making an example of Curry. "It was a case not so much of what Curry had done, but rather an accumulation of disapproval and resentment of similar things that had preceded his alleged offenses." The charges had initially been brought against Curry by the Arkansas Conference. When it came time to try the case, the bishops compromised by assigning Bishop Baber to Arkansas and sending Curry to Oklahoma. Almost immediately, Oklahoma members accused Curry of maladministration. When Fountain received the charges, he disqualified himself. It was then that Reverdy, second in seniority, was called to preside over the trial.[66] Reverdy wrote to Curry on March 21, assuring him that all his "rights and privileges in the proceedings [would] be protected and observed." He planned to arrive in Tulsa on March 13 to make sure the stage was properly set.[67]

The trial lasted two days. This was the first ecclesiastical court ever held in the interval between General Conferences; consequentially, no precedent existed to cover some of the vital decisions Reverdy was called on to make. The committee found Curry guilty but recommended mercy; however, the A.M.E. *Discipline* made no provisions for mercy. Reverdy based his ruling on his "conscience and the teachings of Jesus, as well as the customs of the court of law [which] all extend mercy.... I knew in my heart of hearts that a sinner like me could not refuse to give that which he hopes to receive when he comes at last to stand before the Judge of all the earth." If he had followed the *Discipline* he would have had to suspend Curry permanently. Instead, he suspended Curry for three months until the opening session of the Bishops' Council, June 19 in Kansas City, Kansas. At that time Curry's suspension could be lifted if, during the period of suspension, he had not exercised or tried to exercise Episcopal authority in Oklahoma or anywhere else in the Connection.[68]

At the Bishops' Council meeting in Kansas City in June, Reverdy reported what had occurred at the trial and closed by stating: "I have done my work, the result of which is in your hands. You, from this time forward, must follow your godly judgment concerning any new precedents that may be established or judgments rendered on behalf of Christ and the Church."[69]

In addition to the problems with Curry, Reverdy was drawn into a controversy involving Bishop David H. Sims and the First Episcopal District. Reverdy wrote:

> For the past, more than 150 years of our organization, our foes have been from without; it was not until the appearance of Bishop David Sims as one of our chief administrators . . . that the first real test of our integrity and capacity for self government were seriously challenged.[70]

The bishops were informed of the trouble when they attended the Missionary Meeting June 6–7 in New York City. Two ministers from the New York Annual Conference petitioned them to remove Bishop Sims from the First District. Their complaint stemmed from Sims's purchase of Paradise Lakes in Alloway, New Jersey, allegedly for the Connection. Afterwards he had set up the Paradise Lakes Foundation in the Allen Building at 716 South 19th Street, Philadelphia, with himself as president; Vernon G. Ward, first vice president; Mayme Sims, secretary; and Sadie T. M. Alexander, general counsel. Not only did he encourage his friends to invest in the project, he assessed each church member in his district ten dollars. Because the *Discipline* forbade bishops from assessing churches for any items other than those approved by the General Conference, Rev. J. A. Portlock, pastor of Bethel, and A. Chester Clark, pastor of Emanuel in New York, refused to pay or ask their members to pay. Bethel had a large membership, and it would have had to pay $28,000 a year along with all its other many assessments.[71]

At the New York Annual Conference in 1945, Bishop Sims had moved Portlock and Clark to smaller churches in the district as punishment. Clark took the matter to the New York Supreme Court, and Portlock gathered petitions from the members of Bethel protesting the bishop's changes. Revs. Crawford, Gumbs, Clark, and Walker attempted to obtain an order to restrain the officers of the New York Annual Conference from disbursing any monies received at the conference. The court refused.[72]

Consequently, during the Missionary Meeting in June 1946, the bishops suggested to Sims that he send Portlock and Clark back to their respective churches because the *Discipline* was on their side. Sims met with his ministers and presiding elders and told them he had decided to take the bishops' advice. Afterward, letters poured into the Bishops' Council accusing them of forcing Sims to reverse his decisions against his will and asking them to stop interfering with the First District and their leader.[73] So many allegations, pro and con, were voiced that at the June Bishops' Council meeting in Kansas City that Bishop R. R. Wright was appointed to assist Sims with the First District until things could be straightened out. Sims agreed but, when he returned to

New York, led a protest that culminated in a temporary injunction preventing Wright from assisting in the First District.[74]

There was so much confusion about what the bishops had actually decided in Kansas City, and the newspapers badly misrepresented their actions, that a special Bishops' Council meeting was called for August 15 in Washington, D.C., to write a resolution clarifying their stand. By this time, the council had divided into two factions, the Sims faction that included Sims, Fountain, Davis, Tookes, and Curry; and the Ransom faction that included Ransom, Green, Gregg, Williams, Wright, Reid, Clayborn, and Nichols. Allen had not decided, and Young was too ill to participate. At the Washington meeting, the presiding senior bishop, W. A. Fountain, refused to bring before the group a motion to adopt the resolution of clarification signed by nine bishops.[75] Fountain saw the resolution not so much as a clarification but as a suspension of Sims. If this were so, it was illegal because such a decision called for two-thirds of the bishops' consent, he said.[76]

On September 7, 1946, Reverdy received a letter from Bishop Green who had been in communication with Bishop Wright. Both of them urged Reverdy, "as the Acting Senior, since Bishop Fountain was [now] under charges, to call a special meeting of the Council before they had to appear in court to answer Sims' charges."[77] In reply, Reverdy called a special session of the Bishops' Council for 9 A.M. September 23 at Missionary Headquarters, 112 West 120th Street. In his announcement he wrote, "This matter is so grave that I sincerely urge you to drop every thing and be present on time for this meeting. Because of its urgency, I am postponing my North Ohio Conference. We must save the church." According to Green, the extra session of the council would not have been "necessary, nor imminent, except for the wholly unwarranted and inexcusable actions of [Fountain at] the Washington Council" in not allowing the resolution of clarification to be voted on.[78]

Bishop Davis, secretary of the council, refused to come to the September special session because he said such a session could only be issued jointly by the senior bishop and the secretary. Because he had not called the meeting jointly with Ransom, he did not consider the call legal nor necessary.[79] Clearly the council was in danger of coming apart at the seams, and many felt this marked the end of the African Methodist Episcopal Church. Nevertheless, the council did meet without Davis and others of the Sims faction, who instead sent charges against all of the bishops to the Episcopal Committee of the A.M.E. Church.

Ransom made several attempts to hold a church trial, first at Brooklyn Bridge Church in New York; however, in the middle of the proceedings, Bishops Sims, Fountain, Davis, and several of their supporters marched down the aisle shouting, praying, and making a travesty of the proceedings. Reverdy moved the trial to Union Bethel Church at Schenectady and Dean Avenues. The Sims' group again rushed into the church, this time with a court order to stop the trial.[80] Next the trial was to be held at Allen Temple A.M.E. Church in Cincinnati, but Sims and Fountain got a temporary injunction preventing it from taking place.[81] If the group felt they had defeated the eighty-five-year-old Ransom, they had underestimated his instinct for survival, especially when his indignation was aroused. Because it was obvious no serious trial could be held in New York or Ohio, Reverdy announced that the bishops would call a special session of the General Conference in Little Rock, Arkansas, during November.[82]

Despite the effort of the Sims faction to get a restraining order against holding the conference, the First Special Session of the General Conference of the A.M.E. Church convened November 20–24, 1946 at Robinson Memorial Auditorium, in downtown Little Rock, Arkansas. Over three thousand delegates and visitors "witnessed the performance of a completely unprecedented miracle of ecclesiastical surgery performed on the ailing and strife-worn body of the great African Methodist Episcopal Church."[83] Reverdy had prepared the Episcopal Address on behalf of the bishops. He walked up to the podium, leaning heavily on a cane, straightened up, and with unwavering strength and clarity spoke about the divided house, the A.M.E. Church. History is "replete with records of diverse dissensions, both grave and otherwise—but careful study of the outcome reveals . . . that righteousness eventually arises triumphantly," he asserted.

> It should be understood therefore that far more than the bare refusal of a bishop to comply with the expressed will, judgment and direction of his colleagues . . . is that super offense—that offense which defies description—bold, audacious, heretic, rebellious—both defying and denying without hesitation one of the most fundamental tenets of our doctrine and policy, the General Superintendency.[84]

No lawyer could have presented the case more eloquently. When the conference was over, Bishop Sims had been unfrocked, by a vote of 999 to 35, and Bishop Curry by 812 to 94. Bishop Davis was suspended until the February 1947 meeting of the Bishops' Council. The only one who came away unscathed was Fountain who was exonerated.[85]

More important were the long overdue changes in the *A.M.E. Disciple.* The two-thirds rule that had for so long allowed a minority of bishops to impede the progress of the council was changed to a simple majority. The senior bishop was no longer automatically the head of the council. Instead, the council would elect a president who could serve for only four consecutive terms (years). Every bishop was to make a full and accurate financial report to the Bishops' Council that, in turn, would be published and sent back to the districts for perusal.[86]

Repercussion of the extra session ran throughout 1947. Sims attempted to start an independent A.M.E. Church in New York but was prevented from using the name and taking over the buildings.[87] Every legal step he tried was rebuffed, and soon many of his followers abandoned him and found their way back to the A.M.E Church. Eventually he too would return. There was no doubt the church had suffered from the scandalous behavior, the suits and countersuits, the sensational headlines, and the circus atmosphere prior to the conference, but most important it had survived. The African Methodist Episcopal Church, whose members were offsprings of those removed less than a century from physical and mental slavery, deprived for years of education and leadership training, was experiencing severe growing pains. Those adversities that did not kill her would undoubtedly make her stronger.

Completely exhausted from the church trials and the problems at Wilberforce, Reverdy leaned more and more on Myrtle. He almost always walked with a cane and was pushed in a wheelchair if he had to go any long distance. It did not help that the crisis at Wilberforce peaked rapidly. The same year, the Ohio senate introduced Bill 258 that stated that eight members of the Board of Trustees of the College of Education and Industrial Arts "should be appointed by the governor, by and with the *advice* and consent of the senate, *one* member thereof shall be chosen by the board of trustees of the university." This trustee shall hold office for a term of three years.[88]

Once again, the state had diminished the university's representation on its board. In 1887, there had been equal representation. In 1896, it was changed to five from the state and four from the university; in 1939, it was changed again to six members for the state and three for the university. Now the university would have only one trustee on the state board. Other provisions of Bill 258 were: the state board was empowered to elect its own president, confer degrees, and extend courses including some given before by the College of Liberal Arts.[89] Reverdy could see the handwriting on the wall. The state was planning to take over Wilberforce or force its closure by building its own university on the site.

Prior to sending this bill to the senate, Albert L. Daniels of Greene County, Ohio, had made clear the state's intent when he said, "We shall pass this bill and if this does not do, the State of Ohio will come down there and run Wilberforce." In an article, Joseph Gomez warned Daniels that the State of Ohio would "not never operate a college apart and separate for Negroes, not while free men shall live and speak."[90] Daniels had put into words what the church had begun to suspect. Allegedly, Wesley supported this bill even after he had promised to separate himself from politics and even though he was an ordained minister in the African Methodist Episcopal Church. At any rate, he said or did nothing to protest its passage. The church felt it had been betrayed.

In March of 1947, the university lost its accreditation following the Report of the Board of Review of the Commission of Colleges and Universities. After examining the university on February 6–7, 1947, it had cited the most outstanding weakness of Wilberforce to be the lack of unity between the two boards of trustees. In summary it concluded: "Each of the two boards concerned with the control of Wilberforce University appears to need reconstitution so as to insure a broader basis of representation in the general direction of the institution." Both boards "should be modified to make clear the status of the President as chief executive officer of the University." Of the two, the university-church board was given most of the blame for the situation at Wilberforce.[91]

On April 3, Reverdy called a special session of the university board. He expressed concern about the loss of accreditation and the unfavorable press the church board of trustees was receiving. It was curious that the results of the North Central's decision had come out before the report had been released. Reverdy charged that Dr. Wesley had leaked the report because he was the only one who had a copy beforehand. The headlines talked down the university trustees, praised the state trustees, and seemed to echo Wesley's sentiments. This had set the students in a frenzy, so that when Wesley asked Reverdy to speak to the students in chapel, Reverdy was booed. "This was the first time a president had not stood behind him in support," Reverdy said. There could be no doubt that the university had lost its accreditation under Wesley. He realized there were conditions at Wilberforce that needed to be corrected, and they would, of course, be corrected. "Wilberforce University does not revolve around Bishop Ransom or Dr. Wesley." The trustees must choose the university over any individual, Reverdy challenged.[92]

In reply, Wesley said it was unfortunate that they could not settle matters without personal attacks. The school was suffering nationally from these kinds of attacks. He claimed not to know anything about the bill before the legislature and felt he was being used as a scapegoat. The newspaper leaks did not originate from his office, but if he was in the way he would step down. He denied that he was trying to build a state university at Wilberforce.[93] (It seems highly unlikely that Wesley did not know about the bill because he was in close contact with the state board and the politicians in Columbus. As president, he would have been knowledgeable about everything that affected the university.)

During the afternoon session of the university trustee board meeting, Bishop John Gregg, chairman of the Committee on Recommendation, read a resolution to be sent to the North Central and general public. It said "It has been most surprising to the university board that under the present administration of Dr. Charles H. Wesley, the accreditation is most recently withdrawn." He felt that the university was in good condition, and weaknesses pointed out by the North Central could easily be corrected.

> This board regrets the opinion prevails that it has in any way presumed to assume direction of the administration affairs. It is to be regretted that the administrators have knowingly or unintentionally subjected the University Board to unnecessary

criticism which means that it is going to be difficult to bring about the needed unity for the situation in existence.

He, therefore, referred the "question of harmony to the Joint Executive Board."[94]

Before the session closed, Joseph Gomez read a resolution expressing the board's opposition to the bill that reduced university representation on the state trustee board. He asked that the university trustees be empowered to form a committee to speak before the Ohio Legislature now considering the bill.[95] All of this was to no avail. Despite the speeches and letters to the legislature, Bill 258 became law. Gomez was asked by Governor Thomas J. Herbert to be the one church member on the state board. He vehemently refused to serve as a token representative.[96]

Ira F. Lewis, president of the Pittsburgh Courier Publishing Co., wrote a letter to Reverdy after reading an article Reverdy had written pointing out the real issues and the merits of the controversy at Wilberforce. Lewis's conclusion that the Ohio legislature wanted to create a segregated state university at Wilberforce coincided with Reverdy's and the majority of A.M.E.s:

> There is one point which is so very pertinent and which not only are our folks so quick to overlook; and that is that the enemies of our progress and the enemies of the idea of the full integration of the Negro into the American scheme of things are never asleep. They are always working in some subtle manner to defeat the progress of the Negro.[97]

The denunciation of Wesley was not unanimous. Some A.M.E.s, black Republicans, and most whites sided with him. No doubt, however, those who felt that Wesley had cooperated with the state and the North Central to have the accreditation removed found Wesley's statement to the *Cleveland Call and Post* disingenuous.

> While we have deep regrets that Wilberforce University has been dropped from the list of institutions accredited by the North Central Association . . . [It] is still one of the best institutions of collegiate character in the United States. This is attested by the number of other accreditations and affiliations [it] continues to have.

He pointed to the Joint Committee with equal representation from both boards as the final solution to the problems.[98]

Former President D. Ormonde Walker gave a fiery speech at the St. James, Cleveland, Literary Forum in April that stirred the audience. He was indignant that the accreditation he had obtained for the university in 1939 had been lost. He proceeded to answer the North Central report point by point. He said:

> responsible persons at Wilberforce seeking to cover up their own deficiencies in administration, after learning of the impending loss of accreditation by Wilberforce,

caused publications of news stories that this condition has been brought about by too many bishops and ministers on the trustee boards and too many relatives of bishops employed by the school.

The truth is, of the twenty-two people the North Central complained of, "only three are relatives of bishops and 12 of the 22 persons are the personal choice of the present president of Wilberforce University." The responsibility for the loss of accreditation, he said, rests with Wesley "whose inability as an administrator has been the undoing of Wilberforce's position as an accredited college." The failure of the president and on him alone rests the complaint of too many relatives, too many young persons on the teaching staff, no marking and evaluating system of grading studied, and no systematic use of the library by faculty and students. In answer to a question by someone in the audience, Walker said he would favor a complete withdrawal of the State of Ohio from Wilberforce University.[99]

Reverdy called it "Sales Day" at Wilberforce with the auctioneer being the state board of trustees and the president. Wilberforce could not be bartered for. It was a "spirit, one of those timeless and fondly cherished intangibles that cannot be expressed in the outward forms of endowments, imposing buildings, and the other material trappings." It was not like other schools designed for Negroes. "It was never conceived of as a place to teach 'Negro education.'" For over one hundred years Negroes had kept its flame alive though it was regarded by many as an object of pity or indifference or an effort doomed at failure simply because it is owned, supported, operated, and controlled by Negroes. Even Dr. DuBois had said Wilberforce could not survive as long as it was controlled by the A.M.E. Church and that its only hope was for the state to take it over. Three different superintendents of the Normal and Industrial Department have tried to deliver it to the State of Ohio, he said. Little by little the state has declared elements of power. It has gotten so bad that some believe that the university board has become "so incompetent and so weak, that if not by compromises or bribes, then by force of law it can be compelled to lower the flag and surrender its heritage to the control of the State of Ohio." As long as the African Methodist Episcopal Church existed, this would never happen, he promised.[100]

On June 10, one day before commencement, the university board of trustees met. It moved that "in view of the unsettled conditions at Wilberforce University, the office of President should be declared vacant." The motion was seconded and passed by a vote of eleven to nine. Wesley protested that although he would accept the board's decision, this was not the end so far as he was concerned. He further objected to the use of proxies (Bishop Tookes and Rev. R. B. Smith) and "referred to Robert's Rules and the laws of the State of Ohio." Bishop Greene countered with, "The University is now governed alone by the charter. Since the charter has never been changed to meet any new situation, the charter gives this board the right to elect the President for Wilberforce University." Bishop Reid then moved that the "board go on record as withdrawing all delegated powers to our members on our Joint Executive Committee, as to the election or the dismissal of the President, because of broken faith on the part of the state board." The motion was seconded and passed twelve to three.[101]

During the afternoon session, it was agreed that all official actions of the president be terminated as of midnight, June 12, and that he be so notified. Bishop Greene moved and was seconded by Revs. Bright and Kyle that Dr. Charles Leander Hill become acting president of Wilberforce at that time. Hill was a well-known scholar. He had studied at Hammon School of Divinity at Wittenberg College, received his Ph.D. from Ohio State University, and completed further graduate work in philosophy and theology at the University of Berlin and the University of Bonn. While studying original Latin and German documents, he attended regularly the lectures of Emil Brunner in Zurich. He had been dean of Turner Theological Seminary at Morris Brown College, Atlanta, Georgia. The trustees were satisfied that he was well qualified to be president and voted for his appointment fifteen to one.[102]

In retrospect most agreed that it would have been better if Wesley had been fired after the students had left campus. He would not have been present to make his dramatic statement to the graduation class. "Some day I hope to stand again on this platform as President of Wilberforce University....I will come home if you want me," he said.[103] Afterward his supporters gathered a group of students for a march to Tawawa Chimney Corner to burn Reverdy in effigy. The eighty-six-year-old Reverdy, Bishop Reid, Rev. Gomez, and Myrtle watched from the front window in disbelief as the stuffed likeness blazed and then shriveled until it was dust.[104] For the first time in his life, Reverdy felt old, but he firmly believed he had done what was best if his integrity and that of Wilberforce was to be upheld. Only time would tell if he were right.

CHAPTER 11

Ransom the Historiographer, 1947–1952

Surely he hath borne our griefs, and carried our sorrows; yet we did esteem him stricken, smitten of God and afflicted.

    Isaiah 53: 4

Reverdy faced the crisis at Wilberforce determined that the African Methodist Church would regain control of the university. He was angered that at the 1947 commencement Wesley had asked the students, his friends, and supporters to "join him in developing a state supported College of Education and Industrial Arts, free from any connection with the church."[1] A few days after commencement Wesley was offered the presidency of Morgan State College. His letter of acceptance was printed in the *Baltimore Afro* July 5 in which he stated, "I have given consideration to the invitation and I am herewith accepting the same."[2] At the same time he assured his followers at Wilberforce that he wished to remain until he had saved it from "the group of persons who had neither the desire nor the purpose" to make it a first-class school, but who wanted instead to exploit it for their own political ends.[3] It seemed he was playing the "wait-and-see" game. Meanwhile he moved his office from Shorter Hall, opened a summer school on the state side, and announced it was available to any interested student or professor.

Wesley's actions seemed ironic in light of what he had said in his report to the Board of Trustees at the June 10, 1947 meeting.

> I know of no desire, motive, thought or plan to have the State "take over" the University. I repeat—this is a smoke-screen for an ulterior purpose. In the first place, this could not be done, even if some evil-minded person wanted to do it because of the charter of 1863 which says: "That the institution shall forever remain under the management, direction, and control of the African Methodist Episcopal Church, and for that a majority of the Board of Directors and Trustees shall always be members of said African Methodist Episcopal Church!" I am an A.M.E. Churchman of proven loyalty through long years of service and standing, and I would not join in any such movement nor give it aid or comfort.[4]

In July, Reverdy called a mass meeting on behalf of Wilberforce University. Leaning over the podium in Shorter Hall, he asked every loyal friend of Wilberforce to stand by the university in the name of the founders "who had toiled and made great sacrifices that [they] might have this great heritage today . . . and for generations to come." When he had finished, over fifteen hundred ministers, laymen, and alumni from the Third District gave him a standing ovation. Tears streamed down his face in gratitude. Only a month ago he had watched his figure being burned in effigy; now he felt vindicated. After he sat down, speeches in support of his actions were delivered by Bishops John Gregg and R. R. Wright, former presidents of Wilberforce.[5]

Bishop Frank M. Reid, who was presiding, introduced the new president of Wilberforce, Dr. Charles L. Hill, who pledged to stand by Wilberforce University and be loyal to the African Methodist Episcopal Church with the help of Almighty God. Before adjourning, the assembly formed three committees: a committee for raising funds, a committee for organization and reconstruction, and a committee for publicity and public relations. In addition a resolution was passed to propose to the governor that the church be allowed to buy out the interests of the State of Ohio at Wilberforce.[6]

In an effort to prevent two colleges from being established at Wilberforce, Ransom wrote to Governor Thomas J. Herbert asking him to "appoint a board composed of citizens of recognized character, intelligence and understanding to deal with the situation at Wilberforce" so that they could:

> quickly settle all questions of . . . Division. All that is necessary for you, as our governor, is to remove Charles H. Wesley, former president of Wilberforce University, from all connections with the College of Education and Industrial Arts, and not to appoint Attorney Ray E. Hughes or any other member of the [present] trustees of the College of Education and Industrial Arts.[7]

On July 29 Reverdy received a letter from the Honorable Perry W. Howard who said that according to a news release, Governor Herbert was quoted as saying "that if the church felt that they could operate the total plant, he would be disposed" to let them have it.[8] It would soon become obvious, however, that neither Herbert nor the State of Ohio were interested in removing Wesley, changing the State Board of Trustees, or releasing its interest to the A.M.E. Church. Instead, it made Wesley president of the College of Education and Industrial Arts at Wilberforce.

It was alleged that when Wesley moved his office to Bundy Hall, he took with him "all the important records, his three secretaries, and the personnel deans and their records." Student records and transcripts were not returned until the second week of October, after Wilberforce had begun its fall session. This made it difficult for the registrar. "In August, Dr. Wesley ordered that the books purchased with state funds be removed from the library along with the water fountain, clock, and pencil sharpeners installed in the library building owned by the church." The state board raised his salary and bought him a new car, and the State of Ohio withdrew all of its funds from Wilberforce University and instead supported the College of Education and Industrial Arts at Wilberforce. Although the split had not been formalized, for all practical purposes there were now two separate, hostile schools at Wilberforce, Ohio.[9] After several court trials it was determined that the state could not use the name Wilberforce University as it had initially attempted to do. Nevertheless, it retained all of its property, including O'Neil Hall which was on church property, and enjoyed the largesse of the state's coffers.[10]

Meanwhile a few months after Wesley had opened his separate summer school, Reverdy convened the North Ohio Annual Conference in Warren A.M.E. Church at Toledo, Ohio. Several pleas were made for the support of Wilberforce, the most forceful being those by Charles E. Loeb, associate editor of the *Call and Post*; Joseph Gomez, endorsed candidate for the bishopric; and D. Ormonde Walker, former president of Wilberforce, also a candidate for the bishopric. Loeb said that Governor Herbert had slapped the Negro in the face by glorifying Wesley, a man who was endorsing a Jim Crow state school at Wilberforce. Gomez affirmed that all that he had achieved was given him by the A.M.E. Church, and he was willing to die for its rights. Walker was glad that "God had spared the life of Bishop Ransom to serve in such a time like this in which many events [were] shaking the very foundation of our church." To him Wilberforce was "a spirit," "an opportunity," and "a challenge." The conference dedicated "November 23 as a day of prayer, fasting, and giving for the benefit of the University," and Rev. R. N. Nelson moved that the delegates petition the General Conference to return Ransom to the Third Episcopal District for another four years.[11]

That Reverdy was deeply concerned about the status of the A.M.E. Church was reflected in his President's Address and his Report on the Third Episcopal District at the Bishops' Council, meeting in Dallas, February 18, 1948. "I think there is general agreement that the African Methodist Episcopal Church is sick. There is not a very wide divergence of opinion as to the cause of this sickness," he said. It is the result of the Curry, Davis, and Sims trials and the division in the Bishops' Council. It is time that "we must cleanse the temple. Although it is inevitable that free and intelligent men will differ over vital questions, if we, the bishops, are to administer to a great national and inter-national church, we must subordinate our individual prejudices, attitudes, opinions and desires for the 'peace, welfare, and prosperity of the church we serve,'" he counseled.[12]

He contrasted Wilberforce with schools like Tuskegee Institute that drew their "large endowment and support from wealthy white people because [they] coincided with the kind of education and training that [whites] considered best for the Negroes." For years, Wilberforce had tried to operate a liberal arts university in cooperation with the State of Ohio. Little by little, "the State encroached upon the spirit, the ideals, and the objectives upon which Wilberforce was founded." The problems between the state and church finally came down to "the wrong use of money" that worked to the destruction of the university "just as money, authority and power are seeking to destroy the foundations of the A.M.E. Church today," he said. Ohio is a part of the Northwest Territory that was dedicated to freedom. If Ohio "may legally set up a segregated college for Negroes, than the State of Michigan, Illinois, Indiana, and the entire west to the Pacific Ocean may do likewise. . . . Are we as a race willing to deny ourselves, to sacrifice, to give to save Wilberforce?" He reminded them that one-half of the districts are represented on the University Board of Trustees. Each bishop should send at least ten students to Wilberforce and Payne Theological Seminary next fall. "This would be a valuable and lasting contribution to the church and race," he affirmed.[13]

Reverdy had a busy schedule in the months prior to the 1948 General Conference. On March 3, in Dayton, Ohio, he conducted the Annual Educational Chautauqua meeting of the Third District which, besides pledging its financial support for Wilberforce, also resolved that Ransom should be returned to the Third District.[14] The following day he met with the delegates from the Third District who would be going to the General Conference. The members decided they would hold a testimonial for Bishop and Mrs. Ransom on April 21 to thank them for their leadership during the past four years.[15]

The same month Reverdy wrote an article that went out to the delegates of the General Conference, titled, "Shall We Launch a Forward Movement in 1948: Bureau of History and Statistics." In it he proposed that there should be established at Wilberforce University a Department of Research under one of the bishops of the church, an assistant Ph.D. in history, who would divide his time between research for the A.M.E. Church and teaching at the university, and a paid stenographer and clerk. A yearbook would be published, reviewing the year's work and giving statistics of the church. He reminded his readers that some time ago in Chicago, Rev. Monroe Work, an A.M.E. minister, had tried to sell the idea of research to the church but had failed. Consequently, Booker T. Washington had hired Work and opened a Division of Research and Record. Work published *The Negro Yearbook* and made Tuskegee the center of information on Negroes.[16]

The role of the bishop would be to guide the historian in light of his experiences with the church and to provide an interpretation of its customs and practices. He pointed out that no important organization in the United States was without a Bureau of History and Statistics, and the A.M.E. Church must also create such a department if it is to be in step with the times. In this department facts would be gathered concerning current events and from the history of conferences, departments, and institutions; past biographies; from other churches, their yearbooks, principal publications, interchurch and world movements; and from Negro publications, reports of Negro organizations, tabulations of great events in Negro life and other races. It would be incumbent on the bureau to send out releases to church papers, Negro papers, and selected others; and to supply materials for schools, writers, editors, lawyers, and church leaders. It became obvious that this was the kind of bureau Reverdy would like to head.[17]

Reverdy and Myrtle journeyed to Kansas City, Kansas, in early May, the site of the Thirty-Third Session of the General Conference where over eighteen hundred delegates gathered. As Reverdy was to observe, it was "perhaps the most epochal" conference in many years. At the opening session in Soldiers and Sailors Memorial Auditorium, Reverdy, as president of the Bishops' Council, was presented by Bishop Fountain to pray. His voice was strong and deliberate, despite his frailness; but the delegates could see that the last five years had aged him considerably. "Somewhere our Fathers have lost their way," he prayed. The delegates have come to the conference:

> from Africa, Isles of the Sea, lonely missions and proud cities, to make our confessions. We've given over to our devices; given over to man instead of God. Our ideologies are trying to take the place of the Gospel. . . . Our only hope is when we get to the Gates of God we'll have the blood of Jesus to plead for us.

In the conference minutes, his prayer was described as "fervent," and the recorder said he wore his age with "grace and unction."[18]

Bishop Noah Williams delivered the Quadrennial Sermon from the subject "The Ideal Christian." Using Isaiah 31 as a text, he described a Christian as "a hiding place from the wind, a covert from the wind and tempest, a river of water in a dry place, and a shadow of a great rock in a weary land." At the close of the service, the bishops, general officers, presidents of colleges and deans, and the wives of the bishops were introduced to the conference. In the afternoon the three-hour-fifteen-minute Episcopal Address, containing the recommendations of the bishops, was read by Bishop R. R. Wright, followed that evening by warm welcome addresses from Mayor Clark E. Tucker and Governor Frank E. Carlson of Kansas.[19]

Among the important events of the conference were recognition of the Supreme Court's decision to deny the constitutionality of Restrictive Covenants in housing; the Civil Rights Bill in Congress, especially those sections pertaining to the FEPC and anti-lynching laws; a resolution introduced by D. Ormonde Walker to move all bishops to different districts; the establishment of the Judicial Council as the final authority in all legal matters; and the creation of a Bureau of Research and History to preserve valuable information concerning the church as Reverdy had suggested. On May 12, President Charles Leander Hill and several students from Wilberforce were introduced to the conference. The students assured the delegates that the spirit of Wilberforce was still alive, and they appealed for funds for the library.[20]

During the Thursday afternoon session (May 13), the eighty-seven-year-old Reverdy rose slowly to address the convention. Knowing there was a movement afoot to have him retired, he advised the conference that he had served the church for sixty-three years, had been a bishop for twenty-four years, sixteen of which had been in the Third Episcopal District. He was not asking to be appointed to a district, but to head the new Bureau of Research and History. Bishop Gregg read the following resolution:

> Whereas Bishop Reverdy C. Ransom knows more about the history of the A.M.E. Church and is eminently qualified to conduct a department of research, as his classmate in the Episcopacy, I wish to move that [he] shall remain an active Bishop in the A.M.E. Church, but with special assignment to the above departments.

Others rose to second the motion. Bishop George W. Baber noted there had never been a bishop more "self-sacrificing" than Ransom; Rev. Lutrelle Long said "one of the greatest men in the Church is stepping down today. Between us and Richard Allen is Reverdy Cassius Ransom, who organized the regiment that walked up San Juan Hill," helped organize the Niagara movement that led to the NAACP, and founded the Fraternal Council of Churches.[21]

Bishop Gregg was asked to lead the delegates in singing the Wilberforce Alma Mater he had composed when he was president. With the singing of "'Dear Old W U,' the Sons and Daughters of Allen united their voices in paying tribute to a celebrated orator and Christian statesman who had just received the permission" of the conference to retreat to Tawawa Chimney Corner and "codify the annual deeds of the African Methodist Episcopal Church." Then Rosa Gragg, who Franklin D. Roosevelt had appointed to serve with Ransom on the Commission of National Civil Defense, recited "God Give Us Men." Afterward she lauded Reverdy "for his ability to represent the race in National affairs." Bishop Tookes called him "a builder of men and the African Methodist Episcopal Church"; and A. S. Jackson, secretary of finance, declared that as long as the sun shone in the heavens, Ransom would not be forgotten."[22] Because the conference did not vote for a history scholar to assist him, with the help of his secretary, Reverdy would be a one-man bureau. He would soon learn that the job would be taxing even for a young man.

Reverdy had a special interest in the election of bishops. It was his hope that the delegates would right the injustice perpetrated against Joseph Gomez at the last General Conference. Would the members be willing to elect two West Indians in 1948, Gomez and Walker? If not, which, if either, would be selected? For years, Reverdy had worked in Gomez's behalf; he also wanted Walker elected. To his delight both men won on the first ballot, along with their less worthy opponent L. H. Hemingway, who people said had bought his election. Hemingway received 981 votes, Walker 958, and Gomez 942. Of the 1,905 votes cast, 924 were needed for election. On the second

Bishops of the A.M.E. Church, 1948. *Seated, left to right:* Ransom, Gregg, Greene, Hemmingway, Gibs, Allen. *Standing, left to right:* Gomez, Nichols, Walker, Wright, Baber, Williams, Clayborn, Wilkes, Bonner, Reid.

ballot, I. H. Bonner from Alabama, and W. R. Wilkes of Georgia were elected. C. A. Gibbs was elected on the third ballot.[23]

At the Sunday morning service, the six new bishops were consecrated. The ritual for Gomez was read by Ransom, Gregg, and Reid.[24] When it came time for the "Laying on of Hands," Ransom could not lift himself, so he knelt behind Gomez and his voice trembled. He said later it was fitting that as he was going out, Gomez and Walker were ushering in a new era, one that would be creative and strong. It would be up to them to redeem the ailing A.M.E. Church. Gomez was assigned to the Fifteenth District (South Africa), and Walker to the Fifth (California, The Puget Sound, Colorado, Kansas, and Missouri). Bishops Noah W. Williams and George B. Young were retired.[25]

Shortly after the General Conference, Bishop Tookes, who had been assigned to Texas (Tenth Episcopal District), died. Although the conference had ruled that no one who had been assigned to a foreign district could be reassigned to another district, the Bishops' Council voted to send Gomez to Texas and to make Bishop Bonner responsible for both the Seventeenth and the Fifteenth districts. Bishop Clayborn had insisted that Gomez was ineligible and that he be sent to Texas; however, the ministers of the Tenth rejected Clayborn and strongly requested Gomez instead. Throughout the year of 1948, controversy raged. Finally, at the February Bishops' Council meeting in 1949, the matter was settled, and Gomez remained in Texas. At first Reverdy had written Gomez, "You have an appointment to meet Jesus Christ in South Africa. I beg you to keep that appointment," but later was pleased that Gomez was going to Texas where he would be faced with the challenge of straightening out Paul Quinn College in Waco, one of the A.M.E. schools that was dying from mismanagement.[26] Reverdy would visit the Gomezes on many occasions at their Episcopal residence on the campus of Paul Quinn.

The Ransoms returned from Kansas City happy that the conference had voted overwhelmingly to ordain women; that Wilberforce University was connectionalized, and all the districts were pledged to contribute to its upkeep; and that salaries of bishops and general officers were raised. However, although Reverdy would enjoy being historian of the A.M.E. Church, he would miss having a district, holding Annual Conferences, and being in constant contact with the bishops, ministers, and laymen. On the other hand, he was tired. He believed now he could arrange his own schedule and take his time gathering historical and current church data.

His first task was to establish an office in the student union building at Wilberforce. Bookcases had to be built; file cabinets, typewriters, and copiers purchased. In addition to the material from his own library, he had to locate and compile documents and books, magazines, papers, and photographs that were scattered throughout the

Connection. With the help of Augustus C. Randall, Wilberforce University librarian, he was able "to arrange the material to comply with modern standards."[27] Next, he set about publishing a pocketbook edition of the 1948 General Conference activities.

On August 11, he and Bishop R. R. Wright Jr. signed an agreement allowing him to use for his pocketbook edition any material he deemed necessary from Wright's *Encyclopedia of the African Methodist Episcopal Church* and to purchase the paper left over from the printing of it.[28] In 1944, Reverdy had issued "Acts of the General Conference" but felt it had been incomplete because of "so many broken links in the information it was intended to convey." This time he was able to secure all the vital facts. Wright had used the completed minutes of the General Conference as a supplement to his encyclopaedia and had been assured by Russell Brown, secretary of the General Conference, that they were complete. These he made available to Reverdy.[29]

Not everyone thought Reverdy's project was worthwhile. For example, he received a letter from Bishop L. H. Hemingway who considered the pocketbook edition of the 1948 General Conference to be useless because it carried "no legal authority. It would be a reflection on [Bishop Wright if he] joins anyone in publishing such a meaningless pamphlet."[30] In answer to Hemingway, Reverdy sent out the following rationale titled "Freedom and Liberty under Law." After listing the freedoms guaranteed by the U.S. Constitution to which all organizations must adhere, he wrote:

> Freedom of the press may not be denied, or suppressed. Following our recent General Conference in Kansas City, Kansas, differences of opinion, yea, even controversy has arisen concerning the right or propriety to print and circulate information or reports on the alleged action or proceedings of that General Conference. Under the auspices of the Bureau of Research and History [the pocketbook edition] carries with it no authority, whatever, but it does revitalize the scenes, and makes them come alive as they were enacted from day to day. . . . Regardless of its legal value, this body of information shall become more and more valuable with the ever-widening gap of the unfolding years.[31]

No doubt many found this edition convenient to carry and thorough enough for quick reference. It listed all the delegates, recorded each day's activities, and contained the entire Episcopal Address and excerpts from many of the speeches and committee reports, election results, and resolutions passed.

In 1949, Reverdy deeded his Woodland Park, Michigan, property to the Gomezes. Although he had loved the lake, it was becoming increasingly difficult for him to get there, and Myrtle preferred staying at Tawawa. In addition, this would prove to be an ideal respite each year for the Gomezes before and after their strenuous Texas Annual Conferences.[32] The cottage was filled with memories of Emma whom the Gomezes had been so fond of; therefore, there was no couple Reverdy would rather have occupy it.

The same year, the 140-page *Year Book of the A.M.E. Church 1948–1949 and of Negro Churches,* compiled and edited by Reverdy C. Ransom, was published by the A.M.E. Sunday School Union. Reverdy called it "A record of Religious Activities of American Negroes, and Interracial Co-operation through the medium of the Church, with statistics and records of Negro life and achievements." Topics of interest were population and population characteristics, including Negro migration from 1940–1944; political divisions of Negro Africa, Liberia in the world today, race relations and disabling acts of the Union of South Africa; chronology of African Methodism; an official directory of the A.M.E. Church; a directory of Negro religious bodies in the U.S.; Quadrennial Reports by the various departments in the A.M.E. Church; statistics on Negro colleges and universities, Negroes in the labor union; and policies of churches in the field of human rights.[33]

Reverdy's next project was to complete his autobiography started in 1946. On December 30, 1948, he wrote the Macmillan Company, hoping to interest them in publishing *The Pilgrimage of Harriet Ransom's Son.* He was aware that a book of this nature usually appealed only to a special audience; but the African Methodist Episcopal Church had over one million members. His writer friend, Louis Bromfield, had read the manuscript and expressed his approval. As far as Reverdy knew, "no book [had] been written that gives an intimate look into the administration, aims and objectives of the Negro Church" and therefore might interest black and white members of other denominations as well.[34]

The book's eighteen chapters of 323 pages are divided into nine sections. It abounds with anecdotes that show Reverdy's lively sense of humor and his humanity. It also gives insight into an important era of black religious and secular history. As J. Saunders Redding observed, however, it is "a book without organization in any real sense. . . . What a good book a really good editor could have made of it," he laments. Nevertheless, he admired its "honesty and blunt courage" even though it sometimes seemed "tactless and libelous." If Ransom is frank about the church and other people in the book, he is equally frank about his own follies, Redding pointed out.[35]

Ormond A. Forte said that though the narrative is "ungilded by professional touches or glamour of gripping prose," it is:

> intriguing. It is an earnestly told story of the life of a definitely remarkable personage, who for sixty-four years has moved conspicuously across the stage as one of the builders of the A.M.E. Church—while yet reaching out in other directions to help in the building of a general bridgehead for the forces of working religion in the United States.[36]

The Pilgrimage of Harriet Ransom's Son was to come out finally in 1950 and sold for $2.50. The book received a mixed reaction from the church. There were those who thought its honesty bordered on brashness; some who felt it was too critical of the church; but the majority found it to be refreshing. Today, it seems tame compared with many contemporary autobiographies and is valuable as a primary source for Ransom researchers.

In 1950, Reverdy's *Preface to History of the A.M.E. Church* was also published by the A.M.E. Sunday School Union. He had toyed with the concept for two years and felt that in 1950 the book was long overdue. The full history of the A.M.E. Church had been written by Bishop Daniel A. Payne, Dr. J. T. Jenifer, and Bishop C. S. Smith, covering its activities through 1922. Because history had to be put in prospective after long contemplation, Reverdy did not believe another history of the A.M.E. Church should be written until at least fifty years had passed, hence his *Preface*.[37]

With the assistance of Myrtle who typed and corrected the manuscript, Reverdy approached the task with anticipation and found it "more fascinating" than "a novel." It is a slim 215-page volume of short essays that move back and forth in time. In it he compared the beginnings of the A.M.E. Church with the founding of America, one a democratic government "established to uphold political equality for all men," the other a church where "all men may have freedom and equality at the altars of religion on the basis of human brotherhood, taught by Jesus Christ."[38] In examining the national and racial background of the Negro, Reverdy concluded that though white enslavement was the direct cause of blacks leaving Africa, "God drove the Negro out of Africa to teach him that he had a soul." As he postulated in many of his writings, Reverdy believed God had a special mission for the Afro-American to liberate America from its illnesses. Victimized by slave catchers and cruel holders, the Negro was better prepared than any other group to establish freedom and independence as exemplified by Richard Allen in his founding of the African Methodist Episcopal Church. The creation of that body of black Methodists contradicts forever the concept that, left to their own devices, Negroes are incapable of functioning independently.[39]

In the chapter composed of direct quotes by Richard Allen, the word "Negro" is never used. Instead, Allen refers to the "colored" race. Reverdy pointed out that "African" in the title A.M.E. Church was selected by the founders to distinguish it from the Methodist Episcopal Church from which it had separated.[40] It was Allen and Daniel Coker who, during the yellow fever epidemic in Philadelphia in 1793, "created the spirit and breathed the atmosphere that dedicated the [A.M.E. Church] to Christian Social Service."[41] The "Negro Church" grew out of the "conflicting economic, political, religious and social currents that have shaped" our nation, he wrote.[42]

In a separate section, Reverdy listed the schools, colleges, and universities founded by the A.M.E. Church; the dates of organizations and Annual Conferences in the South; the problems during Reconstruction; and the effect of education on the black pulpit and black journalism.[43] He concludes the book with a meditation:

The African and his descendants are the best spiritual reserves of humanity. It may be that the nations, now empty in the midst of their wealth, weak through the strength of their armies, and now the bewildered prey of the magnificence and wonders their genius has created, shall remain in their social, economic and spiritual valley of dried bones, until as of old, the question comes to some Negro prophet, "Can these bones live?" Then out of the depths of his highly emotional and spiritual nature, he shall prophesy to the dry bones of our civilization until they are united, clothed with the warm blood of our common human brotherhood and be made alive by the spirit of God dwelling in their hearts.[44]

The book was well received.

In a letter to Reverdy quoted in the Foreword, Dr. E. E. Tyler, scholar, wrote:

I am awed at your facile gathering and marshalling of material as is reflected throughout the pages of your most informing preface. If the impact of this work does for the present generation of African Methodist and those who are to follow what it has done for me, then you have placed your stamp upon those now in the service of the church and those who are to follow.[45]

In addition to his writings, between 1949–1950, Ransom was still concerned about politics and the situation at Wilberforce University. In April 1949, certain politicians were attempting to defeat Bill 5 then before the Ohio legislature that in essence would make the College of Education and Industrial Arts again a part of Wilberforce University. Reverdy wrote to Frank J. Lausche, newly elected governor of Ohio and a Democrat. "It is a well known fact," he said, "that for more than twenty years Dr. Bland Stradly, Vice President of Ohio State University, with a few like-minded persons, has advocated and tried to implement the establishment of a State-supported college at Wilberforce." Stradly was also an official for the North Central Accrediting Agency for Colleges and Secondary Schools. "This week, he spearheaded a move to have the State-supported department at Wilberforce University accredited, in order to circumvent or defeat the bill now pending in the Ohio State Legislature." He reminded Lausche that for fifty years Negroes, "with the assistance of influential white friends" have prevented the establishment of State-supported colleges for Negroes on northern soil. The purpose of this "quick accreditation" is designed to remove the pressure on Ohio State to accept Negro students, and to establish at Wilberforce University a college for Negroes supported by the taxpayers of the State of Ohio. Second, the move is designed as a political payoff to the state-appointed board of trustees and to some Negro politicians.[46]

In private conferences with Ransom and others and in campaign speeches, Lausche had promised that if he were elected he would appoint a board of state trustees and would seek a just and fair settlement of the differences between the university and the state. "We believed you and gave you our whole-hearted support. We still believe you," Reverdy wrote.[47] Lausche attempted to keep his promise to prevent the creation of two schools at Wilberforce but with little success. (Later in 1951, when Bill 58 was before the legislature that would create Central State University, Lausche vetoed the bill. In the *Xenia Gazette* of May 9, President Charles Leander Hill of Wilberforce blasted those who criticized Lausche's veto and said "such courageous action . . . lifts him even higher above the political opportunists and demagogy so characteristic of the average cheap politician of the weather-vane caliber."[48] The legislature overrode Lausche's veto and Central State University became a reality.)

Reverdy had mourned with the rest of the country the sudden passing of Franklin D. Roosevelt in 1945 and looked with skepticism on the ascendancy of Harry Truman to the presidency. However, before long, he found that Truman was making a strong stand for civil rights, and Reverdy admired the plucky politician who proclaimed "The Buck Stops Here!" On March 10, 1949, he wrote Truman complimenting his efforts on behalf of civil rights and the McCarran Bill that provided for the appointment of twenty-three federal judges. Reverdy recommended Attorney Raymond Pace Alexander for one of the appointments who he said measured "up to the highest standard" of those Truman might consider. If the president chose Alexander he would bring "encouragement and hope to millions of Americans of African descent who even now [held Truman] in high esteem . . . and cherished [his] administration as President of the United States."[49]

On February 13, 1950, *Time* did a feature story on Reverdy, "Confessions of a Bishop," the title of an article that had appeared in *Ebony*, which *Time* described as "a gentle detached look into some of the trials and triumphs of a man who has ministered well to his people." *Time* outlines the main events in Reverdy's life, calling him "one of the patriarchs of Negro religious life . . . the oldest bishop in one of the country's oldest Negro denomination."[50]

In 1950, another recognition came to Reverdy. Flushing, Ohio, Reverdy's birthplace, held its Homecoming Celebration August 12–13, during which it dedicated its new Municipal Building, its White Way, and Schuler Park. On Sunday afternoon in the park, Ransom was presented to the citizens by Charles Johnson of Cleveland, Ohio. He was asked to lift the covering from a monument, which to his surprise read: REVERDY CASSIUS RANSOM WAS BORN JANUARY 4, 1861, 64 YEARS A BISHOP OF THE A.M.E. CHURCH, 16 YEARS CHAIRMAN TRUSTEES WILBERFORCE UNIVERSITY, MEMBER OHIO BOARD OF PAROL, NOTED NEGRO EDUCATOR. UNVEILED BY BISHOP RANSOM AUGUST 13, 1950. Following the ceremony, Reverdy thanked the twelve hundred citizens for the honor. He acknowledged the goodness of God who had blessed him to live eighty-nine years. He would always hold a special place in his heart for Flushing and wished it continued growth. Before he left, he visited the old Flushing Mill, established in 1877; the American Legion building located on Holland; the Pastime Theatre built by W. W. Bethel in 1915, now called the Flushing Theatre; the Masonic Temple; and the Community National Bank. Although he had been too young to remember much about his childhood in Flushing, he felt nostalgic when he imagined himself walking beside his mother and grandmother down what was now Main Street. [51]

Much of Reverdy's time the year prior to the 1952 General Conference was spent writing articles in *The Christian Recorder.* On February 22, 1951, there appeared "Yard-Stick of Values" based on Ephesians 4:13 "The Measure of the stature of the fullness of Christ." Although Reverdy seemed to ramble, he made one point clear, that "moral, spiritual, and social values are measured by 'the fullness of Christ.'" The A.M.E. Church was founded and nurtured by this yardstick and must continue to "assume the 'Spiritual Leadership' of the Christian world." It has had no competition since Mahatma Gandhi died, "but Jesus is with us, perhaps in some Gethsemane praying in agony of spirit for the things that we must suffer for the sake of the kingdom of God, because we love our fellowman," he said.[52]

The following month he wrote "Solid Rock or Shifting Sand in Human Relations." His purpose was "to state the primary source and bedrock upon which the entire family of the human race was built and must stand forever more." He listed the marriage of one man to one woman as the leading source. In that source there is no distinction made as to "the color of skin, or texture of hair or other accidents of birth—just one man and one woman." From that union comes families, tribes, nations, states, and empires. These groups do not invalidate the fact that all men are created equal "in the sense of having a common origin and fatherhood by the creative act of God"; for there is one race, "the Human Race," he wrote. Next, he traced the unique history of the Negro in the United States. While Europeans form armies in the name of freedom, Negroes call "for mobilization of [their] spiritual and moral strength . . . in churches, pulpits, schools and newspapers to speak about compromise and firmly stand for the destruction of all artificial barriers between man and his fellow man."[53] Notably, this article depicts a less radical warrior. Reverdy of the early 1900s would not have echoed these sentiments. Certainly he would have never advocated compromise.

In a third article, "Ecumenical, What? Ecumenicity, Where? The Shame of Negro Methodism," Reverdy spoke of a movement that involved his interest most of his life. He began by writing about words or phrases that have influenced the thinking of humans during different eras. In the 1890s it was "sociology," "the sociological aspect," "social science," or the "sociological approach to problems." In religion in 1951, the word is "ecumenical" or "ecumenicity." For over one hundred years the A.M.E. and A.M.E. Zion denominations have tried to unite, he said. Later the C.M.E.s also joined in the attempt. All three are the same in polity, hold the same articles of faith, speak the same language, and are the same race. Reverdy listed as the obstacles to their union: "bigotry, narrowness of mind and spirit, selfish personal ambition on the part of church leaders, and lust for personal prestige, honor and power." Among all of the denominations meeting in Oxford, England, for the Ecumenical Council of Churches in a few weeks, the A.M.E.S, A.M.E.Z.S, and C.M.E.S "will represent the most glaring example of the spirit of continued separation," he lamented. He hoped these denominations would bring back with them "the ecumenical spirit that is supposed to underlie the main purpose of their visit to Oxford."[54]

In the summer of 1951, Myrtle and Reverdy traveled to Liberia, West Africa, a country that had been founded by the American Colonization Society of Washington, D.C., in 1822. The "independent towns, villages and settlements united under one central government in Monrovia in 1839." On July 8, 1847, Liberia declared its independence one year after the Colonization Society had withdrawn.[55] Reverdy was thrilled to be standing on African soil, particularly because Liberia had been settled by free America blacks.

The occasion that had brought the Ransoms to Monrovia, the capital, was the celebration of sixty years of missionary work by the A.M.E. Church. President William S. V. Tubman greeted the couple warmly and conferred upon Reverdy the Medal of the Order of Knight Commander of the Humane Order of African Redemption. In addressing the assemblage, Ransom noted that Liberia was "the first attempt in history for Blacks to establish a nation and government of their own" in West Africa.[56]

The sixtieth anniversary celebration of the A.M.E. Church's existence in Liberia and Sierra Leone belongs to history, Reverdy said. "Here at least the stage is being set for the power of leadership for Africans by Africans, in a manner similar to that which is taking place among the Jews in Palestine." Unlike the way Americans treated the native Indians they found when they arrived in America, the American Negroes who migrated to West Africa live in peace and friendship with the native tribes that surround them. He believed that the spiritual future of mankind may well be in the hands of Africans.[57]

Upon his return, Reverdy wrote two articles for *The Christian Recorder,* "Liberia, Faces the Rising Sun," and "God's Last Reserve." In the later, he concluded that "For the past five thousand years Europe, the Orient, and parts of North Africa have had their day of probation," but Africans are just beginning "to open their eyes and awake from their long, long sleep. God has no fresh reserves to call upon except the black millions of the continent of Africa. He has tried everybody else. These are His last reserves."[58] The pilgrimage to Liberia had refreshed him spiritually and given him great hope for the emergence of black power.

Reverdy's sporadic bouts with alcohol occurred in greater and lesser degrees all his life. Alcohol was the albatross around his neck. Few knew the anguish he suffered and the depressions he experienced because of the power it had over him. Those who loved him suffered with him; others saw it as a humorous flaw to be joked about behind closed doors or overlooked. An example of how sensitive an issue it was to Reverdy can be found in a letter he wrote to Bishop R. R. Wright Jr. on July 16, 1951.

> Dear Bishop Wright,
> This letter comes to you as the result of what seemed to be a jovial moment between Bishop Nichols and myself. But the jovial moment was tinged with a razor blade edge of derision bordering almost onto contempt in the deep seeded attitude you carried toward me. I say this because when you speak of me in public as well as in private you cannot refrain reverting to what you seem to regard as my outstanding pit of damnation. In that jovial moment you said how may times you had seen me out of control; then you looked up and said to me that you hoped this wife had been able to stop me from drinking. I cannot act the hypocrite with you so if you get any satisfaction out of these episodes—go your way. But I want no more of your friendly demonstrations. I have helped you more than anybody else to obtain every outstanding position you have held in the A.M.E. Church. I am not now and never was your personal enemy; but from now on I want no more of your.
> .. smiles, or your words that carry poisoned arrows, or the shake of your hand that conceals a dagger that strikes to kill when my name comes up either in private talk or public speech. I am as always, yours very truly.[59]

To Reverdy, Wright's behavior was a betrayal of friendship. And though he was always quick to forgive, no doubt the hurt stayed with him for a long time. After all, Wright had been his assistant pastor in Chicago and had worked with him on many projects. Ransom had championed him in all of his aspirations for higher positions in the Church.

Reverdy's drinking is mentioned "in passing" in biographical studies, articles, and books, mainly because it did not represent the thrust of the man's personality and life. Such a flaw would have probably destroyed a lesser man, but Reverdy was a giant. He was always willing to aid others when they were unfairly attacked. For instance, in October of 1951, Reverdy had a chance to defend his friend and sometime critic, W. E. B. DuBois, who was being accused of not registering The World Peace Center, a so-called subversive organization, with the Department of Justice. Because he was said to be a part of the group, it was alleged that he was in violation of the Foreign Agents Registration Act. The National Council of the Arts and Sciences requested that Reverdy come to Washington and testify in DuBois's behalf. After explaining that his physical health would not allow him to appear, Reverdy wrote a strong letter affirming that he had known DuBois for more than fifty years. DuBois had always "stood for things for which George Washington fought, that Thomas Jefferson wrote in the Declaration of Independence, and the guarantees contained in the Constitution of the United States." Millions of Afro-Americans "aspire to achieve the things advocated" by him—complete integration and equality. If he should come to trial, "It would be the most powerful blow for Negro Freedom and Equality that has happened since Abraham Lincoln issued his proclamation emancipating the slaves." Ransom was sure that DuBois had "never leaned in the direction of Russian Communism." When the laws of this country were administered so as to frighten or attempt to intimidate Negroes, they would not "retreat a single inch. If we could ascend from the depths of slavery" to where we stand today," we can "achieve the goals of brotherhood and peace for which we strive." DuBois was acquitted of the charges that year. No doubt Reverdy's letter, along, with the testimony of other supporters had played a part in that acquittal.[60]

In anticipation of his retirement at the next General Conference, Reverdy wrote an editorial for the *Recorder* titled "Old Men for Counsel, Young Men for War." He acknowledged that a man is not necessarily wise because he is old. "'Methuselah lived for 969 years, and he died.' This is all the scripture has to say concerning the oldest man that ever lived." Nevertheless, most of the aged are to be revered because they represent a link of two or more generations of human life. They have lived through wars, suffering, self-denial, and sacrifices and have witnessed invention and evolutions. They "should know where the pitfalls of life are hidden, where the highway of life runs close to the cliffs." They have known "defeat, suffered heartache and the crucial agony of disappointment and denial." When then is a man through? Reverdy asked. In the workforce and the military, age limits have been drawn, and he saw nothing wrong "in these attempts to lift the strain from tired backs." But he believed the aged should be used as counselors if they have "three dimensional wisdom of breath, depth, height, enriched by experience and mellowed by the years."[61]

"To youth," he said, "belongs virility, strength and courage to stand up and fight without compromise or surrender, to hold our gains and to vastly extend the borders of the conquest of the human mind and spirit in material things, those great intangibles of faith and hope that have been the dream of prophets and seers since the creation of man." No person should get so old that he views with detachment the new issues that face the succeeding generation. Like Jacob, he can lean on his staff, support, and give counsel. Likewise, youth should know that no one can take the place of a person who has passed on. Each generation must produce its own leaders to face its unique problems. There can be no repeat performance or curtain calls for anyone. *Now* is the time for the youth of this day.[62]

Although there are many astute observations in Reverdy's later writings, like his autobiography, they often lack structure and continuity. Nevertheless, it is remarkable that a man of ninety could write anything at all. His thoughts seemed to emerge in such profusion that they often scattered like rays that light on the same plane though they never come together. Reverdy was beginning to feel his years as evidenced not only in his thoughts, but also his body. On many occasions, the cane was not sufficient to hold even his frail body, and he reluctantly agreed to being wheeled in a chair when traveling any distance. Myrtle was his constant companion, as were Louis and Ruth Ransom who lived nearby in Xenia. They saw to it that he was immaculate in attire and well groomed. He maintained his charm, thoughtfulness, and sense of humor. He still attempted to rise whenever a woman came into a room, enjoyed teasing his great-grandchildren, and discussing issues with the young students and seminarians who visited Tawawa Chimney Corner.

On May 7, 1952, Reverdy and Myrtle traveled to the Thirty-fourth General Conference held at the Coliseum in Chicago, Illinois. Reverdy was wheeled in during the opening procession of bishops, general officers, presidents, deans, and chaplains as the delegates sang "All Hail the Power of Jesus' Name." Later he listened to the Quadrennial Sermon preached by Bishop Madison Reid who used as his text John 15, "I am the true vine; Ye are the branches." Reid described Jesus as the "Cultivator" who prunes the vines, and affirmed that Christ was indispensable. Turning to current issues, he said, "America must not wink at segregation." A fair employment practice, equal education, the right to vote, and all other rights that lead to universal brotherhood must exist in a democracy. The A.M.E. Church historically "had always taken a position on all-out equality for all people" and must continue to do so.[63]

During the second day, when Reverdy presided over the assembly, the Episcopal Address was read by Bishop Nichols. That evening, Walter White, former executive secretary of the NAACP, addressed the conference stating that the race question was not a sectional question, but a world problem. The two world wars had destroyed forever the concept of racial superiority. Edward Brown, candidate for Congress from Chicago, and Bishop Joseph Gomez responded to White's address, pledging continued support of the NAACP in its fight for Negro rights.[64]

The third day Reverdy presented the *Social Creed* he had written for the A.M.E. Church. Among his responsibilities as historiographer, he considered this document to be of vital importance. Along with the *Apostles' Creed*, this creed would spell out clearly what the A.M.E. Church believed: in the universal laws of God that supersede all human devices for peace; in the dignity of man and the sacredness of human personality; in the oneness of the human race; that only adultery is a ground for divorce; that racial prejudices and discrimination are injurious to the unity of mankind; that humans should be accorded equal opportunities in educational, social, and cultural development in accordance with their capacities and inclinations; that under all forms of government there should be freedom of speech and of worship; that no one should be denied a right to earn a living because of race, creed or color; that individual ownership of property is in accord with Christian principles and should be encouraged; that the use of alcohol and dope are moral and social evils; that through Jesus, humans must find the grace to return good for evil and patience to employ nonviolent methods to obtain just and lasting peace; in the Protestant principles of the separation of church and state; in the unity of all Christian believers; in the redeemability of sinful humanity through Jesus; and that with the adoption of the creed by the conference, the Bishops' Council should recommend an annual reading of the creed in churches and Sunday schools. After Reverdy had finished, Bishop D. Ormonde Walker moved that the *Social Creed* be referred to the Committee on Revision of the Discipline who would recommend its adoption.[65]

On Saturday May 10, the matter of retirement came up when Rev. A. J. Jennings made a motion that the Retirement Law, passed in 1948 that required that bishops should be retired at seventy-five, be rescinded. Before voting on the motion, Bishop Gregg made a plea that a bishop who is mentally and physically fit should not be retired at seventy-five if he is capable. When the vote was taken, it was decided that the Retirement Law should not be retroactive before its passage in 1948. Three days later, the Episcopal Committee recommended that Bishop Reverdy C. Ransom be retired and Bishop M. H. Davis be located [without a district] for four years. The Conference voted that the recommendation be sent back to the Episcopal Committee. When the committee returned, it once again recommended that Bishop Davis be located for four years and that Ransom be retired along with Bishop W. A. Fountain. In addition, it recommended the election of three new bishops.[66]

Bishop Fountain thanked the committee and the church for the consideration they had given him during his more than thirty years as a bishop. He would retire without malice and with love for the people and the church. "The good old Methodist Christian never dies, he simply fades away," he concluded. Then the ninety-one-year-old Ransom pulled himself up slowly and thanked the church for the honors he received for sixty-six years as pastor, editor, and bishop. He suggested that he be allowed to stay on as historiographer to complete his findings and record them while there was yet time. Gomez spoke in behalf of his request, praising Reverdy for the support he had given him all his life and, waxing poetic, he affirmed, "When the shadows fall and the book of Ransom is closed, his tombstone shall read, 'He was a maker of men.'" Ransom knew the time had come for him to step down, so he accepted gracefully the Episcopal Committees ruling and left the platform. Last of all, Bishop Davis thanked the church and urged continued devotion to the work of God's Church. "The A.M.E. Church made me, and the Church still has me," he vowed.[67]

On Monday, May 19, three new bishops were elected: H. T. Primm, Frederick D. Jordan, and E. C. Hatcher. The next afternoon they were consecrated as the seventy-first, seventy-second, and seventy-third bishops of the A.M.E. Church. Later they were given their Episcopal assignments along with the other bishops.[68] The secretary put the final period on the minutes of this conference which, like all others, proved to be a new beginning for some, and an ending for others.

Thus the 34th Session of the General Conference of the African Methodist Episcopal Church became history. Delegates, visitors, newsmen and people [from] all walks of life joined in greetings mingled with tears of joy and feelings of regret. Candidates [who had lost] could understand the poet who said. "What I aspired to be and was not, comforts me."[69]

Reverdy sang the final hymn with the rest of the delegates, "The Church Is Moving On."

Ransom the Ransomed, 1952–1959

The days of our years are threescore years and ten; and if by reason of strength they be fourscore years, yet is their strength labour and sorrow; for it is soon cut off, and we fly away.

Psalm 90:10

On May 21, 1952, a lean, silver-haired Negro sat back in the black limousine bound from Chicago, Illinois, to Wilberforce, Ohio. The accolades and fond farewells he had received at the General Conference did little to ease his anxiety as he watched the gold and green landscape rush by like so many picture postcards. His destination? Tawawa Chimney Corner, home for over twenty years. He had first come to Wilberforce as a student in 1881 when he was twenty years old.

Reverdy Cassius Ransom, son of Harriet Ransom, former pastor, editor, politician, writer, civil rights leader, trustee board president, historiographer, husband, grandfather, great grandfather, now retired bishop of the African Methodist Episcopal Church, was returning home for the final seven years of his pilgrimage. These would be years of family, of writing, of celebrating birthdays, of remembrances, and sometimes of loneliness.

He revealed his true feelings about his retirement in an article that appeared in *The Christian Recorder*, August 14, titled "The Last Mile." "I have lived through three generations. I have heard the rebel yell, the mourns and groans of slavery and the death rattle in the throat of the expiring monster as he was forever destroyed." He regretted he had so little to offer God and the church "as the fruit of [his] labor." Now he was taking his first step down the path of his last mile. After quoting a letter from the Cleveland Clinic that reported he was in good health, he noted that he also had peace of mind. "There isn't anybody in my church or in the world whom I dislike or to whom I would do any injury," he vowed. It seems to be the opinion of the church that a retired bishop should do nothing; but "it is my opinion that a 'retired bishop' who does nothing day after day will soon become intellectually sterile and physically dead." With Reverdy's love for the written word, it was not likely he would become "intellectually sterile," forgetful perhaps, but not sterile. He was still a minister of the gospel with a commission from Christ; consequently, he had set for himself a " productive task for each day . . . giving it the highest and best . . . within [him]. I do not seek to see the distance scene. One step enough for me," he said.[1]

Another article reflecting Reverdy's thoughts about retirement was published in the January issue of *The Christian Recorder*, "The Albatross Who Lost His Way among the Highways of the Skies." In it he recalled his first trip across the Atlantic over fifty years ago. "Of things observed en route, the one that . . . lingered longest in [his memory was] that of a tired and weary Albatross who had lost his sense of direction among the divergent highways of the skies." He was resting among the rigging, and the crew lifted him down and took care of him until they reached Liverpool "where they loosed him to soar aloft, a chastened and a wiser bird." Reverdy compared the albatross to humans who fly for less than a hundred years then "live forever in the spirit world." Like the bird, they have been given no map, chart or compass but have been given "an inner voice . . . a consciousness of 'the Divine within' us; occasionally, 'a long distance call' in some form of 'spiritual telepathy' gets through to us in [a way] we can feel but do not clearly understand," he wrote. Like the albatross, many humans (including himself) have lost their sense of spiritual, social, and moral direction at some time during their pilgrimage. But for all those who "by faith stand still and firmly hold on, Christ comes to walk on the waves of Galilee saying 'Be not afraid. It is I. . . . Get aboard and I will land you at your desired heaven.'"[2] Reverdy was to spend a great deal of the time writing short philosophical articles and letters, reminiscing, and keeping in touch with his family. Only Reverdy III remained a problem.

In November, he received a letter from Reverdy III stating he wished to come to Wilberforce and visit his grandfather. Reverdy responded on November 27, 1952:

My dear Grandson:

It is a very difficult, and distressing task to write this letter in reply to your communication about your proposed visit here. It is unthinkable that I could extend to you the courtesy of entertainment in my home which is also the home of my wife, Mrs. Myrtle Teal Ransom. I cannot mend the situation, and I cannot end it.

Our Lord Jesus said, "If a person turns against you and repents, forgive them." This has nothing to do with social implications. I have your children always in my heart, and in my prayers, and entertain nothing but good will for your peace, success, and happiness.

Your grandfather[3]

Though deeply distressed by his grandson's past behavior, Reverdy had long since forgiven him. Nevertheless, Myrtle could not forget the humiliation he had caused her by exposing her letters to the public. Most likely Reverdy carried out her wishes not to allow him to visit. Reverdy III did come to Wilberforce with his family but did not visit Tawawa Chimney.[4]

Among the more memorable articles Reverdy wrote during this period, one appeared in the April/June 1954 issue of *The A.M.E. Church Review*, "Paul Laurence Dunbar." It was an expansion of the earlier Dunbar article he had written while editor of the *Review*. He began by calling Dunbar "a product of the first generation of freedom. Whatever talent, endowment of genius he possessed belonged to the rich, warm blood of his African inheritance." He was a child who "passed from us before he came to the full maturity of his powers." Reverdy recalled the times he had ridden with Dunbar in his elevator, where "scattered about him on loose sheets of paper were some of the first of his imperishable lines," and the times they had dined together on "chitterlings and hot corn pone." He remembered when Dunbar would come to his house in the late hours, "in search of a word that might better convey the delicate shades" of his vision. Both Dunbar and Phyllis Wheatley, pure Africans, were pioneers who opened the way for other black poets. In death they wait confidently for the day when "the gifted children of their people will hold the rapt attention of the world, while they flood it with their ravishing strains of music and song."[5]

On January 4, 1955, Reverdy celebrated his ninety-fourth birthday. He told a reporter from the *Journal Herald* that he did not have an ache or pain and was looking forward in a few days to attending a church meeting in Waco, Texas, with his friends Joseph and Hazel Gomez. He also said he had just completed a new book, entitled *A Quilt of Many Colors*, which dealt with church personalities. (There seems to be no copy in existence now.) He attributed his long life to daily afternoon naps and two meals a day. Sitting in his library, surrounded by volumes of books, he was asked about the progress of the Negro. He quipped, "When the slaves were freed only five per cent could read or write. I think they have done pretty well since."[6] Of the many birthday greetings Reverdy received from all over the world, he was particularly fond of one. Robert and Margaret Hardoan had written: "There is a breed of men who are brothers the world around, from every nation, race and creed: the golden breed of gentleman and a scholar. Today, we salute one such on his 94th birthday."[7]

On the cover of the February 1955 *A.M.E. Voice of Missions* is a picture of Reverdy and Dean Rembert Stokes of Payne Theological Seminary. Reverdy pointed to "the Systematic Theology section of 100 books which he has contributed to launch the Seminary drive for 20,000 volumes, an important step toward accreditation." Reverdy vowed that his entire theological collection of six thousand volumes will go eventually to the Payne Seminary Library located in the new Administration Building. On pages 3–4 of the magazine, under the title "An Empire For Service, Influence and Power

Reverdy showing Rembert Stokes, president of Wilberforce University, the books from his library that he planned to give to Payne Theological Seminary, 1955.

in the Kingdom of God," Reverdy wrote about the importance of the Department of Missions to the Church and provided the reader with an interesting description of the controversial A.M.E. advocate of colonization, Bishop Henry McNeal Turner. who spent a great deal of time in Africa.

> Turner was a man of at least four distinct split personalities. Under one guise he was a statesman, under another he was a saint, under another he was a devil, and under another he was a prophet of a new heaven and a new earth. After long intervals he might make a safari into the wilderness of passion and appetite, and then after days and nights of mourning take hold upon God with new veneration and power. Bishop Turner did more than any one else to put the breath of life into our Missionary Department.[8]

Reverdy was still very much concerned with the problems facing Wilberforce University. It was his wish that Joseph Gomez be sent to the Third District at the next General Conference so he could tackle the problems of the university as he had those of Paul Quinn College in Waco, Texas. Since being in Texas, Gomez had resurrected the old school, built five new buildings, drastically improved the curriculum and faculty, and reduced the indebtedness. On January 20, 1956, he wrote Gomez expressing his wish and offering Tawawa Chimney Corner as an Episcopal Residence should he come to the Third District. Those who currently administered to the school, Reverdy said, "seem to be chiefly concerned with their own personal and financial welfare, and not with order, discipline and tradition. . . . From almost every standpoint, you are made to order for the needs and opportunities for which Wilberforce is crying loud." He and Myrtle planned to move from Tawawa into her cottage up the road because Tawawa Chimney was not designed to be the home of a retired bishop. Realizing he was trying to plan Gomez's future for him, he said, "Both you and your wife seem like children of my own, and perhaps, unconsciously, I am trying to establish a little parental direction over your public service and activities."[9]

The Pittsburgh Courier's Eric Roberts honored Reverdy's birthday in an article, titled "Old Man Eloquent, Bishop Ransom, 95, Last of 'First Generation.'" Because the country is celebrating Negro History week, he wrote, "it was requisite that we here bring back into focus the supreme gifts of this nonagenarian great and, for a moment kneel at the feet of one unsurpassed in pulpit, epideictic and deliberate oratory." In an age where men such as Dr. Thurman Arnold, Bishop I. H. King, Dr. Mordecai W. Johnson, Dr. John W. Davis, Dr. Charles Wesley, and Bishop John A. Gregg have disappeared from the scene, "the flame of eloquence still burns in that ancient Ransom bosom who, at his noon, played on human souls as Paderewski played on the keys of a piano."[10]

In May 1956, Reverdy and Myrtle reluctantly headed for Miami, Florida, to attend the Thirty-fifth Session of the General Conference in Dinner Key Auditorium. Reverdy had opposed the Conference being held in Miami because of the city's racial policies. Not long ago, he and Myrtle had been denied restroom facilities in service stations and had even suffered the indignity of being told by one attendant that they should use the woods. Given the church's stance on civil rights, Reverdy felt it was folly for the conference to be held in an atmosphere where such practices still existed.[11] As it turned out, encouraged by Governor Collins, the mayor gave the golden key of the city to the church, housed the delegates in beach hotels, and extended them a cordial invitation to Miami's public places. As Russell S. Brown, secretary of the General Conference, was to record at the end of the conference, "There seemed to be a moratorium on Race conflict. There had not been one eventuality!"[12]

At the opening services, Reverdy was a part of the procession of colorfully robed bishops, general officers, presidents of colleges, deans of seminaries, chaplains, and elders of the church. As they approached the platform, decorated with palm leaves, potted plants, and American and Christian flags, Reverdy must have sensed that this was his last General Conference. Later he listened to Bishop George Baber's dynamic Quadrennial Sermon, "Christ Will Stay with His Church," in this "The Golden Age of Our Zion." There should be vigorous determination to set the church in order. "This is God's church; it is bigger than any man in it," he said, decrying those who would buy offices or positions in God's Church. Following the sermon, over three thousand people were served communion at the cross-shaped altar as the organ played a medley of hymns.[13]

Monday morning, May 7, Reverdy was presented to the conference as the "Sage of Tawawa Springs." He described "in his eloquent way the joy he felt in his heart for the progress of this conference, its seat," and what this southern city's surprising welcome signified for America.[14] Six nights later, after the regular youth program had held its program, Annetta Gomez-Jefferson surprised him by presenting a sketch of his life. Myrtle said afterward she had had a difficult time getting him to come out that evening. She had had to tell him it was a missionary program that she was required to attend. When his wheelchair reached the back of the auditorium, the auditorium was darkened, a large spotlight shone on him, and a voice from the dark called out, "Reverdy Cassius Ransom, This Is Your Life!" The choir sang the Wilberforce Alma Mater as Myrtle wheeled him up to the stage. Patterned after the television program of the same name, the sketch included short bios of men and women who had meant a great deal to him during his lifetime. As their names were called, they came from the wings. When everyone had crowded the stage, the program ending with the singing of "Auld Lang Syne." Reverdy wept as he tried to join in the singing. For once in his life, someone had "put one over on him."[15]

Other pleasurable moments for Reverdy occurred when he listened to Thurgood Marshall, head of the NAACP, speak on "Desegregation and Discrimination"; when, for the first time, the Connectional Budget, presented by the Brotherhood, a layman's activist group, passed; when an agreement was reached to ordain women as local elders; when a repentant David Sims was reinstated as bishop in the A.M.E. Church; when Francis H. Gow, the first native South African, was elected bishop; when Dr. R. V. Hilson, pastor of St. John Church in Montgomery, Alabama, recounted the story of Rosa Parks and the Montgomery bus boycott; and finally, when the conference established a historiographer's fund and elevated him to the position of general officer. On the other hand, Reverdy was disappointed that Gomez was sent to Kentucky and Tennessee instead of Ohio.[16] A few months later, however, providence intervened again. In November Bishop A. J. Allen died, and Gomez was sent to the prestigious Fourth District that included Michigan, Illinois, Indiana, and Ontario.[17]

There were also moments of loneliness for Reverdy, especially when he recalled that the other two bishops elected with him in 1924 were gone. W. J. Gaines had died in 1931, and his close friend, John A. Gregg, in February 1953. Among others he would miss was D. Ormonde Walker, who had died in 1955 in the midst of a brilliant career. Surely there was "a crowd of witnesses" hovering over Keys Auditorium at this 1956 conference.

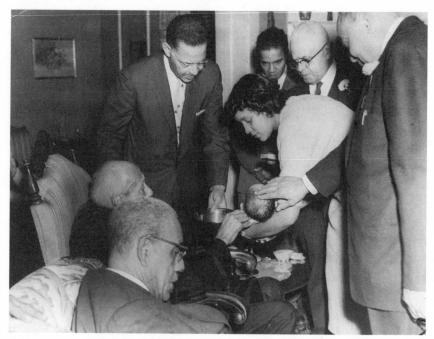

On his ninety-sixth birthday, Reverdy baptizes his great-grandson, Julius High Jr., who is being held by his mother, Emily High, Reverdy's granddaughter. *Seated left to right:* J. Maxwell, Bishop, Reverdy C. Ransom. *Standing:* Hubert M. Robinson, Julius High, Joseph Gomez, Reverdy C. Ransom Jr.

The Ransoms did not move to Myrtle's cottage when they returned to Wilberforce. They returned to Tawawa Chimney Corner and settled into a routine of writing, reading, and receiving family and friends. At dinner, Reverdy insisted on having his usual bean soup before the main course, and he took more naps than he used to. Myrtle kept busy seeing that he was always comfortable and occasionally attending her sorority meetings and bridge club. Those who had disliked her at first had to admire the care she gave to Reverdy.

The Gomezes always visited on Reverdy's birthday and stayed to dine with the family on his ninety-sixth birthday. Among others present were his sons Reverdy Jr., now living in Pennsauken, New York; Harold Ransom, still living in Montclair, New Jersey; Louis and his wife Ruth from Xenia, Ohio; cousins Anna Grinnel from Chicago and Alice Muntz from Flushing, Ohio; and Julius and Emma Ransom High and son, Steward Ransom, and his wife and daughter from Lima, Ohio. In all, six grandchildren and eleven great grandchildren attended. In addition to the family were Hubert and Mami Robinson and daughter Cassandra; Gertrude Holland; Helen Taylor; Eva and Yvonne Walker, wife and daughter of the late Bishop D. Ormonde Walker; Revs. Wallace Wright and W. F. Ogleton of Dayton, Ohio; and Rev. Harry Maxwell. As if to emphasize the sacredness of the occasion, Reverdy donned his favorite robe and christened his newest great grandchildren, Julius High Jr. and Stephany Ransom.[18]

His ninety-sixth birthday was also of special national interest. Among the many greetings he received was a letter from C. Roger Wilson, the grand polemarch of the Kappa Alpha Psi Fraternity. He had seen Reverdy's picture in the May issue of the *Kappa Alpha Psi Journal* and wanted Ransom to know that he was one of his admirers and had been a member of Kappa Alpha Psi (Ransom's fraternity) for a longer period than he could recall.[19]

Before coming to Wilberforce for the birthday celebration, Bishop Hubert Robinson had sent ahead a telegram in which he praised Reverdy's "most noble life, rich in its contributions to the kingdom of God and its inspiration to humanity." He expressed his personal debt for the influence Reverdy had had on his ministry. Indeed he had had a profound impact on the lives of many young ministers.[20] In September Reverdy received a telegram from Chicago signed by Joseph Gomez, Mayor Richard J. Daley, U. S. Robinson, secretary of Publicity, and Rev. R. L. Miller, pastor of Greater Institutional Church. At its Seventy-fourth Chicago Annual Conference the clergy and laypersons had recalled "with fondest recollection the service [Reverdy] rendered and the sacrifices [he] made almost 3 score years ago when he established the Institution A.M.E. Church . . . which has stood as a monument to [his] foresight, ability and faith."[21]

The A.M.E. Church Review featured Reverdy on its cover in its July–September 1958 issue and saluted him as the oldest bishop in the church in an editorial, "Reverdy Cassius Ransom, 'Sage of Tawawa.'" The writer noted as the church approached the bicentennial of the birth of Richard Allen, Reverdy was drawing near the centennial of his life. Ransom had "achieved immortality in the field of belle letters, poetry, literature, history and oratory. . . . He was the incarnation of eloquence . . . a master of the art of witchery of word," and had been an uncompromising fighter for social justice and first-class citizenship. "Through the increasing years he ever strove to 'fill the heavens full of stars of hope' for his people of African descent."[22] Unfortunately, Reverdy was never to reach his centennial.

On April 19, 1959, Myrtle informed the Ransom family and friends that Reverdy was dying. He had had three strokes, and his ninety-eight-year-old heart was finally failing him. People from all over heard that the Sage of Tawawa was waging his last battle with death. On the campus, the students and faculty gathered in small groups, waiting to hear the latest report. Few could believe that the ageless Reverdy was succumbing to time. Finally at 4 P.M. Wednesday, April 22, with his head resting in Hazel Gomez's hands, he stopped breathing. Reverdy Cassius Ransom, forty-eighth Bishop of the African Methodist Episcopal Church was no more.[23]

On April 28, 1959, at the Chapel of the Living Savior of Payne Theological Seminary, his widow, family, friends, and fellow bishops gathered to bid farewell. The service

Left to right: Bishops D. Ward Nichols, Reverdy C. Ransom (seated), and Joseph Gomez. Taken in 1958, one year before Ransom's death.

began at 11 A.M. with an organ rendition of the "Funeral March" by Frédéric Chopin. Next came the invocation and then W. Dawson's "Balm in Gilead," sung by the university choir. Tributes were given by Bishop Frederick D. Jordan representing the Bishops' Council; Dr. Robert Mance for the general officers and laity; Rev. Hubert Robinson for the ministers; President Rembert E. Stokes for the university; Dean Charles S. Spivey Jr. for Payne Theological Seminary.[24]

Following the university choir's interpretation of "God is Our Refuge and Strength," Joseph Gomez stepped up to the podium. It was difficult for him to adequately eulogize the man who had meant so much to him and his family during his life, but he had to make the effort. His subject—"Reverdy Cassius Ransom: Prevailer Extraordinary"—was taken from Genesis 32:28: "For as a Prince hast thou power with God and with men, and hast prevailed." In his opening, he mentioned that after the death he had found in Reverdy's favorite Bible the section dealing with Jacob's life heavily scored. "It is a story deeply personal and intensely human." Everyone is a struggler, but few are prevailers as was Jacob. "The glory of Reverdy Cassius Ransom is the glory of survival; the heritage he bequeaths us is that of the prevailer. Jacob the prototype . . . Ransom the modern pattern of prevailing power," he said.[25]

Ransom would be laid to rest in "one of his Ohio Valleys, at a time when the early spring makes mockery of winter's harsh strength. . . . The overcoming grace of spring is upon us," Gomez said, "indicative of the character and temper of the man we eulogize." Ransom had been born in an era of "stirring movements," which marked the rebirth of a nation as a result of a bloody Civil War. "This child of tempest was to feel the full blast of tempest all his life." Ransom had prevailed in intellectual combat, in politics both church and civic. "He was spiritual, sensitive. He felt deepest because he suffered most. He was most critical of himself. Often he tore the veil from himself and viewed with candor and disarming frankness his own frailties." His preaching was solid, profound, eloquent, rhetorical, chaste in language, passionate, inspirational, and informative.[26]

Gomez also paid tribute to Reverdy's two wives. He described Emma as friend, mother, and advisor. She was "frugal, dignified, sympathetic, a great civic and religious worker" who wore Ransom's "burdens with rare insight, intelligence, understanding and love." Gratitude was also due Myrtle for her "devotion and care in the physically burdened years. . . . Hers was the alabaster box of precious ointment poured out without stint, without regard to stress or strain, time or tide; a devotion so rare and unique and unselfish as to challenge our best praise." The eulogy took a more personal tone, when Gomez called Ransom his "best Friend" and "Father in Spirit," who had been there at every turning point in his career.[27]

He concluded the eulogy by envisioning Ransom knocking on the door of heaven and saying to Peter: "I Ransom the Ransomed of the Lord . . . come with no merits of my own but the strength of Him whose strength has been made perfect in my weakness." Peter answered:

Enter, Thou! Thou battle-scarred veteran of a hundred battlefields, evangel of the cross-ways, hero of the crowded ways of men, thighbone disjointed and sword broken, but with hilt still in hand, and the light of victory in thine eyes. Come!

Thou shall now stand upon the sea of glass mingled with fire. Thou shalt receive the palm of the victor; for thou hast prevailed over the beast and the dragon and finally conquered death. Hesitate not, Ransom the Ransomed. Thou hast found favor with God and man and hast prevailed.[28]

When Gomez finished, Roberta Alexander sang Malotte's "Lord's Prayer." Then the active pallbearers, young men who had served under Reverdy, carried the casket out to the hearse that transferred the body to the Massie Creek Cemetery, a few miles from Wilberforce. There Reverdy Cassius Ransom was interred beside his beloved Emma. He had left a wife; two sons, Reverdy Jr. and Harold; their wives; eleven grandchildren; thirty-seven great-grandchildren; and one great-great-grandchild.[29]

The Southern Christian Recorder captured the sentiments of African Methodists when it reported that Ransom was one of the few persons who had merited the title "Venerable." "Ninety-eight years of rich life and enviable contributions is a feat seldom attained in life." Most A.M.E. ministers, past and present, who knew him, attributed much of their inspiration to Ransom. His flaming heart, passion for fraternity, and innumerable conquests as writer, scholar, preacher, and defender qualified him to be classified as one of the greatest personalities in the church. "No father in the gospel could have been more blessed and pleased than he who lived long and enjoyed the development and success of many of his sons on whom he had let fall his mantle."[30] Other papers and journals enumerated his many accomplishments in politics and civil rights, his involvement in causes, and his acquaintance with renowned historical figures such as: W. E. B. DuBois, Booker T. Washington, William Monroe Trotter, Frederick Douglass, Paul Laurence Dunbar, Sojourner Truth, Ida B. Wells, Henry Wadsworth Longfellow, Henry Ward Beecher, Andrew Carnegie, William McKinley, Harry S. Truman, Franklin D. Roosevelt, Mark Hanna, and so many more.[31]

In his autobiography, Reverdy summed up his own life better, perhaps, than anyone else could.

The drama of life never gives a repeat performance. Similar scenes may be enacted, but always with entirely new settings for the stage. I am not one of those who would like to live their lives over again, thinking they would do a better job if they had a second chance. No—the hazards are too great. I am content to let the record stand just as it is, with all of its laughter and tears, its sickness, sorrow and pain, its disappointments, defeats and oft willful desertion from the highest and noblest things of mind and spirit. The chart and compass of my soul has always brought me back to the King's Highway.[32]

🔙

Notes

1. Reverdy C. Ransom, *School Days at Wilberforce* (Springfield, Ohio: The New Era Co., 1892), 1. (Wilberforce Univ. Archives)

2. Reverdy C. Ransom, *The Pilgrimage of Harriet Ransom's Son* (Nashville, Tenn.: A.M.E. Sunday School Union, 1950), 17.

3. Ibid., 15.

4. Ibid.

5. David A. Gerber, *Black Ohio and the Color Line 1860–1915* (Urbana, Ill.: Univ. of Illinois Press, 1976), 4; Frank I. Quillin, *The Color Line in Ohio* (1913; reprint, New York: Negro Univ. Press, 1969), 21–24.

6. Gerber, *Black Ohio*, 4.

7. Ransom, *Pilgrimage*, 15.; Bureau of the Census, *Negro Population 1790–1915* (New York: New York Times, 1968), 44.

8. *Special Flushing (Ohio) Hometown Edition*, Aug.12–13, 1950.

9. *Bureau of the Census, Negro Population 1790–1915*, 44.

10. Ransom, *Pilgrimage*, 19–20.

11. Ibid., 19

12. Ibid., 20.

13. Ibid.

14. Gerber, *Black Ohio*, 4–5.

15. Ransom, *Pilgrimage*, 20–21.

16. Ibid., 21–22.

17. Ibid., 17.

18. Calvin S. Morris, *Reverdy C. Ransom, A Pioneer Black Social Gospeler* (Ph.D. diss., Boston Univ., 1982, printed UMI Dissertation Information Service), n. 15, 19.

19. Ransom, *Pilgrimage*, 16.

20. Ibid., 22.

21. Gerber, *Black Ohio*, 46.

22. Ransom, *Pilgrimage*, 24.

23. Ibid., 25.

24. Ibid., 23, 26.

25. Ibid., 23.

26. Reverdy C. Ransom, Album of pressed leaves and flowers, Cambridge, Ohio, around 1876. (author's file)

27. Reverdy C. Ransom, "Confessions of a Bishop," *Ebony*, Feb. 1950, 73.

28. Teacher's Certificate of Guernsey County, Ohio, Aug. 28, 1880. (author's file)

29. Ransom. *Pilgrimage*, 27.

30. Ransom, *School Days*, 1.

1. GREEN AND GOLDEN COLLEGE DAYS, 1881–1886

1. Frederick A. McGinnis, *A History and An Interpretation of Wilberforce University* (Blanchester, Ohio: Brown Publishing, 1941), 9.

2. Daniel A. Payne, *History of the African Methodist Episcopal Church* (Nashville, Tenn.: A.M.E. Sunday School Union, 1891), 423–28.

3. B.W. Arnett, comp., *Wilberforce Alumnal—A Comprehensive Review* (Xenia, Ohio: Printed at the Gazette Office, 1885), 26–27. (Wilberforce Univ. Archives)

4. Payne, *History*, 428.

5. Ibid., 428–29.

6. Reverdy C. Ransom, *School Days*, 8–9.

7. Payne, *History*, 429.

8. Ransom, *School Days*, 1–2.

9. Ibid.

10. Ibid., 2; R.R. Wright, *Bishops of the A.M.E. Church* (Nashville, Tenn.: A.M.E. Sunday School Union, 1963), 253–55.

11. Ransom, *School Days*, 2–3.

12. Ibid., 3.

13. Ibid., 12.

14. Arnett, *Wilberforce Alumnal*, 26–27.

15. Hallie Q. Brown, *Pen Pictures of Pioneers of Wilberforce* (Xenia, Ohio: Aldine Press, 1937), 13.

16. Ransom, *School Days*, 44.

17. Ibid., 42–43.

18. Arnett, *Wilberforce Alumnal*, 27–28.

19. Ransom, *School Days*, 37–38.

20. Ibid.

21. Ibid., 12.

22. *Biennial Catalogue, Wilberforce University*, 1883–84, 1884–85 (Wilberforce Univ. Archives); Ransom, *School Days*, 12–13.

23. Ransom, *School Days*, 13–14.

24. *Biennial Catalogue, Wilberforce University*, 1883–84, 184–85.

25. Ransom, *School Days*, 30.

26. Hanley Hickey, interview with author, Wilberforce, Ohio, April 7, 1999.

27. Ransom, *School Days*, 30; Reverdy C. Ransom, "Confessions of a Bishop," *Ebony*, Feb. 1950, 73.

28. James H. Fairchild, *Oberlin the Colony and the College* (Oberlin, Ohio: E.J. Goodrich, 1883), 52–53.

29. Ibid., 53.

30. Ibid., 62.

31. Ibid., 64.

32. David A. Gerber, *Black Ohio and the Color Line 1869–1915* (Urbana, Ill.: Univ. of Illinois Press, 1976), 12.

33. Ransom, *School Days,* 19.

34. Sara C.B. Scarborough and Bernice Sanders, eds., *Autobiography of the Life of William Sanders Scarborough* (unedited typescript in the possession of T.K. Gibson, 5) cited by Gerber, *Black Ohio,* 55.

35. Letter of Character from President Benjamin G. Lee concerning Reverdy C. Ransom, Jan. 20, 1882. (author's files)

36. Fairchild, *Oberlin,* 9.

37. *Oberlin College Catalogue,* 1882–1883, 77–78.

38. Ransom, *Pilgrimage,* 33.

39. *Oberlin Catalogue,* 1882–1883, 73.

40. Ibid., 73–74.

41. Ibid., 73, 76.

42. Ibid. 80.

43. Ransom, *Pilgrimage,* 34.

44. Ibid., 27.

45. Letter to "Honorable Faculty of Oberlin College" from Oberlin Negro Students, around 1882, exact date not recorded. (James A. Fairchild Papers, Oberlin College Archive)

46. Letter to President James A. Fairchild from Julia A. Wilson, Baxter Springs, Kansas, Mar. 16, 1882. Letterhead: "Mission to the Colored Refugees" in connection with the Women's Home Missionary Association, Boston, Mass. (James A. Fairchild Papers, Oberlin College Archives)

47. "Is There a Color Line In Oberlin?" *Oberlin Review,* Feb. 3, 1883, 115. (Oberlin College Archives)

48. Ransom, *Pilgrimage,* 33.

49. Letter to President James A. Fairchild from B.A. Ames, Memphis, Tenn., Oct. 16, 1882. (James A. Fairchild Papers, Oberlin College Archives)

50. Letter to President James A. Fairchild from L.A. Roberson (city and state not noted), Oct. 11, 1882. (James A. Fairchild Papers, Oberlin College Archives)

51. "Communications," *Oberlin Review,* Mar. 3, 1883, 136. (Oberlin College Archives)

52. Interview with author and Hanley Hickey, Wilberforce, Ohio, April 7, 1999.

53. Ransom, *Pilgrimage,* 37.

54. Ransom, *School Days,* 8.

55. Ibid., 9.

56. Ransom, *Pilgrimage,* 38.

57. McGinnis, *A History,* 56.

58. *Biennial Catalogue, Wilberforce* 1883–84, 1884–85; Ransom, *Pilgrimage,* 38.

59. Ibid., *Biennial Catalogue.*

60. Ibid.

61. Ransom, *Pilgrimage,* 42.

62. Ibid., 38.

63. Ibid.

64. Ibid., 42.

65. Ibid., 31.

66. Reverdy C. Ransom, "T.H. Jackson," editorial, *The A.M.E. Church Review,* Jan. 1922, 130.

67. Brown, *Pen Pictures*, 7–13.

68. Reverdy C. Ransom, "Daniel Payne: The Prophet of an Era," *Making the Gospel Plain: the Writings of Reverdy C. Ransom*, edited by Anthony B. Pinn (Harrisburg, Pa.: Trinity Press International, 1999), 222–25.

69. George A. Singleton, *The Romance of African Methodism* (New York: Exposition Press, 1952), 129.

70. Arnett, *Wilberforce Alumnal*, 40–42.

71. Ransom, *School Days*, 53–55.

72. Arnett, *Wilberforce Alumnal*, 45.

73. Reverdy C. Ransom, "The Class of 1886" typescript. (author's files)

74. Reverdy C. Ransom, "Civil and Divine Law" typescript. Delivered at his Commencement, June 17, 1886. (Ransom Papers, Wilberforce Univ. Archives)

75. Ibid.

76. Ibid.

77. Ibid.

78. John G. Brown, "Wilberforce University: Twenty-third Commencement Exercise—A Brilliant Closing," *The Christian Recorder*, July 8, 1886; Ransom, *Pilgrimage*, 41.

79. Ransom, *Pilgrimage*, 43

2. EARLY ITINERANT MINISTRY, 1886–1896

1. Ransom, *Pilgrimage*, 43–44.

2. Charles L. Blockson, *Pennsylvania's Black History* (Philadelphia, Pa.: Portfolio Assoc., 1975), 38.

3. Ransom, *Pilgrimage*, 44.

4. Ibid.

5. Ibid.

6. Blockson, *Pennsylvania's Black History*, 47.

7. Ransom, *Pilgrimage*, 44–45

8. Reverdy C. Ransom, "Two Cultured for His Flock," *The Christian Recorder*, Nov. 18, 1886.

9. Booker T. Washington, "Atlanta Exposition Speech," *The Black American: A Documentary History*, edited by Leslie H. Fishel Jr., Benjamin Quarles (New York: Scott Foresman, 1970), 343.

10. Reverdy C. Ransom, "Concerning Wilberforce University," *The Christian Recorder*, Mar. 24, 1887.

11. Donald A. Drewett, *Ransom on Race and Racism: The Racial and Social Thought of Reverdy Cassius Ransom—Preacher, Editor and Bishop of the African Methodist Episcopal Church*, (Ph.D. diss., Drew Univ., 1988, printed UMI Dissertation Information Service), 88.

12. Reverdy C. Ransom, "The Student," *The A.M.E. Church Review*, Jan. 1948, 33–35.

13. Ransom, *Pilgrimage*, 45.

14. Ibid., 290–91.

15. Ibid., 45–46.

16. Reverdy C. Ransom, Handwritten journal, 1888–1894, 3. (author's file)

17. Ransom, *Pilgrimage*, 46.

18. Charles Spencer Smith, *A History of the African Methodist Episcopal Church* (Philadelphia, Pa.: A.M.E. Book Concern, 1922), 161.

19. Ransom, *Pilgrimage*, 47.

20. Ibid., 47, 49.

21. Ransom, Journal, 1888–1894, 5.

22. Ransom, *Pilgrimage,* 47.

23. Ibid., 48–49; Ransom, Journal, 1888–1894, 11.

24. Morris, *Reverdy C. Ransom: A Pioneer Black Social Gospeler,* 48.

25. Ransom, Journal, 1888–1894, 6.

26. Ransom, *Pilgrimage,* 49–50.

27. David Wills, "Reverdy C. Ransom: The Making of an A.M.E. Bishop," *Apostles: Afro American Clergy Confront the Twentieth Century,* edited by Randall K. Burkett, Richard Newman (Boston: G.K. Hall, 1989), 193.

28. Ransom, *Pilgrimage,* 50.

29. Reverdy C. Ransom, "Notes and Comments from the Smoky City," *The Christian Recorder,* Mar. 20, 1890.

30. Ransom, Journal, 1888–1894, 8–9.

31. Ibid., 9.

32. Ibid.

33. Ransom, *Pilgrimage,* 52–55.

34. Ibid., 55.

35. Gerber, *Black Ohio and the Color Line, 1860–1915,* 274–75.

36. Ibid., 144.

37. Ransom, *Pilgrimage,* 58.

38. W. E. B. DuBois, "A Tribute to Reverdy Cassius Ransom," *Making the Gospel Plain,* edited by Pinn, xix.

39. Reverdy C. Ransom, "Concerning Wilberforce," *The Christian Recorder,* Jan. 11, 1891.

40. Smith, *A History,* 368–69.

41. Letter from T.D. Scott, W.A. Anderson, J.P. Maxwell, Wilberforce, Ohio, to Rev. Reverdy C. Ransom, Springfield, Ohio, Feb. 11, 1893. (author's file)

42. Reverdy C. Ransom, "The Fifteenth Amendment," *The Wilberforce Alumnal,* Vol. 1, No. 5 (Ohio: Wilberforce Univ., Feb. 1893), 1–5. (Wilberforce Univ. Archives)

43. Ibid.

44. Ibid.

45. Ibid.

46. Ibid.

47. Robert A. Divine, T.H. Breen, George M. Fredrickson, R. Hal Williams, *American Past and Present* (Glenview, Ill., Scott, Foresman, 1984), 584–85.

48. Grover Cleveland, "Inaugural Address," cited in George Sinkler, *The Racial Attitudes of American Presidents: From Abraham Lincoln to Theodore Roosevelt* (New York: Doubleday, 1971), 221.

49. Ibid.

50. Ransom, *Pilgrimage,* 59–60.

51. *The Cleveland Gazette,* Dec. 23, 1893.

52. Ransom, *Pilgrimage,* 60.

53. Rayford W. Logan, Michael R. Winston, eds., *Dictionary of American Negro Biography* (New York: W.W. Norton, 1982), 200–03.

54. Ibid., 202.

55. Jean Wagner, *Black Poets of the United States,* (Urbana, Ill.: Univ. of Illinois Press, 1972), 80–92.

56. Paul Laurence Dunbar, "The Poet," cited in Wagner, *Black Poets,* 109. [emphasis added]

57. Ransom, *Pilgrimage,* 61.

58. Reverdy C. Ransom, "Paul Laurence Dunbar," editorial, *The A.M.E. Church Review*, Oct. 1914, 194–95.

59. Ransom, *Pilgrimage*, 64.

60. Countee Cullen, "Yet Do I Marvel," cited in Wagner, *Black Poets*, 307. [emphasis added]

61. Kenneth L. Kusner, *A Ghetto Takes Shape: Black Cleveland, 1879–1930* (Urbana, Ill.: Univ. of Illinois Press, 1976), 30.

62. Ransom, *Pilgrimage*, 68–69.

63. Ibid., 68.

64. Reverdy C. Ransom, "Out of the Midnight Sky: A Thanksgiving Address,"*Making the Gospel Plain*, 59–67.

65. Ibid.

66. Ibid.

67. Ibid.

68. Ibid.

69. Ibid.

70. Stephen Ward Angell, *Bishop Henry McNeal Turner and African-American Religion in the South*, (Knoxville, Tenn.: Univ. of Tennessee Press, 1992), 119–22.

71. H.M. Turner, "A National Convention," *The Cleveland Gazette*, Nov. 25, 1893.

72. Reverdy C. Ransom, *Preface to History of the A.M.E. Church* (Nashville, Tenn.: A.M.E. Sunday School Union, 1950), 166.

73. Angell, *Bishop Henry McNeal Turner*, 220–21.

74. Ibid., 221.

75. Ibid., Introduction, 1.

76. "Bishop Payne's Funeral," *The Cleveland Gazette*, Dec. 9, 1893.

77. Ransom, *Preface*, 128.

78. "St. John A.M.E. Church," *The Cleveland Gazette*, Mar. 31. 1894.

79. Reverdy C. Ransom, "Two Great Women at Variance: The National Convention of the WCTU in Cleveland, Notes and Comments," (article found in Ransom trunk—n.d. and no name of paper, probably published in Nov. 1895 in either *The Cleveland Gazette* or *The Christian Recorder*).

80. "Miss Wells Lectures," *The Cleveland Gazette*, Nov. 24, 1894.

81. Ransom, "Two Great Women"; Ida B. Wells, *Crusade for Justice: The Autobiography of Ida B. Wells*, edited by Alfreda M. Duster (Chicago: Univ. of Chicago Press, 1970), 109.

82. Ransom, *Pilgrimage*, 69.

83. "Reverdy C. Ransom," *The Christian Recorder*, Aug. 26, 1897.

84. Reverdy C. Ransom, "The Institutional Idea in Church Work," *The Christian Recorder*, Nov. 28, 1895.

85. Ibid.

86. Ibid.

87. Ransom, *Pilgrimage*, 73; L.L. Berry, *A Century of Missions of the African Methodist Episcopal Church 1840–1940* (New York: Gutenberg Printing, 1942), 158.

88. Ransom, *Pilgrimage*, 73–74.

89. Reverdy C. Ransom, "Mission of Religious Press" (delivered before the A.M.E. General Conference, Kansas City, Mo., May 16, 1912); Reverdy C. Ransom, *The Spirit of Freedom and Justice: Orations and Speeches* (Nashville, Tenn.: A.M.E. Sunday School Union, 1926), 88–97.

90. Berry, *A Century*, 91, 101.

91. Ibid., 105–14.

92. Ibid., 107.

93. Reverdy C. Ransom, *The Disadvantages and Opportunities of the Colored Youth* (Cleveland, Ohio: Thomas & Mattell Printers, 1894), Preface, 3.

94. Ibid., "Race Soil," 5–13.

95. Ibid.

96. Ibid.

97. Ibid., "Are We Able to Go Up and Possess the Land?" 14–22.

98. Ibid.

99. Ibid., "Lions by the Way," 23–32.

100. Ibid.

101. Ibid.

102. Ibid.

103. Ibid., "Grapes from the Land of Canaan," 33–41.

104. Ibid.

105. Ibid.

106. Ibid.

107. Ibid.

108. Ibid.

109. "Frederick Douglass," *The Cleveland Gazette,* Mar. 9, 1895.

110. Ibid.

111. "Shame!!!" *The Cleveland Gazette,* Mar. 16, 1895.

112. Ibid.

113. Reverdy C. Ransom, "Sign of the Times: Our Hold Upon the People," *The Christian Recorder,* Sept. 5, 1895.

114. Ibid.

115. Kusmer, *A Ghetto Takes Shape,* 117.

116. Ransom, *Pilgrimage,* 71–72.

117. Kusmer, *A Ghetto Takes Shape,* 118–22.

118. Ransom, *Pilgrimage,* 69–70.

119. Ibid., 66–67.

120. "Hallie Q. Brown," *The Cleveland Gazette,* Mar. 2, 1893.

121. Smith, *A History,* 187.

122. Ransom, *Pilgrimage,* 74–76.

123. William Seraile, *Fire in His Heart: Bishop Benjamin Tucker Tanner and the A.M.E. Church* (Knoxville, Tenn.: Univ. of Tennessee Press, 1998), 111.

124. Smith, *A History,* 187–89.

125. B.W. Roberts, "A Trip to Wilmington, North Carolina, General Conference—Scenes and Happenings To and From," editorial, *The Christian Recorder,* July 23, 1896; Seraile, *Fire in His Heart,* 146.

126. Smith, *A History,* 195–99.

127. Ibid., 199.

128. Ransom, *Pilgrimage,* 75–77.

129. Smith, *A History,* 195–99.

130. Ibid.

131. Ransom, *Pilgrimage,* 75.

3. THE INSTITUTIONAL CHURCH, 1896–1904

1. Allan H. Spear, *Black Chicago: The Making of a Negro Ghetto 1890–1920* (Chicago: Univ. of Chicago Press, 1967), 2.

2. Ibid., 5.

3. Ibid.; St. Claire Drake, Horace Cayton, *Black Metropolis: A Study of Negro Life in a Northern City* (New York: Harcourt, Brace, 1945), 12–17.

4. Spear, *Black Chicago*, 6–8; Harold F. Gosnell, *Negro Politicians: The Rise of Negro Politics in Chicago* (Chicago: Univ. of Chicago Press, 1935), xix–xxi.

5. Spear, *Black Chicago*, 91.

6. Reverdy C. Ransom, *Pilgrimage*, 81–82.

7. Ibid., 83.

8. Ibid.

9. Ida B. Wells-Barnett, "Rev. R.C. Ransom, B.D.," *The Christian Recorder*, Jan. 25, 1900.

10. Reverdy C. Ransom, "Negro's Path A Thorny One," *The Indianapolis Freeman*, Dec. 19, 1896.

11. Reverdy C. Ransom. "The Industrial and Social Condition of the Negro," A Thanksgiving Sermon given at Bethel A.M.E. Church, Chicago, Nov. 26, 1896, printed pamphlet. (Wilberforce Univ. Archives)

12. Ibid.

13. Ibid.

14. Ibid.

15. Reverdy C. Ransom, "The Negro and Socialism," *The A.M.E. Church Review*, Oct. 1896, 194–95.

16. Ibid.

17. William H. Coston, "The Negro and Socialism," *The Christian Recorder*, Feb. 18, 1897.

18. Reverdy C. Ransom, "Socialism and the Social Spirit," *The Christian Recorder*, Mar. 18, 1897.

19. Drewett, *Ransom on Race and Racism*, 168.

20. Reverdy C. Ransom, "Deborah and Jael," (sermon delivered to the Ida B. Wells Women's Club at Bethel A.M.E. Church, Chicago, June 6, 1897); Ida B. Wells, *Crusade for Justice*, xix.

21. Ransom, "Deborah and Jael," 1–8.

22. Ibid.

23. Ibid.

24. Ibid.

25. Ibid.

26. Ibid.

27. Ibid.

28. Interview between Annetta Gomez-Jefferson and Hanley Hickey, Wilberforce, Ohio, Apr. 7, 1999.

29. Divine, Breen, Fredrickson, Williams, *America Past and Present*, 617–20.

30. Ransom, *Pilgrimage*, 85–86

31. Reverdy C. Ransom, "To Black Soldiers of the Spanish American War," (Handwritten poem). (author's file)

32. Divine, Breen, Fredrickson, Williams, *America Past and Present*, 617–20.

33. "Eighth Comes Home," *The Inter Ocean*, Mar. 19, 1899.; "To Meet the Eighth," *Indianapolis Freeman*, Mar. 15, 1899.

34. "Reception to the Eighth," *The Colored American*, Apr. 22, 1899.

35. George Sinkler, *Racial Attitudes of American Presidents*, 297–300.

36. Ibid., 299.

37. Ibid.

38. National Peace Jubilee (printed program) Chicago, Oct. 16, 1898. (author's file)

39. Drewett, *Ransom on Race*, 100–03; Spear, *Black Chicago*, 59–60.

40. Ransom, *Pilgrimage*, 85.

41. (No author or title noted), *The Chicago Tribune*, Aug. 20, 1899.

42. Wills, "The Makings of an A.M.E. Bishop," 199–200; Louis Harlan, *Booker T. Washington: The Making of a Black Leader 1856–1901*, (New York: Oxford Univ. Press, 1972) 263–66.

43. "The Afro-American Quarrel, Booker T. Washington Defines His Attitude for His Critics," *New York Times*, Aug. 21, 1899. (A.P. from Saratoga, Aug. 20)

44. Cited by Wills, "The Makings of an A.M.E. Bishop," 200.

45. W. E. B. DuBois, *The Souls of Black Folk* (Chicago: A.C. Mc Clurg, 1903), 59.

46. Letter from Reverdy C. Ransom to Booker T. Washington, Aug. 31, 1899, Louis R. Harlan, Raymond W. Smock, eds. *The Booker T. Washington Papers, Vol.* 5, 1899–1900 (Urbana, Ill.: Univ. of Illinois Press, 1976), 194–95.

47. Ransom, *Pilgrimage*, 91–93.

48. Spear, *Black Chicago*, 103.

49. Ransom, *Pilgrimage*, 86–87.

50. Ibid., 87.

51. Pinn, *Making the Gospel Plain*, 135–39.

52. Reverdy C. Ransom, "The Institutional Church," *The Christian Recorder*, Dec. 21, 1899.

53. Ransom, *Pilgrimage*, 103.

54. Smith, *A History*, 204–5.

55. Ibid., 209–13.

56. Ibid., 215–16, 219.

57. Reverdy C. Ransom, *First Quadrennial Report of the Pastor and Warden of the Institutional Church to the Twenty Second General Conference*, Quinn Chapel A.M.E. Church, Chicago, 1904. n.p.; Ransom, *Pilgrimage*, 104–5.

58. Ibid.

59. Ibid.

60. Ibid., *Pilgrimage*, 104–5.

61. Ibid.

62. Katherine Leckie, "A South Side Institution," *Chicago American*, Mar. 1, 1901, cited in Ransom, *Pilgrimage*, 105–10.

63. Ransom, *Pilgrimage*, 111–12.

64. Ransom, *First Quadrennial Report*, 1904. n.p.

65. Ibid.

66. Leckie, "A South Side Institution," cited in Ransom, *Pilgrimage*, 106–8.

67. Ransom, *Pilgrimage*, 93–99; Smith, *The History*, 224.

68. Ibid., *Pilgrimage*.

69. Reverdy C. Ransom, "Letter to the Editor," *Chicago Conservator*, Aug. 15, 1901.

70. Letters to Emma from Reverdy C. Ransom, Sept. 9, 15, 1901. (Wilberforce Univ. Archives)

71. Reverdy C. Ransom. *Work of the Methodist Churches in the Twenty First Century from an Address by Reverdy C. Ransom before the Third Ecumenical Conference in John Wesley's Chapel, City Road, Sep. 4, 1901*, cited in Ransom, *Pilgrimage*, 98–99.

72. Smith, *A History,* 224.

73. Ransom, *Pilgrimage,* 94.

74. Ibid., 96–97.

75. Ibid., 95.

76. Ibid., 95–96.

77. Ibid., 117–18.

78. Reverdy C. Ransom, Sermon outline, Feb. 15, 1902. (author's file).

79. *Chicago Tribune,* May 4, 1903, cited in Ransom, *Pilgrimage,* 119–20.

80. *Chicago Evening Post,* May 4, 1903, cited in Ransom, *Pilgrimage,* 124–25.

81. Ibid., 117–18.

82. *Chicago American,* May 4, 1903, cited in Ransom, *Pilgrimage,* 125–26.

83. *Chicago Record-Herald,* May 11, 1903, cited in Ransom, *Pilgrimage,* 122–23.

84. *Chicago Tribune,* May 4, 1903, cited in Ransom, *Pilgrimage,* 121.

85. Spear, *Black Chicago,* 36–37.

86. Ransom, *Pilgrimage,* 113–14.

87. Ibid., 114.

88. Ibid., 135

89. Reverdy C. Ransom, Sermon outline, 1899. (author's file)

90. Ransom, *Pilgrimage,* 135.

4. NEW ENGLAND YEARS, 1904–1907

1. Ransom. *Pilgrimage,* 148.

2. Ibid., 143,146.

3. Frederick Douglass. *Douglass Autobiographies: Narrative of the Life, My Bondage and My Freedom, Life and Times* (New York: The Library of America, 1894, reprint 1994), 93–94.

4. Ransom, *Pilgrimage,* 143.

5. Ibid., 144–48.

6. John Daniels, *In Freedom's Birthplace: A Study of Boston Negroes* (New York: Houghton, Mifflin, 1914), 1, 8–9.

7. Ibid., 23–24.

8. Ibid., Appendix, 458.

9. Ibid., 36–38, 54–56.

10. R.R. Wright, Jr., comp. *Encyclopaedia of African Methodism, 1948* (Philadelphia, Pa.: A.M.E. Book Concern, 1947), 342.

11. Ransom, *Pilgrimage,* 150.

12. Wright, Jr., *Encyclopaedia, 1948,* 342.

13. Daniels, *In Freedom's Birthplace,* 17, 143–45.

14. Ransom, *Pilgrimage,* 151.

15. Ibid., 149.

16. "The Northeast Conference," *Alexanders Magazine,* Aug. 15, 1905.

17. Ransom, *Pilgrimage,* 153.

18. *The Charles Street Church Weekly Bulletin,* Sept. 3, 1905. (author's file).

19. "Charles Street Church's New Pastor," *Voice of Missions,* Aug. 1905, 11.

20. Ransom, *Pilgrimage,* 150–51.

21. Emma S. Ransom, "The Home-Made Girl," (An address delivered before the Convention of the Northeastern Federation of Women's clubs, Potter Hall, New Century Building, Boston, Mass., Aug. 11, 1905, pamphlet), 1–8.

22. Ibid.

23. Ibid.

24. Ibid.

25. Ibid.

26. *The Charles Street Church Weekly Bulletin,* Sept. 24, 1905. (author's file).

27. Ibid., Oct.1, Oct. 8, 1905.

28. Reverdy C. Ransom, "How Should the Christian State Deal with the Race Problem," *The Spirit of Freedom and Justice,* 128–37.

29. Ibid.

30. Ibid.

31. Ibid.

32. Ibid.

33. Ransom, *Pilgrimage,* 154,

34. Ibid., 154–56.

35. William Monroe Trotter, editorial, *The Boston Guardian,* Dec. 20, 1902.

36. William Monroe Trotter, editorial, *The Boston Guardian,* Apr, 4, 1903.

37. Reverdy C. Ransom, editorial, *The A.M.E. Church Review,* Oct. 1919, 379–80.

38. W. E. B. DuBois, *From Dusk to Dawn: An Essay Toward an Autobiography of the Race Concept* (New York: Harcourt, Brace. 1940), 73.

39. Ransom, *Pilgrimage,* 169.

40. Reverdy C. Ransom, "William Lloyd Garrison," Ransom, *The Spirit of Freedom,* 5–14.

41. Ibid.

42. Ibid.

43. Ibid.

44. Ibid.

45. Ibid.

46. Ibid.

47. Ibid.

48. Cited in *The Boston Herald,* Dec. 12, 1905. Also cited in Ransom, *Pilgrimage,* 169.

49. "Colored Folks' Fervor," *The Boston Herald,* Dec. 12, 1905. Also cited in Ransom, *Pilgrimage.* 170–71.

50. Ransom, *Pilgrimage,* 169.

51. Reverdy C. Ransom, "Centennial Oration of R.C. Ransom at Faneuil Hall, Boston, Dec. 11, 1905 on William Lloyd Garrison" (printed and published pamphlet by Boston Suffrage League, 12 pages). (author's file)

52. *The New York Evening Sun,* Jan. 3, 1906.

53. *The Christian Recorder,* January 11, 1906.

54. Ransom, *Pilgrimage,* 176–81.

55. Ibid.

56. Ibid.

57. *The Knoxville Journal, The Knoxville Tribune,* May 28, 1906, cited in Ransom, *Pilgrimage,* 173–74.

58. Ransom, *Pilgrimage,* 192.

59. T. Timothy Fortune, "Ransom Corrupter of Youth," *New York Age*, July 2, 1906.

60. Ransom, *Pilgrimage*, 186.

61. Letter from Booker T. Washington to T. Timothy Fortune, June 19, 1906. (B.T.W. Papers, Vol. 9, Library of Congress, Manuscript Division, 34–35)

62. T. Timothy Fortune, "Running Amok in Boston," *New York Age*, July 2, 1906.

63. "Boston Friends Aroused at Action of Pullman Company," *The Boston Post*, May 29, 1906; "Boston Pastor Is Ejected From Car." *The Boston Herald*, May 29, 1906; both cited in Ransom, *Pilgrimage*, 174–176.

64. "Ransom's Insult," *Alexanders Magazine*, June 1906, 14–15.

65. George W. Forbes, *The Boston Guardian*, 1906, n.d., cited in Ransom, *Pilgrimage*, 185.

66. Monroe Trotter's letter to the editor of *The Boston Globe*, 1906, n.d., cited in Ransom, *Pilgrimage*, 185–86.

67. Ransom, *Pilgrimage*, 181.

68. Bishop Henry McNeal Turner, Written Review of the Fifty-Fifth Session of the New England Annual Conference, July 5–9, 1906, Providence, R.I.), cited in Ransom, *Pilgrimage*, 188–89; *Minutes of the Fifty-Fifth Session of the New England Annual Conference*, 29.

69. Turner, Written Review. See n. 68.

70. Letter from Bishop Henry McNeal Turner to Reverdy C. Ransom, Aug. 5, 1906. (Wilberforce Univ. Archives)

71. "Bibulous Ransom Preaches on 'How to Keep Sober,'" *New York Age*, Aug. 16, 1906.

72. Letter from Bishop Henry McNeal Turner to Reverdy C. Ransom, n.d., cited in Ransom, *Pilgrimage*, 186–87.

73. *The Charles Street Weekly Bulletin*, July 1, 1906. (author's file)

74. *The Charles Street Weekly Bulletin*, July 19, 1906. (author's file)

75. W. E. B. DuBois, *The Autobiography of W. E. B. DuBois* (New York: International Publishers, 1968), 248–49.

76. Ibid., 138,

77. R.R. Wright, Jr., *Eighty-Seven Years Behind the Black Curtain* (Nashville, Tenn.: A.M.E. Sunday School Union, 1965), 97.

78. C. Eric Lincoln, Lawrence H. Mamiya, *The Black Church in the African American Experience* (Durham, N.C.: Duke Univ. Press, 1990) 230.

79. Letter from F.H.N. Murray to Reverdy C. Ransom, July 30, 1906. (author's file)

80. Ransom, *Pilgrimage*, 196.

81. Reverdy C. Ransom, "The Spirit of John Brown," *The Spirit of Freedom and Justice*, 16–25.

82. Ibid.

83. Ibid.

84. Ibid.

85. Ibid.

86. J. Max Barber, "The Niagara Movement at Harper's Ferry," *The Voice of the Negro*, Oct. 1906, 408.

87. W. E. B. DuBois, "The Word," Reverdy C. Ransom, *"The Negro: The Hope or the Despair of Christianity"* (Boston: Ruth Hill, 1935), front of book, n.p.

88. DuBois. *Autobiography*, 253.

89. Gunnar Myrdal, *An American Dilemma: The Negro Problem and Modern Democracy, Vol. 2* (New York: Random House), 1972, 567, 680.

90. Langston Hughes, *Fight for Freedom: The Story of the NAACP* (New York: W.W. Norton, 1962) 57–58.

91. Reverdy C. Ransom, "The Atlanta Riot," *The Spirit of Freedom and Justice*, 117–21.

92. Ibid.

93. Ibid.

94. Ibid.

95. Ibid.

96. Eileen Southern, *The Music of Black Americans* (New York: W.W. Norton, 1971), 307–8.

97. Letter from Samuel Coleridge-Taylor to Reverdy C. Ransom, Oct. 2, 1906. (author's file)

98. Ransom, *Pilgrimage*, 194–95.

99. Ibid.

100. Ibid.

101. Reverdy C. Ransom, "Bon Voyage," (New Year's printed message, Jan. 1907). (author's file)

102. Reverdy C. Ransom, "Staid Boston Enthusiastic Over Distinguished Visitors," *The Christian Recorder*, May 30, 1907.

103. Letter from Bishop Henry McNeal Turner to Reverdy C. Ransom, May 7, 1907, cited in Ransom, *Pilgrimage*, 199–200.

104. Letter from Bishop Henry McNeal Turner to Reverdy C. Ransom, May 27, 1907, cited in Ransom, *Pilgrimage*, 200–1.

105. Certificate of Reverdy C. Ransom's Pastoral Appointment to Charles Street A.M.E. Church, Boston, Mass., New England Annual Conference, signed by Bishop Henry McNeal Turner, July 7, 1907. (author's file)

5. NEW YORK MINISTRY, 1907–1912

1. Seth M. Scheiner, *Negro Mecca, History of the Negro in New York City 1865–1920* (New York: New York Univ. Press, 1965), 17–20; Ransom, *Pilgrimage*, 202.

2. David Levering Lewis, *When Harlem Was in Vogue* (New York: Oxford Univ. Press, 1981), 25.

3. Ransom, *Pilgrimage*, 202.

4. Jervis Anderson, *This Was Harlem 1900–1950* (New York: Farrar, Straus & Giroux, 1982), 5.

5. Ransom, *Pilgrimage*, 201.

6. Anderson, *This Was Harlem*, 23–24.

7. Ibid., 24–26.

8. Scheiner, *Negro Mecca*, 222–23 (Tables).

9. James Weldon Johnson, *Black Manhattan* (r.p. Salem, N.H.: Ayer, 1988), 128–31.

10. "Welcome to Rev. Ransom," *New York Age*, Aug. 15, 1907.

11. Ransom, *Pilgrimage*, 205–7.

12. Reverdy C. Ransom, "Concerning the Editorship of The Christian Recorder," *Voice of Missions*, Feb. 1907, 2.

13. "The Iconoclast," "Reverdy C. Ransom Great Religious Leader of the Race," *Voice of Missions*, Sept. 1907, 2.

14. Reverdy C. Ransom, "John Greenleaf Whittier: Plea for Political Equality" (Centennial Oration delivered Faneuil Hall, Boston, Mass., Dec. 17, 1907). Included in Ransom's *The Spirit of Freedom and Justice*, 31–41.

15. Ibid.

16. Ibid.

17. Ibid.

18. "Ransom's Boston Whittier Centennial Oration," *The Advocate-Verdict* (Harrisburg, Pa.), Dec. 27, 1907.

19. Ruth Ransom, interview with author, Xenia, Ohio, July 19, 2000.

20. Anderson, *This Was Harlem*, 19–21.

21. Annetta L. Gomez-Jefferson, *In Darkness With God: The Life of Joseph Gomez, a Bishop in the African Methodist Episcopal Church* (Kent, Ohio: Kent State Univ. Press, 1998). 18–30.

22. Anderson, *This Was Harlem*, 22.

23. Johnson, *Black Manhattan*, 90.

24. Ibid., 90–92.

25. Paper found in Ransom's trunk at Tawawa Chimney Corner, given to the author by Georgia Myrtle Teal Ransom before she died. (n.d.)

26. Ransom, *Pilgrimage*, 207.

27. Ernest Hogan, "The Church and the Stage," *New York Age*, Dec. 24, 1908.

28. Reverdy C. Ransom, "Answer to Ernest Hogan," *New York Age*, Jan. 28, 1909.

29. Smith, *A History*, 244–63.

30. Ibid.

31. Divine, Breen, Fredrickson, Williams, *America Past and Present*, 645–48.

32. "Negroes for Roosevelt," *The Inter Ocean*, May 21, 1904.

33. *New York Age*, Sept. 10, 1908.

34. "Almost a Riot and in a Church," *The Cleveland Gazette*, Oct. 17, 1908.

35. George Brown Tindall, *America: A Narrative History* (New York: W.W. Norton, 1988), 959.

36. "Bethel A.M.E. Church," *New York Age*, Dec. 25, 1908.

37. Reverdy C. Ransom, Printed address at Joint Hearing Before Senate Committee on Taxation and Retrenchment and Assembly Excise Committee on the Bracket–Gray Local Option Bill, delivered Apr. 14, 1908, Albany, NY. (author's file)

38. Ibid.

39. "Negro Police for New York," *New York Age*, Aug. 5, 1909.

40. "Subject of Negro Police," *New York Age*, Aug. 19, 1909.

41. "Will Not Take Examination," *New York Age*, Sept. 2, 1909.

42. "Subject of Negro Police," *New York Age*, Aug. 19, 1909.

43. Ransom, *Pilgrimage*, 215–16.

44. Langston Hughes, *Fight for Freedom*, 20–22.

45. "Whites and Blacks Confer as Equals," *New York Times*, June 1, 1909.

46. "Address of Chairman William Hayes Ward," *Proceedings of the National Negro Conference* 1909, *May* 31 *and June* 1, New York City, 9–13. Given to Joseph Gomez from Ransom library. (author's file)

47. Ibid., Livingston Farrand, "Race Differentiation-Race Characteristics," 14–21.

48. Ibid., Burt G. Wilder, "The Brain of the American Negro," 22–70.

49. Ibid., John Dewey, "An Address," 71–78.

50. Ibid., W. E. B. DuBois, "Evaluation of the Race Problem," 142–58.

51. Ida B. Wells, "Lynching Our National Crime," 174–79.

52. Ibid., Bishop Alexander Walters, "Civil and Political Status of the Negro," 167–73.

53. Ibid., "Resolutions," 222–25 (also see footnotes).

54. "Negro Rights Discussed," *New York Evening Post*, June 1, 1909.

55. Hughes, *Fight for Freedom*, 23.

56. Ransom, *Pilgrimage*, 203–5.

57. Reverdy C. Ransom, "A Thanksgiving Sermon," *The Spirit,* 62–70; Booker T. Washington, *Up from Slavery: An Autobiography* (New York: Houghton Mifflin, 1902), passim.; W. E. B. DuBois, *The Souls of Black Folk* (Chicago: A.C. McClurg, 1918), passim.

58. Ibid.

59. Ibid.

60. Ibid.

61. "Negro Criticizes Taft," *Boston Evening News,* Dec. 3, 1909.

62. Reverdy C. Ransom, "Martyrdom of John Brown," *The Spirit,* 104–12.

63. Ibid.

64. Obituary, Reverdy C. Ransom Jr., Funeral Program, Bethel A.M.E. Church, Ashbury Park, NJ., May 22, 1967.

65. Logan, Winston, *Dictionary of American Negro Biography,* 583–84.

66. "Mary Church Terrell at Bethel," *New York Age,* Feb. 17, 1910.

67. "Press Criticizes Speech of DuBois,"*New York Age,* Mar. 10, 1910.

68. "Dr. Washington at Bethel," *New York Age,* Mar. 24, 1910.

69. Ibid.

70. "Our Aims," *Original Rights Magazine, Vol.*1, No. 2, Apr. 10, 1910, Title Page, 4, 61 (Moorland–Spingarn Research Center, Howard Univ.); Drewett, *Ransom on Race,* 200–3, footnote.

71. Ibid.

72. Ibid., Reverdy C. Ransom, "The Bad Negro, Vol 1. No. 2 "The Reno Prize Fight," Vol. 1, No, 6 (Aug. 1910); Ransom, *Pilgrimage,* 208–14.

73. "White Ministers Flayed by Ransom," *New York Age,* June 9, 1910.

74. Ransom, "The Reno Prize Fight." See notes 70–72.

75. Ibid.

76. "Define Power of the Bishops' Council," *New York Age,* July 28, 1910.

77. Ibid.

78. Reverdy C. Ransom, "Let the Bishops Rotate," *The Christian Recorder,* Aug. 4, 1910.

79. John S. Bowman, ed., *The Cambridge Dictionary of American Biography* (Cambridge: Cambridge Univ. Press, 1995), 711.

80. Reverdy C. Ransom, "Oration Plea for Charles Sumner," Ransom, *The Spirit,* 51–61; Pinn, *Making the Gospel Plain,* 112–22.

81. Louis Harlan, *Booker T. Washington: The Wizard of Tuskegee 1901–1915* (New York: Oxford Univ. Press, 1983), 379–82.

82. "Booker T. Washington," *New York Age,* Mar. 23 1911.

83. Ransom, *Pilgrimage,* 223–25.

84. "Express Faith in Their Leader," *New York Age,* Mar. 30, 1911.

85. Ransom, *Pilgrimage,* 224.

86. Ibid.

87. Harlan, *Booker T. Washington,* 391.

88. Ransom, *Pilgrimage,* 225.

89. Reverdy C. Ransom, Certificate, Ministerial Delegate to Twenty-Fourth A.M.E. General Conference, Kansas City, May 1912. Elected by Ninety-First Session of the New York Annual Conference, May 18, 1911. Signed by Bishop Wesley J. Gaines. (author's file)

90. Letter from William Pickett of Pickett and Miller Law Offices, Brooklyn, New York to Reverdy C. Ransom, Aug. 21, 1911. (author's file)

91. Copy of letter from Parker (first name not indicated) of Nail and Parker Realtors, New York City to Reverdy C. Ransom, Aug. 23, 1911. (author's file)

92. Copy of letter from J.E. Spingarn, President of the New York Branch of the NAACP, to Reverdy C. Ransom, Aug. 23, 1911. (author's file)

93. Gomez-Jefferson, *In Darkness with God*, 26, 27, 30.

94. Wedding Invitation: Aida Stewart to Reverdy C. Ransom Jr., Bethel A.M.E. Church, New York, N.Y., Dec. 25, 1911. (Copy author's file, original Ruth Ransom file)

95. Smith, *A History*, 264–66.

96. Ibid., 226–79.

97. Ibid., 174.

98. Reverdy C. Ransom, "The Mission of the Religious Press," Pinn, *Making the Gospel Plain*, 209–22; Ransom, *The Spirit*, 88–97.

99. Ibid.

100. Ibid., 275–76.

101. Ibid., 278, 279.

102. Letter from W. E. B. DuBois to Reverdy C. Ransom, Apr. 27, 1912. (author's file)

6. RANSOM THE EDITOR, 1912–1916

1. "Four New A.M.E. Bishops Chosen: Dr. Ransom Elected Editor, *New York Age*, May 23, 1912.

2. William Seraile, *Fire in His Heart*, 100–01.

3. R.T. Wright, *Encyclopaedia*, 1948, 498.

4. Ransom, *Pilgrimage*, 227; Reverdy C. Ransom, "Our Church Competitor," *The A.M.E. Church Review*, July 1912, 81.

5. Ibid.

6. Reverdy C. Ransom, "The Review in Philadelphia," editorial, *The A.M.E. Church Review*, July 1912, 83.

7. Reverdy C. Ransom, "The Preacher Editor," editorial, *The A.M.E. Church Review*, July 1912, 80–81.

8. Morris, *Reverdy Ransom: a Pioneer Black Social Gospeler*, 119.

9. Ransom, "The Preacher Editor," 80–81.

10. *New York Age*, editorial, July 11, 1912.

11. Raymond Washington Logan, *The Betrayal of the Negro* (New York: Colliers, 1963), 360.

12. Divine, Breen, Fredrickson, Wilson, *American Past and Present*, 676–77.

13. Reverdy C. Ransom, "The National Republican Convention," *The Spirit*, 676–77.

14. Ibid.

15. Ibid.

16. Logan, *The Betrayal*, 360–61.

17. Henry Lee Moon, *The Emerging Thought of W. E. B. DuBois: Essays and Editorials from the Crisis* (New York: International Publishing, 1978), 264.

18. James L. Curtis, "Side Lights on the Baltimore Democratic National Convention," *The A.M.E. Church Review*, July 1912, 84–85.

19. Reverdy C. Ransom, "The Negro's Political Conscience," editorial, *The A.M.E. Church Review*, July 1912, 84–85.

20. Divine, Breen, Fredrickson, Wilson, *America Past and Present*, 676–77.

21. Reverdy C. Ransom, "The Psychology of a General Conference," editorial, *The A.M.E. Church Review*, July 1912, 82.

22. Reverdy, C. Ransom, "A Step toward Denominational Union," editorial, *The A.M.E. Church Review*, July 1912, 85.

23. Letter from Bishop Evans Tyree to Reverdy C. Ransom, Aug. 22, 1912. (author's file).

24. R.R. Wright, "Samuel Coleridge-Taylor," *The A.M.E. Church Review*, Oct. 1912, 124–29.

25. Census Bureau, "Proportion of Mulattoes in the Negro Population of the United States: Preliminary 13th Census Statistics," *The A.M.E. Church Review*, Oct. 1912, 137–39.

26. Reverdy C. Ransom, "The Census Negro," editorial, *The A.M.E. Church Review*, Oct. 1912, 144–46.

27. Logan, *The Betrayal*, 360.

28. Fred R. Moore, "The Republican Party and the Negro," *The A.M.E. Church Review*, Oct. 1912, 123–24.

29. James L. Curtis, "Will Sentiment or Reason Determine the Course of Negro Voters in This Campaign?" *The A.M.E. Church Review*, Oct. 1912, 118–23.

30. Reverdy C. Ransom, "Hunting Big Game Out of Africa," *The A.M.E. Church Review*, Oct. 1912, 141–42.

31. Theodore Roosevelt, "Progressivism and the Colored Man," *Outlook* 101, cited in George Sinkler's *Racial Attitudes of American Presidents*, 361.

32. Ransom, "Hunting Big Game Out of Africa," 141–42.

33. *The A.M.E. Church Review*, Jan. 1913, passim.

34. Booker T. Washington, "Industrial Education and Negro Progress," *The A.M.E. Church Review*, Jan. 1913, 226–28.

35. Reverdy C. Ransom, "The New Emancipation," *The A.M.E. Church Review*, Jan. 1913, 260–64.

36. Oswald Garrison Villard, "Message for the Next Fifty Year," *The A.M.E. Church Review*, Jan. 1913, 225.

37. Reverdy C. Ransom, "The New Emancipation," 263–64.

38. Bishop C.S. Smith, "The Noachian Curse," printed commencement address, Wilberforce Univ. June 1913. (author's file)

39. Reverdy C. Ransom, "A Black Soul Among Prophets, *The A.M.E. Church Review*, Oct. 1913, 151–53.

40. Ransom, *Pilgrimage*, 228–34.

41. Reverdy C. Ransom, "The Editor's Vision and Task in New York's Black Tenderloin," *The A.M.E. Church Review*, Oct. 1913, 149–51.

42. Ibid.

43. Ibid.

44. Frank Lincoln Mather, *Who's Who of the Colored Race: Half Century of Negro Freedom in the United States, Chicago 1917*, Memento Edition (Detroit, Mich.: Book Tower, 1976), 224.

45. Letter from Chaplain George W. Prioleaux to Reverdy C. Ransom, Apr. 27, 1914. (author's file)

46. Gomez-Jefferson, *In Darkness with God*, 48–50.

47. Ibid.

48. Open letter from Reverdy C. Ransom announcing First Anniversary Ceremony of Simon of Cyrene, Sept. 4, 1914. (author's file)

49. "Dr. Ransom's Mission in Conference at Last," *New York Age*, June 3, 1915.

50. Reverdy C. Ransom, "Notice of Changes," *The A.M.E. Church Review*, July 1914, 31.

51. Reverdy C. Ransom, "The Negro Bishops and Their Opportunity for Race Leadership," editorial, *The A.M.E. Church Review*, July 1914, 64–67.

52. Reverdy C. Ransom, "Bishop Timber," editorial, *The A.M.E. Church Review*, July 1914, 69–70.

53. Reverdy C. Ransom, "What Will Bishop Walters Do Now?" editorial, *The A.M.E. Church Review*, July 1914, 73–75.

54. Divine, Breen, Fredrickson, Williams, *America Past and Present,* 680–81.

55. Reverdy C. Ransom, "What Will Bishop Walters Do Now?" 73–75.

56. Bishop Alexander Walters, "Letter to Editor Ransom," *The A.M.E. Church Review,* Oct. 1914, 208–11.

57. W. E. B. DuBois, *From Dusk to Dawn,* 234; Logan, *The Betrayal,* 360.

58. Logan, *The Betrayal,* 360.

59. Reverdy C. Ransom, "What Constitutes an American?" *The A.M.E. Church Review,* July 1914, 80–84.

60. Reverdy C. Ransom, "Travel Talks," *The A.M.E. Church Review,* 324–30.

61. Ibid.

62. Ibid.

63. Ibid.

64. Ibid.

65. Alice M. Dunbar, "The Poet and His Song," *The A.M.E. Church Review,* Oct. 1914, 121–35.

66. W.S. Scarborough, "Poet Laureate of the Negro Race," *The A.M.E. Church Review,* Oct. 1914, 135–43.

67. Bibliography of Dunbar's Works, (follows section on Dunbar), *The A.M.E. Church Review,* 144.

68. Reverdy C. Ransom, "The Thin Veneer of Christianity on European Civilization," editorial, *The A.M.E. Church Review,* Oct. 1914, 195–99.

69. Reverdy C. Ransom, "The Ape That Speaks Like a Man," editorial, *The A.M.E. Church Review,* Jan. 1915, 303–7.

70. Copy of letter sent by Reverdy C. Ransom to city editor of the *New York Age,* Dec. 11, 1914. (author's file)

71. Ransom, "The Ape That Speaks Like a Man," 303–7.

72. Ibid.

73. G.W. Forbes, "President Wilson, Trotter and the American People," *The A.M.E. Church Review,* Jan. 1915, 309–18.

74. Reverdy C. Ransom, "Strengthen Thy Stakes, But Lengthen Not Thy Cords," editorial, *The A.M.E. Church Review,* Jan. 1915, 319–22.

75. Reverdy C. Ransom, "Amanda Smith," editorial, *The A.M.E. Church Review,* Apr, 1915, 405–7.

76. Reverdy C. Ransom, "News Item," *The A.M.E. Church Review,* Apr. 1915, 407–8.

77. Ibid.

78. Reverdy C. Ransom, "Senator Borah and That Dirty Rag," editorial, *The A.M.E. Church Review,* Apr. 1915, 408–9.

79. Reverdy C. Ransom, "We Salute the Serbians," editorial, *The A.M.E. Church Review,* Apr. 1915, 409–10.

80. Reverdy C. Ransom, "That Old Borah Knife," editorial, *The A.M.E. Church Review,* Apr. 1915, 411.

81. Logan, Winston, *Dictionary of American Negro Biography,* 267–68.

82. Richard R. Greener, "An Edgefield Idyll—A South Carolina Reminiscence," *The A.M.E. Church Review,* Apr. 1915, 361–67.

83. Reverdy C. Ransom, "Dr. Greener, in the Golden Afterglow," editorial, *The A.M.E. Church Review,* Apr. 1915, 399–400.

84. Reverdy C. Ransom, "Our New Dress," editorial, *The A.M.E. Church Review,* July 1915, 58.

85. Angell, *Bishop Henry McNeal Turner,* 248–49.

86. George W. Forbes, "Bishop Turner, the Grandest Old Roman of Them All," *A.M.E. Church Review,* July 1915, 63–64.

87. Reverdy C. Ransom, "Bishop Henry McNeal Turner," editorial, *The A.M.E. Church Review*, July 1915, 45–47.

88. (n.a., just says "contributed"), "Boston's Fight Against the Slanderous Play," (cites speech of Hon. William H. Lewis protesting "Birth of a Nation"),*The A.M.E. Church Review*, July 1915, 30–33.

89. Reverdy C. Ransom, "The Birth of a Race vs. 'The Birth of a Nation,'" *The A.M.E. Church Review*, July 1915, 47–48.

90. Letter from Richard Theodore Greener to Reverdy C. Ransom, Chicago Ill., Oct. 11, 1915. (author's file)

91. Richard R. Greener, "Russia's Financial Position During the Russo-Japanese War—How She Builds Railroads," *The A.M.E. Church Review*, Oct. 1915. 93–98.

92. Reverdy C. Ransom, "Black and White," *A.M.E. Church Review*, Oct. 1915, 127–28.

93. (n.a., just says "contributed"), "American Intervention in Haiti," *A.M.E. Church Review*, Oct. 1915, 98–100.

94. Reverdy C. Ransom, "Toussaint L'Overture's Rusty Sword," *The A.M.E. Church Review*, Oct. 1915, 121–23.

95. Reverdy C. Ransom, "Ecclesiastical Imperialism," *The A.M.E. Church Review*, Oct. 1915, 119–21.

96. Booker T. Washington, *Booker T. Washington's Own Story of His Life and Work: Including an Authoritative Sixty-Four Page Supplement by Albon L. Holsey*, 1901, r.p., J. Nichols & Co., 1915, 451–458. (author's library)

97. Booker T. Washington, "The Mission Work of the Negro Church," *The A.M.E. Church Review*, Jan. 1916, 186–89.

98. George W. Forbes, "The Passing of Dr. Booker T. Washington," *The A.M.E. Church Review*, 190–96.

99. Reverdy C. Ransom, "The Passing of a New Age," editorial, *A.M.E. Church Review*, Jan, 1916, 208–9.

7. FROM EDITOR TO BISHOP, 1916–1924

1. Reverdy C. Ransom, "The Celebration of the Centennial of the A.M.E. Church," editorial, *The A.M.E. Church Review*, July 1916, 30–31.

2. Smith, *A History*, 290–92.

3. Ibid., 292–97.

4. Ibid.

5. Ransom, "The Celebration," 30–31.

6. *Minutes of the Twenty-Fifth Centennial General Conference of the A.M.E. Church*, Bethel A.M.E. Church, Philadelphia, PA., May 3–21, 1916, 17.

7. Program, *Star of Ethiopia* (pageant), Horizon Guild, W. E. B. DuBois, manager, Philadelphia, Pa. May 1916. (author's file)

8. Smith, *A History*, 300.

9. Reverdy C. Ransom, "Our Newly Elected Bishops," editorial, *The A.M.E. Church Review*, July 1916, 37.

10. Reverdy C. Ransom, "To Our Erstwhile Competition," editorial, *The A.M.E. Church Review*, July 1916, 40–41.

11. Reverdy C. Ransom, "The Centennial General Conference," *The A.M.E. Church Review*, July 1916, 27–29.

12. Roy Nash, "Waco Horror Stirs to Action—NAACP Subscription to $10,000 Lynching Fund," *The A.M.E. Church Review*, July 1916, 21–25; *Waco Times-Tribune, Waco Times Herald*, May 15, 1916.

13. Reverdy C. Ransom, "National Preparedness and Lynching Called to the Attention of the General Conference," editorial, *The A.M.E. Church Review*, July 1916, 29.

14. Tindall, *America*, 994.

15. Reverdy C. Ransom, "That Old Black Mule," editorial, *The A.M.E. Church Review*, Oct. 1916, 98–99.

16. Tindall, *America*, 995–96.

17. Reverdy C. Ransom, John R. Hawkins, eds. *A Handbook of the A.M.E. Church* (Nashville, Tenn.: A.M.E. Sunday School Union, 1916), passim.

18. Reverdy C. Ransom, "Travel Talks," *The A.M.E. Church Review*, Jan. 1917, 169–72.

19. Ibid.

20. Reverdy C. Ransom, "Oceanport—By the Sea," *The A.M.E. Church Review*, Oct. 1923, 101–2.

21. Reverdy C. Ransom, handwritten Oceanport Journal, 1917. (author's file)

22. Picture of farmhouse at Oceanport supplied by Ruth Ransom, Xenia Ohio. (author's file)

23. Ransom, Oceanport journal.

24. Ibid.

25. Ibid.

26. Reverdy C. Ransom, "The Exodus," editorial, *The A.M.E. Church Journal*, Jan. 1917, 149–52.

27. Ransom, Oceanport journal.

28. Ibid.

29. Ibid.

30. Ibid.

31. Tindall, *America*, 998, 1001.

32. W. E. B. DuBois, *The Autobiography*, 266–67.

33. Reverdy C. Ransom, "One Country One Flag," editorial, *The A.M.E. Church Review*, Apr. 1917, 241–42.

34. W. E. B. DuBois, "Close Ranks," *Crisis*, July 1918, cited in *The Emerging Thought of W. E. B. DuBois: Essays and Editorials from the Crisis with an Introduction, Commentaries and Personal Memoirs by Henry Lee Moon* (New York: Simon &Schuster, 1972), 254.

35. Ibid., DuBois, "The Perpetual Dilemma," *Crisis*, Apr. 1917, 249–50.

36. Reverdy C. Ransom, "Travel Talk," *The A.M.E. Church Review*, July 1917, 40–43.

37. Ibid.

38. Ibid.

39. Ibid.

40. Ibid.

41. Ransom, Oceanport journal.

42. Reverdy C. Ransom, "Inter-denominational Duty and Opportunity," editorial, *The A.M.E. Church Review*, Jan. 1918, 174–76.

43. W. E. B. DuBois, *Autobiography*, 268–69; Langston Hughes, *Fight For Freedom*, 40–41.

44. Reverdy C. Ransom, "Good-bye Boys!" editorial, *The A.M.E. Church Review*, Jan. 1918, 177–79.

45. Reverdy C. Ransom, "Seeking a Seat in Congress and a Voice in Government," editorial, *The A.M.E. Church Review*, Apr. 1918, 228–31.

46. Ransom, *Pilgrimage*, 235.

47. Ibid., "New York and New Horizons," 234–57; "Negro Dark Horse in Congress Race," *The New York Sun*, Feb. 27, 1918, cited in *Pilgrimage*, 236–37.

48. "Hayes Asks About Negro's Nomination," *New York Evening Post*, Feb. 27, 1918, cited in *Pilgrimage*, 237–39.

49. Ransom, "Seeking a Seat," 228–31.

50. "Negroes Hear Mrs. Gould," *The New York Times*, Feb. 27, 1918; "Mrs. Gould Speaks in Dr. Ransom's Interest," *New York Age*, Mar. 2, 1918.

51. Ransom, *Pilgrimage*, 246–57; Ransom, "Seeking a Seat," 228–31.

52. Ibid.

53. Ibid.

54. Ibid.

55. Ibid.

56. W. E. B. DuBois, "Close Ranks," *Crisis*, July 1918, cited in DuBois, *The Emerging Thought*, 254.

57. Reverdy C. Ransom, "Close Ranks," editorial, *The A.M.E. Church Review*, Oct. 1918, 113–14.

58. Emmet J. Scott, "Facts Concerning the Activities of the Negro in Work of the World War," *The A.M.E. Church Review*, Jan. 1919, 145–48.

59. Ralph W. Tyler, "Record of Colored Fighting Troops to Make Bright Days in History," *The A.M.E. Church Review*, Jan. 1919, 150–51.

60. Imogene Burch,"Colored Women in Industry," *The A.M.E. Church Review*, Jan. 1919, 152–53.

61. Tindall, *America*, 1012–13.

62. Reverdy C. Ransom, "Peace," editorial, *The A.M.E. Church Review*, Jan. 1919, 162–163.

63. Fishel, Quarles, "Reaction and Renaissance," (Introduction to Chapter 10), *The Black American*, 402.

64. Reverdy C. Ransom, "Old Things Have Passed Away," *The A.M.E. Church Review*, Oct. 1919, 372–74.

65. Ibid.

66. W. E. B. DuBois, "Returning Soldiers," *Crisis*, May 1919; DuBois, *The Emerging Thought*, 259–61.

67. Hughes, *Fight for Freedom*, 46–47.

68. Reverdy C. Ransom, "Our Printer, the A.M.E. Sunday School Union," *The A.M.E. Church Review*, Jan. 1919, 168.

69. Ransom, *Pilgrimage*, 261.

70. "Commencement Address of Dr. Emmett J. Scott at Wilberforce," *The A.M.E. Church Review*, July 1919, 275–80.

71. Reverdy C. Ransom, "Wilberforce," editorial, *The A.M.E. Church Review*, July 1919, 300–1.

72. Reverdy C. Ransom, "Candidates and Policies to Meet and Serve the New Age," editorial, *The A.M.E. Church Review*, Jan. 1920, 429–30.

73. Reverdy C. Ransom, "Sensational Preaching," editorial, *The A.M.E. Church Review*, Apr. 1920, 432–33.

74. Reverdy C. Ransom, "The Victory Rally for Wilberforce," editorial, *The A.M.E. Church Review*, Apr. 1920, 510.

75. Reverdy C. Ransom, "Has the A.M.E. Church Forgotten Its Mission?" editorial, *The A.M.E. Church Review*, Oct. 1919, 368–70.

76. Bishop L.J. Coppin, "Organic Union of Methodists," *The A.M.E. Church Review*, Apr. 1920, 502–3.

77. Reverdy C. Ransom, "The Bishops Council at Baltimore," *The A.M.E. Church Review*, Apr. 1920, 508.

78. *Journal of Proceedings of the Twenty-Sixth Quadrennial Session of the General Conference of the A.M.E. Church*, St. Louis, Mo., May 3–16, 1920, 44, 54.

79. Reverdy C. Ransom, "The Coming Vision," *The A.M.E. Church Review*, Jan. 1921, 135–39.

80. *Journal Twenty-Sixth Quadrennial*, 73.

81. Ibid., 103–5

82. Ibid., 117–20.

83. Ibid., 122–23.

84. Gomez-Jefferson, *In Darkness with God*, 77–78.

85. Ransom, *Pilgrimage*, 262.

86. *Journal Twenty-Sixth Quadrennial*, 137–39.

87. Ransom, *Pilgrimage*, 262.

88. *Journal Twenty-Sixth Quadrennial*, 138.

89. Ransom, *Pilgrimage*, 262.

90. Reverdy C. Ransom, "The General Conference of 1920," *The A.M.E. Church Review*, July 1920, 36–37.

91. *Journal Twenty-Sixth Quadrennial*, 142–43.

92. Gomez-Jefferson, *In Darkness with God*, 79.

93. Ransom, "The General Conference of 1920," 36–37.

94. Ibid.

95. Reverdy C. Ransom, "Back to Africa, a Militant Call," editorial, *The A.M.E. Church Review*, Oct. 1920, 88–89.

96. Ibid.

97. Ibid.

98. Marcus Garvey Jr., "Garveyism: Some Reflections or its Significance for Today," *Marcus Garvey and the Vision of Africa*, edited by John Henrik Clark (New York: Random House, 1974), 379.

99. Gayraud S. Wilmore, *Black Religion and Black Radicalism*, 2nd ed. (Maryknoll, N.Y.: Orbis, 1991), 149–51.

100. Cited in C. Eric Lincoln, Lawrence H. Mamiya, *The Black Church in the African American Experience* (Durham, N.C.: Duke Univ. Press, 1990), 177.

101. George W. Forbes, "Garvey Plight—The Pity of It All," *The A.M.E. Church Review*, July 1923, 49–50.

102. George W. Forbes, "Cox Boomeranged with Negro and Religious Questions," *The A.M.E. Church Review*, Jan. 1921, 164–65.

103. George W. Forbes, "Tanner's First in Boston," 253, "The Triumph of Charles S Gilpin," 253, "Bert Williams and Others in Boston," 254–255, all in *The A.M.E. Church Review*, Apr. 1921.

104. Reverdy C. Ransom, "Brieflets—Personal and Otherwise," *The A.M.E. Church Review*, July 1921, 34–36.

105. Reverdy C. Ransom, "Notes to Subscribers of the *A.M.E. Review*," *The A.M.E. Church Review*, Oct. 1921, Preface.

106. Reverdy C. Ransom, "A Quadrilateral View of the Attitude and Outlook for Negroes Throughout the World," editorial, *The A.M.E. Church Review*, Oct. 1921, 82–85.

107. Reverdy C. Ransom, "Gandhi, Indian Messiah and Saint," *The A.M.E. Church Review*, Oct. 1921, 87–88.

108. Reverdy C. Ransom, "The Menace of the Ku Klux Klan," editorial, *The A.M.E. Church Review*, Jan. 1922, 102–5.

109. Reverdy C. Ransom, "An A.M.E. Year Book for 1922," editorial, *The A.M.E. Church Review*, Apr. 1922, 107–8.

110. Reverdy C. Ransom, "A Teaching Church," editorial, *The A.M.E. Church Review*, Apr. 1922, 198–99.

111. Reverdy C. Ransom, "A Missionary Department for the Women of Our Church," editorial, *The A.M.E. Church Review*, Apr. 1922, 199–200.

112. Reverdy C. Ransom, "In Peace or War, The Negro the Deciding Element of the Nation's Strength," editorial, *The A.M.E. Church Review*, Apr. 1922, 204–5.

113. Reverdy C. Ransom, "I Do Not Mourn Bert Williams as the Last of the Line," *The A.M.E. Church Review*, Apr. 1922, 205–6.

114. Fishel, Quarles, eds. *The Black American*, Introduction to Dyer Speech, 427; Tindall, *America*, 1048.

115. Reverdy C. Ransom, "Lawless America True to Form in Its Defeat of the Dyer Anti-Lynching Bill," editorial, *The A.M.E. Church Review*, Jan. 1923, 178–77.

116. Reverdy C. Ransom, "Benjamin Tucker Tanner," editorial, *The A.M.E. Church Review*, Apr. 1923, 233–36.

117. Reverdy C. Ransom, "Charles Spencer Smith," editorial, *The A.M.E. Church Review*, Apr. 1923, 237–39.

118. Bishop L.C. Coppin, "Fortieth Anniversary of the A.M.E. Church Review," *The A.M.E. Church Review*, July 1923, 3–4.

119. Reverdy C. Ransom, "The Fortieth Anniversary of the A.M.E. Church Review: A Literature of Protest and Aspiration," editorial, *The A.M.E. Church Review*, July 1923, 41–42.

120. Reverdy C. Ransom, "Three Quadrennials of the A.M.E. Review," *The A.M.E. Church Review*, Apr. 1924, 216.

121. Ransom, *Pilgrimage*, 264.

122. *Journal of Proceedings of the Twenty-Seventh Quadrennial Session of the General Conference of the A.M.E. Church*, Louisville Ky., May 5–21, 1924, 50–58, 71.

123. Reverdy C. Ransom, "The Leaf," No. 1 (flyer), May 6, 1924. (author's file)

124. *Journal Twenty-Seventh Quadrennial*, Ransom, "Report: The A.M.E. Church Review," 384–86.

125. Ibid., 114–116.

126. Ransom, *Pilgrimage*, 263–64.

127. *Journal Twenty-Seventh Quadrennial*, 114–16.

128. Ransom, *Pilgrimage*, 263–64.

129. *Journal Twenty-Seventh Quadrennial*, 114–16.

130. Ibid., 135; Program—Consecration of Bishops, General Conference of the A.M.E. Church, Louisville Ky., Sunday, May 18, 1924. (author's file)

131. Ibid., *Journal Twenty-Seventh Quadrennial*, 144–45.

132. Ransom, *Pilgrimage*, 264.

8. EPISCOPAL DISTRICTS, 1924–1932

1. Alain Locke, "The New Negro," *Black Voices: An Anthology of Afro-American Literature*, edited by Abram Chapman (New York: New American Library, 1968), 512–23.

2. Reverdy C. Ransom, "The New Negro," *The A.M.E. Church Review*, Jan. 1923, 152.

3. Lewis, *When Harlem Was in Vogue*, passim.

4. Tindall, *America*, 1045.

5. Wright Jr., *Encyclopaedia 1948*, 514–16.

6. Reverdy C. Ransom, *Pilgrimage*, 264–66.

7. Ibid., 265.

8. "Turner College," *Journal of Proceedings of the Twenty-Eighth Quadrennial Session of the General Conference of the A.M.E. Church*, 342–43.

9. Reverdy C. Ransom, "The Fourteenth Episcopal District Notes," *The Christian Recorder*, June 12, 1924.

10. "Turner College to Become Junior College," *The Christian Recorder*, June 11, 1925.

11. Ransom, *Pilgrimage*, 265–66.

12. Ibid., 266.

13. Ibid., 265–66.

14. Wright Jr., *Encyclopaedia*, 296–97.

15. Ransom, *Pilgrimage*, 266.

16. Tindall, *America*, 1033–34.

17. *Journal of the Proceedings of the Fifty-Eighth Annual Session of the Kentucky Conference of the A.M.E. Church*, St. James A.M.E. Church, Danville, Kentucky, Sept. 30–Oct. 4, 1925, 76–77, 82.

18. Reverdy C. Ransom, "Future Influence of Negro Scholarship in America," *The Spirit of Freedom and Justice*, 165–68.

19. Ibid.

20. Ibid.

21. Ibid.

22. Bishop Joseph Gomez, "Reverdy Cassius Ransom: Prevailer Extraordinary," *Through Love to Light: Excerpts from the Sermons, Addresses and Prayers of Joseph Gomez, a Bishop in the African Methodist Episcopal Church*, edited by Annetta L. Gomez-Jefferson, (Nashville, Tenn.: A.M.E. Christian Education Department, 1997), 11–18.

23. Reverdy C. Ransom, "Shall We Have Eighteen Ecclesiastical Principalities or a Connectional Church?" *The Southern Christian Recorder*, Dec. 16, 1926.

24. Reverdy C. Ransom, "The Cross and the Dollar Sign," *The Southern Christian Recorder*, Mar. 24, 1927.

25. R.R. Wright Jr., "View From Look Out Mountain" and Reverdy C. Ransom, "As Seen Through Editor Wright's Dark Thunder Clouds," *The Christian Recorder*, May 5, 1927.

26. *Journal of the Proceedings of the Forty-Seventh Annual Session of the West Kentucky Conference*, Quinn Chapel A.M.E. Church, Louisville, Ky., Oct. 5–9, 1927, 20.

27. Ransom, *The Spirit*, Introduction.

28. *Journal* (West Ky.), 18–19.

29. "Bishop Ransom's Anniversary," *The Nashville Globe*, Oct. 27, 1927.

30. Death Certificate of Harriet Ransom (spelled Haretta on certificate), Cambridge, Ohio, Nov. 2, 1927. (Information given by Health Department of Cambridge over phone, Sept. 25, 2000)

31. Ransom, *Pilgrimage*, 15.

32. George A. Singleton, *The Romance of African Methodism* (New York: Exposition Press, 1952), 162–63.

33. Ibid., 163–66.

34. Ransom, *Pilgrimage*, 267.

35. *Journal of the Twenty-Eighth Quadrennial Session of the General Conference of the A.M.E. Church*, May 7–23, 1928. Chicago, Ill., 40–53.

36. Ibid., 78–99.

37. Ibid., 119–20.

38. Ibid.

39. Singleton, *Romance*, 165–67.

40. Ibid., 167.

41. Ransom, *Pilgrimage*, 268.

42. *Journal Twenty-Eighth Quadrennial*, 137, 156–57.

43. Ibid., 165–72.

44. Ibid., 206–11, 235.

45. Ransom, *Pilgrimage*, 269.

46. Singleton, *Romance*, 168.

47. Divine, Breen, Fredrickson, Williams, *America Past and Present*, 740–41.

48. "Ransom Flays G.O.P.," *Baltimore Afro American*, Aug. 30, 1928.

49. Ibid.

50. Ibid.

51. Robert Weisbrot, *Father Divine and the Struggle for Racial Equality* (Urbana and Chicago, Ill.: Univ. of Illinois Press, 1983), passim.

52. Ransom, *Pilgrimage*, 280–81.

53. "Ransom Flays G.O.P."

54. "Bishop Ransom Answered," *The Christian Recorder*, Sept. 13, 1928.

55. Divine, Breen, Fredrickson, Williams, *America*, 741–42.

56. Reverdy C. Ransom, handwritten recipe for pneumonia.

57. Poem, "After 40 Years," 1929, Louisiana. (author's file)

58. Ransom, *Pilgrimage*, 269–70.

59. Divine, Breen, Fredrickson, Williams, *America*, 746.

60. Ransom, *Pilgrimage*, 270–71.

61. I.A. Newby, *Black Carolinians: A History of Blacks in South Carolina from 1895 to 1968* (Columbia, S.C.: Univ. of South Carolina Press, 1973), 220.

62. Ibid., 146.

63. *Bicentennial Focus*, Published by the Seventh Episcopal District (Printed by Tappan, New York Custombook, Inc., 1987), 25–37.

64. Ibid.

65. Wright Jr., *Encyclopaedia 1948*, 509–10.

66. Ibid., 328.

67. Newby, *Black Carolinians*, 15.

68. Ransom, *Pilgrimage*, 270–71.

69. Ibid.

70. William S. Pollitzer, *The Gullah People and Their African Heritage* (Athens, Ga.: Univ. Of Georgia Press, 1999) 149.

71. "Crispus Attucks," an address delivered by Bishop R.C. Ransom at the Metropolitan Opera House, Philadelphia, Pa., Mar. 6, 1930. Printed by the A.M.E. Book Concern, Nashville, Tenn.

72. Ibid.

73. Ibid.

74. "Rt. Rev. Reverdy C. Ransom, *The Palmetto Leader* (Columbia, SC), Feb. 13, 1932.

75. Ibid.

76. Ransom, *Pilgrimage*, 271–72.

77. Ibid., 272.

78. "Battle of Laymen Goes to Committee," *The Cleveland News,* May 4, 1932.

79. *Journal of Proceedings of the Twenty-Ninth Quadrennial Session of the General Conference of the* A.M.E. *Church,* May 2–16, Cleveland, Ohio, passim.

80. Ransom, *Pilgrimage,* 272–74: *The Cleveland Press* (A.M.E. Special Edition), May 10, 1932.

81. Ransom, *Pilgrimage,* 273.

82. Ibid., 274,

83. Ibid., 277–78.

9. THE THIRD DISTRICT AND WILBERFORCE, 1932–1940

1. Interview with Ruth Ransom, Sept. 2001, Xenia, Ohio.

2. Frederick A. McGinnis, *A History and An Interpretation of Wilberforce University* (Blanchester, OH: Brown Publishing, 1941), 57.

3. *State Relations at Wilberforce University* (Wilberforce, Ohio: Committee on Study of State Relations at Wilberforce Univ., 1947), 2.

4. McGinnis, *A History,* 78.

5. "The Wilberforce Dilemma: A Critical and Objective Evaluation of Dr. Wesley's Administration," *Wilberforce University Bulletin, Volume XXXII,* Jan. 1948, 7–8.

6. McGinnis, *A History,* 72–75.

7. Ibid., 66–68, 71–72.

8. Reverdy C. Ransom, *Pilgrimage,* 278.

9. Letter from George W. Henderson to Bishop Reverdy Cassius Ransom, May 24, 1932. (Wilberforce Univ. Archives)

10. McGinnis, *A History,* 90.

11. Letter from Charles W. Wesley to Bishop Reverdy Cassius Ransom, May 24, 1932. (Wilberforce Univ. Archives)

12. Ibid.

13. Letter from Charles W. Wesley to Bishop Reverdy Cassius Ransom, June 2, 1932. (Wilberforce Univ. Archives)

14. Minutes of the Meeting of the Board of Trustees of Wilberforce University, June 6–7, 1932. (author's file); McGinnis, *A History,* 89–90.

15. "The Wilberforce Presidency," *The Palmetto Leader* (Columbia, S.C.), June 11, 1932.

16. Letter from Charles W. Wesley to Bishop Reverdy Cassius Ransom, June 11, 1932. (Wilberforce Univ. Archives)

17. Ibid.

18. Letter from Charles W. Wesley to Bishop Reverdy Cassius Ransom, June 15, 1932. (Wilberforce Univ. Archives)

19. Ransom, *Pilgrimage,* 278–79.

20. Letter from Charles W. Wesley to Bishop Reverdy Cassius Ransom, July 4, 1932. (Wilberforce Univ. Archives)

21. Ibid.

22. Ransom, *Pilgrimage,* 278–79.

23. Wright, Jr., *Encyclopaedia 1948,* 311–12.

24. McGinnis, *A History,* 91.

25. R. R. Wright Jr., *Eighty Seven Years Behind the Black Curtain* (Nashville, Tenn.: A.M.E. Sunday School Union, 1965), 188.

26. Ransom, *Pilgrimage*, 279.

27. *Official Minutes of the Sixty-Fifth Session of the Pittsburgh Annual Conference of the* A.M.E. *Church*, Park Place, Homestead, Pa., Oct. 12–16, 1932, 11–12.

28. Ibid.

29. Ibid., 21.

30. Ibid., 22–23.

31. Ibid., 36.

32. Tindall, *America*, 1109.

33. Speech delivered by Bishop Reverdy C. Ransom, Springfield, Ohio, Oct. 1932. (typed copy, author's file)

34. Reverdy C. Ransom, "Why Vote for Roosevelt," *Crisis*, Nov. 1932, 343.

35. Ransom, *Pilgrimage*, 296–97.

36. "The Fraternal Council of Negro Churches," *The Negro Journal of Religion*, Wilberforce, Ohio, May 1934, 3.

37. Reverdy C. Ransom, "A Message to the Churches and to the Public from the Fraternal Council of Negro Churches," Cleveland, Ohio, Aug. 21–23. 1935. Printed in Ransom, *Pilgrimage*, 297–300.

38. Ibid.

39. Reverdy C. Ransom, "Heroes of Peace:" A memorial address under the auspices of the Peace Heroes Memorial Society, Cincinnati, Ohio, May 30, 1935. (typed copy, author's file)

40. Singleton, *The Romance*, 146.

41. Reverdy C. Ransom, "The Church that Shall Survive," Quadrennial Sermon delivered at the A.M.E. General Conference, New York City, May 6, 1936. (Cited in Singleton's *The Romance*, 146–56.)

44. *Journal of Proceedings of the Thirtieth Quadrennial Session of the General Conference of the* A.M.E. *Church*, New York City, May 6–19, 1936. passim.

45. Ransom, "*The Negro the Hope or Despair of Christianity*, 1–7. See also statement on book jacket by R.R. Wright Jr.

46. *Journal Thirtieth Quadrennial*, 112.

47. Ibid., 119,

48. Ibid., 123, 127.

49. R.R. Wright Jr. *Bishops of the* A.M.E. *Church* (Nashville, Tenn.: A.M.E. Sunday School Union, 1963), 347–49.

50. Ibid.

51. Ibid.

52. Ransom, *Pilgrimage*, 28–33.

53. *Official Minutes of the Sixty-Ninth Session of the Pittsburgh Annual Conference of the* A.M.E. *Church*, Brown Chapel, N.S. Pittsburgh, Pa., Sept. 23–27, 1936, 23, 25–26.

54. "Gomez Bids Farewell," *St. Louis Argus*, May 29, 1936.

55. *Official Minutes of the Fifty-Fifth Session of the North Ohio Annual Conference of the* A.M.E. *Church*, St. James A.M.E. Church, Cleveland, Ohio, Sept. 30–Oct. 4, 1936, 31.

56. Ransom, *The Negro the Hope*, Inscription to Joseph Gomez by Ransom (copy in author's library)

57. *Minutes Fifty-Fifth North Ohio*, 31.

58. Program, Inauguration of Dougal Ormande Beaconsfield Walker President of Wilberforce Univ., March 18, 1937, passim.

59. Ibid., 12.

60. Ibid., Walker's Inaugural Address printed in Inauguration Program, 13–28.

61. Ibid.

62. Ibid.

63. Letter from Reverdy C. Ransom to Rev. Joseph Gomez, July 7, 1937. (author's file).

64. *Official Minutes of the Fifty-Sixth Session of the North Ohio Annual Conference of the A.M.E. Church*, Bethel A.M.E. Church, Akron, Ohio, Sept. 29–Oct. 3, 1937, 16–17.

65. Ibid., 31,38.

66. Ibid., 42.

67. *Official Minutes of the One Hundred Eighth Session of the Ohio Annual Conference of the A.M.E. Church*, St. Paul A.M.E. Church, Zanesville, Ohio, Oct. 5–9, 1938, 27–28.

68. "50th Wedding Anniversary of Bishop and Mrs. R.C. Ransom," *The Cleveland Call and Post*, Nov. 4, 1937.

69. Ransom, *Pilgrimage*, 288; G. Lincoln Caddell, *Brief History of the North Annual Conference, Third Episcopal District of the A.M.E. Church*, (printed pamphlet, author's file)

70. *Minutes Fifty-Sixth North Ohio*, 29.

71. Ransom, *Pilgrimage*, 288–90.

72. Ibid., 290.

73. *Official Minutes of the Seventy-First Session of the Pittsburgh Annual Conference of the A.M.E. Church*, St. Paul A.M.E. Church, Washington, Pa., Sept. 20–24, 1938, 13.

74. *Official Minutes of the Fifty-Seventh Session of the North Ohio Annual Conference of the A.M.E. Church*, Cyrene A.M.E. Church, Piqua, Ohio, Sept. 28–Oct. 2, 1938, 14.

75. Ibid., 18–19.

76. *Minutes Seventy-First Pittsburgh*, 14.

77. "The Wilberforce Dilemma," *Wilberforce University Bulletin*, Jan. 1948, 9.

78. Minutes of Wilberforce University Board of Trustees, Mar. 21–22, 1939; Letter from John A. Gregg to Governor John W. Bricker of Ohio, quoted in entirety, 4–5, 12–17.

79. Ibid.

80. Letter from Governor John W. Bricker to John A. Gregg, Apr. 13, 1939. (Wilberforce Univ. Archives)

81. *Official Minutes of the Fifty-Eighth Session of the North Ohio Annual Conference of the A.M.E. Church*, St. John A.M.E. Church, Cleveland, Ohio, Oct. 18–22, 1939, 28.

82. *Journal of Proceedings of the Thirty-First Quadrennial Session of the General Conference of the A.M.E. Church*, Detroit, Mich., May 1–15, 1940, 66–69.

83. Reverdy C. Ransom, James H. Robinson, comp. & eds. *Year Book of NEGRO CHURCHES, 1939–1940* (Philadelphia, Pa.: A.M.E. Book Concern, 1940), passim.

84. Letter from Mary McLeod Bethune to Reverdy Cassius Ransom, Apr. 25, 1940. (Wilberforce Univ. Archives)

85. Report of the Proceedings of the Democratic National Convention, Chicago, Ill., July 15–18, 1940, 31–32.

10. THE WILBERFORCE DILEMMA AND SIMS TRIAL, 1940–47

1. Divine, Breen, Fredrickson, Williams, *America Past and Present*, 782–83.

2. Reverdy C. Ransom, director, *Bulletin No. 2* (Wilberforce, Ohio: African Methodist Episcopal Church, Bureau of Research and Publicity, Feb. 1941), 16–17.

3. Deed to cottage in Woodland Park, Mich., from Hallie Q. Brown to Reverdy C. Ransom, June 3, 1941. (author's file)

4. Letter from President Franklin D. Roosevelt to Reverdy C. Ransom, July 18, 1941. Cited in Ransom, *Pilgrimage*, 293–94.

5. Telegram from Mayor F.J. LaGuardia, U.S. Director of Civilian Defense, to Reverdy C. Ransom, July 21, 1941. Cited in Ransom, *Pilgrimage*, 295.

6. *State Relations at Wilberforce University* (pages not numbered); "The Wilberforce Dilemma," 8–11.

7. Ibid.

8. Ransom, *Pilgrimage*, 281–283.

9. "The Wilberforce Dilemma," 8–11.

10. Ransom, *Pilgrimage*, 283.

11. "Wilberforce Trustees Vacate Presidency," *The Cleveland Call and Post*, June 13, 1942.

12. "The Wilberforce Dilemma," 40 –41.

13. "Dean Wesley Named Wilberforce Head," *The Cleveland Call and Post,"* June 13, 1942.

14. Ibid.

15. Divine, Breen, Fredrickson, Williams, *America Past*, 785.

16. Hughes, *Fight for Freedom*, 90–91.

17. Divine, Breen, Fredrickson, Williams, *America Past*, 793–94.

18. Ruth Ransom, telephone interview with author, Xenia, Ohio, Sept. 27, 2000.

19. Program, Wilberforce University Seventy-Ninth Commencement, Jones Memorial Chapel, June 11, 1942.

20. "The Wilberforce Dilemma," 26–27.

21. *Official Minutes of the Sixty-First Annual Session of the North Ohio Conference*, St. James A.M.E. Church, Sept. 29–Oct. 4, 1942, 63–65.

22. Ibid., 20.

23. "A.M.E. Bishops Urge Church to Fight for Negro Rights," *The Cleveland Call and Post*, Mar. 6, 1943.

24. Program, Bishop Reverdy C. Ransom Celebration of 57 Years of Ministry—12 Years in Third Episcopal District, St. Paul A.M.E. Church, Columbus, Ohio, Mar. 25, 1943; "Bishop Ransom honored by 200 Religious Leaders," *The Cleveland Call and Post*, Apr. 6, 1943; *The Spokesman, Vol.* 1, Official Organ of the Third Episcopal District, Wilberforce, Ohio, Jan. 1943.

25. Ibid.

26. Ibid.

27. Letter from Bishop Reverdy C. Ransom to Mae Basey, Apr. 26, 1943. (author's file)

28. Gomez-Jefferson, *In Darkness with God*, 176.

29. Ransom, *Pilgrimage*, 291.

30. Funeral program of Emma Ransom, May 18, 1943, Wilberforce, Ohio.

31. Minutes of Bishops' Council, Birmingham, Ala., Feb. 17, 1944; Bishop R.C. Ransom's Report of the Third District to the Bishops' Council, Birmingham, Ala., Feb. 17, 1944.

32. *Journal of Proceedings of the Thirty Second Quadrennial Session of the General Conference of the A.M.E. Church*, Philadelphia, Pa., May 3–14, 1944, 5, 8–9.

33. Ibid., 11, 15, 17.

34. Ibid., 27.

35. Ibid., 31–32.

36. "Ohio's 'Favorite Son' is Defeated on Fifth Ballot, Clayborn Triumph," *The Cleveland Call and Post*, May 13, 1944.

37. Ransom, *Pilgrimage*, 323.

38. Minutes of the State Board of Trustees, Wilberforce, Ohio, June 15, 1944. (Ransom Papers, Wilberforce Univ. Archives)

39. "The Wilberforce Dilemma," 17–18.

40. Letter from Reverdy C. Ransom to Charles Wesley, June 19, 1944 (Ransom Papers, Wilberforce Univ. Archives)

41. Ibid.

42. Letter from Charles Wesley to Reverdy C. Ransom, June 22, 1944. (Ransom Papers, Wilberforce Univ. Archives)

43. Ibid.

44. *Uncovering the Facts," Vol.* 1, *No.* 1, Aug. 10, 1944, Wilberforce Ohio, 8 pages. (Ransom Papers, Wilberforce Univ. Archives)

45. Ibid., Letter from Myrtle Teal to Reverdy Ransom, July 3, 1944, 1.

46. Ibid., Letter from Myrtle Teal To Reverdy Ransom, July 5, 1944, 2.

47. Ibid., Letter from Myrtle Teal to Reverdy Ransom, July 9, 1944. 5.

48. Ibid., Letter from Myrtle Teal to Reverdy Ransom, July10, July 25, 1944, 2–6.

49. Ibid., Letters from Myrtle Teal to Reverdy Ransom, July 4, 9, 20, 27, 29, 1944, 2–5.

50. Ibid., Introduction.

51. Letter from Reverdy C. Ransom to John D. Russell, Nov. 9, 1944; Letter from Charles Wesley to John D. Russell, Nov. 14, 1944; Letter from John D. Russell to Charles Wesley, Nov. 4, 1944. (All three letters copied and bound in the Annual Minutes of the Board of Trustees of Wilberforce Univ., author's file)

52. Ibid.

53. Ibid.

54. Ruth Ransom, telephone interview with author, Xenia, Ohio, Sept. 3, 2000.

55. Letter from Reverdy C. Ransom to John D. Russell, Nov. 9, 1944.

56. Ibid.

57. Letter from John D. Russell to Charles Wesley, Dec. 19, 1944. (See notes 51–53 above.)

58. Letter from John D, Russell to Charles Wesley, Apr. 5, 1945. (Wilberforce Univ. Archives)

59. "The Wilberforce Dilemma," 25–17, 23, 35, 45.

60. Ibid.

61. Ibid.

62. Ibid.

63. Ibid.

64. "Bishop Ransom Has 'Last Word' In Wilberforce Controversy," *The Cleveland Call and Post,* May 31, 1947.

65. Letter from Bishop W.A. Fountain to Bishop Reverdy C. Ransom, Apr. 14, 1946. (author's file)

66. Ransom, *Pilgrimage,* 303–5.

67. Letter from Reverdy C. Ransom to Bishop George E. Curry, Mar. 2, 1946. (author's file)

68. Reverdy C. Ransom, Report to the Bishops' Council (typed copy), Kansas City, Kan., June 19, 1946, 1–3. (author's file)

69. Ibid.

70. Ransom, *Pilgrimage,* 306.

71. Letterhead of the Paradise Lake Foundation; Letter from Council of Presiding Elders to Bishop William A. Fountain, senior bishop, and the Bishops' Council of the A.M.E. Church, June 10, 1946; Letter from Mt. Pisgah A.M.E. Church, Salem, N.J., June 9, 1946. (all in author's file); Ransom, *Pilgrimage,* 306–8.

72. Ibid.

73. Ibid.

74. Minutes of the Bishops' Council, Kansas City, Kan., June 23, 1946.

75. Minutes of Special Meeting of the Bishops' Council, Washington, D.C., Aug. 15, 1946; Letter from Bishop M.H. Davis to Bishop Reverdy C. Ransom, Sept. 13, 1946. (author's file)

76. Ibid.

77. Dispatch from Bishop S.L. Green to Bishop Reverdy C. Ransom, Sept. 7, 1946. (author's file)

78. Letter from Reverdy C. Ransom to Bishops of the A.M.E. Church, Sept. 1946. (Exact date not noted, author's file)

79. Letter from Bishop M.H. Davis to Bishop Reverdy C. Ransom, Sept. 13, 1946. (author's file)

80. "Trial is Halted by Singing Filibuster," *The Cleveland Call and Post,* Oct. 5, 1946.

81. "Legal Action Halts Trials of A.M.E. Bishops at Cincinnati," *The Cleveland Call and Post,* Oct. 26, 1946.

82. Special communication to ministers and members of the A.M.E. Church by Bishop Reverdy C. Ransom, Oct. 5, 1946.

83. *Minutes of the Special Session of the A.M.E. Church General Conference,* Little Rock, Ark., Nov. 20–24, 1946; "Episcopal Address of the Majority Report of the Bishops of the A.M.E. Church," Nov. 20, 1946; "Call Post Sends Editor to the A.M.E. Confab at Little Rock," *The Cleveland Call and Post,* Nov. 23, 1946; "Unfrocked Sims and Curry are Ousted, M. Davis Draws Suspension," "Toss Out Two-Thirds Rule from A.M.E. Bishops' Council, (both articles) *Cleveland Call and Post,* Nov. 30, 1946.

84. Ibid.

85. Ibid.

86. Ibid.

87. Charles H. Loeb, "A.M.E. Split Looms as Bishop Sims Calls Confab," *The Cleveland Call and Post,* Dec. 7, 1946; "Supreme Court Upholds Ouster of Bishop David H. Sims, *The Cleveland Call and Post,* Dec. 14, 1946; Copy of Decision of Supreme Court of New York, Honorable Samuel Dickestein, presiding, David H. Sims et al., Plaintiffs, Richard Robert Wright, Jr., Defendant, Dec. 10, 1946. (author's file)

88. "Amended Senate Bill No. 258," *State Relations at Wilberforce University,* (pages not numbered).

89. Ibid., passim.

90. "Church Leader Strongly Opposes Bills to Re-organize Wilberforce," *The Cleveland Call and Post,* Apr. 26, 1947.

91. Report of the Board of Review of the Commission on Colleges and Universities, North Central Association of Colleges and Secondary Schools, Wilberforce Univ., Wilberforce, Ohio, Feb. 6–7, 1947, Passim.

92. Minutes of the Special Session of the Wilberforce University Board of Trustees, Apr. 3, 1947.

93. Ibid.

94. Ibid.

95. Ibid.

96. Letter from Rev. Joseph Gomez to Governor Thomas J. Herbert, Sept. 8, 1947. (author's file)

97. Letter from Ira F. Lewis to Bishop Reverdy C. Ransom, May 29, 1947. (author's file)

98. "Wesley Points out 'Force' Is Still Good School: Sees Re-Accreditation," *The Cleveland Call and Post,* Apr. 19, 1947.

99. D.O. Walker, "A Struggle for Control of Wilberforce University" (printed speech), Apr. 27, 1947. (author's file)

100. "Bishop Ransom Has 'Last Word' in Wilberforce University Controversy," *The Cleveland Call and Post,* May 31, 1947.

101. Minutes of the Wilberforce University Board of Trustees, June 10, 1947.

102. Ibid.

103. *Dr. Wesley's Case Against Dr. Wesley,* (printed pamphlet, author not listed); Myrtle Teal Ransom, interview with author, Wilberforce, Ohio, Sept. 1996.

104. "Ransom Burned in Effigy," *The Cleveland Call and Post,* June 21, 1947.

11. RANSOM THE HISTORIOGRAPHER, 1947–1952

1. Lathardus Goggins, *Central State University: The First One Hundred Years 1887–1987* (Wilberforce, Ohio, Central State Univ., 1987), 27.

2. "The Wilberforce Dilemma," 33.

3. Goggins, *Central State University,* 20.

4. "The Wilberforce Dilemma," 30; President Wesley's Annual Report to the Trustees, Minutes of the University Trustees, June 10, 1047. (Wilberforce Univ. Archives)

5. Minutes of Special Mass Meeting on Behalf of Wilberforce University, Shorter Hall, June 26, 1947. (Wilberforce Univ. Archives)

6. Ibid.

7. Letter from Reverdy C. Ransom to Governor Thomas J. Herbert, June 26, 1947. (typed copy, author's file)

8. Letter from Attorney Perry W. Howard to Bishop Reverdy C. Ransom, July 29, 1947. (author's file)

9. "The Wilberforce Dilemma," 37–38.

10. Goggins, *Central State University,* 28–31; "Cut off $42,000 at 'Force,' Baptist Speak for Wesley," *The Cleveland Call and Post,* Aug. 16, 1947.

11. *Minutes of the Sixty-Sixth Annual Session of the North Ohio Conference of the A.M.E. Church,* Warren A.M.E. Church, Toledo, Ohio, Oct. 7–12, 27–30, 34–35.

12. Bishop Reverdy C. Ransom, The President's Address to the Bishops' Council, Dallas, Texas, Feb. 18, 1948. (author's file)

13. Report of Bishop Reverdy C. Ransom to the Bishops' Council, Dallas, Texas, Feb. 18, 1948. (author's file)

14. Minutes of the Annual Educational Chautauqua of the Third Episcopal District, Wayman Chapel, Dayton, Ohio, Mar. 3, 1948. (author's file)

15. Minutes of the Organizational Meeting of Delegates to the General Conference, Wayman Chapel, Dayton, Ohio, Mar. 3, 1948.

16. Reverdy C. Ransom, "Shall We Launch a Forward Movement in 1948?" Bureau of History and Statistics of the A.M.E. Church, Apr. 1948. (Wilberforce Univ. Archives)

17. Ibid.

18. *Official Minutes of the Thirty-third Session of the General Conference of the A.M.E. Church,* Kansas City, Kansas, May 5–17, 1948, 37–38.

19. Ibid., 38, 41–43.

20. Ibid., 66, 70–71, 77, 89.

21. Ibid., 94–95.

22. Ibid.

23. Ibid., 104–106.

24. Ibid., 108.

25. Ibid., 120.

26. Minutes of the Bishops' Council, Washington, D.C., Feb. 1949; Letter from Reverdy C. Ransom to Ira T. Bryant, Sept. 29, 1948. (author's file)

27. Report of Bureau of Research and History to the General Conference of the A.M.E. Church, Chicago, Ill. May 7, 1952.

28. Agreement between Reverdy C. Ransom and R.R. Wright Jr., Cleveland, Ohio, Aug. 11, 1948.

29. Letter from Reverdy C. Ransom to Ira T. Bryant, Sept. 29, 1948. (author's file)

30. Letter from Bishop L.H. Hemingway to Bishop Reverdy C. Ransom, Sept. 11, 1948. (author's file)

31. Reverdy C. Ransom, "Freedom and Liberty under Law," (essay written September 1948). (author's file)

32. Letter from Reverdy C. Ransom to Joseph Gomez, Dec. 5, 1949. (author's file).

33. Reverdy C. Ransom, comp., ed., *Year Book of the A.M.E. Church 1948–1949* (Nashville, Tenn.: A.M.E. Sunday School Union, 1949), passim.

34. Letter from Reverdy C. Ransom to MacMillan and Company, Dec. 30, 1948. (author's file)

35. J. Sanders Redding, "Harriet Ransom's Son is a Blunt Story of A.M.E. Church Corruption," (book review found in Ransom papers, Wilberforce Archives, n.d. or paper listed).

36. Ormande A. Forte, "Following 'A Pilgrimage,'" (book review found in Ransom papers, Wilberforce Archives, n.d. or paper listed).

37. Reverdy C. Ransom, *Preface to History of the A.M.E. Church* (Nashville, Tenn.: A.M.E. Sunday School Union, 1950), foreword.

38. Ibid., 13.

39. Ibid., 18.

40. Ibid., 37–50.

41. Ibid., 79.

42. Ibid., 91.

43. Ibid., passim.

44. Ibid., 215.

45. Ibid., foreword.

46. Letter from Reverdy C. Ransom to Governor Frank Lausche, Apr. 1, 1949. (author's file)

47. Ibid.

48. "President Charles Leander Hill Blasts Those Who Criticize Lausche's Veto," *Xenia* (Ohio) *Gazette,* May 9, 1951.

49. Letter from Reverdy C. Ransom to President Harry S. Truman, Mar. 10, 1949. (copy, author's file)

50. "Confessions of a Bishop," *Time Magazine,* Feb. 13, 1950, 58–59.

51. *Special Flushing Hometown Edition,* Flushing, Ohio, Aug. 1950; Flushing Homecoming Program; *Freeport Press,* Freeport, Ohio, Aug. 17, 1950. (author's file).

52. Reverdy C. Ransom, "Yard-Stick of Values," *The Christian Recorder,* Feb. 22, 1951.

53. Reverdy C. Ransom, "Solid Rock or Shifting Sand in Human Relations," *The Christian Recorder,* Mar. 13, 1951.

54. Reverdy C. Ransom, "Ecumenical, What? Ecumenicity, Where? The Shame of Negro Methodism," *The Christian Recorder,* Aug. 9, 1951.

55. Berry, *A Century of Missions,* 142–43.

56. Reverdy C. Ransom, "Liberia Faces the Rising Sun," *The Christian Recorder,* June 28, 1951.

57. Reverdy C. Ransom, "The Sixtieth Anniversary of the Founding of the A.M.E. Church in West Africa," (Speech), Monrovia, Liberia, June 1951. (author's file); See also speech in *The Christian Recorder*, July 12, 1951.

58. Ransom, "Liberia Faces the Rising Sun," *The Christian Recorder*, June 28, 1951; Reverdy C. Ransom, "God's Last Reserve," *The Christian Recorder*, July 19, 1951.

59. Letter from Reverdy C. Ransom to Bishop R.R. Wright Jr., July 16, 1951. (author's file)

60. Letter from Reverdy C. Ransom to the National Council of Arts and Sciences, Oct. 25, 1951. (copy, author's file); Philip S. Foner, ed., *The Voice of Black America: Major Speeches of Blacks in the United States 1797–1973*, *Vol. 2* (New York: Capricorn Books, 1972), 866.

61. Reverdy C. Ransom, "Old Men for Counsel, Young Men for War," *The Christian Recorder* (Ransom papers, Wilberforce Archives, n.d. but most likely written in late 1951 or early 1952 before General Conference in May).

62. Ibid.

63. *Official Minutes of Thirty-fourth Session of the General Conference of the A.M.E. Church*, Chicago, Ill. May 7–20, 1952. (found in *Combined Minutes of the General Conferences*, A.M.E. Church, 1948, 1952, 1956*)* 151–61.

64. Ibid., 167–69.

65. Ibid., 172–73,

66. Ibid., 179–80, 195.

67. Ibid., 225.

68. Ibid., 245–48.

69. Ibid., 262.

EPILOGUE

1. Reverdy C. Ransom, "The Last Mile," *The Christian Recorder*, Aug. 14, 1952.

2. Reverdy C. Ransom, "The Albatross Who lost His Way Among the Highway of the Skies," *The Christian Recorder*, Jan. 31, 1953.

3. Letter from Reverdy C. Ransom to his grandson, Reverdy III, Nov. 27, 1952. (author's file).

4. Ruth Ransom, telephone interview with author, Xenia, Ohio, Sept. 13, 2000.

5. Reverdy C. Ransom, "Paul Laurence Dunbar," *The A.M.E. Church Review*, April/June 1954, 56–58.

6. George Van Gieson, "Durable Bishop Ransom Passes 94th Milestone," *Journal Herald*, (n.d., n.p. but probably written in Jan. 1955.) (Wilberforce Univ. Archives)

7. Birthday greetings from Robert and Margaret Hardoan to Reverdy C. Ransom, Jan. 4, 1955. (author's file)

8. Reverdy C. Ransom, "An Empire for Service, Influence and Power in the Kingdom of God,"*Voice of Missions*, Feb. 1955, 3–4. (picture on cover).

9. Letter from Reverdy C. Ransom to Bishop Joseph Gomez, Jan. 20, 1956.

10. Eric Roberts, "Old Man Eloquent Bishop Ransom 95, Last of 'First Generation,'" *The Pittsburgh Courier*, Feb. 18, 1956.

11. Reverdy C. Ransom, "Have We Made a Wise Choice for the Seat of the General Conference," *The Christian Recorder*, Dec. 15, 1955.

12. *The Official Minutes of the Thirty-fifth Session of the General Conference of the A.M.E. Church*, Miami, Fla., May 1956. (found in the *Combined Minutes of the General Conferences of the A.M.E. Church*, 1948, 1952, 1956*)*, 502.

13. Ibid., 336–38.

14. Ibid., 368.

15. Ibid., 368; Interview with Myrtle Teal Ransom, Wilberforce, Ohio, Apr. 3, 1992; Annetta Gomez-Jefferson "Reverdy Cassius Ransom, This is Your Life," 1956. (script).

16. *Official Minutes General Conference* 1956, 355, 383, 391, 393, 432–33, 470.

17. Gomez-Jefferson, *In Darkness with God,* 279.

18. "96th Birthday," *The Cleveland Call and Post,* Jan. 6, 1957.

19. Letter from Roger Wilson, Grant Polemarch of Kappa Alpha Psi, to Bishop Reverdy C. Ransom, Feb. 21, 1957. (author's file)

20. Telegram from Bishop and Mrs. Hubert N. Robinson to Bishop Reverdy C. Ransom, Dec. 31, 1956. (author's file)

21. Telegram from Bishop Joseph Gomez, Mayor Richard Daley, Revs. U.S. Robinson and Roy L. Miller to Bishop Reverdy C. Ransom, Sept. 19, 1957. (author's file)

22. *The A.M.E. Church Review,* July/Sept. 1958, cover.

23. Gomez-Jefferson, *In Darkness with God.,* 282–83.

24. Funeral program of Bishop Reverdy Cassius Ransom, Chapel of the Living Savior, Payne Theological Seminary, Wilberforce, Ohio, Apr. 28, 1959, 11 A.M.

25–28. Bishop Joseph Gomez, "Reverdy Cassius Ransom: Prevailer Extraordinary," Gomez-Jefferson, ed. *Through Love to Light,* 11–18.

29. Funeral program of Bishop Reverdy Cassius Ransom.

30. "American Methodist's Venerable Leaves Rich Heritage," *The Southern Christian Recorder,* May 9, 1959.

31. *Dayton Journal Herald,* Apr. 23, 1959; *The Chicago Defender,* Apr. 23, 1959, *The Springfield* [Ohio] *Sun,* Apr. 23, 1959.

32. Ransom, *Pilgrimage,* 322–323.

Selected Bibliography

BOOKS BY REVERDY C. RANSOM

"The Quilt of Many Colors." Unpublished manuscript, ca 1955.

The Disadvantages and Opportunities of Negro Youth. Cleveland, Ohio: Thomas & Mattell, 1894.

The Negro: The Hope or the Despair of Christianity. Boston: Ruth Hill, 1935.

The Pilgrimage of Harriet Ransom's Son. Nashville, Tenn.: A.M.E. Sunday School Union, 1950.

Preface to History of the A.M.E. Church. Nashville, Tenn.: A.M.E. Sunday School Union, 1950.

School Days at Wilberforce. Springfield, Ohio: The New Era Co., 1892.

Spirit of Freedom and Justice: Orations and Speeches by Reverdy C. Ransom. Nashville, Tenn.: A.M.E. Sunday School Union, 1926.

Year Book of A.M.E. Church, 1918. Nashville, Tenn.: A.M.E. Sunday School Union.

Year Book of A.M.E. Church, 1922–23. Nashville, Tenn.: A.M.E. Sunday School Union.

Year Book of Negro Churches, 1935–36. Printed at Wilberforce University, 1936.

Year Book of Negro Churches, 1938–49. Nashville, Tenn.: A.M.E. Sunday School Union, 1949.

Year Book of Negro Churches, 1939–40. Philadelphia, Pa.: A.M.E. Book Concern, 1940.

PUBLISHED SOURCES

Angell, Stephen Ward. *Bishop Henry McNeal Turner and African-American Religion in the South*. Knoxville, Tenn.: Univ. of Tennessee Press, 1992.

Arnett, B. W., comp. *Wilberforce Alumnal—A Comprehensive Review*. Xenia, Ohio: Gazette, 1885.

Berry, L. L. *A Century of Missions of the African Methodist Episcopal Church—1840–1940*. New York: Gutenberg Printing Co., 1942.

Blockson, Charles L. *Pennsylvania's Black History*. Philadelphia, Pa.: Portfolio Assoc., 1975.

Bowman, John S., ed. *The Cambridge Dictionary of American Biography*. Cambridge: Cambridge Univ. Press, 1995.

Brown, Hallie Q. *Pen Pictures of Pioneers of Wilberforce*. Xenia, Ohio: Aldine Press, 1937.

Burkett, Randall K. and Newman, Richards, eds, *Apostles: Afro American Clergy Confront the Twentieth Century*. Boston: G. K. Hall, 1989.

Chapman, Abram, ed. *Black Voices: An Anthology of Afro-American Literature*. New York: New American Library, 1968.

Clark, John Henrik, ed. *Marcus Garvey and the Vision of Africa*. New York: Random House, 1974.

Daniels, John. *In Freedom's Birthplace: A Study of Boston Negroes*. New York: Houghton, Mifflin, 1914.

Divine, Robert A., Breen T. H., Frederickson, George M., and Williams, R. Hal. *America Past and Present*. New York: Scott, Foresman, 1984.

Douglass, Frederick. *Douglass Autobiographies: Narrative of the Life, My Bondage and My Freedom, Life and Times*. New York: The Library of America, 1894. Reprint 1994.

Drewett, Donald A. *Ransom on Race and Racism: The Racial and Social Thought of Reverdy Cassius Ransom—Preacher, Editor and Bishop of the African Methodist Episcopal Church*. Ph.D. dissertation, Drew University, 1988.

Du Bois, W.E.B. *The Autobiography of W.E.B. Du Bois*. New York: International Publishers, 1968.

———. *From Dusk to Dawn: An Essay Toward an Autobiography of a Race Concept*. New York: Harcourt & Brace, 1940.

———. *The Souls of Black Folk*. Chicago: A.C. Mc Clurg, 1903.

Fairchild, James H. *Oberlin the Colony and the College*. Oberlin, Ohio: E. J. Goodrich, 1883.

Fishel, Leslie H. and Quarles, Benjamin, eds. *The Black American: A Documentary History*. New York: Scott, Foresman, 1970.

Gerber, David A. *Black Ohio and the Color Line 1860–1915*. Urbana, Ill.: Univ. of Illinois Press, 1976.

Gomez-Jefferson, Annetta L. *In Darkness with God: The Life of Joseph Gomez, a Bishop in the African Methodist Episcopal Church*. Kent, Ohio: Kent State Univ. Press, 1998.

———. *Through Love to Light: Excerpts from the Sermons, Addresses and Prayers of Joseph Gomez, a Bishop in the African Methodist Episcopal Church*. Nashville, Tenn.: A.M.E. Christian Education Department, 1997.

Goggins, Lathardus. *Central State University: The First One Hundred Years 1887-1987*. Wilberforce, Ohio: Central State Univ., 1987.

Gosnell, Harold F. *Negro Politicians: The Rise of Negro Politics in Chicago*. Chicago: Univ. of Chicago Press, 1935.

Harlan, Louis. *Booker T. Washington: The Making of a Black Leader 1856–1901*. New York: Oxford Univ. Press, 1972.

———. *Booker T. Washington: The Wizard of Tuskegee 1901–1915*. New York: Oxford Univ. Press, 1983.

Hughes, Langston. *Fight for Freedom: The Story of the NAACP*. New York: W. W. Norton, 1962.

Johnson, James Weldon. *Black Manhattan*. Reprint ed. Salem, N.H.: Ayer Co., 1988.

Kusmer, Kenneth. *A Ghetto Takes Shape: Black Cleveland, 1879–1930*. Urbana, Ill.: Univ. of Illinois Press, 1972.

Lewis, David Levering. *When Harlem was in Vogue*. New York: Farrar, Straus & Giroux, 1981.

Lincoln, C. Eric and Lawrence H. Mamiya. *The Black Church in the African American Experience*. Durham, N.C.: Duke Univ. Press, 1990.

Logan, Raymond Washington. *The Betrayal of the Negro*. New York: Colliers, 1963.

Logan, Rayford W. and Michael R. Winston, eds. *Dictionary of American Negro Biography*. New York: W. W. Norton, 1982.

Mather, Frank Lincoln, ed. *Who's Who of the Colored Race: Half Century Anniversary of Negro Freedom in the United States*. Chicago 1915. Memento ed. Detroit: Book Tower, 1976.

McGinnis, Frederick A. *A History and Interpretation of Wilberforce University*. Blanchester, Ohio: Brown Publishing, 1941.

Moon, Henry Lee. *The Emerging Thought of W.E.B. Du Bois: Essays and Editorial from The Crisis*. New York: Simon & Schuster, 1972.

Morris, Calvin S. *Reverdy C. Ransom: A Pioneer Black Social Gospeler*. Ph.D. Dissertation, Boston Univ., 1982.

Myrdal, Gunnar. *An American Dilemma: The Negro Problem and Modern Democracy, Vol. 2*. New York: Random House, 1972.

Newby, I. A. *Black Carolinians: A History of Blacks in South Carolina from 1895 to 1968*. Columbia, S.C.: Univ. of South Carolina Press, 1973,

Payne, Daniel A. *History of the African Methodist Episcopal Church*. Nashville, Tenn.: A.M.E. Sunday School Union, 1891.

Pinn, Anthony B., ed. *Making the Gospel Plain: The Writings of Reverdy C. Ransom*. Harrisburg, Pa.: Trinity Press International, 1999.

Pollitzer, William S. *The Gullah People and Their African Heritage*. Athens, Ga.: Univ. of Georgia Press, 1999.

Scheiner, Seth M. *Negro Mecca: A History of the Negro in New York City 1865-1920*. New York: New York Univ. Press, 1965.

Seraile, William. *Fire in His Heart: Bishop Benjamin Tucker Tanner and the A.M.E. Church*. Knoxville, Tenn.: Univ. of Tennessee Press, 1998.

Singleton, George A. *The Romance of African Methodism*. New York: Exposition Press, 1952.

Sinkler, George. *The Racial Attitudes of American Presidents: From Abraham Lincoln to Theodore Roosevelt*. New York: Doubleday, 1971.

Smith, Charles Spencer. *A History of the African Methodist Episcopal Church 1856–1922*. Philadelphia, Pa.: A.M.E. Book Concern, 1922.

Southern, Eileen. *The Music of Black Americans*. New York: W. W. Norton, 1971.

Spear, Allan H. *Black Chicago: The Making of a Negro Ghetto 1890–1920*. Chicago: Univ. of Chicago Press, 1967.

Tindall, George Brown. *America: A Narrative History*. 2nd ed. New York: W. W. Norton, 1988.

Wagner, Jean. *Black Poets of the United States*. Urbana, Ill.: Univ. of Illinois Press, 1972.

Washington, Booker T. *Booker T. Washington's Own Story of His Life and Work: Including An Authoritative Sixty Four Page Supplement by Albon L. Holsey*. The Authentic edition, 1901. Copyright by J.R. Nichols & Co., 1915.

Weisbrot, Robert. *Father Divine and the Struggle for Racial Equality*. Urbana and Chicago: Univ. of Illinois Press, 1983.

Wells, Ida B. *Crusade for Justice: The Autobiography of Ida B. Wells*. Alfreda M. Duster, ed. Chicago: Univ. of Chicago Press, 1970.

Wilmore, Gayraud S. *Black Religion and Black Radicalism*, 2nd ed. Maryknoll, N.Y.: Orbis, 1991.

Wright, R. R. *Bishops of the A.M.E. Church*. Nashville, Tenn.: A.M.E. Sunday School Union, 1963.

———. *Eighty-Seven Years Behind the Black Curtain*. Nashville, Tenn.: A.M.E. Sunday School Union, 1965.

———. ed. *Encyclopaedia of African Methodism, 1948*. Philadelphia, Pa.: A.M.E. Book Concern, 1947.

Index